A PROPHET IN POLITICS

JAMES SHAVER WOODSWORTH
(1874–1942)

A PROPHET IN POLITICS

A Biography
of J. S. Woodsworth

By

KENNETH McNAUGHT

University of Toronto Press

Preface

J. S. WOODSWORTH WAS KNOWN to Canadians in a number of ways—as a Methodist preacher, as a social worker, as a voluble pacifist, and as a socialist politician who was the father of the Co-operative Commonwealth Federation.

Since his death in 1942 there have been many and varying estimates of his achievement. Such estimates do not run the same wide gamut permissible to violent partisanship during his lifetime (when he was known in some circles as "a dirty bolshevist" and a "red rabble-rouser in the pay of Moscow"). Nearly all agree that he was an outstanding man. But some, using the criteria of success, of the willingness to compromise on major as well as on minor issues, call him a "saintly failure." Others say he was an absolute pacifist in an age of war, and thus he failed to resolve "a contradiction in his own philosophy" of liberal-socialism.

The fact is that Woodsworth was a success by any standard other than that of expediency. His pacifism was no contradiction, but rather the keystone of the arch which unified all his thinking. One does not "resolve" anything by simple compromise; this was his message to Canadians.

Perhaps his greatest achievement was his consistent battle against the demands of institutional conformity—a battle waged so effectively that even while denying the right of anyone to expect conformity from others he was able to bring forth solid progressive measures and to guarantee for future generations a position from which to obtain still further progress. His is a story of moral courage unsurpassed in Canadian history. To tell that story, in its context, is the purpose of this book.

In the preparation of this biography many people have given assistance. I wish particularly to thank Professor Frank H. Underhill who encouraged me in the writing of a preliminary study as a thesis for the University of Toronto; Mrs. J. S. Woodsworth, Mrs. Angus MacInnis, and Mr. Charles Woodsworth for their interest and help; and the following who read the manuscript at various stages: my wife; Professor J. H. Stewart Reid; and Mr. and Mrs. R. G. Prodrick.

I am happy to acknowledge my debt also to the Rockefeller Foundation for financial assistance during periods of research, to the Canadian Social Science Research Council for a grant in aid of publication, and to the Publications Fund of the University of Toronto Press.

Finally, I am very grateful for the courtesy and skill of the editorial department of the University of Toronto Press.

KENNETH MCNAUGHT

Contents

PART I: 1874-1921

1

FRONTIER EVANGELISM

"APPLEWOOD" WAS THE NAME of the fine Ontario farm home in which
James Shaver Woodsworth was born in July of 1874. The farm
belonged to the Shaver family, pioneers of the Etobicoke district on
the western fringes of Toronto. It had been established by Peter and
Esther Shaver who, through their daughter, Esther Josephine, passed
on to J. S. Woodsworth a German-Dutch lineage. The Schaeffers had
come to New York from "High Germany" in 1765 and had moved on
through Pennsylvania to Upper Canada. At Ancaster, near Hamilton,
one of the Schaeffer sons, William, obtained a grant of Crown land.
William's son, Peter, changed the spelling of the family name, moved
on to Etobicoke, and married Esther Vansickle, whose ancestors had
come from the Netherlands. It was Peter and Esther Shaver who built
"Applewood" with its prosperous pioneer air of orderliness, co-operation, and Methodist piety.

James Woodsworth, who married the daughter of this house, gave
to his son a lineage no less important. His grandfather, Richard
Woodsworth, had come to Upper Canada from Yorkshire in 1830. At
York, Richard Woodsworth became a leader in the Wesleyan church
and, as an architect and builder, made a name for himself in the
colonial capital. He was a staunch loyalist and remained a supporter
of the British Wesleyan connection rather than the independent
Methodist Episcopal Church. The latter supported the Reformers in
the election of 1836, the former the Governor; in the following year
Richard received a sword to assist in the defence of Sir Francis Bond
Head.

Richard Woodsworth's loyalism was not diminished by his marriage
to Mary Ann Watson. The Watsons had left London for New England
in 1807; by 1819 they had had enough of anti-British sentiment and

they too found their way to Upper Canada. Richard married Mary
Ann Watson in 1831. James Woodsworth, born in 1843, was the
seventh of their twelve children.

Thus, when James Woodsworth married Esther Josephine Shaver in
1868 their union brought together a rich and varied heritage. To a
strong feeling of loyalty and conservatism was added a pioneer vigour
and a deep sense of spiritual values.

James had started life in business, but he soon began reading for the
ministry and in due course was ordained by a visiting British preacher.
It was while filling one of his first charges that he lived with the
Shavers at "Applewood." After his marriage, and the birth of James
Shaver, the first of his six children, the Woodsworths moved on to a
series of Methodist circuits in New Ontario centring in Parry Sound
and Bracebridge. But for the Woodsworth children the best adventure
came in 1882 when James took his family south of the Great Lakes,
up through Minnesota and on to a new appointment at Portage la
Prairie.

In 1882 the whole country between Belleville and British Columbia
was included by Methodists in the Toronto Conference. In the following year the Manitoba and North-West Conference was organized in
recognition of the immense potential growth of western Canada. The
Canadian Pacific Railway was beginning to hit its stride on the plains,
real estate speculation was at a feverish pitch, and there were even
some genuine settlers entering the area. The Conservative national
government had said that the opening of the West was one of the
three central pillars of its house. James Woodsworth shared in the
general optimism. He pursued his pastoral duties at Portage la Prairie
and developed a strong belief in the future of the West. Just at the
close of his three-year Portage pastorate there occurred the second
Riel Rebellion and his written comment on that event illustrates his
political position well. "Many lives were lost in this unfortunate disturbance. On the other hand, much good resulted. Disaffected half-
breeds and rebellious Indians were taught a salutary lesson; they
learned something of the strength of British rule, and likewise experienced something of its clemency and righteousness."[1] But to quote
this alone would be misleading, for in James Woodsworth perhaps the
most outstanding characteristics were kindliness and tolerance. If the
principle of British order remained the keynote in his political thought,
it was always qualified by insistence on high standards of morality and

[1]James Woodsworth, *Thirty Years in the Canadian North-West* (Toronto,
1917), p. 12.

responsibility in both private and public life. Certainly he regarded his own mission in the West as the carrying forward, side by side with the advance of commerce and agriculture, of the moral precepts of Methodist Christianity. In him the missionary spirit drew strong breath, and as a result of his zeal he was appointed, in 1886, first Superintendent of Methodist Missions in the North-West, his territory extending at one time from the Head of the Lakes to the Pacific coast.

This frail man, slightly stooped, with an aristocratic air suggested by his neat Vandyke beard, became a familiar figure to all who frequented the prairie trails. His tours to Indian missions and struggling Methodist churches took him by buckboard, canoe, and stern-wheeler to all parts of the West, sometimes accompanied by his eldest son. It would be no licence if the younger Woodsworth later claimed to be the genuine product of the Canadian frontier—a frontier that stretched intermittently from the rocky lakes of New Ontario to the freshly broken wheat lands around Brandon.

The Woodsworths established a home in Brandon in 1885. With the lightly rolling prairie stretching away from their back garden the children of the house were never at a loss for something to do. Fishing, swimming in the Assiniboine, trapping gophers, gathering wild flowers, and the occasional camping trip to Lake Clementi or Shoal Lake, or in the winter, skating, the building of snow forts, and sleigh-riding—all this made life in Brandon far from dull. Although parties, cards, and the like were not to be thought of, the children found outlets in a "literary society," reading, and family games. Of the Brandon home J. S. Woodsworth later wrote, "Though built on puritan foundations there was nothing austere in its lines. Its hospitable door was always open alike to friends and strangers. It radiated a genial warmth throughout the neighborhood. . . ."

The position of the eldest son in that home was one of considerable importance. With Dr. Woodsworth away much of the time, James had to help in directing the vigorous younger children, and this gave him many responsibilities. His mother's very orderly mind and tireless devotion to the duties of rearing a large family in orthodox piety worked an important influence upon her son. From the first it was his mother's great hope that James should enter the Methodist ministry, and from her he received some of his most basic convictions: a deep belief in order and efficiency, a determination to follow the dictates of conscience, and a definite concept of leadership.

If his mother stressed the principles of authority and non-compromise, his father introduced a strong note of doubt into his son's mind.

Authority, yes, but always tempered with tolerance, compassion, and
the idea of service. Orthodox piety, good, but with some reservations.
In religious matters Dr. Woodsworth was a moderate liberal and discussions at the family dinner-table prepared the children for the
heresies of the "higher criticism" which they would all sooner or later
have to face. There was much less preparation along the lines of the
"social gospel" that was beginning to be important in the United
States; for in Canada the Methodist church in the 1880's and 1890's
was consolidating itself as a church of the well-to-do. Its message in
the West tended to be a call to a new puritanism.

Young James completed his high-school work in 1891, and that
autumn he entered Wesley College at Winnipeg. Study in the Department of Mental and Moral Science absorbed most of his time, but he
also became a leader in football and in student organizations. In 1893,
to help the family budget, he took a short normal school course in
Brandon and taught for a year in rural schools. In the following year,
1896, he returned to Wesley to be elected Senior Stick, and to win
the bronze medal for second position in his graduating class.

At Wesley he had encountered the semi-classical education of a
small church college of the day. Every encouragement to join the
ministry had been given him. The natural inclinations of his parents,
his own strong desire to serve, and the influence of his professors led
him almost automatically into the ministry. Here he followed the
normal procedure and spent two years as a probationer or circuit-rider
in the mission field of southwestern Manitoba.

In July, 1896, Woodsworth left Brandon to enter this new work.
He did so with a high sense of dedication, and yet it would be incorrect
to say that the choice had been made entirely without misgivings.
The following two years contained for him many periods of struggle
and doubt. He was well aware that the ordinary Methodist minister
had experienced a personal religious "conversion," that there was
much of revivalism in western Methodism. He also knew that by
temperament he found emotional religious experience difficult to
achieve. His period as probationer was a continual struggle to convince himself that he had experienced a personal conversion. There
can be no doubt of the intensity of this struggle: the attempts to hold
himself to the most puritanical existence, the conducting of tiny
prayer meetings in isolated prairie farms with their revivalistic ritual,
the passionate prayer for greater power to convince others of sin and
the need of salvation.

At one point he greatly doubted the wisdom of the course he was
following and noted in his diary, "It appears to me that in my life I

am often looking within and striving to make my experience conform to those of men who are eminent for their high Christian life rather than just allowing God to work out His own will in me in His own way...."[2]

Some of his observations during the long rides in buggy or saddle formed the basis of future action. The poverty of the educational system, the lack of community organization, and the significant differences in wealth—all these posed problems which had not received emphasis in the Brandon pulpit. In his diary he wrote on one occasion:

Had quite a conversation with Hughes. He is the type of [the] comparatively uneducated class—narrow and bigoted and jealous of upper classes. Still there is a good deal of truth in many of the complaints of such people. From their standpoint the wealthy seem to have little right to their riches. "If I work as hard as a lawyer I ought to have the same reward" is the principle. They forget, or rather cannot comprehend the different abilities— the quality as well as the quantity. Still, when a man is struggling along making a bare living and sees others living in luxury from profits made in business transactions with him he is apt to think there is something wrong. Still, in my own case, I am not envious of those wealthy businessmen I have met.

On another occasion he thought that there might be too many churches already in Canada, and that this accounted for the pitifully small number of people at any particular service. His thoughts turned to the foreign mission field. But he did not dwell upon that prospect for long, and he noted in his diary, "When I think of the work abroad I am always thrown back upon the great need at home." Yet there is little wonder that he should sometimes hesitate and question the value of his western circuit work. It was one of the most arduous tasks in the Canadian ministry; more important, it apparently showed a minimum return. Riding for miles the unmarked prairie trails in winter storms when the temperature ranged between forty and fifty degrees below zero, only to find an empty meeting house, was not the sort of experience to encourage even the most ardent youth.[3] Returning to his lodgings in the sub-zero moonlight, perhaps as late as two or three o'clock in the morning, after struggling through mountainous snow-drifts with a weary horse and rickety cutter, the young preacher was frequently beset with basic questions. Granting the great need to spread the gospel and bring individuals to Christ, there must yet be

[2]J. S. Woodsworth, diary, 1896–8. (The Woodsworth papers, composed of letters, diaries, and scrapbooks, are in the control of Woodsworth House, Ottawa.)
[3]After one bitter drive through heavy drifts, only to find two empty churches in succession, he returned to find that his cheeks and ears were "slightly frozen." "How true is the saying re this glorious land, 'Well it's cold but you don't feel it.'"

something wrong with the appeal. "Still it seems strange that despite one's greatest efforts the people all sit apparently unmoved. Where does the fault lie? Oh that God would enable me to bring men to repentance and Christ." Or again, "Could we but have a revival of scriptural and spiritual Christianity in our midst! Were it not for my own home and some of my friendships I should at times become cynical. Oh, that some more had the blessed privilege of feeling the blessings of a truly Christian home and Christian friendships."[4] Although the terms might later be altered, this last wish was to remain the driving force of his entire life. In the slums of Toronto or London or Winnipeg it was this hope and aim that gave him constancy.

During these two years he was forming many questions and some doubts; doubts about the validity of his own position as an evangelistic Methodist preacher and about the wisdom of approaching the problem of decent social living only through the avenue of isolated individuals. At the same time he felt no lessening of the desire to dedicate himself to the salvation of his fellow men. He might wonder about the precise meaning of the word "salvation," but the desire to serve was overwhelming. He regretted time that he "fooled away" upon novels or aimless thought as this might diminish his self-preparation. After one day which he felt to have been largely wasted he wrote in his diary, "My period of severe repentance has not quite come on. Still, what nonsense this is. I must exert more will power or my life will be a failure through simply following inclinations. I am rather too apt to pride myself upon such amiable weaknesses instead of detesting them as they deserve."

Although entertaining some doubts as to his own vocation he determined to go ahead, not quite blindly, believing that with the right purpose he must be doing good. In later years he was to set up the "sin of indifference" as the cardinal violation of human goodness, and for his own purpose he early recognized this as a prime principle.

Oh, how prone to wander away. Is this very proneness not yet a remnant of the sinful life? I do not mean an inclination or desire for positive sin but rather an apathy which does not allow the soul to pray without ceasing. . . . What is to be my present attitude? To wait till all my inquiries may be satisfactorily settled? No, my present life *must* be right, for if God is good he will reveal to me my present duty.[5]

In the autumn of 1898 the young candidate for the ministry entered the theological course at Victoria College in Toronto. His year there

---

[4]Woodsworth, diary, 1896–8.   [5]*Ibid.*

was one of quiet and serious study, with many hours devoted to the intricacies of the Hebrew language. He became more acutely aware of the controversy then raging in the church over the question of "modernism." In that debate Woodsworth was in sympathy with the group led by Rev. George Jackson, minister of Sherbourne Street Church in Toronto, who was preaching the new historical-critical approach to biblical sources. Partly because of early discussions in his home, he was unable to accept the fundamentalist position which was being vigorously asserted by Rev. Albert Carman, Superintendent of the Methodist Church. In his work at Victoria, Woodsworth gave considerable attention to the writings of "higher criticism" and began to formulate still further questions about his own and the church's position on such matters.

Another line of investigation he also discovered at this time—the ideas of the social gospel as they had been tentatively laid out by the American, Washington Gladden, and his sympathizers. He took pains to observe the growing slum conditions in Toronto and admired the work there of the Fred Victor Mission.

By the end of his course at Victoria he had a mind full of questions and a deep-seated purpose to answer as many of them as possible. He was, furthermore, a child of the age, in that he was increasingly reluctant to accept any answers on faith alone. At home he had been given an absolute body of doctrine with the implied admonition that the faith of his fathers was an adequate faith for the children of his day. But he had also heard the faint stirrings of criticism of some of that body of doctrine. In his father he greatly admired the stimulating qualities of an enquiring mind. If Woodsworth had inherited a great pride both in his church and in his country, it was a pride which did not refuse to recognize blemishes in either, but which desired fervently to remove those blemishes.

Woodsworth decided to pause for reflection before committing himself to the ministry. On the advice of Chancellor Burwash of Victoria and with the approval of his parents, he decided to go to Oxford and there make himself familiar with the spirit of the Old World, as well as think through some of his own problems. He was quite clear before he left for England that he was not going to spend a year of continuous study at the British university. He was going, primarily, to allow himself time to digest the content of his previous reading and experience, and to tap, if possible, the wells of an older culture.

In great measure he achieved this dual purpose.

2

OXFORD

AND THE BRITISH SLUMS

WHEN WOODSWORTH WENT OVERSEAS he had a background of experience spreading over half a continent and stretching from rudest frontier conditions to the ambitious culture of Ontario's capital. The young Canadian was probably much better prepared to receive a varied new education than he himself suspected. But there were some qualifications to this. His was not the background, for instance, of a Henry Adams in a search for "education." What Woodsworth was to see would be received through the eyes of a Methodist and a colonial. The adjustment of focus would require more than one journey overseas and immense effort at reassessing inherited values.

In the second week of October, 1899, he boarded the S.S. *California* at Montreal, and on arrival in England went at once to Oxford. "It all seems like dreamland," he wrote on his first day there, "and I wonder sometimes just where I am—or how I got here and how it will all end."[1] He faced this dreamland with characteristic efficiency. Within two days he had secured permanent rooms in Walton Well Road, and had received permission to attend the lectures of Dr. Fairbairn of Mansfield College in theology and Dr. Caird of Balliol in philosophy. This permission he regarded as a real favour since he had decided not to matriculate into the University and thus was paying no fees. Reporting on his position, Woodsworth wrote home, "The information orally is the smallest part of the benefit. . . . You know I told you I was not going to Oxford to study—I can do that at home."

[1] Most of the material in this chapter is taken from correspondence between Woodsworth and his family.

Even in his choice of lodgings he selected an "unlicensed" house, one that was not recognized by the University. Such unlicensed rooms were cheaper, and Woodsworth obtained his board and room for nineteen shillings a week. Whether he realized that these arrangements would mean that he would not experience fully the inner life of the University is not clear. He did manage to meet a number of regular students socially—usually at the tea hour—in his or their lodgings. But as Oxford graduates will quickly assert, this kind of attendance at the University is quite different from regular enrolment.

Apart from lecture hours he spent most of the first term getting to "know" Oxford. He explored the various colleges, the art galleries and museum collections, the libraries and the surrounding countryside. His reaction to much of this was complex. For example, while he deplored automatically the drinking habits of Oxford, he had also a growing awareness that these were part and parcel of a way of life—a way of life which he, in the main, could not help but admire. Returning from a bicycle trip to Blenheim, he wrote home to his sister, "I am sorry I don't drink 'ale' or I would enjoy to the full these old English inns. . . ." Whenever he associated with members of the Oxford Wesley Guild or attended their meetings his reaction was distinctly cool. The achievement of the four Methodist "schools" was not impressive and Woodsworth's general conclusion was that "most Methodist ministers in England have little culture and Methodism has no place in higher education." Although he was elected an honorary member of the Wesley Guild, and preached on several occasions at local village meetings, Woodsworth tended to prefer the Church of England sermons while he was in Oxford.

Toward the end of the first term he arranged to spend a fortnight during the Christmas holiday at the Mansfield College settlement in London. The settlement was a familiar topic of conversation at Oxford, and, holding to his original intention to see English life rather than the tourist glaze, he decided that there was no better method than that of actually living in a university social-service settlement. Probably when he first determined to go to Mansfield House, knowing that the idea of the social settlement had at least some tinge of radicalism and that the establishments themselves were situated in the most poverty-stricken areas, he expected to undergo some discomfort. In this he was once more surprised. Describing the settlement to his father, he wrote: "In the first place, men live here with every comfort. It costs about the same as a hotel I think. But everything is run in what is to me so strange a style that I hardly yet know where I am—at any rate

I am more than delighted. . . ." In letters to his family he was cautious,
for at least part of his delight in Mansfield House was its very practical
approach to the problem of Sunday afternoons. This was not the
traditional approach of Canadian Methodists. The P.S.A., or Pleasant
Sunday Afternoon, at Mansfield House, he noted, was "a political or
social rather than a religious meeting. . . ." And the classes held on the
same day in other places were by no means comparable to the familiar
afternoon Sunday Schools.

Some were on the Bible—on sociology—on Shakespeare and I know not
what all. It seems a peculiar medley. But this is not a city mission. The
ordinary religious meetings fail to meet certain classes and these men are
trying to help them. I cannot now discuss methods. I cannot now understand them. I am trying to study the whole thing which is certainly a sincere
effort to uplift humanity. . . . It is really worth more than months of study.

Mansfield House was close to the docks, and the kind of people, as
well as the conditions in which they existed, provided entirely new
experiences. Woodsworth used his opportunity well and struggled to
understand the picture that was unfolded to him. In one noon hour
he helped to serve a free dinner to several hundred school-children
of the district and came to know "the pathetic eagerness with which
the little lads watched me pouring out the soup, or pleaded for just a
little more of the thicker soup near the bottom. . . ." Another service
of the settlement was free legal advice, volunteered by lawyers who
visited the House on certain evenings each month. On one such evening
Woodsworth acted as clerk for one of the lawyers and heard the
detailed stories of fifteen cases, all of which centred around the problems of debt and drink. On another evening a reception was held at
the House for the "better classes." If the slums of London were beyond
anything Woodsworth had observed in Toronto, so too the customs of
the London bourgeoisie were distinct from those of prairie Methodism.
The Canadian was presented with one more piece to be fitted into
the intricate pattern of his English experience. Today his observations,
contained in a letter to his family, seem curious, but that is the measure
of the adjustment that had to be made between life in London and
life in Brandon. Reporting the reception at Mansfield House, Woodsworth wrote, "Still, you would be shocked at many things. Facilities
were provided in one of the rooms for smoking and cards. Many
people take quite different views on these matters to what we do. . . ."

He could accept the kind of Sunday afternoon offered by the settlement in view of the undoubted fact that the public houses remained
open and "anything is better than that the men should hang around

drinking all the day." But what of the content of the lectures and the predominant opinions of his associates in Mansfield House? One talk he heard was by a pastor of a certain brotherhood church, a representative of Christian Socialism. Another was delivered by a member of Parliament who strongly denounced the South African war, "and this attitude was applauded by the audience—of course working men." Perhaps it was because Methodist training had been more intensive on the subject of drink than on the topics of war and politics that Woodsworth was frankly open-minded on the latter subjects, while on the former he had considerable difficulty. On occasion he was even prepared to offer a tentative defence of certain positions.

Most of the men here in the House are much opposed to the war. They think the English are in the wrong. Indeed it does seem a very great question as to whether we are justified or not. Now I know Harold will object to this. Let us remember that the Boers are his cousins and that they are fighting for their liberty. Why should England be supreme in South Africa? Our losses have been dreadful. Then here in England we have the widows and children. . . .

Woodsworth's survey of London working-class life was amplified during a visit to a friend who had married a Canadian girl and was in charge of a mission church. Here, accompanying the pastor on his rounds, he obtained intimate glimpses of working-class living conditions. At such close quarters the social problem seemed virtually insoluble. Later, writing home from the quiet of a Christmas day in Yorkshire, he commented, "It was really sickening to see the poverty and distress. . . . Of course a good share of the poverty is due to improvidence and drunkenness but that does not make it any the less real or pitiable. Then it seems that nothing permanent can be done. One can give a few coppers—alleviate the distress a little—that is all. Thousands of people in this district are doomed to drag out such a life of misery. . . ." Personal contact with the English people who were suffering from, as well as those who were thinking about the war, and conscientious observation of the London slums intensified Woodsworth's concern to discover a systematic basis of Christian ethics; this was to be the central objective of his second term at Oxford.

Before leaving London, however, interests other than those of the sociologist led Woodsworth to the more conventional places. One afternoon he spent with the private secretary of Leonard Courtney (a prominent Liberal of radical views), visiting the chief Dickens landmarks in the city. Time was also devoted to the "sacred ground" of Bunhill cemetery with its graves of Bunyan and Susannah Wesley, and the City Road Chapel with Wesley's adjoining house—a tour described in careful detail for his parents.

Contrasts presented to Woodsworth during a second sojourn in London in the first days of 1900 sharpened his interest in English social problems. The first part he spent, in billet, with a well-to-do Wesleyan family in the West End, where, in the evenings, four servants came in to prayers. For the latter part he lived with one of the parishioners of the mission church he had previously visited. Here the house also contained its owner's cobbling shop. From there he returned to the East London mission field, even taking over the pastor's work for one day. The discrepancy between his West End billet and his tiny bedroom over the cobbler's shop was striking. The "class distinction" which he found extending deep into ministerial ranks disconcerted him. With surprise he noted, "I certainly can get the people to talk to me as they do not to their own ministers." And the prairie democrat privately berated "most English ministers" for refusing to consider themselves "of the people."

Returning to Oxford by way of Cambridge, Woodsworth reviewed his work with some degree of satisfaction. He had come to England to gain as many points of view as possible, to study life rather than see places. And, deliberately inspecting English life in as many of its expressions as were open to him, he was aware always of a purpose behind his endeavours—a purpose formulated in a letter to his father at the outset of the second Oxford term. "I think I am gaining an idea of a culture deeper than scholarship which many of us have utterly ignored. I do not want to accept all I see. I do not despise what we have at home in Canada—I would not exchange Canada for England. But my ideals for Canada are being raised...."

Christian ethics had been the original focal point of Woodsworth's academic work at Oxford. His purpose did not change, but he soon discovered that his chosen subject was much more nebulous than he had at first suspected. The systematic study of the "science" by Protestants was only beginning and there were no university courses devoted directly to it. Even in the Bodleian Library there was no separate classification for the subject. He found the problem fascinating and peculiarly important for his personal philosophy. It was in essence the same problem that had faced him while riding circuit on the prairie: the almost desperate search for a system that would guide men through the conditions of modern living, and would at the same time embody the quintessence of Christ's moral and ethical teachings.

Along what lines should the reformation of society, distinct from, yet including, the regeneration of the individual soul, be conducted? In short, what was Christian ethics, and how was this scheme of behaviour to be applied in the modern world?

The question must be answered if he were to continue work within the church. Outside the church there were many possible answers. At Mansfield House he had heard some of the "utilitarian" answers, and the London slums had further emphasized the pressing nature of the problem. Reviewing the complexity of the question, he wrote:

While studying philosophy, ethics was presented in entire independence of Christianity. Blewett [of Victoria College, Toronto], one day speaking of this phase of the work, laughingly described himself as a pagan. Indeed, it is true we take no account of Christian revelation. . . . Then (in theology) we are told of sin—of Christ as the only one to deliver from sin. What does it all mean? My ethics has told me nothing of this. How can I reconcile the two, or are they irreconcilable? I turn to the libraries. The books on the subject have their leaves uncut. No one is interested. Everyone is too busy with Latin or Greek and Higher Criticism and Theology. . . . Surely there must be one great system of morality. Nor need this exclude Christianity. Rather, if Christianity is as universal as it claims to be it must combine in itself all morality—must allow for its highest development and be an essential factor in that development. . . .

No doubt its breadth was for Woodsworth one of the attractions of the Church of England, which at this time had identified itself through men like Bishop Gore and Canon Scott Holland with the cause of social reform, while the English Wesleyans were still concerned primarily with a personal evangelism.

He was not the first to be puzzled by the problem, but there was something of originality in the intensity of his desire to solve it. If Woodsworth later proved himself to be more the man of action than of original and systematic theory, he was the better prepared for his task through early recognition of the value of systematic thought. If he was to be increasingly sceptical of all final answers, he also possessed a full appreciation of the suggestive functions of intellectual systems.

In his letters Woodsworth reported many meetings and special lectures with impartiality and little background information. A February debate in the Oxford Union was impressive, but the fact that a Cecil and an Asquith led opposing sides on the question of the war, and even the arguments advanced, received less mention than the reaction of the townspeople following news of the relief of Ladysmith.

There is little evidence of any particular influence exerted upon him either by Caird or Fairbairn. One suspects, however, that Caird's idealism in philosophy and the notable German influences in Oxford would not repel him. Caird, he noted, was the greatest man of his day in English philosophy.

Toward the end of March, Woodsworth visited Edinburgh. He thought it the most beautiful city he had seen, and with Scottish people he felt thoroughly comfortable. "We in Canada are much more like Scotch people, I think, than like English people. I am sure I could feel at home sooner here. . . ." He explored Glasgow and the Trossachs and made several walking trips from Edinburgh. With the chief librarian he inspected the university and its library. To an admirer of Sir Walter Scott all this had a special relish; he even took care to view fair Melrose by the pale moonlight. But again came the qualifications. Concerning the ruined chapel of Roslin he wrote, "I had always thought everything good about the Scottish reformers and Cromwell and the Puritans, but really, it is a shame to see the way they destroyed some beautiful work." A rather more acid comment was prompted by a service he had attended in an Edinburgh mission hall. "Talk about methodist enthusiasm, testimonials, etc. Why, these evangelical Scotch are away ahead of our modern Methodists. . . ." And, as his sensitive eye surveyed the conditions in working-class Edinburgh, he was once again brought up short. Even though his visit was brief, he found time to accompany a medical student on a round of visits, and again encountered the ubiquitous slum.

In the latter part of April, Woodsworth yielded to the lure of Paris and the great Exhibition. With the latter he was somewhat disappointed, as many of the buildings were still incomplete. With Paris and Versailles he was entranced and on the Champs Elysées he discovered "all the gaiety and life of the French capital in its perfection. . . ." French customs were even more startling to him than those of England, but the conditioning of the preceding months had been excellent preparation. The Louvre and the art collections at Versailles moved him to regret his lack of earlier exposure to them. It might be noted here that despite partial colour blindness, Woodsworth was genuinely appreciative of graphic as well as other forms of art. He used to claim that the handicap was an advantage as he could distinguish finer gradations of colour in some areas of the spectrum than could most people.

Woodsworth's initiation into the life of the Old World necessitated frequent reflection and assessment. If he seemed at times to be overwhelmed, there was always an illuminating ray of sceptical good sense. In a letter written in Yorkshire during a pause in his travels there is clear evidence of this inherent stability.

I wish I understood something about music. One feels there are worlds all around, about which he is in dense ignorance. When I hear beautiful music —watch a painter or sculptor—see something of architecture—the great industries on every hand—learn the hundreds of different subjects that men are reading or studying, I almost feel that it is useless to try to learn much because it can be such a small proportion of the world's knowledge. . . . And yet, sometimes one ignorant man practically sets up the claim that his ideas and standards should be the measure of the universe. . . .

While he was prepared to give due praise to endeavour in any field, the threat of tyranny in any remained a thing to be abhorred and opposed.

Returning to Oxford from Paris, Woodsworth sought to review his year's experience. He had gained perspective; previous knowledge had been allowed to settle. At Victoria College many questions had arisen, and familiar standards had seemed no longer valid. "Well now I find things are becoming somewhat steady again. My somersaults may have changed my position somewhat, but after all, things around are steady, even if my viewpoint has altered a little. . . ."

His overseas experience had by no means destroyed his faith in the general structure and purpose of Canadian Methodism. He suspected, perhaps, that he himself lacked the deep and immediate inspiration required in Methodist ministers, but that did not mean that he could not continue either in some non-pastoral work or in his search for pastoral inspiration. The first alternative was his preference. Examining the question of his future course he decided that his "gift" was that of teacher rather than preacher or administrator. Perhaps the way in which he defined the problem to his father suggests his growing fear that he could never accept unreservedly the position of a regular minister—and his anxiety was partly due to his desire not unnecessarily to disappoint his parents. "Now, while our church, especially, has emphasized preaching, I believe that there is room in the Christian ministry for the exercise of various other gifts. Still, under our present policy, and in the present state of the work, the teacher, if he remain in the regular work, does not have the best opportunities for the exercise of his distinctive talents. . . ." Beyond doubt, Woodsworth was correct in his self-analysis. He was born to teach, and those who insisted in seeing only the preacher in him, to the end, failed in their understanding of him. It remained true, certainly, that he wished always to influence the thought and lives of other men; but the influence was to result from assisting them to discover and understand realities, not by telling them what was or was not so.

At this time he suggested to his father that he might join the faculty of Wesley College. He emphasized the strategic position occupied by the college teacher. One great need of the Canadian West, thought Woodsworth, was for scholars who were in touch with the requirements of the time and who lived in its spirit. Again, there would be opportunities, he felt, for assisting in city mission work and perhaps for extending the influence of the college throughout the prairie countryside. Woodsworth's father was at the time a member of the Board of Wesley College, and the son suggested that the matter might be mentioned unofficially to the chairman. He noted that such procedure was no different from that which might laudably be followed in entering foreign mission work. The end in view was fully as justifiable. This proposal came to nothing, either because Woodsworth's father hesitated, as a member of the Board, to forward it, or because there was no opening on the college faculty. It did represent, however, a broad definition of intention.

Before leaving for Canada Woodsworth expanded his itinerary to include a brief visit to Germany and a trip on the Rhine between Rotterdam and Mannheim. Although this was a journey more purely for enjoyment than any of his previous overseas activities, some of his contemporary comments are characteristic. The most consistent note struck in his letters from Germany was one of admiration, not only for the beauty of the Rhine with its castled crags and mediaeval atmosphere, but also for the German people and their way of life. Describing Cologne, its cathedral, and the trim charm of the city, he wrote, "Then there does not seem to be that degraded element which is everywhere in evidence in the great cities of England." The efficiency of the state-owned railways appealed to him as did the generally ordered air of the towns. He did not find the military atmosphere distasteful, and commented, "Today at Duisberg I saw a fine company of German soldiers. . . . They were all mounted and carried their lances upright. As they rode along the high stone paved streets one almost imagined that he was back in the days of chivalry." And again, "The presence of large numbers of soldiers gives a lively appearance to a crowd." At Heidelberg he met casually two German students who spoke English and he was tremendously impressed by their courteous manner. When they invited him to watch a duel, Woodsworth accepted and went to the "clubhouse" of the duelling society where he observed the procedure which accounted for the great scars on many of the students' faces. Pleased with the hospitality shown him, he wrote: "I confess that I shall always have a kindlier feeling towards those organizations which English students generally call 'Duelling societies' and 'Beer Drinking Clubs.' " The enthusiasm with which he greeted the principle of order with its apparent results of efficiency and absence of abject poverty was, however, the most significant feature of his brief visit to Germany. His views on the military were soon to change. His ideas about order, efficiency, and welfare in society, though they became much more complex, were to remain basically unaltered.

In July, 1900, Woodsworth returned to Canada, received his degree in divinity from Victoria College, and went then to Brandon where he was ordained a Methodist minister by a special committee in August.[2]

For James and Josephine Woodsworth the twenty-sixth of August, 1900, was a day of fulfilment. The note in the front of the Bible which was presented to their son on that occasion reads, "James S. Woodsworth, dedicated to God by his parents at his birth, and now commended by them to Him for keeping and blessing. . . ." For their son it was no less a time of consecration. But there must also have been disturbing overtones of doubt. On the circuit he had questioned the validity of his ministerial inspiration; at Victoria he had been faced with the problem of higher criticism of the Bible; at Oxford he had wrestled with the question of Christian ethics and its relation to the modern world. He had observed overseas a social *milieu* and an intellectual atmosphere much of which appeared admirable; he had also been warned of social problems then only in their birth throes in Canada. Could he, within the pastoral work of the church, find adequate outlet for his deep humanitarianism and for his burning desire to prevent in his own country a repetition of the evils he had seen in London, Edinburgh, the black country, and elsewhere? Was he, even granting the rest, certain of his vocation?

[2]This procedure was arranged because he was absent during the annual Conference meeting in June.

3

TRIAL

TURNED ASIDE FROM THE contemplated rôle of church college professor, Woodsworth almost automatically entered work in a western mission field. A year at Carieval in Assiniboia was followed by a similar appointment as pastor of a small church in Keewatin, Ontario.

Here again was the evangelical work of the frontier, and once more the struggle for conviction. All the old questions recurred. Could he really accept the dogmas of the Methodist "Discipline"? Was the continual effort to "save" the individual, while ignoring his social context, really practical Christianity? Apathy on the part of the members of his congregation, and perhaps a sense of isolation, helped to imbue these questions with a great urgency. During the long winter at Keewatin, Woodsworth came to a position where he could no longer believe literally some of the church's basic theological statements. The mystery of the Trinity, the doctrine of the two natures in one person, he rejected as "both inconclusive and unnecessary."[1] But this alienation from orthodoxy seemed only to strengthen his acceptance of the spiritual revelation through Christ. This, he claimed, was morally certain: "Jesus has given us a revelation of God which bears upon it the impress of truth and is witnessed to by our spiritual needs and experience."[2]

His own experience and reading had emphasized the social nature of most of man's problems. The need which he felt to attack these problems and the equally personal insistence that his relationship to individuals and groups be completely honest, led inevitably to a crisis. The course he followed toward this crisis is portrayed in an allegorical

[1]Woodsworth papers, 1901.
[2]*Ibid.*, 1902.

reflection penned in his contemporary notebook. He had, he observed, been reading Wendt[3] and Gibbon,

but these writers were not the cause of my change—at most they but precipitated the inevitable end of my course of thought. It was as if I had been travelling along an uneven mountain path. Lately the way had been smoother. I walked confidently, notwithstanding the drifting mists. Suddenly the mists cleared and I found myself on the very verge of a precipice. I looked down but could not see the bottom. There was no turning to right or left. I could not retrace my steps. . . . I thought of my parents—my dearest friends—their grief—I was leaving them. My life was a failure. . . . I found myself in the valley again and started forward with uncertain steps. . . . The mist was thicker in the valley but the path still ran on much the same as before and I was none the worse. Sometimes I shuddered at the thought of my long fall. Again, I forgot that I was not on the mountain path, and still again I wondered if the valley might not be safer and more beautiful than the mountain. So I go on my way assured that I am still on God's earth. . . .[4]

The "fall," however, appeared to imply certain specific consequences. Woodsworth decided that he believed "fully and sincerely" only those Methodist doctrines directed against Romish and "other false teachings," and those which taught the necessity of a moral life; and even the details of these he was soon to question. He knew now that he could not "endeavour fully and faithfully to preach" the others, as required by his ordination vows. On June 10, 1902, he addressed a formal letter of resignation to the President of the Manitoba and North West Conference. His decision to break with the past, and perhaps with many of his old friends, was not easy. That he believed such separation might be involved is evident in his contemporary speculation about going to the United States to teach. That he felt dissatisfied in pastoral work is apparent in a letter which he sent to his cousin and college friend, C. B. Sissons. With reference to the ministry he wrote: ". . . take the advice of one who says 'keep out of

[3]This probably refers to Hans H. Wendt, *The Teaching of Jesus*, published in English in 1896. Wendt was a German critic of New Testament sources, and a follower of Albrecht Ritschl.

[4]Woodsworth papers, 1902. In this year Woodsworth read, among other titles: F. D. Maurice, *Modern Doubt and Christian Belief*; W. E. H. Lecky, *History of European Morals*; Gibbon, *Decline and Fall of the Roman Empire*; Darwin, *The Origin of Species*; B. T. Washington, *Up from Slavery*; and works by Kingsley, Hugo, Carlyle, N. W. Willis, and H. Van Dyke. In the preceding year a lengthy reading list included: B. F. Browne, *The Philosophy of Theism*; D. Kidd, *Social Evolution*; Josiah Strong, *The Twentieth Century City*; W. T. Stead, *If Christ Came to Chicago*; J. Ruskin, *Ethics in the Dust*; Froude, *Oceana*; and Carlyle, *Past and Present* and *Heroes and Hero-Worship*.

it if you can'. . . . You know I am dreadfully heretical on many points. . . . Next year I should like to get to Winnipeg for some city mission work."[5]

Woodsworth arrived at the Conference meeting of June, 1902, with the letter of resignation in his pocket. That letter was never delivered. His proposed action being known in advance, largely because his family was so intimately connected with the affairs and leaders of western Methodism, the President of the Conference and several other members dissuaded him from carrying to conclusion so drastic a step.

Several pressures bore upon Woodsworth influencing him to alter his decision. His family's feeling in the matter was important, for although both his mother and father made it clear that their prime concern was that he should follow truly the dictates of his own conscience, he could not be entirely unconcerned about the distress he would cause them by openly breaking with their church. Much more important than the personal factor were the arguments of respected men, spokesmen for the church, assuring him that there was scope for his kind of belief within the Methodist ministry. He was convinced that in accepting their assurances he was in no way compromising with himself. Perhaps he saw the situation in these terms: having declared his position unequivocally to the proper authorities, it was no longer entirely his responsibility to prove that he could work within the church. It was also the church's opportunity to show that it could use the services of men with progressive ideas. A bold and, superficially perhaps, an egotistical conception. But one would do less than justice to Woodsworth in painting him only as modest and well-meaning. While for himself he entertained only the most restricted ambitions, for his ideas and the essential justice of his cause at any time he was willing to be uncompromising and even belligerent. In any event, having cleared the air for himself he was prepared to try again the work of the regular ministry.

The Conference appointed him assistant pastor to Rev. R. F. Bowles of Grace Church, Winnipeg. Without hesitation he threw himself into the new pastoral work, giving most of his time during the first two years there to visiting and to the Young People's organization. In the first half of his association with Grace Church he began to feel that he had really found a working basis within Methodism—that the sincerity and zeal with which he carried out his duties showed an adequate return in the increased interest in the church exhibited by those with

[5]J. S. Woodsworth to C. B. Sissons, Feb. 14, 1901 (one of a small collection of Woodsworth-Sissons letters in the Victoria University Archives).

whom he worked. At least the spiritual returns appeared to be more substantial than those observed in Carieval or Keewatin.

In the summer of 1904 Woodsworth journeyed east to Bethany, Ontario, where he married Lucy Lilian Staples, whom he had come to know at Victoria College and upon whose sympathy and support he was to rely with ever growing confidence.[6] For the newly married couple the year 1904 must have been one of nearly perfect content-ment. They returned to Winnipeg in late September to be warmly received by the Woodsworth family and by friends in Grace Church. Their home quickly became a gathering place for the younger people of the congregation, and the paths to the future seemed clear.

Winnipeg in 1904 was at the very heart of Canada's great "wheat boom." The economic potentialities of the Canadian West and of its railway metropolis seemed unlimited. Between 1891 and 1901 the population of Manitoba expanded from 152,506 to 255,211, and reached 461,392 by 1911. Between 1901 and 1906 the population of Winnipeg grew from 42,340 to 90,153 and by 1908 had reached 139,863. In Winnipeg, in 1908, it was estimated that between one-quarter and one-third of the population was foreign-born—a mag-nificent labour market for the western Canadian entrepreneurs, agrarian or industrial. As the gateway to the West and a great railway focal point Winnipeg stood to gain immensely from the federal railway policies formulated in 1903 and 1904, those years of hysterical economic optimism. Between 1901 and 1914 railway milage in the prairie provinces increased from 18,140 to 30,795. The business of the Winni-peg Grain Exchange mushroomed, while the winners (or losers) in the vast new game of real estate gambling congregated in Winnipeg to make the most of their new-found affluence (or to swell the ranks of the unemployed). In short, by 1904, Winnipeg was well on the way to being the Chicago of western Canada. What young minister would not count himself fortunate to obtain a post at the centre of this land of opportunity? As early as 1902, Woodsworth had written to his cousin in Toronto urging him to come west: "You have no idea of the

[6]Mrs. Woodsworth's ancestors came to Canada from Ireland in 1825 and settled on a farm at Cavan, Durham County, Ontario. She received a well-rounded education, progressing from the country school, to Lindsay Collegiate, to the Ottawa Normal School. She graduated from Victoria College in 1901 with an honours degree in Moderns and History. In 1902 she received the honours degree in Moderns and History from the Ontario Normal College. Before attending Victoria she had taught for several years.

enthusiasm people have here about the prospects. My only fear is that we may not stop short of a boom. . . ."[7]

Clouds, however, soon appeared. Grace Church was one of the wealthiest places of worship in Winnipeg, counting among its illustrious membership R. T. Riley, J. H. Ashdown, J. A. M. Aikins, and other leaders in the business and legal community. These leading Methodists represented the backbone of Winnipeg respectability. They were prepared to sponsor and contribute to charitable undertakings, but most certainly did not constitute the *avant garde* of the social gospel in the West. Most of them were well acquainted with the young assistant minister's parents, and although they undoubtedly knew something of his unorthodoxy, accepted him partly because of his background. The basis of this tolerance was steadily undermined. More and more the elders of Grace Church were aware of the precarious balance maintained between the acceptability of Woodsworth's conservative background and the irritation they experienced whenever he stepped into the pulpit. For although the young minister found himself on good terms with Dr. W. A. Sparling, who succeeded Dr. Bowles at Grace, he did not cease reading nor was his mind inactive on the problems that previously had plagued him.[8] Comment upon these questions inevitably found its way into Woodsworth's sermons. And no matter how moderate his treatment of the matter under discussion, there was a considerable volume of advice proferred the junior minister by his father's friends. One professor intimated in unmistakable terms that the young man was ruining his career. A notable conservative lawyer suggested suavely that the junior minister should give "less ill-digested sociology and more simple gospel preaching." In short, the son of Dr. James Woodsworth was creating some uneasiness among the influential people of the congregation. The feeling was not dispelled when, during the summer of 1905 while Woodsworth was acting pastor, he invited the "radical" Dr. Salem Bland of Wesley College to supply one service each Sunday. During that summer Bland preached a series of sermons on "The Ideal City" and Woodsworth one on "Business Life."[9]

[7]J. S. Woodsworth to C. B. Sissons, Aug. 21, 1902.

[8]Among the books which Woodsworth read from 1903 to 1906 are the following titles: J. Strong, *The Next Great Awakening*; F. G. Peabody, *Jesus Christ and the Social Question*; R. Blatchford, *Britain for the British*; W. A. Wycloff, *The Workers*; H. D. Lloyd, *Newest England*; E. Haeckel, *The Riddle of the Universe*; J. A. Hobson, *Problems of Poverty*; Bryce, *The American Commonwealth*; G. Smith, *Commonwealth or Empire*; Froude, *Erasmus*; Morley, *Compromise*; Bingham, *Shaftesbury*; Davenport, *Primitive Traits in Religious Revivals*; and Hugo, *Les Miserables.*   [9]J. S. Woodsworth to C. B. Sissons, Aug. 9, 1905.

There is preserved a notebook in which Woodsworth wrote the outlines for a number of his sermons during this period of mounting tension. No question which he considered important was skirted and certainly he made no intellectual compromises as pastor for a wealthy flock. Perhaps recalling his reading of the *American Commonwealth*, he tackled the subject of political machines in a sermon delivered early in 1904. "In this democracy of ours," he said, "we often hear the expression, 'it is money that talks.' Yes, often it is money that votes. It is money that rules us. Surely it is time for us to awake from our lethargy. Shall we stand by while this old landmark of British freedom is undermined by those who live under its protection?" To those who financed the machinery of the national parties in Winnipeg, this was unpalatable, especially as many of their sons and daughters thought highly of Woodsworth and talked appreciatively of evenings spent in his home or in the Young People's club rooms.

Other sermons followed on the corrupting effects of wealth. "The Kingdom of God is a kingdom of self-control—a kingdom of self-denial —and these are not virtues that are easily developed in a wealthy home. . . ." Throughout his sermon notes there is a characteristic emphasis on personal purity and the avoidance of sensuality. Indeed an irrepressible idealism was always hand in hand with his practical reforming zeal, and on occasion he set a standard for his hearers that was reminiscent of an older puritanism. In art, he asserted, perfection of form and colour could never satisfy higher needs. These things, as ends, were not of the Father but of the world. Ostentatious display was still more abhorrent. "I fear that in our own city we have not yet learned the vulgarity of a lavish expenditure of newly acquired wealth. Costly dresses, magnificent houses, expensive entertainments— those are the things we seek after. And the snobbishness that goes with such vulgarity! The pride of wealth. . . ." The standards which he proclaimed were not beyond his own reach. He willingly accepted a very modest income, and yet was eager for the pleasures that come from good books and art, the satisfaction of raising a family,[10] and of performing, as far as is humanly possible, a selfless service to society.

As living values these constituted the antithesis of the growing commercialism he saw on every side, and they represented for him, as for the Protestants of earlier days, a return to original Christian principles. In the booming Canadian West, and in the Methodist Church which was so integral a part of it, slight attention seemed to be paid to such values. The greater the wealth amassed, the less the

[10]The Woodsworths' first child, Grace, was born in July, 1905.

sense of responsibility—this seemed to be almost axiomatic. Woodsworth's sermons attacked the perverted development in specific terms. "The Sin of Indifference" was his favourite title for exhortation in this vein. As in the days of the Old Testament, he would begin,

A curse still hangs over inactivity. A severe condemnation still rests upon indifference. . . . Christianity stands for social righteousness as well as personal righteousness. . . . It is quite right for me to be anxious to save my never dying soul; but it is of greater importance to try to serve the present age. Indeed, my friend, you will save your own precious soul only as you give your life in the service of others. . . . There have been socialists and positivists and secularists and agnostics who, by their sincerity and earnestness and self-sacrificing spirit, have put to shame many of the professed followers of Christ. . . . If it is right to help the sick it is right to do away with filth and overcrowding and to provide sunlight and good air and good food. We have tried to provide *for the poor.* Yet, have we tried to alter the social conditions that lead to poverty? . . . You can't separate a man from his surroundings and deal separately with each. What nonsense we talk! We allow a false psychology or a narrow theology, or a misapplied logic to carry us into all kinds of absurdities. . . .

Here was the social gospel that was then sweeping through the lower branches of church hierarchies all over America. It was the timeless warning of social reformers everywhere.

In Woodsworth's case the personal intensity of the message was reinforced by wide reading, travel, and observation. Spiritually and intellectually he had arrived at the station which he was never to desert. The true Christian society, for him, could never be other than organic in its nature, and certainly it could never be founded upon the principle of competition. "Jesus said very little about saving souls—He spoke often about the establishment of the Kingdom." Or again, "Need constitutes a claim—this is Christian Socialism, Christian charity, Christian love. This is the great principle that must be applied to our social problems. No Christian liveth to himself. . . ." He would elaborate this theme as the years passed, and would fill in many gaps in his information about the business man's society that was being consolidated in Canada. But he was to deviate in no essential from the position which he had resolutely taken by 1906.

At a time when the well-to-do of Winnipeg were scrambling for a share in the appreciated land values of the period, making substantial profits in the remarkable railway undertakings of McKenzie and Mann, or enjoying an unprecedented expansion in commercial activity, the young minister was attacking their indifference to the growing slums and the harsh competitive morality which he saw lying at the root of all these enterprises. The heartless economic struggle which was producing greater and greater inequalities of wealth and opportunity, he already believed, was also the fundamental cause of war. He accepted, in this connection, the teaching of both Tolstoi and Hobson—a combination perhaps, which illustrated his chronic dichotomy of purpose and thought, combining the emotional with the material. The undeclared, but none the less real and bitter war between individuals and classes "within the bosom of a single state," as well as the ramification of this struggle in international and imperial war, claimed a growing share of his attention.

In this struggle, Woodsworth was painfully aware that the Christian aims of social justice and of peace seldom received their proper emphasis in the councils of the churches. Furthermore, since the problem of church policy and outlook resolved itself in the final analysis into one of personal sincerity and enlightenment, the whole question of church doctrine must be faced in specific terms. That is, if Christianity was really to be applied, its major aims and beliefs should be stated in such a manner that men of sincerity, intelligence, and goodwill could fully accept and teach them. It was not enough that certain absolute formulae should be laid down and then interpreted so broadly that they ceased to hold the meaning that their words seemed to carry.

Perhaps this fundamental trait—a kind of perfectionism—was impractical. Perhaps, even, it indicated a reluctance to work with, or under the direction of men with whom he did not agree. Certainly Woodsworth was a leader and not a follower, as the whole of his later activity was to show. Just as sure, however, is the conclusion that the driving force supplied by his humanitarian idealism made practicable many things which to a mere opportunist would have remained chimerical impossibilities.

By the summer of 1906, the moral and intellectual issues combined forces with ill health to demand a leave of absence from regular church duties. Woodsworth's father had decided to make periodic trips to the British Isles in search of recruits for the mission field of western Canada. Now, in July of 1906, the son decided to take his wife and accompany his father and sister to the Old World.[11] The earlier journey to Oxford, and now this venture of some six months' duration

[11]His commonplace book notes a change in his reading for the year 1906; it included: Jerome K. Jerome, *Three Men in a Boat*; Mark Twain, *A Tramp Abroad*, and *Innocents Abroad*; Ruskin, *Crown of Wild Olives*; Swift, *Gulliver's Travels*; and biographies of Southey and Wordsworth.

established firmly the belief that no education is complete if it lacks the element of travel.

Together, in 1906, the Woodsworths visited the British Isles, France, the Low Countries, and Germany, and then, in October, it was decided that he should remain overseas until the end of the year, while his wife returned to her family's farm at Cavan, where their little daughter had been left. From October to December, Woodsworth travelled through Switzerland, Italy, Egypt, and Palestine. In Florence he bought a small bronze bust of Savonarola, that religious reformer being one of his "prophets." He saw much and brought back a fund of experience, which was later incorporated in writings, speeches and even in bed-time stories for his children. Charles Woodsworth, in an unpublished memoir of his father, has written, "As children we never wearied of hearing him recount how, on a visit to the pyramids, he had meekly exchanged his lordly but spine-jolting camel for the guide's lowlier but more comfortable mule, and how he used the crook of his umbrella to pull himself up from one huge stone block to the next in climbing the pyramid of Giseh. What Father was doing in Egypt's arid climate with an umbrella we never stopped to question."

The basic importance of the trip, however, was the free time it gave for thought, and the environment congenial to objective reflection.

During the past six months [Woodsworth wrote at the end of his trip], when away from the many duties of church work, and mixing with all sorts and conditions of men, I have been able to view matters with a certain detachment. . . . It is more and more difficult for me to believe in the "supernatural" events as recorded in the Old and New Testaments. I have been seeing so much superstition, so much that is mere tradition, that I have been forced to find some standard by which I could determine what was true and what false—and I can't see how the supernatural can find a place. . . .[12]

Questions that had bulked so large for Voltaire and, indeed, for the writers of the "higher criticism," now pressed with growing insistence upon him. Miracle stories were common to most religions—why reject all but one group? "I haven't found an answer to this 'why.' "[13] While at Grace Church he had thought he had found a working compromise. Although he had not accepted the Methodist doctrines precisely, he had felt himself in possession of the essential truth. "But now the question is not so much as to this or that particular doctrine, but it is this—when my views are so, confessedly, different from those contained in the standards of our church and held by the majority, am I justified

[12]J. S. Woodsworth to his brother, Joseph, Jan. 7, 1907.
[13]*Ibid.*

in remaining in the church. Would not that course be hypocritical or Jesuitical?"[14]

Such was Woodsworth's state of mind in December of 1906. He was then in Jerusalem. He received a cable from friends in Revelstoke, British Columbia, asking his help in an emergency that had developed in their church. At first he did not clearly understand the purpose of the Revelstoke offer, but this much was sure: return to Canada and another effort to clear the air were immediately necessary.

He undertook the return journey at once, and while resting briefly at Cavan with his wife and baby, received a letter from his cousin, C. B. Sissons, who had kept in close touch with Woodsworth and had been his best man in 1904. At this time Sissons was principal of the Revelstoke High School and wrote explaining the present situation. Difficulties had been encountered with the local Methodist pastor; it was necessary to find someone prepared to enter a disrupted congregation in this railway and lumbering outpost and restore harmony. The close friendship between the two cousins, and Sissons' knowledge of Woodsworth's vigorous devotion to any work that was at hand, made the choice a natural one.

Temporarily, Woodsworth was thus provided with a solution, and accepted the post as an appointment from January to June, 1907. He was determined to present his resignation at the annual meeting of the Manitoba Conference, which was not until June. In the meantime it was an opportunity to do useful work in surroundings suited to the exhausting effort of analysing again his relation to the church. That analysis would necessarily accompany his second letter of resignation in the spring.

[14]*Ibid.*

4

THE SOCIAL GOSPEL

IN THE MOUNTAINS AROUND Revelstoke winter reluctantly gave way to spring and Woodsworth found a physical release for his pent-up emotions of the preceding months. In the last week of April he went to Rogers Pass and in the following two days walked the forty-six miles back to Revelstoke. He found the tramp exhilarating and in a long letter to his wife and parents pictured the excursion for them. No one can read that letter without sensing its author's pantheistic appreciation of natural beauty. The English poets, he thought, could never have caught the inner turbulence of a Canadian mountain river. He wished passionately that he could sketch; and the thrill of making his way through the opaque darkness of a tortuous railway snow shed, or of half falling, half climbing down steep mountain slopes was not soon to be forgotten.

Returning to Revelstoke, he found a letter from his father. It was the best possible conclusion to a correspondence whose main theme had been the son's impending resignation. Dr. Woodsworth made no attempt to conceal his feelings, yet considerately relieved his son of any over-burdening sense of family disapproval. The point is important. Although Woodsworth was then in his thirty-third year, and by other standards might easily have followed his own course without much misgiving as to his parents' convictions, his whole tradition and training prohibited this. The Woodsworth family possessed a strong sense of solidarity. The tradition of open discussion within the family circle was deep-rooted, and the family correspondence in this period was significant for the nascent rebel. He could spend a winter buttressing his own position by acute analysis; he could come to his own conclusions; he could even obtain a sense of divine approval through communion with nature; but in the final stage the opinion of the family was extremely important. There was never any possibility that either parent would attempt to interfere with his decision, once it was announced, as that, too, would have been alien to the whole spirit of the family. But the intimacy of their relationship constituted a complicating emotional element in the situation.

The expected sanction was provided in his father's letter:

... it is only natural that we should feel very badly that what seemed to be your life work should thus be interrupted—and even the word "interrupted" may not be in place. . . . Feeling as you do I do not see that any other course is open to you—and I am under the impression that the Conference will feel obliged to accept your resignation. . . . However, a Methodist Conference is not all the world. The day may come when there will be greater liberty of thought and action. . . . While we all regret the occasion that has led you to take this step, there is no dishonour involved, and we admire your courage and honesty. . . .[1]

This had not been the family's immediate reaction to his decision, at least as far as his mother was concerned. In January he had received a letter from her which must have weighed heavily upon him during the winter's work.

... your letter this afternoon was not one of the pacific kind, it made me feel weak and sick at heart. . . . I just believe that you are where you were five years ago—worn out in body, and the same old temptation has come to torture you again. And now the case seems to be so much worse, for there are so many more to be brought into suffering with you. . . . Do you think all this training for a life work would have been allowed you if it were not in the right way? In the meantime let us not lose hold of the power of prayer.[2]

There had followed the hard weeks of pastoral work among the railway men and in the lumber camps: successful work for the church while he was convinced that he must resign from the ministry and while he was hammering out the details of his statement for the Conference. Matters were not made easier by the absence of his wife, who had to remain with her relatives in Cavan, where her second child was born in May, 1907. But in letters he received her unqualified support for the step he was about to take, and the courage with which she faced their troubled future became a part of his own moral determination.

Finally, with spring, his statement was completed, his family's

[1]Dr. James Woodsworth to J. S. Woodsworth, April 24, 1907.
[2]Mrs. James Woodsworth to J. S. Woodsworth, Jan. 7, 1907.

acceptance of the necessity of resignation was made known to him,[3] and the day for the assembling of his District Meeting was at hand. Without delay Woodsworth handed his letter of resignation and the supplementary statement to Dr. Stewart, the acting chairman. Only the letter was read to the meeting. Then the matter was referred to a committee.[4] The committee members urged him strongly to withdraw his resignation, but at adjournment the District Meeting had to report failure. He was urged also, by close friends, to withold his statement and allow the Manitoba Conference, to whose deliberation the case automatically went, to make its decision without the obstacle of the detailed statement. Woodsworth again refused; the whole matter must be made completely clear to his colleagues.

At the Conference, Dr. James Elliott moved that the problem be again referred to a committee. Rev. F. B. Stacey, Rev. Thompson Ferrier, and Dr. Elliott were named to confer with Woodsworth. In private he read his prepared statement to them, explained his position still more fully and answered questions which they put to him. There could be no mistaking the sympathetic attitude of these men, but probably Woodsworth was more surprised than many members of the Conference when the three committee-men presented to the Conference president the following report: "Having had a full and frank conversation with Bro. James S. Woodsworth re the cause of his resignation, we find that there is nothing in his doctrinal beliefs and adhesion to our discipline to warrant his separation from the ministry of the Methodist Church, and therefore recommend that his resignation be not accepted and that his character be now passed." The committee's report was put to a vote of the Conference and accepted. The Methodist use of the word "character" has reference to the individual's acceptance and practice of the Methodist Discipline. In the Minutes of the Manitoba Conference (1907) the notation is "Resigned: James S. Woodsworth—moved by Dr. Elliott, seconded by Dr. Rose that the chair appoint a committee to confer with Bro. Woodsworth before final action be taken. *Carried.* . . . On returning the committee reported through F. B. Stacey that they found Bro. Woodsworth in harmony with Methodist doctrine and that he had withdrawn his resignation and character clear."

[3]His mother, in a letter of April 26, 1907, had written: "I had hoped and prayed that faith or light might come in some way to avert this step. This does not seem possible with your condition of mind. We know and sympathize with you in the long delayed struggle that has led to this decision."
[4]The District Meeting committee consisted of Principal Sparling, Dr. S. P. Rose, and Dr. William Sparling.

Woodsworth was unprepared for this decision. He had known that there would be considerable pressure from many quarters to prevent his resignation, and he had seen in 1902 the willingness of the Methodist leaders to be lenient toward the details of private belief. But this time he had presented his colleagues with what amounted to an unqualified indictment of basic sections of the Discipline. Even his father had agreed that the Conference would have no alternative to accepting his resignation. The content of his statement is of more than passing interest, as it not only defines his own position; its acceptance by the committee, and through the committee, by the Conference, throws an interesting light on the apparent flexibility of western Methodism in those years.

He began with a reference to the General Rules of the church, which prohibited, among other things, "playing at games of chance, encouraging lotteries, attending theatres, horse-races, circuses, dancing parties, patronizing dancing schools, taking such other amusements as are obviously of a misleading or questionable moral tendency, and all acts of disobedience to the Order and Discipline of the Church." Here Woodsworth stated conclusively, "I do not believe in these rules. I cannot enforce them."[5] Again, he took exception to the Order of Baptism for infants, where the compulsory opening prayer was, "Almighty and Everlasting God, Who of Thy great mercy didst save Noah and his family in the Ark from perishing by water; and also didst safely lead the children of Israel, Thy People, through the Red Sea, figuring thereby Thy Holy Baptism. . . ." Woodsworth found most of this objectionable, but contented himself with the comment, "I do not believe that in any sense these incidents 'figure' Christian Baptism. . . ."

Similarly the Order for the Administration of the Lord's Supper presented a clearly defined theory, which he could not accept, and he would not make "a mockery of the form." With the central theological doctrine, as phrased in the questions put to candidates for the ministry, he could not agree.

Do you sincerely and fully believe the doctrines of Methodism as contained in our twenty-five Articles of Religion, and as taught by Mr. Wesley in his Notes on the New Testament and volumes of sermons, especially the following leading ones; the total depravity of all men by nature, in consequence of Adam's fall; the atonement made by Christ for the sins of all the human race; the direct witness of the Spirit; the possibility of falling from a state

---

[5]The original copy of this statement is in the Woodsworth papers. It was published by him in 1926 as part of a pamphlet entitled *Following the Gleam*.

of justification and holiness and perishing everlastingly; the absolute necessity of holiness both of heart and life and the proper eternity of future rewards and punishments?

About most of this he was in doubt. The Methodist conception of the nature of Christ, the Virgin birth, and the physical resurrection and ascension he did not believe. How then could he preach it? He was well aware that many ministers agreed with some or all of his own reservations, but thought it necessary to believe only "the essential underlying truths." To this position, he replied:

But who is to determine what are the essential underlying truths? Words have well-recognized meanings. We cannot play fast and loose with them. So long as I hold the office to which such statements admitted me, and to which today I would not receive admission without making the same statements, I am bound in common honesty to continue to believe and preach these doctrines. So soon as I am unable to "sincerely and fully believe them" and to "fully and faithfully preach them," it seems to me that but one course is open. . . .

Not only on questions of doctrine did Woodsworth feel himself to be in a false position. There was the oldest and, from the Methodist point of view, perhaps the most important question of all: his personal religious experience. He had never been "converted"; he had not "faith in Christ" as that phrase was formally defined; he did not "expect to be made perfect in love in this life." He did not believe in fasting as a religious exercise. "In this matter of personal experience lies the root of the difficulty. My experience has not been what among Methodists is considered normal. . . . My experience has determined my theology, and my theology my attitude toward the Discipline. And all three, according to our standards, are un-Methodistical."

Had not the character of the statement's author been known, all this might have been interpreted as a harsh, slashing attack upon the church. Woodsworth himself was aware that men who knew he held such views might question his sincerity in having remained in the ministry after 1902, even knowing the circumstances of that year. Thus, he included several paragraphs of personal explanation.

With me it was not a case of *entering* the church. I was born and brought up in the Methodist Church and easily found my way into its Ministry. It was not difficult to give assent to the doctrines as a whole—though, I may say, I never gave an affirmative answer to all the questions proposed to candidates. I have always tried to be frank in stating my experiences and views to my brethren, whether in private conversation, or, when occasion permitted, in our ministerial gatherings. I have preached only what I believed to be the truth. . . .

In his conclusion he pointed out that his contemplated resignation of 1902 had really only been deferred, that in the meantime he had come to realize that his position in the church was "an impossible one." And, significant of his strong emotional attachment to his church, he added, "If it were possible, I would still be willing to work under the direction of the Methodist Church. But I must be free to think and speak out my own thoughts, and live out my own life. I take this step with no feeling of bitterness toward the Church and no sense of disloyalty to the Master, but with the conviction that I must be sincere at any cost, and with the belief that He who has been my Guide in the past will still be my Guide—unto the end."

Human motives are never free from complexity. Nor are any person's decisions and actions to be understood in the single light either of inherited abilities and instincts or of a conditioning environment. A multitude of factors were at work in this drama of abortive action. In the first place it is clear that Woodsworth, intellectually, had severed himself completely from the formal position of the church. But it is at least questionable if he was emotionally prepared to suffer the break from an institution and a way of life in which he had been completely immersed. Although he had compelled himself to take a step which his intellect demanded, he would be emotionally relieved if an honest alternative could be discovered. The alternative (and it was his real desire) was that the church should somehow come around to his way of thinking. The intensity of this desire was, of course, what made him for a number of years the outstanding Canadian exponent of the social gospel. His position was that which such forceful advocates of "boring from within" as Dr. Salem Bland continued to occupy.

But was it only wishful thinking that made him withdraw his resignation once again? Certainly he had put the church to the severest possible test—had openly and unreservedly denied either the usefulness or the validity of most of its tenets as defined in the Order and Discipline. And, as before, he was confronted with the opinion of outstanding Methodist leaders that one could hold such reservations and still, without loss of integrity, work within the framework of the church.[6] Intellectually he was puzzled, and still a rebel. Emotionally he strongly desired to remain within the familiar fold. But of over-

---

[6]See C. E. Silcox, *Church Union in Canada* (New York, 1933), p. 70: "Canada has known few heresy trials, and theological radicalism did not find there a congenial soil. . . ." This is one way of saying that Protestant Canadian churchmen tend to be lenient on matters of dogma.

riding importance, he desired passionately to help his fellow men and to give effective assistance in bringing about a Christian social order.

It was on this last point that his defences against those who were pressing him to remain went down. When he was offered the post of superintendent of the Methodist city mission in Winnipeg and a free hand to reorganize and revitalize it—in effect the opportunity to use a church agency in an attack upon the ever worsening social conditions of an expanding metropolis—he was compelled to reconsider the situation. His mind undoubtedly flew back over his past experience, his reading on social problems, his knowledge of Mansfield House and the London slums, his observation of immigration problems in Winnipeg, and came to light irresistibly on his prime urge to do immediately something to mitigate the emergent social problems of his own country. He decided to take a chance; emotionally, he welcomed it. And so Woodsworth accepted appointment as Superintendent of All Peoples' Mission in the late spring of 1907.

In a letter to his wife he reported the way in which his case had been handled by the Conference.

Of course I don't think the step consistent on the part of the Conference— but anyway there is no deception on my part. . . . In one way I feel much freer. They know, more or less, what I am. Of course I suppose in a sense I am a marked man. Before the matter came to the Conference it was pretty generally known. But a number, already, even of the most orthodox, have expressed concern that I should remain in. . . . Certainly the Church is broad and generous and sympathetic, whatever the standards are. And I haven't hesitated to make the sacrifice—nor have you. . . .[7]

At the conclusion of the Conference he had paused and asked the question, was it all a storm in a teacup? It was only a momentary thought and once formulated was quickly refuted. But it is perhaps natural that we should wonder whether this sort of intense inner conflict about matters of principle was a common phenomenon amongst Canadians of the time who were imbued with a sense of public service.

In Canadian history there are remarkably few signposts by which one can be directed to the answer of such a question. There comes to mind, of course, the somewhat seamy story of our political and economic development through the last years of the nineteenth century and up to the First World War, and of the leaders in that development, what we know of them. Even within the ministerial brotherhood there was an almost blatant recognition that the major economic,

[7] J. S. Woodsworth to his wife, June 13, 1907.

political, and social influences in Canada had, inevitably, to be served —and on their own terms. What writing has so far been done about this period leaves little doubt in anyone's mind that this was, for Canada, the time of the "great barbecue." It was a period for the maturation of the acquisitive society. And this society did not much care about questions of public or private morality, so long as its *entrepreneurs* were permitted full rein in their ambitious plans for garnering the wealth of the country. If anything was considered immoral in those years it was the extremely rare reluctance of governments at any level to come quickly to the assistance of those who desired to further the country's welfare by making themselves rich. It was the day of the dollar. This background, against which Woodsworth gradually entered public life, is important. He was, as has been said elsewhere, an "untypical Canadian."[8]

True, there were men who regretted what they saw taking place in Canada—men both within and without the churches. There were even some who, while choosing invariably the direct route to wealth and power, could tell their diaries that the Hand of God was leading them. But most of these, if they reached any prominence, admitted tacitly the necessity of constant compromise. The churches themselves were extremely slow to challenge the dominant forms and forces. They contented themselves with vague formal resolutions, passed in general assemblies, about social justice. Such resolutions are typified by the following of 1898: "There can be no struggle, whether for juster laws, more equitable distribution of the reward of labour, or for conditions of a healthier, happier and fuller life, which the church can regard without a deep sympathy."[9] Many ministers, especially the younger ones, had read Henry George and were beginning to read the works of the exponents of the social gospel.

Some of the funds of the Methodist Church began to go to social research and city missions. But it was not until 1914 that the Methodist Department of Temperance, Prohibition, and Moral Reform was renamed the Department of Social Service and Evangelism. The reluctance of substantial Methodist laymen to accept such progressive innovation is illustrated by the fact that at the 1902 General Conference which established this department, Hon. N. W. Rowell objected "on the high ground that social betterment was an integral part of

[8]F. H. Underhill, *James Shaver Woodsworth, Untypical Canadian* (Toronto, 1944).

[9]Declaration of the 1898 General Conference of the Methodist Church, quoted in M. V. Royce, "The Contribution of the Methodist Church to Social Welfare in Canada" (unpublished Ph.D. thesis, Toronto, 1938), p. 102.

Christian life and should not be segregated in a special department."[10]
There seemed to be official fear of the very word "social," and in 1918
the department was again re-named, reversing the order of the words
in its title.[11] Official organs of the churches argued vehemently for the
status quo.[12] The rich were rich because they deserved to be so; the
poor need only stop drinking, save their money, and all would be well.
Only slowly did the social gospel find its way into church pulpit and
publication. When its influence spread in the Methodist Church,
Woodsworth, and others who thought like him, were responsible. Few,
however, went as far along these lines as did Woodsworth, and
perhaps none was so vigorous in advocating them.

In political and business life the great leaders of the day saw eye to
eye with the great churchmen, and had no small influence upon them.
One writer puts it thus: "The failure [of the churches] to develop a
social philosophy offering any solution to the pressing problems of
industrial workers—in the factory or in mining communities—had the
effect of lessening the dependence of this section of the people upon
religion. Successful business people tended to dominate in church
politics. . . ."[13]

In many ways, but in no sense of invidious comparison, the career
of another Brandon son may be taken as typical. Woodsworth and
Clifford Sifton expressed different aspects of the Canadian West in
the opening years of this century. Both were products of Brandon
Methodism and both had attended Victoria College. Of Sifton his
biographer has said, "he had not in any marked degree the disposition
of the social or political reformer. . . . He regarded things as they
were as about the best that the world could do up to date—not as a
finality but as a practical starting point. He knew when he entered
public life that acceptance of the standards and methods of his time
would be necessary if he was to have a political career. . . ."[14] Sifton's
point of view was shared by the great majority of Canadians of his
time, and he was perhaps its leading exponent. Woodsworth's dia-
metrically opposite point of view was shared by a much smaller
number of people, and he was increasingly its chief spokesman. It was

[10]Silcox, *Church Union in Canada*, p. 90. Silcox also observes that "the work
of this department was at first, however, almost wholly confined to the promotion
of prohibition and later to an attack on commercialized vice, and these were its
characteristic activities during the term of office of Dr. Chown, 1902–1910."

[11]Royce, "Contribution of the Methodist Church," p. 102.

[12]S. D. Clark, *Church and Sect in Canada* (Toronto, 1948), pp. 394–5.

[13]S. D. Clark, *The Social Development of Canada* (Toronto, 1942), p. 391.

[14]J. W. Dafoe, *Sir Clifford Sifton in Relation to His Times* (Toronto, 1931),
p. xiii.

in reality the Sifton policies, and the accepted beliefs that lay behind
them, that Woodsworth was determined to upset.

The detailed questions of theology which had constituted the bulk
of his criticism of the church were certainly important in themselves,
but it was a larger question, of which these were but symptoms, that
was most prominent in his reasoning. This was the apparent reluctance
of the church to accept new thought and new evidence. It was an
inherent institutional conservatism which insisted on facing new conditions with outmoded ideas and policies, or simply not facing new
conditions at all. Similarly it was the retention of an outmoded theory
of laissez-faire in political life that was to stimulate in Woodsworth a
repugnance to the policies of the political leaders. The country was
being overwhelmed by a flood of optimism and immigration.

"Perhaps," writes one student of the period, "there never was a time
when satisfaction with existing conditions and confidence in the future
was so general in Canada as in the year 1904. There was hardly a
cloud in the sky. . . . In the preceding year 57,000 homesteaders had
been successfully placed. In the same year 130,000 people came into
Western Canada; and this new immigration was absorbed by the
country without any local congestion anywhere of unemployment. . . ."[15] But this passage simply ignores certain salient facts—or
rather, contradicts them. And no one at the time appeared to be much
concerned about the way in which the necessary adjustments would
be made. Already slum conditions were evident in Winnipeg and few
officials of any importance would even recognize the situation, still less
its monstrous potentialities.

For the individual, Woodsworth thought that honesty, a belief in
progress, and the spirit of *bienfaisance*, implemented by the willingness
to work were the prime requirements. His chief worry had been that
the church, in holding to what he considered obscurantist dogma, was
doing so through its fear of any change—within or without the church—
and that it would prove therefore to be a barrier in the way of social
progress. A passion for clarity was one of Woodsworth's outstanding
characteristics. Whenever he felt that obscure thinking or circumlocu-
tion was being consciously employed for ulterior ends, this passion
reached fever pitch. F. H. Underhill, commenting on this aspect of
Woodsworth's character, has written:

In Canada, in spite of the clearness of our physical atmosphere, we prefer
to live in a mental atmosphere of haze and mist. We never make issues
clear to ourselves. Our national instinct is against defining differences so

---
[15]*Ibid.*, p. 271.

that they can be clearly understood or reconciled. . . . We prefer not to face
the fact that our national society is divided vertically into sections and
horizontally into classes. At its worst this attitude becomes a dangerous
hypocrisy. We need a constant supply of Woodsworths to plague us into
the unpleasant duty of facing clearly up to the issues that confront us.[16]

The opportunity which was offered him in 1907 by the appointment
to All People's Mission compelled Woodsworth to defer his final
decision about the church. This is not to say that he went reluctantly
to the little Winnipeg mission on the wrong side of the C.P.R. tracks.
On the contrary he was, as suggested earlier, sincerely grateful for
the opportunity he believed it afforded him, and entered the new
work with zest.

All Peoples' had been established in 1898 to do the traditional work
of a city mission. It was supported financially by the Methodist
General Board of Missions, the Women's Missionary Society, contributions from Winnipeg Methodist churches, collections at Mission church
services, and special collections. It had grown somewhat in the following nine years, but its motivating philosophy had undergone no significant change. It had remained a small part of the disjointed
machinery of Winnipeg's Christian charity. The idea of associated
charities was in its infancy and despite the devoted work of Miss
Dolly McGuire, the mission's founder, All Peoples' made only a limited
contribution to the area it served. Commenting on the condition of
Canadian social welfare agencies at this time, S. D. Clark has written,
"Straitened financial resources, a reliance upon obsolete techniques
of charity, and an almost complete lack of trained workers were
characteristics of the institutions of social welfare before the Great
War."[17]

To remove such shortcomings was the steady aim of Woodsworth's
six years' association with All Peoples' Mission. From the first he was
determined that the mission would be run in no spirit of narrow
denominationalism, and also that he would employ as much of the
experience of social workers in older cities as he could draw upon,
either from personal observation or from their publications. In some
respects he and other Canadians who were thinking along similar
lines possessed one advantage in grappling with the social results of
industrial revolution and an ever growing immigration. But it was a
qualified advantage. "The fact that industrial entrepreneurship and
organization extended into Canada from Britain and the United States
gave her the advantage of the experience of these countries. A con-

[16]Underhill, *J. S. Woodsworth*, p. 9.
[17]Clark, *Social Development of Canada*, p. 383.

siderable familiarity with the nature of the problems of industrialism was secured even before these problems had appeared in Canadian communities. But if Canada profited from the experience of her neighbours, vested interests operated as an effectual check to the easy diffusion of ideas from outside."[18] Woodsworth certainly discovered a reluctance to accept his analysis and the proposals for solving the problems he defined. But also, along many lines, he was successful and managed to gain considerable support from church and secular quarters.

In his first two years at All Peoples' he concentrated on unifying the work of the scattered branches of the mission, and expanding the facilities and staff. Some additional buildings were acquired, and two new "Institutes" were built. The staff was increased from twelve regular workers (plus volunteers) in 1907 to more than twenty full-time staff members and a large number of well-organized student and church volunteers in 1913. Within this framework he developed consistently the twin ideas of the "institutional church" and the "social settlement." Less attention was paid to sectarian religious activity than to the provision of adequate facilities for the assimilation of foreigners and a decent social life for the young and old of Winnipeg's north end. In 1909 he moved his family into the mission house, and his home became virtually a part of the mission. In his commonplace book, in that year, he noted that the work of All Peoples' Mission was more clearly defined and that it had gained a recognized position. "After two years of unremitting work have won standing ground for myself. Now for the long steady fight. . . . After five years of married life about to move into our own home in close touch with our work."

The facets of his work in these years, and his complete immersion in that work cannot be dealt with briefly in any strictly chronological order. He realized at the outset that if the work was to grow and succeed, it must have an ever broadening basis of support in the community. Thus, in addition to directing the mission's activities he became an accomplished publicist. The *Christian Guardian* and other church publications, as well as the local and then the national press, began to blossom with signed and unsigned accounts of the work of All Peoples'. As his knowledge of the social problem grew, his endeavour spread from the mission to allied fields in Winnipeg and to co-operation with and study of social workers and their problems in the rest of Canada and in the United States. Also, from the beginning, he recognized that the crux of Winnipeg's social problem was the tremendous influx of foreign born. It was not simply a question of the

[18]*Ibid.*, p. 381.

movement of population from country to city, such as had characterized the industrial revolution in England. It was the vastly more
complicated one of digesting a new and very different population.
The work of the mission was directed primarily towards solving this
problem. The personal observation and the reading accomplished by
its director soon made him the foremost authority on Canadian immigration as well as one of the leading sociologists in the country.

All Peoples' was a pioneer—despite its chronically inadequate resources—in its attempt to reach and serve a section of the population
which was largely isolated from the denominational churches; in its
germinating of new or imported ideas; and in its attempts to close the
gap between rich and poor, alien and native.

At a time when Winnipeg's educational authorities maintained no
pre-school facilities, All Peoples' operated two flourishing kinder-
gartens. While respectable Winnipeggers who happened to own
houses in the city's north end were moving out as fast as they could
and leaving the area to the tender regard of the builders who spread
broadcast their miserable cottages and wooden tenements, the mission
was creating the physical facilities and the social atmosphere in which
newly arrived people could acquaint themselves with Canadian ways
and receive Canadian help. The mission's deaconesses were tireless in
their visiting of immigrant "homes" and with each new experience of
the interior life of the spreading slums were galvanized into still
further effort. Classes were organized for older girls, and for the boys
of the families in the districts served by the mission. A fresh-air camp
was established, swimming pool and gymnasium facilities were
secured, night classes in English and "civics" were inaugurated, evening "socials" were arranged—all the branches, that is, of an "institutional church" were carefully fostered. In addition free legal advice
and more direct forms of charity became important in the Mission's
work. In 1912, North End House, a residence for settlement workers,
was purchased at Woodsworth's instigation. When it was discovered
that it was impossible to obtain adequately trained foreign workers,
one of the mission's staff was sent to Poland and Austria to learn the
language and background of one section of the new population.

In all this work the Woodsworths were completely absorbed. Mrs.
Nellie McClung wrote of them at this time, "The Superintendent and
his family live beside the Stella Avenue Mission. Their home is open
to the people. They try in many ways to bring the south and the north
ends of the city together, believing that they will be mutually helpful.
They do not believe in the 'segregation of virtue.' "[19] Certainly Woods-

[19]*Organized Helpfulness*, Report of All Peoples' Mission, 1911–12.

worth did not believe that the church had fulfilled its duties by simply posting a student chaplain at a desk in Immigration Hall and directing him to give all Methodist immigrants an introduction to the minister at their place of destination. But even the work of the mission had painfully obvious shortcomings. Its contacts, after all, could be only with a small minority of Winnipeg's vast new population. And its work even with this small group was carried on within a severely conditioning environment.

To that environment, and to particular weaknesses in it, Woodsworth gave more and more of his attention. His growing consciousness of shortcomings in the mission system can be seen in the annual reports of All Peoples'. In the report for 1909–10, Woodsworth noted that general conditions had been improving and that the Associated Charities were doing good work. But compulsory education was needed as well as other immediate reforms particularly with respect to the drink traffic, cheap theatres, and segregated districts. "These evils, perhaps more than others, are creating the conditions against which our workers are struggling. Preventive rather than remedial measures are necessary to social progress. . . ." In the report of 1911–12, a similar note was struck. "In future the work must be both more intensive and more extensive—more intensive in really moulding the lives of a small group—more extensive in bringing about such changes in our whole social system as will enable men and women and little children to live out their highest lives. . . . The local task is only one part of the work of All Peoples' Mission. Even it can be accomplished only through participation in far-reaching movements."

Following these ideas he worked consistently with the Children's Aid Society and helped to organize the Associated Charities of Winnipeg in 1907, of which J. H. T. Falk became the first secretary.[20] He agitated amongst his friends, and in letters to the press, for the establishment of a juvenile court, and in 1908 was gratified by the city's establishing the first such court in Canada.[21] He conducted a similar agitation for playgrounds. In an article for the *Free Press*,

[20]In this venture he enlisted the assistance of Mayor Ashdown. See the *Manitoba Free Press*, Dec. 4, 1907, *et seq.*

[21]See particularly his letter to the *Free Press*, March 19, 1908, in which he argued from American examples of juvenile treatment. S. D. Clark has noted the reluctance of the time to adopt penal and legal reform: "The distinction between the juvenile and the adult in methods of determining guilt, and of reformation, came only with the establishment of juvenile courts and with legislation dealing with juvenile delinquency. . . . In the field of prevention, reform efforts consisted largely of the playground movement and the establishment of juvenile and youth organizations chiefly under church leadership. . . ." (*Social Development of Canada*, p. 384.)

March 26, 1909, entitled "Social Progress in Winnipeg" he entered his
familiar plea for the recognition of human values. The concentration
on railways, bank clearings, real estate, and commerce, he wrote, "has
led to the crowding out of much that makes for the permanent welfare
of the people. . . . With a thousand miles of prairies to the west, why
such narrow, shallow, crowded lots?" Subsequently a playground commission was established; he was a member, and to obtain statistical
information he undertook a social survey of one street in Winnipeg.
Later, he co-operated in a similar survey of a section of Regina. In
1912 the municipal government made playgrounds its own responsibility.

A still broader question of general educational policy was never far
from his thoughts. He was interested in the establishment of a branch
of the Workers Educational Association, and played host to the first
organizational meeting. Through the sponsorship of All Peoples'
Mission he inaugurated the People's Forum movement which rapidly
spread to other cities, often with his direct assistance. Probably pat-
terned after the Sunday activities he had seen at Mansfield House in
London, these Sunday meetings were calculated to serve a multiple
purpose. They were to bring together all sections of the population,
irrespective of race, religion, or class; they were to be of positive
educational value; and they were to provide an alternative to less
desirable Sunday activities. Woodsworth early referred to the Forum
as the people's church, and certainly it was one expression of his
growing distaste for denominationalism and for absolute theological
doctrine of any kind. The meetings of the People's Forum were very
popular. The music of Polish, Ukrainian, Hungarian, Russian, Nor-
wegian choirs and instrumentalists, and the worthwhile lectures provided a continuous attraction. A community committee was formed
in 1910 and the movement flourished. Speakers of eminence in their
various fields were willing to assist. In 1912 the roster included Joseph
Fels of Chicago, A. W. Puttee, editor of the Winnipeg labour paper
and ex-M.P., Professors Osborne, Wallace, Crawford, and Maclean of
the University of Manitoba, Professor S. G. Bland of Wesley College,
Mayor Evans, and R. A. Rigg, S. J. Farmer and F. J. Dixon of the
Winnipeg labour movement. The press and the general public gave
a wholesome support to the Forum until, with the war, such things
were viewed with the jaundiced eye of a narrow patriotism—the Forum
catered to "enemy aliens."[22]

[22]In the early days of Woodsworth's connection with All Peoples' even the
Winnipeg *Telegram*, a Conservative paper, gave generous space to all the activi-

Woodsworth, in his attempt to infuse an element of realism into provincial and municipal educational policy, asserted that the Manitoba schools question was by no means dead. In an article in the *Christian Guardian* he argued that if the basic problems of assimilation and of city life were to be approached with a long-range view, there must be compulsory attendance at "truly national schools."[23] The Roman Catholic Church, he maintained, "with the foreign vote behind it, has set itself against compulsory education." It was futile to try to assimilate immigrants, he argued, if teaching was not directed towards the learning and use of the English language. The Conservative government of the province had, "as far as practical politics is concerned, declared against compulsory education." The Liberals had allowed one of their members, D. A. Rose, to introduce a bill on the subject, but since it provided for a system of local option, it was a farce. "Protestantism is divided by political allegiances. There is not yet a sufficiently large number of men with whom their country's best interests hold first place." It was a vigorous article and pulled no punches. The *Guardian* backed him up editorially, and the local press, Conservative and Liberal, took exception, each from its own point of view.

On July 5, 1912, the Winnipeg papers reported a speech made by Woodsworth at Whitby in which he condemned Manitoba's educational policy. He had remarked that bilingual schools were a curse and that there were about 30,000 children not attending *any* school. Editorially the *Free Press* praised the speech, while the *Telegram* termed it an injustice to Manitoba, called for "proofs or apologies," and reported Hon. George R. Caldwell as stating that similar conditions existed in other states and provinces. The *Free Press* followed with a long editorial (July 7) defending Woodsworth against "Sir Rodmond Roblin's newspaper." The attack in the *Telegram* was the beginning of a permanent and very bitter disapproval of Woodsworth by that paper. After this the *Telegram* saw him alternately as a hireling of the Liberal party and press, and as a red revolutionary. He continued, however, to argue strenuously for a genuinely public system of education, both juvenile and adult.

To help consolidate opinion among the city's social workers on this and other questions, Woodsworth called a meeting at All Peoples' in

---

ties of the Mission, and praised Woodsworth's work unreservedly. As will be shown, the *Telegram*'s attitude changed markedly as time passed. For an example of the earlier attitude see the spread given to the annual Mission report, Dec. 10, 1910.   [23]*Christian Guardian*, April 21, 1912.

January, 1910. Here on the motion of Hon. T. A. Daly was established the League of Social Workers, with J. H. T. Falk of the Associated Charities as secretary.[24]

As Woodsworth increased his interest in "the problem of the community," and particularly in that community known as the Canadian melting pot, he read more and more, and became a still better publicist. A hundred speeches a year, in Manitoba, across Canada, and even in the United States, was his approximate average between 1907 and 1913.

To gather his knowledge together, and to present it in educational form, he wrote a textbook on the problem of immigration in 1909. The publication, *Strangers within Our Gates*, was sponsored by the Young People's Forward Movement of the Methodist Church,[25] and received considerable praise across the country as the pioneer work in its field. Basically a statement of facts, it contained also some of the conclusions at which the author had arrived. The chief of these was that Canada must evolve some effective selection agency, or be overwhelmed by a stream of unassimilable people from the British Isles and Europe. Even when immigrants had been properly "screened" before arrival there was still, he argued, a tremendous responsibility to be accepted by Canada. It simply was not sensible to bring a foreigner into the country, take him to a piece of land, and leave him to adjust as best he might. As a corrective to the official thought of the period, the book was useful. Remarks such as the following might well have been heeded by an exuberant Ottawa:

Immigration and transportation are the two questions of greatest importance to Canada. From the situation, extent and character of the country, transportation must always be one of the leading factors in industrial and commercial development. But as men are greater than things, so immigration is greater than transportation. . . . Within a few years the people with lower standards of living will drive out other competitors. The economic question becomes a social question. Our resources must be developed, but why such haste? Can we afford, for the sake of immediate gain, to sacrifice those standards and ideals which we have most carefully cherished? True prosperity cannot be measured by the volume of trade or bank clearings. It consists in the social and moral welfare of the people.[26]

We should be diligent, he asserted, in extending to the newcomers the benefits of community organization, education, and social service.

[24]*Manitoba Free Press*, Jan. 20, 1910.

[25]For this study he read extensively in government publications, current American periodicals, and the best American monographs on immigration. In the suggested reading list he included Josiah Strong, *The Challenge of the City*, and Jacob Riis, *How the Other Half Lives*.

[26]*Strangers within Our Gates*, pp. 195, 226.

Although Canada had much to gain from the cultural contributions of the immigrants, she had also her own heritage and destiny to consider. Certainly she must not accept from the Old World a preponderance of the bad, any more than she should open her gates unconditionally to the potentially inundating floods of Asia. Woodsworth observed that one of the main drives for a "progressive" (that is, wide-open) immigration policy in Canada, as had been the case in the United States, came from employers in search of cheap labour, and that a very considerable proportion of the immigrants never found their way to prairie farms. He believed that the public school system should be extended beyond the mere night classes in English "by establishing industrial classes and literary clubs, thus becoming the centre of the life of the community." As it was, he claimed, it was not in the school but on the street and in the shop that foreigners acquired their knowledge.

One of the most effective agencies for breaking down national differences is the labour union. Men of all languages and creeds band themselves together to maintain their "rights" against employers. Every strike reveals the strength of trades and labour unions. Few think of the education that has been going on for months before united action is possible. Whatever its faults, the union is doing an immense amount in breaking down at least certain national prejudices and educating the foreigner to think.[27]

In appealing for an adequate programme of selection he did not exclude consideration of English immigrants. "Someone has said that 'the English are the least readily assimilated of the English-speaking nationalities.' But the trouble has been largely with the *class* of immigrants who have come. Canada has needed farmers and labourers, and these should be resourceful and enterprising. England has sent us largely the failures of the cities. . . ."[28] All across Canada there were many indications of such a problem, the most notable being the numerous signs, "No English Need Apply." Among the letters which Woodsworth received concerning his book, some were irate about his "anti-English prejudice." One minister of a Congregational church in Ontario wrote, "It will help to deepen a prejudice against Englishmen in Canada that is altogether too apparent now. I beg you to reflect whether on this whole subject of our country's relation to prospective immigrants, you have followed the ethics of Jesus or of certain American political economists." This particular critic must have missed a key sentence in Woodsworth's book: "We need more of our own

27*Ibid.*, p. 285.
28*Ibid.*, p. 51.

blood to assist us to maintain in Canada our British traditions and to mould the incoming armies of foreigners into loyal British subjects."[29]

In the immigration book there was included a chapter on "The City." The very rapid growth of Canadian municipalities, the deterioration of living conditions within them, and the failure to develop community activities and services that could measure up to any standard based on human values absorbed Woodsworth's attention increasingly.

In 1911 he brought out a second book, *My Neighbor*.[30] Although in form this was also a textbook, and as full of facts and figures as the first, it showed greater conviction and confidence. It is perhaps the clearest statement of the social gospel of Christianity to appear in Canada before the inter-war period and certainly the most comprehensive. In one sense it was not an original book. But it was a pioneer work in this country. He made full use of the investigations of American sociologists, social gospel writers and "muck-rakers," and of British socialist writing.[31]

The social gospel of Christianity is as difficult to define, for general acceptance, as is socialism itself; but for our present purpose certain generalizations may be made. Its central purpose was to work for "the Kingdom" in this world. It laid heavy emphasis upon the doctrine of

[29]*Ibid.*, p. 50.

[30]Also published by the Methodist Young People's Forward Movement and adopted by that organization as its "text-book No. 7." In the work of publishing both these books Woodsworth had the helpful and sympathetic co-operation of F. C. Stephenson, secretary of the Y.P.F.M. Professor G. J. Blewett wrote to Woodsworth upon the appearance of the first book: "You and Fred Stephenson and men like you and he, are the true light and heart of our church in its work for the country." In a letter to the present writer, Dr. George Dorey, of the United Church Board of Home Missions, said about *Strangers within Our Gates* that it "was a very significant thing in the life of the Methodist Church. . . . What the book did was to focus the attention of the Church on the problem it was facing in North Winnipeg, and in some respects the effect was revolutionary. To begin with, nobody knew about the conditions which were revealed in the book, and the same thing might almost be said about the kind of people who had come to Winnipeg and the problems which they represented. . . ."

[31]Some of the books included in the bibliography, and which quite evidently had been digested by the author, were the following: Shailer Matthews, *The Social Teaching of Jesus*; F. G. Peabody, *Jesus Christ and the Social Question*; Walter Rauschenbusch, *Christianity and the Social Crisis*; R. T. Ely, *The Coming City*; H. G. Wells, *Anticipation of the Reaction of Mechanical and Scientific Progress upon Human Life and Thought*; E. Howard, *Garden Cities of Tomorrow*; H. R. Meyer, *Municipal Ownership in Great Britain*; G. B. Shaw, *The Common Sense of Municipal Trading*; G. Booth, *Life and Labour of the People of London*; J. A. Hobson, *The Problem of Poverty*; R. T. Ely, *The Labour Movement in America*; S. and B. Webb, *History of Trade Unionism*; J. R. MacDonald, *Socialism*; Jane Addams, *The Spirit of Youth and the City Streets*; and Lincoln Steffens, *The Shame of the Cities*.

love and proclaimed the principle of co-operation as opposed to that of competition. It asserted the brotherhood of man and decried excessive individualism and the adoration of the profit motive in economic life. It placed greater emphasis upon the temporal welfare of individuals and society than upon the salvation of particular immortal souls. Beyond this there was variation. Most exponents of the social gospel agreed that the influence of wealth in church councils, as in civil government, should be curbed. But if most also agreed that "institutional churches" and active encouragement of social welfare work were essential, there were differences of opinion as to what brand of socialism (or progressivism) was best calculated to move society towards the realization of the Kingdom. And few, very few, advocated ministerial participation in politics.[32]

This was the test that disillusioned many ministers of the social gospel. They thought they could see clearly the reforms and policies that were necessary but they faced this dilemma: inside the church they were frustrated by dependence upon wealthy men, and if they exerted an influence politically, were informed that a minister's job could not include such activity. In Canada there were many who were more or less under the influence of the social gospel—and as many variations in their conception of it. Some, like Dr. Salem Bland, when they taught their doctrine with too thin a veil, lost their jobs but remained within the ministry; some, like William Ivens, emphasizing the pacifist side of the gospel during the war, lost their jobs and their ministerial membership also; some, like A. E. Smith, when they reached a point of sufficient frustration, resigned from the ministry. The majority preached either with greater caution or under peculiarly amenable conditions and did not reach any particular crisis. Writing,

[32]Walter Rauschenbusch, *Christianity and the Social Crisis* (New York, 1907), is the leading American statement of the social gospel. There is no suggestion in it that the minister should ever find it necessary to give up his denominational affiliation, although a picture is there painted of commercialism in the church that might well raise that question. Politically, Rauschenbusch seemed satisfied with Theodore Roosevelt. His position was that of a Christian socialist and he took pains to distinguish between socialism and Christian socialism: "The religious belief in the Fatherhood of God, in the fraternal solidarity of man, and in the ultimate social redemption of the race through Christ lends a religious quality to the Socialist ideals." Quoted in Hopkins, *The Rise of the Social Gospel in American Protestantism, 1865–1915* (New Haven, 1940), p. 227. This caution in the Rauschenbusch approach is also emphasized in D. R. Sharpe, *Walter Rauschenbusch* (New York, 1942), p. 9: "Himself a Christian socialist, he opposed the materialism and atheism which accompanied Marxism, and was fearful that a time might come when a sudden revolution would bring socialism on a people unprepared for it, without spiritual backing for it, and under the control of leaders untrained in government affairs."

in a private letter, of Woodsworth's case, one western minister who knew him in those years says, "The action of the Manitoba Conference when he tried to resign from the ministry [in 1907] was quite in keeping with Methodist policy. A man might preach what he liked so long as his name was not challenged at the District Meeting when the question was asked: 'Does he believe and teach all our doctrines?' A man in his ordination vows did not have to promise to preach the orthodox code of the church. Unless he was challenged by his peers, he went ahead. That is how I escaped for so many years."

All across the Canadian West these men helped prepare a fertile ground for the Progressive movement, the Social Credit party, and the Co-operative Commonwealth Federation. The social gospel had in it a strong non-denominational strain, and this did not hinder its spread in the West. One contemporary observer wrote:

Religion is too utterly inconvenient and opposed to the general atmosphere of the country to come easily to Westerners. . . . It is often noticeable that church people tend to become imbued with a sort of undenominational fervour and are equally ready to attend any service that may be held in the district—Anglican, Methodist, Presbyterian, Baptist, or what not. The freedom of the West infects every phase of their life, and, in showing themselves disloyal to the church principles, they imagine they are being magnanimous and charitable toward the other religious bodies.[33]

In the field of agrarian revolt, the social gospel was particularly significant.[34] In the area of urban labour organization it was less so, and those ministers who sympathized with the urban aspects of "the revolt against the new feudalism" found themselves more quickly disciplined.

[33]J. B. Bickersteth, The Land of Open Doors (Toronto, 1914), pp. 200–43, quoted in H. S. Crowe, "Contemporary Views on the Significance of the Canadian West, 1896–1914" (unpublished M.A. thesis, Toronto, 1946), p. 47. See also Silcox, Church Union in Canada, p. 72. Silcox emphasizes the exigencies of Protestant organization in the West as leading toward church union. It is significant that the project of union was started at the 1902 General Conference of the Methodist Church which was held, for the first time, in Winnipeg. Silcox also indicates Methodism as the most important seed-bed of the social gospel in Canada: "Methodism in the early years of the twentieth century had surrendered its revivalistic fire for a social gospel, largely under the influence of a similar movement in American Methodism" (p. 70).

[34]Paul F. Sharp, The Agrarian Revolt in Western Canada (Minneapolis, 1948), emphasizes the influence of the social gospel in the Canadian west. See especially chap. IV. Here, Bland and Woodsworth are indicated as the chief leaders of the social gospel movement. R. C. Henders of the Manitoba Grain Growers Association and William Irvine began as ministers. Henry Wise Wood and Percival Baker of the United Farmers of Alberta were trained in American theological colleges and both had done lay preaching for the Disciples of Christ. See also W. K. Rolph, Henry Wise Wood of Alberta (Toronto, 1950), chap. I and IV; and W. L. Morton, The Progressive Party in Canada (Toronto, 1950), pp. 28–9.

If the social gospel interpretation of what was wrong with the church was correct, it was natural that city ministers would face more directly the opposition of employers who were represented in church councils and who financed the major expenses of the denominational churches.

Woodsworth, in *My Neighbor*, presented the urban aspect of the social gospel, but it was sifted through a compilation of factual material in such a way that conservative church authorities could not object openly, assuming that they did not concur in his implied or stated conclusions. The labour paper, the Winnipeg *Voice*, saw in it an obvious leaning toward socialism.[35] In the book, there is a thorough discussion of the church and lay wings of social service work, and the author made it quite clear that what was required was an attack on the social-economic system broader than the mere alleviation of distress.

We can hardly be accused of underestimating the value of social settlements, institutional churches and city missions, but more and more we are convinced that such agencies will never meet the great social needs of the city. They serve a present need; they point out 'the line of advance. Then by all means let us multiply them and extend the scope of their work. But the needs will remain until the community at large is dominated by the social ideal. This surely is the mission of the Church, yet the Church itself is hardly awake to the situation, much less fitted to meet it. . . .[36]

But apparently the book was open to other interpretations: for example S. D. Chown wrote in the Introduction, "Yet it is gratifying to see that the author never loses faith in the ultimate success of the reclaiming and uplifting agencies at work."[37]

There is in *My Neighbor* a revealing section in the chapter on "The Struggling Masses" sub-titled "Our Stand." The chapter discusses the various ways in which men are organized economically, together with several proposed solutions to the problem of social justice.

We hold firmly that personal morality is the basis of public morality and yet admit that the morality of the community, as expressed in its customs and institutions, is the most potent factor in determining the morality of the individual. We dream of a specialistic state and yet sympathize with Mr. Brooks when he says that the "Mecca of the Co-operative Commonwealth is not to be reached by setting class against class, but by bearing common burdens through toilsome stages along which all who wish well to their

---

[35]Winnipeg *Voice*, Nov. 10, 1911.
[36]*My Neighbour*, p. 334.
[37]*Ibid.*, p. 5. Dr. Chown was, at the time, about to vacate the post of general secretary of the Methodist Department of Temperance, Prohibition, and Moral Reform.

fellows can journey together." If there must be a fight then it is a fight for the rights of the many weak against the privileges of the few strong, and we stand with the many weak.[38]

My Neighbor presents the social gospel in its ultimate form—and even so there is room for argument as to whether Woodsworth as early as 1911 was not already beyond that position. Although he was prepared to remain within the ministry as long as he was given free scope for his thought and work he felt strongly the restrictions imposed by denominational ties, the influence of wealth within the church, and the continuing sectarian rivalry which was but thinly veiled by co-operation in such bodies as the Associated Charities. He moved more and more into work with and interest in non-religious groups, and also to criticism of the existing denominational organizations. In 1912 he wrote an article for the *Christian Guardian* entering a strong plea for church union on a broad base. "Many of our young ministers—and older ones too—are keen to get something done, but they are continually held down by the restrictions of the discipline and the dead-weight of the system. It takes so much time to keep the machine going that they have no time to do any work. . . . A rigorous discipline may be salutary—it may curb rash and erratic action—but it may be terribly deadening."[39]

In a series of articles for the *Voice*, in the spring and summer of 1909, under the pen-name "Pastor Newbottle," he poked fun at the church, and also offered some criticism. In one of these he wrote that the churches should forget their property interests and remember that they exist to make the world better, not to perpetuate their own existence in particular places. "The church leaders in Manitoba established the university—all honour to them. But why should they be so loath now to hand over the burden to the government?" Some preachers, he continued, feared that there would remain little for them to do. "Anything left to do? Monopolies that grind the life out of the poor. . . . Social inequalities that cry to heaven. . . . As an institution as at present constituted [the church] may die, but the real life for which she stands will maintain itself in richer and more varied forms than now we can dream of."[40] One need not be familiar with the problems facing Canadian university federations to understand that this sentiment was spectacularly unorthodox for any clergyman to express. As for the suggestion that the contemporary kind of church organization might die—Woodsworth was certainly placing himself

[38]*Ibid.*, p. 88.
[39]*Christian Guardian*, March 6, 1912.   [40]Winnipeg *Voice*, June 25, 1909.

publicly on the very outer fringes of the church, even beyond the area held by the sects.

In 1910 he examined more closely the problems of organized labour. This was made possible when the Winnipeg Ministerial Association appointed him a delegate to the city's Trades and Labour Council. But he accepted the appointment not only in order to learn. In the *Voice* of these years there appear regular references to his activity in support of the labour cause. The labour paper even reported a sermon, delivered by Woodsworth at Zion church in 1911, which underlined the importance of trade unionism and defined the immediately pressing issues of the day.[41] When a strike, followed by a lockout, occurred in the autumn of 1911 at the Great West Saddlery Company on the issues of working conditions and the employer's requirement of a "yellow-dog" contract, Woodsworth impelled the Ministerial Association to form a conciliation committee. The committee, composed of himself, Rev. J. L. Gordon, and Dr. Sinclair, interviewed the management, inspected the plant, and submitted a report condemning the company's action as threatening the rights of the workers to organize. Although real success seldom attended such action on behalf of labour, the trade union world deeply appreciated Woodsworth's endeavours on its behalf, and his name became very familiar to the working men of Winnipeg. Equally important, Woodsworth came to know many of the union leaders, and to discover amongst them a surprising amount of socialist thought.

There is not yet a full study of Canadian socialism. Elaborate explanations have been suggested for the tardy growth of a large-scale labour organization, and the C.C.F. was, until recently, understood to be an uneasy alliance between the great body of embattled western farmers and amorphous groups of city workers. But the enduring socialist elements of the C.C.F. spring not so much from the agrarian revolt (although some obviously do as in the case of the Non-Partisan League), as from urban labour and urban intellectuals. The background of this urban socialist thought, which has imposed itself upon a reluctant agrarian movement with limited economic aims, is of considerable importance. One finds little reference to it in the contemporary daily press or even in the journals of opinion. Yet it was existent, already had a tradition in this country, and was being steadily reinforced by each arrival of a British workman and with each book on the theme that was read by progressive Canadians; it had even provoked a reasoned, if violent condemnation from Dr. O. D. Skelton.[42]

[41]*Ibid.*, Sept. 8, 1911.   [42]O. D. Skelton, *Socialism* (Boston, 1911).

One of the best contemporary foreign books about Canada, by a Scottish visitor, E. B. Mitchell, contains a reference to the subject. After noting the supreme official disregard of the growth of slums and suggesting that Canadians were likely to recreate some aspects of American history, the author saw signs of an awakening, critical spirit in both town and country.

To begin with, organized militant socialism has begun to spread its doctrines. One had always heard that there was no serpent of Socialism in that Paradise, because everyone was busy getting property for himself, and so could not possibly wish to attack the "rights of property"; and in the smaller western cities and towns I believe this is practically true. But even at M——— I very soon began to hear about the Socialist bogey, appearing in the oddest possible place. Catechists in the country were horribly bothered by extreme anti-everything Socialist views, and this not in one district only but in many. . . . Land-owning farmers are supposed to be immune from the Socialist germ, but in the prairie districts that I knew it was virulently present at least in many individuals, faithful readers in *Cotton's Weekly*; while an able and widely-read farmers' paper had at any rate a strong socialist tendency and declared that there was nothing to choose between the two old parties. . . .

In Ontario, continues this comment, there is a growing proletariat with Socialist tendencies. "Thus the old secure social and political idea of Canada is threatened by low subterranean rumblings."[43] Had the author been able to attend the meetings of trades and labour councils from Winnipeg to Vancouver, she would have made her remarks still more inclusive.

Woodsworth found in Winnipeg labour circles a significant strain of socialist thought. The Trades and Labour Council endorsed the socialist *Voice*, edited by Arthur W. Puttee, which had been publishing since 1894.[44] The *Voice* was one of the best Left newspapers ever published in this country and the contacts of its editor were wide. The socialist struggle in other countries was followed closely and the visits to Winnipeg of leading British socialists like Keir Hardie and Ramsay MacDonald were reported enthusiastically. Indeed one key to the growth of socialist thought in Canada is to be found in the report of a speech delivered in Winnipeg by Hardie in 1907. It was a great pleasure, he said, "to meet again the men and women who had fought for years in the old country the battle of labor emancipation, and who now in Canada joined in rejoicing with the British Labor party in

[43]E. B. Mitchell, *In Western Canada before the War* (London, 1915), p. 201.
[44]In Vancouver, R. Parm Pettipiece was doing a similar job editing the *B.C. Federationist*.

their partial success in Great Britain."[45] The editorial policy of the *Voice* was broad, although it leaned to the side of social democracy rather than to that of "scientific" socialism. It gave space liberally to the Socialist Party of Canada,[46] and to the Social Democratic party,[47] as well as to all union activities and such national issues of interest to labour as exclusion of Orientals.[48]

Woodsworth gained intimate contact with labour leaders through his attendance at Trades and Labour Council meetings and began to take a political stand. In 1910 he became a member of the Provincial Labour Representation Committee which was organized by S. J. Farmer and others to gain support for the Social Democratic candidate, F. J. Dixon, in the provincial elections of that year. Dixon himself soon became one of Woodsworth's closest friends.

The minister did not escape censure, both public and private, for his broadening sympathies and actions. On one occasion, when he ventured to make known his views concerning a candidate in the municipal elections of 1910, and those views did not coincide with the opinion and interest of prominent Methodist business men (and old family friends), he was favoured with a considerable amount of critical comment. One letter he received read in part,

. . . it occurred to me that being twice your age I might be pardoned if I offered a little advice. I believe you are a man doing a great deal of good and that you have no other intention and I wish you every success, but I

---

[45]Winnipeg *Voice*, Aug. 2, 1907.

[46]The Socialist Part of Canada grew out of the Socialist Party of B.C. The latter was formed in 1902, the former in 1904. For a discussion of its history see R. G. Grantham "Some Aspects of the Socialist Movement in British Columbia, 1898–1933" (unpublished M.A. thesis, U.B.C., 1935). The party had branches in most industrial and mining centres west of Toronto. Its leaders, like Hawthorn-thwaite, Kingsley, Pettipiece, and Coxson, were doctrinaire Marxians, but did not consider themselves the advocates of forceful revolution.

[47]The Social Democratic party was formed in April, 1909, in Vancouver, as a dissident group from the S.P.C. It, too, established branches across the country. In the *Voice* of April 30, 1909, the S.D.P.'s reasons for the break were set forth: "We realize that socialism will come, if it comes at all, as an evolutionary process, as all changes in the past have come; and the more of the public utilities we can get into our own hands while this system lasts the easier will be the transformation when the time is ripe for the final overthrow of capitalism. It is absurd to argue, as some of the leaders of the Socialist Party of Canada do, that there is no value at all in 'immediate demands.' "

[48]Canadian labour leaders who also held socialist views experienced considerable difficulties on this point. Editorially the *Voice* observed on Jan. 17, 1907: "The socialists themselves are not naturally exclusionists and strongly resent the policy in some parts of the Empire, but when a people are up against a problem they have to find a solution, and Asiatic exclusion is the solution for the North American continent."

think you limit your powers for doing good in the future by entering into any question where good people are divided in their opinions. . . . I may say that in looking back for years in every case where ministers took part in such [electoral] matters it has proven a failure. A minister is considered an easy mark, and if there is a deceitful bum he never goes to a business man because a business man would immediately see through him, but he goes to a minister and gains his sympathy. . . . For you, a minister of the Gospel, to intimate that you were satisfied with statements made by Mr. —— would not look well to our best people. . . .

Through all the intensity of these years Woodsworth was feeling his way, with characteristic caution, toward a more comprehensive line of advance than that represented by All Peoples' Mission, even with its ramifications. Certain incidents of this period suggest the moral drive, tempered by a distinct aversion to incompetence and inefficiency, which was responsible for his reforming zeal. One of the most revealing is described in a letter which he wrote to the *Manitoba Free Press* in 1909, concerning poverty and unemployment in the city. It is full of the feelings aroused in him when faced with the conditions which many of his contemporaries managed to disregard. Written after he had taken a friend through some slum dwellings, it was a lengthy letter which would today be placed in the newspaper category, "sob-sister." But it was written before such things in Canada became the professional duty of fresh air fund scribes, and is transparently genuine. Discussing local slum conditions, he wrote:

Some of these people may be lazy and shiftless. Small wonder when they are forced into conditions which foster idleness, immorality and crime. And behind all, the fact remains that there is not work for them. Let me tell you of one little foreign girl. She lives in a room in a disreputable old tenement— one of those human warrens which are multiplying with great rapidity in our city. Her father has no work. The men boarders have no work. The place is incredibly filthy. The little girl has been ill for months—all that time living on the bed in which three or four persons must sleep and which also serves the purpose of table and chairs. For weeks this little girl has had itch which has spread to the children of the surrounding rooms. She has torn the flesh on her arms and legs into great sores which have become poisoned. The other day I saw the mother dip a horrible dish rag into the potato dish and wash the sores! I took a friend to see the child. The mother started to show us the child's arm. The dirty dress was stuck in the great open sores. As the scabs were pulled away from the quivering flesh the little one writhed and screamed in agony. My friend who has dear little girlies of his own, half gasped, half cried, "My God! This is damnable!" As we stumbled down the stairs I heard him muttering between clenched teeth, "God, to think of my Isabelle in a place like that!" The little one still lives there in her misery. Is there not some man or some woman who has a heart and a head who will help that child? . . . Yes, and many of the well-to-do are drawing large revenues from this same misery. A few months ago it was openly stated before the police Commission that the owners of some of the vilest dens in the city were our "best"(!) people—our society people, our church people, and that for these houses they obtain in some cases, double the legitimate rentals. . . .[49]

Anyone who makes it his job to investigate misery of that kind can perhaps be pardoned a certain zeal for an efficient economic and social scheme of things. Viewing such distress Woodsworth could not bring himself to fasten any serious degree of responsibility upon the sufferers themselves. Although he remained strict to the point of puritanism with respect to himself and his family, towards those who lived in underprivileged conditions his attitude was invariably lenient. To some extent this leniency sprang from his confidence in human nature, in his refusal to see degraded human beings as merely the product of their participation in the original sin. A part, too, of this optimistic humanism was his basic belief that the approach to people is almost certain to condition their response.

It was in the midst of scenes of misery such as that described in the letter to the *Manitoba Free Press* that Woodsworth carried on his work from 1907 to the summer of 1913. His experience in those years had led him to accept the ideas of the social gospel, and had even carried him beyond, tentatively, into the field of politics. His contact with labour organizations led him to consider the general question of socialism; and his feeling of frustration while working within the denominational church framework had influenced him to move further and further from the centre of Manitoban Methodism. Increasingly his interests were becoming secular and, at the same time, his knowledge of the problem facing Canadian welfare workers made him think in terms of a wider sphere of action than that represented either by Winnipeg or by a single religious denomination. It was time to find, or, if necessary, to construct a new agency through which to advance the cause of social justice.

[49]*Manitoba Free Press*, March 12, 1909.

5

PRACTICAL EXPERIMENTS

WITH ALARMING PERSISTENCE the ideas of the social gospel seemed to permeate Canadian Methodism in the years preceding the armistice of 1918. With immense tenacity those who held to more orthodox theology and to denominational interest took their stand. The prime, or even the only concern of the church, they asserted, was the regeneration of the individual. There were other groups in the national life that could be held responsible for social well-being. If the individuals concerned could be made truly Christian, the social problem would be solved automatically.

In Woodsworth's eyes the orthodox approach was barren, for the church had developed too many vested interests of its own, and he did not agree, in any case, with those of influence within the church as to what might constitute a "truly Christian individual." The whole problem was circular and he veered away from any path which might lead him further into denominational activity, whatever its ostensible goal.

He was at this period in close touch with those men at the centre of Methodism who were interested in the social gospel—men like T. A. Moore, F. C. Stephenson, and Ernest Thomas—and it was natural that when the Department of Temperance and Moral Reform was expanding Woodsworth should be offered work within it. In February of 1913 he received a letter asking his permission to nominate him for the position of a field secretary for the department. His reply was a refusal in which he remarked that "the two greatest social needs today in Canada are schools for training social workers and the organization and direction in each community of social forces already in existence. These can best be met by independent organizations working in co-operation with the churches." He would consider the departmental work only if a "broader scheme" were possible. There was a reply to his refusal, noting that the scope of the department was already broad, "though it is certainly denominational," and that it was hoped to organize a bureau of lecturers to inform churches on "the social content of the Gospel of Jesus Christ."

This departmental programme was perhaps promising, but Woodsworth felt that it would be frustrated, even granting its own enlightenment, by the conservative forces within the church. Discussing the matter with non-clerical social workers, during February and March of 1913, he came to the decision that a new nation-wide social welfare organization was essential, and that it must not be tied to any religious denomination. A letter received in March from a prominent Quebec social worker indicates the course of thought and investigation that preceded this decision. "Our first judgment was right. Leadership for a national social welfare association must come from outside the church. Our conference at Toronto last week was absolutely of no effect and resolved itself into more or less an agreement of those present (with the exception of a minority consisting of Dr. Mac-Murchy, President Falconer, Miss Saunders and myself) that the Dominion Social and Moral Reform Council was performing all the functions which we had outlined." The council referred to had been established in 1907 to bring about co-operation between the major Protestant churches in the field of social research. Other associations such as the Trades and Labour Congress and the Dominion Grange were represented on it, but it had been somewhat lethargic and was, despite the initial attempt to broaden it, basically a body of churchmen.

On May 7, 1913, the *Free Press* announced Woodsworth's resignation as Superintendent of All Peoples' Mission[1] and on May 31 there

[1]Woodsworth's resignation from the Mission occasioned in the Winnipeg papers many expressions of admiration for the work he had accomplished. He received a letter from the president of the Women's Missionary Society of the Methodist Church, one of the chief financial supports of the Mission, deeply regretting his action: ". . . we hope you may see your way clear to remain in a position for which you are so eminently fitted and which you have made far-reaching in its influence. Lofty ideals, vision, enthusiasm are not given to every man, and but few combine vision and the practical mind which enables them to bring their dreams to life. . . . Before your day the Women's Missionary Society gave of its money to All Peoples'. But the continually changing personnel was very trying and did not tend to increase confidence either in its effectiveness or its stability, but your advent brought a new day in which we have been glad to help in every way possible and stand ready to increase our grant when it becomes necessary. . . . I wish we had a superintendent like yourself for Montreal. They really have not made a beginning there."

appeared in the *Canadian* a leading article by the editor commenting on a letter from Woodsworth which was also printed. The letter was an appeal for "a social clearing house," a voluntary organization for social research, the dissemination of information about social problems and the stimulating of community action on these problems. The editor, who was strongly in favour of this plan, included a coupon with spaces for the names of individuals and organizations that might co-operate, and for contributions. The letter observed that the ideal would be a government department but that unfortunately public men had failed to recognize the great need for this, and that a voluntary association was therefore an urgent necessity.

By the first week of June the response to this appeal, and the personal contacts established by its mover, were so encouraging that a preliminary organization for a Canadian Welfare League was accomplished in Winnipeg. Woodsworth was the secretary of the new body and during the summer he laboured to consolidate support for the League and to expand his circle of acquaintances in the world of professional social workers and sociologists. He attended the meeting of the National Conference of Charities and Corrections in the United States in July and that of the similar Canadian Conference in September. It was at the latter meeting in Winnipeg that the Canadian Welfare League was established as a permanent organization. The opportunity offered by the assembling of leading Canadians in this field was seized and the Welfare League organizational meetings were alternated with those of the Conference on Charities and Corrections. The officers elected by the new group were Dr. J. Halpenny of Winnipeg, president; A. Chevalier of Montreal, vice-president; A. B. Cushing of Calgary, second vice-president; and J. S. Woodsworth, secretary. A strong executive committee included Dr. Helen MacMurchy, J. J. Kelso, W. W. Lee, Dr. D. McIntyre, J. H. T. Falk, and L. Kon. In December an office was opened in Winnipeg and the League's work was directed by Woodsworth from that central location.

During the strenuous months of organizational work Woodsworth had been in the public eye not only as the advocate of a welfare league. In the spring and summer of 1913 he wrote a series of articles for the *Christian Guardian* revealing his deepening interest in the living standards of Canadian workers. The first analysed "A Workman's Budget" and the concluding piece was "A Programme of Social Reform." His conclusions were more definite than in any of his previously published writing. A legal minimum wage, he argued, was a prerequisite, and this would represent a long step in the direction of public control of economic life and toward public ownership. "Probably it will be found that there is no satisfactory way of protecting the poor and the less able against the exploitation of the rich and the clever except public ownership, and only through community ownership can there be secured to the poor all things necessary to a proper, healthful and happy human life at cost price. . . ."[2]

Just as the resolve to fight for equality of opportunity and justice in the distribution of the material and cultural benefits of society led him to take up a position well to the left in Canadian politics, so too his intense dislike of dishonesty and corruption early led him to open criticism of our political mores.

The stage for one spectacular sortie into the field of political criticism was set by the publication of a serial discussion of immigration problems which he wrote for the *Free Press* in May and June of 1913. Under the title "Canadians of Tomorrow," he launched an attack upon the apathy which he felt to be characteristic of the Canadian approach to the problem of unassimilated immigrants. He summed up his earlier arguments and laid heavy emphasis on the need for community action, broadened school programmes, and active provincial support for a scheme of assimilation. He also drew a rather unhappy picture of what happened when the average immigrant was simply left to his own devices, and suggested that this condition was a threat to Canada's future. To this discussion the Winnipeg *Telegram* reacted violently. Following publication of the first two articles the *Telegram* attacked him editorially, claiming that he lied when he wrote that Canada had debauched the immigrant. "There is not a foreigner in Canada," wrote the *Telegram*, "who, by coming here, has not acquired higher ideals of citizenship and been compelled to submit to stricter rules of conduct than ever he was in the country of his origin."[3] The bitterness on the *Telegram*'s part stemmed from its belief that the charge of debauching the immigrant (through electoral activities) was aimed at Hon. Rodmond Roblin's Conservative party, for the Woodsworth articles began to appear just as rumours of excessive political corruption were circulating in connection with a recent by-election in the Gimli constituency. Referring to Woodsworth's comment that many newly arrived immigrants fell prey to the saloon, the ward boss, and machine politicians, the *Telegram* labelled his articles "the most all-

[2]*Christian Guardian*, Aug. 27, 1913.
[3]Winnipeg *Telegram*, May 31, 1913. The editorial proceeded to contradict its own argument by saying that the Liberals were responsible for cajoling and bribing the immigrant.

embracing, succinct and nefarious libel on Canada ever printed."[4]
One week later the same paper dubbed him "a Canadian Cassandra."[5]

The *Telegram* was correct in believing that Woodsworth had the
Gimli by-election particularly in mind. On January 9, the *Free Press*
came to his assistance, referring specifically to that election where, it
claimed, barrels of whiskey labelled "salt pork" had been freely dis-
pensed by the Conservative victors. Woodsworth found himself in the
middle of a first-class political mud-slinging contest; and here he
proved his audacity in the political arena. Instead of beating a retreat
he advanced with an outspoken condemnation of the alleged malpractices of the Gimli election. This was startling to all concerned, for the
successful candidate in that election was E. L. Taylor, a prominent
Methodist and a man long known to Woodsworth personally. Further,
the new criticism was levelled not through the press but within the
Manitoba Methodist Conference in its annual meeting.

Taylor was known as a strong temperance advocate and the charges
of wholesale corruption, floods of liquor, hired thugs, bogus policemen,
threats of "no roads if . . . ," and open bribery, had made a singular
impression upon Woodsworth.[6] He decided that whether they were
true or false they deserved further investigation—that if true, Taylor
should be censured, and if false they should be scotched. Either way
they represented a sorry state in provincial political morals. Introducing a resolution on the subject in Conference he said, "Mr. Taylor
I have known personally for years and hence am loath to credit statements against his moral character. On the other hand I have too high
a respect for some of the gentlemen responsible for the matter which
appears in the *Free Press* and *Tribune* to believe that they would
publish either malicious or unfounded statements. Still further, from
independent sources I have knowledge that similar statements are
made and believed among the non-English residents of the Gimli
constituency. . . ."[7] The resolution called upon Taylor to disprove the
charges and stated that if he could not do so he could scarcely retain
his seat and remain guiltless. It was, perhaps an unfortunate way in
which to frame the resolution and, under the guidance of Dr. S. D.
Chown, it was re-written so as to leave the responsibility of proof with

[4]*Ibid.*, June 5, 1913.
[5]A letter from a friend who had helped organize the People's Forum read:
"Hearty congratulations! You have now your letter of mark. You have been
stabbed at by the hired journalistic assassins of the Roblin government. . . ."
[6]For these charges see the Winnipeg *Tribune* and the *Manitoba Free Press*
for June 12, 1913.
[7]A copy of the speech introducing the resolution is in the Woodsworth papers.

those who printed the statements. In its second form the resolution was passed by Conference.

The incident provoked the Conservative paper to rage and the *Free Press* to cynical disavowal of responsibility. And in the midst Woodsworth was left somewhat puzzled and considerably disillusioned. The *Telegram* alleged connivance between him and the *Free Press*. "Will the senior Grit organ of Winnipeg deny that the assassin-like attack made by Woodsworth to injure Mr. Taylor was known to them before it was read by the man who wielded the knife at Brandon?"[8] The *Free Press*, faced with the official request of the church to prove its charges, termed the resolution "a mere piece of empty firing into the air."[9] The *Tribune*, the most nearly independent of the Winnipeg papers, flailed "the organ of the Roblin government" for its unscrupulous attack on an "honest, courageous, self-sacrificing Canadian."[10] In a later issue it also made an interesting point when it criticized the Methodist ministers of western Canada for not coming to the defence of Woodsworth.[11]

Unquestionably the *Free Press* was right in describing the practical effects of the Conference resolution. But what was Woodsworth to conclude from the whole imbroglio? Was the church endeavouring to shield one of its own? Was the *Free Press* only interested in party advantage? Were the other ministers too timid to venture forth from their quiet pastures in the interests of public morality? Perhaps his original resolution had been "impractical," but was there no way of securing church action in the matter? In any event he had fought for the truth and the double rebuff was valuable education. He had also the satisfaction of receiving, privately, praise from a number of friends for his action in bringing the matter before Conference.

Woodsworth felt that many of his colleagues held back the truths they knew about political and social conditions, and while launching the work of the Canadian Welfare League, he found time to write an article for the *Christian Guardian* entitled "Convictions and Freedom of Speech."[12] Here he claimed that too many ministers remained silent through fear of offending board members, or of being removed or expelled. Again, when the work of the League was well advanced, he

[8]Winnipeg *Telegram*, June 19, 1913. This paper also asserted (June 18) that Woodsworth was an ardent Liberal and, again (June 19) that "being on the payroll" of the *Free Press* he was pulling *Free Press* chestnuts out of the fire.
[9]*Manitoba Free Press*, June 19, 1913.
[10]Winnipeg *Tribune*, June 21, 1913.
[11]*Ibid.*, June 23, 1913.
[12]*Christian Guardian*, Feb. 18, 1914.

returned to the theme under the title "The Functions of the Church."[13] Since the restrictions imposed upon ministers were so rigid, he argued, one could not effectively work for social welfare within the organized churches. He concluded that the church's function was severely limited, even if the limitation were, to some extent, self-imposed. There was naturally a good deal of resentment amongst the more orthodox readers of the *Guardian*. A letter in the issue of September 23 complained because he was continually knocking the church. "Mr. Woodsworth has done a good work, and has been earnest and active in following his convictions; but the church has given him every help and encouragement in so doing, and it would be quite a rest if he would get on the other horse for a while and tell us something of the good the church has done in the world. If he still thinks it dead and nearly useless why not go where there is no such institution? . . ." Woodsworth could counter in two ways. First, he argued, there was already a sufficient number of church publicists engaged in lauding their institutions. Secondly, having accepted church support at All Peoples' Mission he had discovered for himself that such support was inadequate for the problem at hand.

In December, 1914, he made a speech to the Winnipeg Ministerial Association warning of the increased influence of "commercialism" in the church, alleging that the church catered to the well-to-do and completely failed to understand the problems of the working man. The paper was severely criticized by Dr. T. A. Moore, Secretary of the General Conference, and other church leaders present, who agreed that the mission of the church was to save men and not to feed them.[14] The majority, it was also discovered, did not agree with Woodsworth that intemperance was largely a symptom rather than a cause of social conditions.

While this controversy between Woodsworth and Methodist spokesmen was running its course, the former was engaged in the creation of a clearing house for information on social problems. Room 10 at the Winnipeg Industrial Bureau became the centre of a nation-wide correspondence under the auspices of the Canadian Welfare League. The secretary was in touch with social agencies in the United States and Britain, issued weekly bulletins to the press, wrote special articles for newspapers and journals across the country and supervised the compiling of a publication, *Studies in Rural Citizenship*, designed to foster community organizations in country areas. In the first year he delivered some 190 addresses to a variety of organizations including

<hr/>

[13]*Ibid.*, Sept. 2, 1914. [14]*Manitoba Free Press*, Dec. 2, 1914.

churches, trade unions, grain growers' associations, universities, and
Y.M.C.A.'s. He helped establish the first Winnipeg training course for
social workers at the University of Manitoba,[15] and gave short courses
on immigration and community problems at the Universities of Saskatchewan and Alberta.

Adult education was the central theme of the Welfare League, and
its book, *Studies in Rural Citizenship*, stands as one of the first important Canadian documents in this field. In the Foreword to the book,
R. C. Henders, president of the Manitoba Grain Growers' Association,
observed that up to that time the western farmers had been concerned
primarily with the economic questions of transportation and marketing. But with maturity, he continued, Westerners must concentrate on
education, the understanding of social conditions and aims, and of
how these are influenced by legislation. The book was authorized as
the basis for study courses by the Canadian Council of Agriculture
which at that time comprised the executives of the Dominion Grange,
the Manitoba Grain Growers' Association, the Saskatchewan Grain
Growers' Association, and the United Farmers of Alberta.

For the plan and contents of the book Woodsworth was primarily
responsible. In the Preface he admitted that his own work had been
largely concerned with city problems, "but a number of friends have
come to my help, so that in the end this little outline is the work of a
group of specialists. After all, our social problems, whether of the city
or the country, are at root the same." He explained the purpose of the
volume thus: "Most people need a bit of a jolt to set their thinking
apparatus in motion. Our task is to give the jolt, not to think for anyone." With this aim stated there was no particular attempt at impartiality in outlining any of the topics for discussion. The first study,
"Changed Conditions Demand a New Programme," suggested there
was an increasing social stratification across Canada and that the
machinery of production in both country and city was passing into
the hands of the few. Other studies emphasized the need for new community organizations, more and better teachers, the establishment of
larger school districts and the use of school buildings for community
purposes, and increasing co-operation; independence, it was claimed,
was now a vice. There was a pointed argument for public ownership

[15]The other chief organizer of this pioneer venture was J. H. T. Falk of the
Associated Charities. Although this was not formally a university course, the
University granted $400 toward defraying the cost. In addition to fifty-three
lectures, of which eight were given by Woodsworth, the students were taken to
inspect local commercial and industrial establishments and welfare agencies,
attended a meeting of the Trades and Labour Council, etc.

and control of railways, marketing facilities, banks and other "public utilities," bolstered by an analysis of interlocking directorates in Canadian companies which made reference to the "twenty-three men who control Canada's economic structure." F. J. Dixon contributed a study on direct legislation and Mrs. Nellie McClung was responsible for a strong pacifist statement. A number of resolutions for debate were suggested, and some of these were omens of impending trouble for the editor of the volume: "Resolved that attendance at political conventions will do as much to bring in the Kingdom of God as attendance at prayer meetings; is war justified by the teachings of Jesus? Resolved that commercial interests are at the bottom of modern wars." Despite the "inflammatory" character of some of the studies the book received considerable acclaim in the press, and such a respectable publication as the *Municipal Journal* wrote, "Every country school should be utilized as the meeting place of the parents in the evenings . . . and we certainly can think of nothing so attractive as the studies prepared by Mr. Woodsworth."[16]

One could have predicted at this time that a prolonged war would sooner or later mean a personal crisis for Woodsworth. In the first year of the war he was almost completely absorbed in the work of the Welfare League and its ramifications. By 1915 he could no longer hope that the world-wide conflict was an evil that would pass quickly and leave time for further peaceful development. It impinged at too many points upon the domestic scene. It was bad enough that war was evil, that it was something entirely contrary to the teaching of Jesus, but in its modern form it was not even an evil whose influence one might hope to avoid. The problem of social justice was entwined with those of militarism, imperialism, and war. More and more, in Woodsworth's thought, speeches, and writing the latter questions became prominent. Here, again, his trend of reasoning was not so very different from that of many other Canadians. But his ultimate refusal to compromise was distinctive. The western agrarians as a class, for example, were mistrustful of the purposes of the war and apathetic toward its conduct. Political corruption in the war years, and painful inequality of sacrifice tended to alienate this class as well as a large section of the working class.[17] But most members of these classes eventually accepted some compromise position.

[16]*Canadian Municipal Journal* (Montreal), Feb., 1915.

[17]See Paul Sharp, *The Agrarian Revolt in Western Canada* (Minneapolis, 1948), chap. VII. The Winnipeg *Voice*, expressing the majority opinion of organized labour in Manitoba, opened its editorial comment in the first issue after war was declared with: "Now, from the workers' point of view, what quarrel have we

Reinforcing the lukewarm attitude to the war which was widely evident by the end of 1915 was the pacifist strain in the social gospel. Men like Dr. Salem Bland and Rev. William Ivens opposed the war on the ground that war was contrary to the teaching of Jesus. But even among the declared pacifists there was a mixture of the doctrine of pacifism with the argument of socialism. War was not only immoral: it obstructed social progress, and created unlimited opportunity for the exploitation of the common man and the consolidation of capitalist business organization. It was from the mixture of these two lines of thought that Woodsworth's pacifism sprang.

As early as 1906 he had taken the turn toward pacifism. Before that time he had read of wars, of empires, and had heard the arguments concerning the South African struggle. He had touched upon the writings of J. A. Hobson and had thought about the Christian position with respect to war. But it was not until he was aboard the steamer returning from Palestine in December, 1906, that he felt bound to take a definite stand. It is significant that the pivotal incident concerned the effects rather than the fact of war. That is, in the first instance, and perhaps in the succeeding development, he was concerned with the evil social results of war even more than with the actual killing which revolts the pure pacifist. This by no means suggests that his convictions as a pacifist were any the less deep-rooted, but that they were more complex than those of simple religious pacifism.

In an article published shortly after the outbreak of the Second World War Woodsworth reviewed the evolution of his pacifism.[18] In his college days, he observed, war was not a very important issue, and although Oxford and the Boer War had widened his range of thought, "somehow I accepted the existing order of things." He went on to describe a chance conversation with a British civil engineer on the boat from Palestine. The man had told him, from a background of colonial experience, some of the details of the European colonization

---

with Germany? . . ." Winnipeg, it continued, was war mad, and the position of the labour paper must be that of a "war upon war." The editorial policy calmed down considerably after this opening blast, but never reached the point of enthusiasm for the war, and maintained a vigilant watch over profiteering. It opposed conscription and, in Jan., 1917, advocated peace negotiations with Germany. It gave full approval to the famous anti-war speech made in the Manitoba legislature in Jan., 1917, by R. A. Rigg, terming it "the perfect statement of the socialist position." The workers, said the editorial on that occasion (Jan. 26, 1917), were being sacrificed to the "five-per-cent-war-holding patriot."

[18]"My Convictions about War," published Dec., 1939, in *Vox*, the undergraduate magazine of United (formerly Wesley) College, Winnipeg.

of Africa. Later, upon arrival in London, Woodsworth paid a visit to the Army and Navy Museum where he saw the blood-stained relics of imperial wars. The combination of impressions had a deep effect upon him. "Subsequent study only confirmed the impressions of that day." It would be unprofitable to spend time attempting to disentangle the amalgam of his growing pacifist conviction; the cruelty of war, the social inefficiency, the effect upon private and public morality all were important. One cannot hope to convey the sincerity and the passion which were part of this complex pacifism as it grew in Woodsworth during the long months and years between August, 1914, and November, 1918. Only his own words, to which reference will shortly be made, can do that.

During the first two years of the war, most of his enterprises brought him up, sooner or later, against the ramifications of that struggle. In the last three months of 1915, as secretary of the Canadian Welfare League, he undertook a "Montreal Campaign." This consisted of thirty regular lectures in the co-operating theological colleges of that city, seventy-seven addresses to private groups, clubs, and societies, and an extension course of seven evening lectures sponsored by McGill University.[19] The theme of the extension lectures was "Canadian Immigration Problems," while the other lectures and talks ranged far and wide through immigration and social problems.

This trip meant much to him and undoubtedly gave him the feeling that his work and thought were beginning to influence people. Despite a certain hesitation in assaulting the ramparts of a long-established academic institution, he braced himself, and made of the entire visit a distinct success. To his wife he wrote,

These are the *very first extension lectures* given in McGill, so that in itself sets a valuable precedent in popular education in Montreal. . . . If only I can "make good" at these lectures! But I sometimes feel with my limited knowledge and remote academic training that I am almost "working a bluff" on these university people. For example, the Philosophical (student) Society has asked me for a paper. I hate to say I don't know anything about philosophy or psychology—and I would very well like to meet this group—so I think I'll accept. . . .

In Montreal, particularly in addressing the smaller groups and societies, he met a complete cross-section of that metropolitan popula-

[19]Reporting the first of these, the Montreal *Mail* (Oct. 23, 1915) noted that Professor J. A. Dale presided, and the President, Sir William Peterson, was present: "The lecture was well received. This is the first time McGill University has offered an extension course."

tion.[20] Not the least interesting contact he made was with *Le Devoir*, Henri Bourassa's newspaper. There he was given a weekly column while he was in Montreal, and editorially was described as the first English-speaking Canadian to have taken hold of the true ideal for Canada. He attended a meeting of the Reform Club and heard there an address by his friend F. J. Dixon. His comments on this occasion reveal a good deal about the basis of his political judgment. "Remained afterwards for a chat with McMaster, the president, and Hon. Sidney Fisher. These men are liberals in a sense, but they haven't caught the spirit of the New Western Democracy. Dixon's message may be a bit crude—too simple to cover all the case—but there is a downright earnestness and a faith in the people which to me makes a strong appeal."[21]

To the question of the "New Western Democracy" Woodsworth was devoting most of his thought. While in Montreal he read Graham Wallas's *The Great Society* and was profoundly impressed by it.

Again [Wallas says], the very existence of the Great Society (that is modern complex civilization as it has grown out of the industrial revolution and world-wide intercourse and relationships) required that there should be found in each generation a certain number of men and women whose desire for the good of others is sufficiently reliable and continuous to ensure that they will carry on the duty of originating leadership (mere dextrous self-advancement does not originate) either in administration or thought. . . .[22]

This was the book's most significant passage in Woodsworth's eyes, for here was stated his own belief: a missionary conviction, which, in his

[20]Some random impressions, recorded in a letter to his wife (Oct. 4, 1915), are interesting. He attended a Unitarian service where the sermon was on intellectual freedom: ". . . said nothing about freedom to enunciate new social teaching. The Unitarian church is, after all, just another form of institutionalized religion. . . ." He was conducted through a slum area and visited a city mission: "This is professedly a faith venture—is evangelistic in type, but is too sentimental and vague and narrow to appeal to me. . . . The university settlement is built on sand and is offering a stone instead of bread. . . ." And, with respect to a second mission: "The little group of foreign children who compose the S.S. were treated to candy; told not to spend their coppers for gum or moving pictures, both of which were bad, but to bring them for collection. They were told of this glorious Canada in which we live and that if they were good they would soon be prosperous. Tucker is, I think, a good man and his sympathy may help some poor soul, but he will never get anywhere. . . ."
[21]Woodsworth to his wife, Oct. 21, 1915. Dixon's speech probably concentrated on the single tax and direct legislation.
[22]In addition to this book, Woodsworth noted the following titles which he had read during the year 1915: Wilson, *The New Freedom*; E. S. Ames, *The Psychology of Religious Experience*; Baroness Von Sattner, *Disarm!*; Tolstoi, *Resurrection*; G. B. Shaw, *Man and Superman*; E. Porritt, *Sixty Years of Protection in Canada*; and Sir R. Cartwright, *Reminiscences*.

case, had been carried from the religious to the secular field of action (or rather, had made the religious include the secular).

His Montreal trip showed the missionary vein at every turn. In the midst of lectures, talks, and the preparation of newspaper articles he took time to help found the Montreal People's Forum[23] and made a side trip to Ottawa to address the Forum in that city.[24] If only this idea of adult education could be properly rooted, he thought, the future would hold a bright prospect. But that future was heavily overcast by the continuance of the war, and perhaps the strongest impression left with Woodsworth from his Montreal visit concerned that problem.

Soon after his arrival in the city he had attended a service in the leading Methodist church. To that evening his mind returned many times in later years and beyond doubt it was one of the prime influences upon his future course of action. He described the experience in some detail in a letter to his wife (Oct. 4, 1915):

In the evening I went to St. James' Methodist Church to a recruiting meeting. Really, Lucy, if I wasn't on principle opposed to spectacular methods I would have gotten up and denounced the whole performance as a perversion—a damnable perversion if you like—of the teachings of Jesus and a profanation of the day and the hour set aside for Divine worship. War exhortations favour the Hebrew prophets. It was significant that there was no New Testament lesson. War anthems and hymns with war phrases sung as war hymns, the national airs of the allied nations rendered by the organ. In the pulpit Sir —— Tait, the head of the citizens recruiting committee, Sir William Peterson, president of the University, General Meighen and Rev. Williams—a bad combination, business, the University, the army and the church! . . . A deliberate attempt was made through a recital of the abominable acts of the Germans to stir up the spirit of hatred and retaliation. The climax was reached when the pastor in an impassioned appeal stated that if any young man could go and did not go he was neither a Christian nor a patriot. No! the climax was the announcement that recruiting sergeants were stationed at the doors of the church and that any man of spirit—any lover of his country—any follower of Jesus—should make his decision then and there.

I felt like doing something desperate—forswearing church attendance—repudiating any connection with the church. . . . After the service I went into the vestibule to see the results of the recruiting. I was rather glad that there seemed to be very little response. And yet after that appeal it meant that many of the church people who accepted the minister's positions had refused his appeal for self-sacrifice. Anyway you look at it, a melancholy

---

[23]*McGill Daily*, Nov. 18, 1915, reported his address to the organizational meeting of the Montreal Forum, and his work in this respect received praise in the Montreal *Mail*.

[24]On the two Sundays following Woodsworth's address to the Ottawa Forum (Oct. 30, 1915), the speakers were, respectively, H. J. Laski and Clifford Sifton.

spectacle! I ran across Wellington Jeffers and walked with him for over an hour till the nervous tension was over. But Lucy, my love for institutional religion is well-nigh dead. How can one love what one cannot respect? And what about the next generation! . . . [The old religion] will not reach the thousands whom I saw yesterday in the theatres and dance halls and labor temple, and thronging through the streets or hanging out of the windows in the Immigrant quarter. Surely "the age does not see its way clearly." We must simply try to be true—no easy task—and be ready to follow the gleam—even if it appears in an unexpected direction!

He had gone, in a strange city, to a church where he had hoped to find at least some of the values and atmosphere that he had been accustomed to respect. Again he felt disillusioned. When, during these months, the Ottawa Forum came under criticism from "church people" for its discussion of critical political and social questions, he could write with sarcasm, "They don't like discussion on 'secular subjects' and yet they have recruiting meetings in the churches! . . ."[25]

But confirmation rather than disillusionment was the essential outcome of the first war years for Woodsworth: confirmation of his belief that war itself must be resisted, and a renewed sense of dedication to the "secular" cause of social progress. The reception given to his lectures and addresses left him even buoyant. "Sometimes I can almost dream that we are on the eve of a new social and moral movement akin to the Reformation or the other great movements of history. It's' no fun to be crying in the wilderness but still there would be compensations if one were doing something of the work of a John the Baptist."[26]

Another statement of this general theme can be found in the series of articles contributed by Woodsworth to the Grain Growers' Guide during the spring and summer of 1915. The articles were printed under the title "Sermons for the Unsatisfied," and preached the social gospel. They were designed, at least in part, to supplement the Studies in Rural Citizenship and reached much the same audience. In the "Sermon" of June 23 he wrote, " 'The way my father did!' As a matter of fact my father was a progressive man, that is why I admire him. I am worthy to be called his son only as I have caught his spirit. My duty is not to follow in his steps, but to start in where he left off, to blaze a path deeper into the wilderness." And on the social gospel (June 30), ". . . in the church of the future, saving souls will, more and more, come to be understood as saving men, women and children. At least in this world, souls are always incorporated in bodies and to save a man you must save him body, soul and spirit. To really save

25Woodsworth to his wife, Nov. 26, 1915.   26Ibid., Nov. 29, 1915.

one man you must transform the community in which he lives. No man lives or can live unto himself." On the problem of social morality:

We are quite sure that it is a sin to steal a pin, but we rather admire a man who can steal a railroad or a townsite. . . . "My mine"—what a sacrilege! This little man who was born yesterday and will die tomorrow claims what it took God Almighty millions of years to provide. "My mine"—light and warmth and power for the millions claimed by one man! A poor shivering wretch picks up a few pieces of coal from the tracks. He is a thief—a thief according to the law as made by the mine-owners; a thief according to the code of ethics taught in the colleges endowed by the mine-owner; a thief according to the religion proclaimed by the ministers supported by the mine-owner. . . . But in the eyes of Him who made the coal mine for his children, who is the thief? . . . Confessedly the problem of "mine" and "thine" cannot be settled off-hand. But does our present system at all approximate to justice? Gigantic trusts appropriate the greater part of the loaf, distributing large slices to a privileged few. The great mass of the people eke out a mere existence on the crumbs that fall from the rich man's table. Many, in fact, are denied even a job. . . .

One of the major aims of the campaigning secretary of the Welfare League was to stimulate government action in the field of social research. In March, 1916, it appeared that this purpose was to be fulfilled. On March 17, the *Free Press* announced the appointment of Woodsworth as director of a Bureau of Social Research. The occasion for the establishment of the Bureau was the recognition by the governments of Manitoba, Saskatchewan, and Alberta of the necessity of co-operation in making provision for various classes of mental defectives.[27] The three governments decided to set up an office which could investigate the problem and provide them with the background information necessary for legislation. Preliminary arrangements were left to A. B. Hudson, the Attorney General of Manitoba.

In the negotiation preceding Wordsworth's appointment as director, the purposes of the Bureau were widened considerably to include, in addition to the original aim, a practical study of community problems with a view to promoting more interest in social welfare, provision for rendering expert advice and assistance to any community in its endeavour to improve citizenship standards, and the securing of data to form the basis of sound and progressive legislation.[28] An office was

27It has been suggested by Olive Ziegler, *Woodsworth, Social Pioneer* (Toronto, 1934), p. 65, that the presence of H. J. Laski in Winnipeg at that time, where he was giving a lecture course in the Training School for Social Workers, had a bearing on the establishment of the Bureau.

28See the statement of purpose in the report of the first year's work of the Bureau of Social Research, governments of Manitoba, Saskatchewan, and Alberta (Winnipeg, Dec. 1916).

opened in Winnipeg and the *Free Press* commented upon the Woodsworth appointment, "It will occur to most people that if the three governments had toothcombed the West for a man to undertake this new work no more suitable man than James S. Woodsworth could have been found."[29]

To assist the work of the new Bureau each province established an advisory council and the director was given the services of a secretary and a "special foreign investigator."[30] During 1916 a survey of social conditions in prairie rural communities was conducted and two other investigations were made: an intensive study of a number of Ukrainian communities and a preliminary enquiry concerning mental defectives. The information obtained was studied, classified, and put into a series of ten articles which appeared in the *Grain Growers' Guide*. Another series, based on this material, was prepared for the leading western dailies, and special articles were written for various other publications.[31]

Most of Woodsworth's attention was occupied in directing this work from the Winnipeg office, compiling material, and writing articles. But he noted in the *Report* that he had also spent three and a half months in field work and that up to December had given, as director, 124 addresses to schools, colleges, and local organizations across the prairies.

The survey of selected Ukrainian settlements was carried out by means of a house-to-house questionnaire canvass embracing over five hundred homes in certain districts of each province.[32] Professor A. S. Morton of the University of Saskatchewan and other specialists in prairie development contributed additional information, and a report was prepared.[33] Woodsworth considered this the major job and he was

[29]*Manitoba Free Press*, March 17, 1916.

[30]The advisory councils were composed of the following, Manitoba: Hon. Dr. Thornton (Minister of Education), Dr. J. Halpenny, Mrs. W. L. Copeland, J. H. T. Falk, R. C. Henders, and Louis Kon; Saskatchewan: Hon. J. A. Calder (Minister of Railways), Dr. W. C. Murray, J. B. Musselman, C. A. Eymann, Irma Stocking, and T. M. Molloy; Alberta: Hon. J. R. Boyle (Minister of Education), who was requested to obtain the co-operation of individuals who received no listing. The secretary of the Bureau was Miss Gertrude Dobson, and the special investigator, W. Swystun.

[31]Including the *Canadian Municipal Journal*, *Canadian Finance*, Winnipeg *Voice*, *Prairie Farm and Home*, *Farm and Ranch Review*, *Farmers' Magazine*, *Sheaf*, *Statesman*, *Women's Century*, and most non-English-language newspapers in the prairie provinces.

[32]Including Lamont and Lundar in Alberta; Hafford, Canora, Insinger, and Prince Albert in Saskatchewan; and Sandy Lake in Manitoba.

[33]*Ukrainian Rural Settlements; Report of Bureau of Social Research* (Winnipeg, Jan. 25, 1917).

filled with enthusiasm for expanding such research work. What was the use, amidst the overwhelming complexity of modern civilization, in using the obsolete hit-or-miss governing methods of an earlier and simpler age? If democracy were to survive and remain vital it must develop the tools necessary to cope with the "Great Society." "It is hoped that [the report on Ukrainian settlements] may prove a contribution to the better understanding of the complicated problems resulting from our large and varied immigration. Why not a similar study of the Germans, the Icelanders, the Jews and the other groups that comprise our population?"[34] Furthering the idea of general adult education in community problems the Bureau published four widely circulated little pamphlets,[35] provided a reference library in its office, and encouraged consultation on any sociological question.

The most startling fact about this maze of activity is that it was encompassed in the brief span of ten months in 1916. Perhaps the most enduring importance of this period was that it greatly expanded Woodsworth's contacts with and understanding of western rural communities. Although his work and thought had been primarily with the urban working class, his continuing country contacts helped him to keep always in sight the national implications of social problems. His visits to country meetings, his intercourse with agrarian leaders, his advocacy of the "lighted schoolhouse" as a good common aim for both country and city— all this was important in preparing him for life on a broader stage. As director of the Bureau, he had, for example, participated in the Conference for Rural Leadership which met at the University of Alberta during the second week in August, 1916. There he delivered several speeches and met Henry Wise Wood and other Alberta farm leaders.[36]

[34]*Ibid.* It was also noted that the survey in connection with mental defectives was conducted by the questionnaire method and that the material obtained was published in seven articles appearing in the *Manitoba Free Press*, *Regina Leader*, *Saskatoon Star*, *Edmonton Journal*, *Calgary Albertan*, and *Lethbridge Herald*. A sixty-five page typed report was presented to each of the prairie governments.
[35]The pamphlets, forerunners of later adult education and other series, were entitled *Mental Defectives*, *Our Immigrants*, *Child Welfare Creed*, and *Community Organizations*.
[36]At the Conference Woodsworth centred his remarks on the theme of co-operation and the organization of community resources. Wood spoke twice, on "The Minister and Rural Economic Problems" and "The Farmers' Movement." The Conference passed unanimously a resolution requesting Alberta's Premier, A. L. Sifton, to continue government support of the Bureau of Social Research. At this time, also, the women's section of the Saskatchewan Grain Growers' Association resolved that their social service committee "work immediately under Mr. Woodsworth" (*Report* of the Bureau).

But however encouraging the work might seem to him, it had always to compete with insistent demands created by the war: demands that made it difficult to find funds for anything other than work directly connected with the war effort; and demands that individuals in public places must conform, at least outwardly, to the psychology of the great national purpose. It was the latter requirement that brought about the death of the Bureau of Social Research.

During 1916 Woodsworth was in correspondence with a number of pacifists, and was becoming increasingly steadfast in his anti-war convictions. In June he addressed the Young Men's Club of Grace Church in Winnipeg and expressed the view that military force would not secure peace. The speech was reported (June 5) in the *Free Press* and the following day the *Telegram* led off the attack with an editorial entitled, "Is Mr. Woodsworth a Pacifist?" Many of his best friends, thought this newspaper, would regret that he had spoken as he did. The editorial had an ominous ring. Political memories are not short, nor are the passions of war temperate. "Does Mr. Woodsworth really mean that the Allies are wrong in trying to whip Germany? . . . Perhaps Mr. Woodsworth feels that it is his duty to speak out the thoughts within his soul, but he is on the wrong track and makes the judicious patriot and the recruiting agent grieve." Commenting on the *Telegram's* attack the Winnipeg *Voice*, whose editorial policy was virtually identical with Woodsworth's views, wrote, "Regular church-goers have got so used to hearing of the glories of force and war that it sounded like heresy to hear a man say he did not believe in moral issues being settled by physical force." In December the Manitoba government was not taken by surprise when Woodsworth wrote a letter to the *Free Press* in which he condemned the policy of national registration.

The situation on the Canadian "home front" by the end of 1916 was bleak, in the eyes of the Borden ministers and of supporters across the country. Having endorsed the extravagant commitment to maintain a Canadian Corps of four divisions in France, the national government was shocked by a decline in the rate of recruiting from one thousand a day in the first three months of the year to three hundred a day in the latter half of the year. The future rate threatened to become a mere trickle. The recruiting campaign was stepped up and in October an order-in-council established the National Service Board with R. B. Bennett as chairman.[37] Bennett, after protracted consultation with his thirteen Directors of National Service, obtained a rather inadequate authority to institute a manpower survey and announced that in

[37]*Canadian Annual Review*, 1917, p. 302.

January, 1917, national registration cards would be circulated. He hoped that all men between the ages of 16 and 65 would complete and return their cards to the board. There was no legal compulsion involved.

Organized labour across the country reacted violently against the announcement and many leaders advised non-compliance with its request.[38] Virtually all the union locals and trades and labour councils declared against registration. The result of the widespread agitation (and the complicated reaction in Quebec to registration) was incomplete returns, and the board went out of existence in the late summer of 1917. When the Prime Minister, at the end of 1916, declared that registration was not a preliminary to conscription there was, to judge from the columns of the labour press, not a workingman in Canada who believed him. At the multitude of anti-registration meetings this was the key point: registration meant conscription and conscription meant the coercion of labour by capital for the sake of more efficient exploitation. Labour leaders openly announced that they were "not going to die for a myth" and Premier Norris of Manitoba felt obliged publicly to urge compliance with the registration scheme.[39]

Under such circumstances the Manitoba government was distressed, if forewarned, by the publication of Woodsworth's anti-registration letter in the *Free Press* on December 28, 1916. The letter is of particular interest not because it expressed any kind of religious pacifism, but because it was virtually identical with the stand adopted by all the labour "radicals" across Canada. Its opposition to registration (implying conscription) was frankly based upon the requirements of social justice.

Sir:—Yesterday morning there came to me a circular letter asking my help in making the National Registration scheme a success. As I am opposed to that scheme, it would seem my duty as a citizen to state that opposition and the grounds on which it is based. . . . (1) The citizens of Canada have been given no opportunity of expressing themselves with regard to the far-reaching principle involved in this matter. (2) Since "life is more than meat and the body more than raiment" conscription of material possessions should in all justice precede an attempt to force men to risk their lives and the welfare of their families. (3) It is not at all clear who is to decide whether or not a man's present work is of national importance. It is stated that the brewery workers in England are exempt. What guarantee have we that

---

[38]To name but a few: James Simpson, Vice-President of the Trades and Labour Congress; F. J. Dixon and R. A. Rigg, both M.L.A.'s of Winnipeg; J. H. McVety of Vancouver; Alphonse Verville, labour M.P. from Montreal; and Joseph Naylor of Vancouver.

[39]*Canadian Annual Review*, 1917, p. 308.

Canadian decisions will be any more sound, and who are the members of the board that decides the question of such importance to the individual? (4) How is registration or subsequent conscription, physical or moral, to be enforced? Is intimidation to be used? Is blacklisting to be employed? What other method?

Is this measure to be equally enforced across the country? For example, in Quebec, or among the Mennonites in the West?

This registration is no mere census. It seems to look in the direction of a measure of conscription. As some of us cannot conscientiously engage in military service, we are bound to resist what, if the war continues, will invariably lead to forced service.

Perhaps because the letter was so in tune with what the *Canadian Annual Review* termed the "pronounced labour opposition to Registration" the Manitoba government took immediate action. Within a day or two after the letter's publication Woodsworth was summoned to the office of his cabinet minister,[40] Hon. Dr. Thornton. He was informed that the cabinet had discussed the matter and was worried about the adverse public criticism. He was given a chance to "be good" and "keep quiet," which he refused. During that interview he expressed his opinion concerning the relation of government employees to their employers.[41] He declared that the issue upon which he had written was not connected with the work of the Bureau of Social Research. To this there was no reply, for by that time no government was prepared to admit that any of its work was entirely divorced from the war effort. The duty of a citizen to announce his convictions on critical national matters was beside the point when conformity was the overriding desideratum.

Shortly after the interview Woodsworth received a letter directing him to "complete" the work of the Bureau and close its office by January 31, 1917. "The work of years," he later observed, "ended abruptly. I was bitterly denounced. My closest associates said I was a fool."[42] For him it had been evident for some time that a crisis was unavoidable. Before writing his criticism of registration he had discussed with his wife the problem of the uncertain, even precarious, future they and their children would face. But no honest alternative had presented itself. As if to contribute to the crescendo of emotional tension, he received his notice to close the Bureau on the day following his father's death.[43]

[40]See J. S. Woodsworth's pamphlet, *Following the Gleam* (1926).
[41]See Olive Ziegler, *Woodsworth*, p. 73.
[42]Woodsworth, *Following the Gleam*.
[43]Woodsworth papers, commonplace book.

He had chosen voluntarily the thorny path, exposing himself once more to the easy condemnation of those who could never have matched his own sacrifice. Was he wrong to take up his lance only to have it smashed against the stolid wall of conformity? Did he subconsciously seek martyrdom? Or had he simply fallen from a state of grace, as the older family friends believed? Certainly, to most respectable people, he was now a dangerous man. Or perhaps one might see him as more deeply religious, in the sense of consecration to ideals, than the majority of his orthodox critics. In his commonplace book, at the end of 1915, he wrote: "The dreadful war still drags on. . . . Strenuous and precarious living. Yet 'we have been taken care of' as Lucy says. We'll hold to the ideal a bit longer!"

6

DECISION

THE FIRST MONTHS OF 1917 were not easy. All about him Woodsworth saw society coarsening—a result, in part, of the war. Perhaps, after all, the sensible thing would be to withdraw, at least temporarily, from the vortex of reaction. He thought then of the pacifist Doukhobors. He admired their communal pattern of living and even made tentative overtures toward joining one of their communities. But just as he had earlier rejected the foreign in favour of the home mission field, he could not now persuade himself to abandon the struggle.[1] Nor could the suggestion that he might leave Canada and go to the United States, even when couched in tempting terms by a friend in New York, take him from the work which he had chosen for himself in his own country.[2] Although not a patriot in the narrow or military sense of the word, he continually expressed a love of country which was the deeper for its lack of bigotry. The spectacle of a wholesale witch-hunt revolted him, but did not cause him to lose courage.

Woodsworth was not surprised in June, 1917, to read of the dismissal of Professors Salem Bland and A. J. Irwin from the faculty of Wesley College. Bland, in particular, had been prominent as a preacher of the social gospel ideas, and as a friend of labour. Woodsworth had felt that it was unlikely that such a man would survive in a college

[1]The Doukhobors themselves did not encourage the idea, believing that Woodsworth would not be able to stand up to the rigours of their kind of agrarian life. See Mrs. James Woodsworth to J. S. Woodsworth, April 23, 1917.

[2]A. V. Thomas to J. S. Woodsworth, March 29, 1917: "Surely Canadian nationalism wouldn't keep you in Canada. . . . There is democracy here that is spiritually higher than anything I have yet encountered. . . ." Thomas had left Winnipeg after a difference of opinion with the editor of the *Manitoba Free Press* for whom he had worked. He had helped Woodsworth establish the Forum movement.

where the governors cherished the same ideas as those which had caused his own dismissal by the provincial government.

The dismissal of Dr. Bland occasioned marked resentment in labour circles, as well as in the student body and in the *Grain Growers' Guide* (June 13), and Woodsworth agreed with the vigorous editorials printed on the question by the *Voice*. A special committee to deal with staff reorganization had been formed by the College Board, composed of J. H. Ashdown, Dr. Popham, Dr. Halpenny, Rev. A. E. Smith, Dr. Hughson, Dr. Darwin, and E. L. Taylor. This committee announced the necessity of saving the $7,000 represented by the salaries of the two professors. The *Voice* wrote (June 8, 1917): "Wesley College is sacrificing the strongest man west of the Great Lakes on the altar of obedience to vested interests and political pull. . . . Such an institution has no place and no function in the free west. . . . They plead poverty. Yet they own millions. Shame on the Church. Shame on the institution. Shame on the men, millionaires, men of brains and business, who put up such a plea." In the meetings of the College Board of Directors which determined this course of action, emphasis was put upon the College's bank overdraft of $28,000 and the necessity to economize.

The Board committee's vote on the dismissal of Bland was unanimous after Rev. A. E. Smith had been persuaded to withdraw his earlier negative. The notices of dismissal to Irwin and Bland stated financial exigency as the only reason. But on September 20, the two professors were given a hearing before the College Board. At this meeting, also, communications were received from the Manitoba Conference supporting the dismissals, and from the Saskatchewan Conference questioning them. The Saskatchewan communication read, in part,

the dismissal of Dr. Bland and Dr. Irwin should be referred to the Wesley Board of Governors and it is the Board and not a committee of the Board that should deal with the appointment or dismissal of staff. And, further, in the opinion of this Conference, the truest economy would be to strengthen rather than to weaken the Theological Department of Wesley College and in view of the unquestioned ability of Dr. Bland and the excellence and loyalty of his service for the past fourteen years, we trust every effort will be made by the Board to retain his services.

The various communications and the statements of the two professors were debated by the Board and a resolution passed: "That this Board having heard the statements of Professors Bland and Irwin and thoroughly reviewed the facts in this case do hereby endorse the action of the Committee on Staff." At the same meeting Rev. A. E. Smith failed to obtain a seconder for his motion to reinstate Bland and Irwin. The case was carried to the Methodist Court of Appeal in

Toronto which ruled that the College Board had acted within its authority, "but against the usage and law of the church."[3]

Such an atmosphere in Winnipeg, and his own position in the city, obviously diminished Woodsworth's effectiveness in Manitoba. The final step of resignation from the ministry he was not yet prepared to try again. Together with poor health these factors influenced him to move his family to the Pacific coast.

At the suggestion of friends in the British Columbia Conference, he decided to "supply" in a small mission twenty miles north of Vancouver, at Gibson's Landing. Here there were opportunities to resume the kind of work, on a much smaller scale, that he had been supervising as Director of the Bureau of Social Research. For the population at the Landing was composed mostly of recent immigrants, Finns being in the majority. There was also an opportunity to work with the still more conglomerate population of the adjacent lumber camps and mills. In addition, the sheer beauty of the Pacific coast, and the sense of unhurried living, isolated from metropolitan pressures, were refreshing.

Because the problems of community living are essentially the same no matter how large or how small the community, Woodsworth very soon found himself supporting causes which were just as objectionable to the élite of Gibson's Landing as had been his earlier activities to the Manitoba government. He bought a small amount of stock in the cooperative store and gave to the developing ideas of co-operation his whole-hearted support. He encouraged "community nights" and study groups in the schoolhouse, and at the latter it was no doubt evident that he was in sympathy with the opinion of the Finnish socialists present. The outlying districts of his territory Woodsworth visited regularly in the mission launch which he re-christened the "Goodwill." His children retain lively memories of perilous passages in this vessel under the command of one who knew little either of marine engines or the currents and winds of the Pacific coast. There can be no doubt that Woodsworth entered this new mission field with zest and that he came close to the hearts of the working people of Gibson's Landing. But in addition to conscientious attention to his mission territory he had delivered more than twenty lectures in Vancouver by the end of 1917.[4] He could not remain still, and was earning again the reputation of a "dangerous man."

[3]*Canadian Annual Review*, 1918; the account of the Board's action is taken from the Minutes, Board of Directors, Wesley College, 1915–38.

[4]The groups addressed included the Social Welfare Institute, business men's luncheon clubs, the Women's University Club, the People's Forum, high schools, Methodist ministers, Wesley Church and University groups.

The chief merchant of Gibson's Landing was also the leading lay Methodist. As owner of the largest store in the community this man viewed the co-operative concern with undisguised hostility; as a patriotic Methodist he led a small group in resenting Woodsworth's refusal to display recruiting posters in the church. A familiar pattern was beginning to emerge, and in the smaller setting it was sharply in focus. A letter was written to the British Columbia Conference, purporting to come from the whole circuit, asking for Woodsworth's withdrawal. His mission appointment was not renewed at the meeting of the Conference in the spring of 1918.

For the Woodsworths there followed long and heart-searching discussion. Assured that both he and his wife were agreed on the final necessity of resignation from the church, Woodsworth wrote a lengthy letter which reviewed his own relation to Methodism. The letter in its entirety is essential to an understanding of his future activity and thought.

JUNE 8, 1918,
GIBSON'S LANDING,
BRITISH COLUMBIA.

Rev. A. E. Smith,
President, Manitoba Conference,
Methodist Church,
Winnipeg, Man.

DEAR MR. SMITH:—

After serious consideration I have decided that I should resign from the ministry of the Methodist Church. It is perhaps due both to the Conference and myself that I state, at least in outline, the considerations that have led me to this action.

Within a short time after my ordination I was much troubled because my beliefs were not those that were commonly held and preached. The implications of the newer theological training which I received during my B.D. course and at Oxford revealed themselves with growing clearness and carried me far from the old orthodox position.

In 1902 I came to the Conference with my resignation in my pocket, but the urgent advice of the President and others of the senior ministers persuaded me to defer action. I accepted an invitation to become junior minister at Grace Church and for four years devoted myself largely to the practical activities of a large down-town church.

Ill health made necessary a year without station. This gave me an opportunity of getting out of the routine and seeing things in a somewhat truer perspective. While in Palestine I decided that, come what might, I must be true to my convictions of truth. It seemed to me that in the church I was in a false position. As a minister I was supposed to believe and to teach doctrines which either I had ceased to believe or which expressed very inadequately my real beliefs. I carefully prepared a statement of my position and sent it with my resignation to the Conference of 1907. A special committee appointed to confer with me reported that in their judgment my beliefs were sufficiently in harmony with Methodist standards to make my resignation unnecessary, and recommended that it be not accepted. The Conference without dissent accepted the recommendation.

What could I do? Left intellectually free, I gratefully accepted the renewed opportunity for service. For six years as superintendent of All Peoples' Mission I threw myself heartily into all kinds of social service work. Encouraged by my own experience I thought that the church was awakening to modern needs and was preparing, if slowly, for her new task.

But as years went by, certain disquieting conclusions gradually took form. I began to see that the organized church had become a great institution with institutional aims and ambitions. With the existence of a number of denominations, this meant keen rivalry. In many cases the interests of the community were made subservient to the interests of the church. Further, the church, as many other institutions, was becoming increasingly commercialised. This meant control of the policies of the church by men of wealth, and in many cases, the temptation for the minister to become a financial agent rather than a moral and spiritual leader. It meant also that anything like a radical programme of social reform became in practice almost impossible. In my own particular work amongst the immigrant peoples I felt that I, at least, could give more effective service outside denominational lines. Intellectual freedom was not enough—I must be free to work.

For three years I acted as secretary of the Canadian Welfare League and for one year as director of the Bureau of Social Research of the Governments of Manitoba, Saskatchewan and Alberta. Last year, owing to the closing of the Bureau, and another breakdown in health, I came to British Columbia. At the suggestion of one of the ministers and by courtesy of the British Columbia Conference I was appointed "supply" on a little coast mission field. Here I have again had the opportunity of trying out church work and learning in still another field how difficult it is to help the people through the church.

In the meantime another factor makes my position increasingly difficult. The war has gone on now for four years. As far back as 1906 I had been led to realize something of the horror and futility and wickedness of war. When the proposals were being made for Canada to assist in the naval defence of the Empire, I spoke and wrote against such a policy. Since the sudden outbreak of the war there has been little opportunity to protest against our nation and empire participating in the war. However, as the war progressed, I have protested against the curtailment of our liberties which is going on under the pressure of military necessity and the passions of war.

According to my understanding of economics and sociology, war is the inevitable outcome of the existing social organization with its undemocratic form of government and competitive system of industry. For me it is ignorance, or a closed mind, or camouflage, or hypocrisy, to solemnly assert that a murder in Servia or the invasion of Belgium or the glaring injustices and horrible outrages are the cause of the war.

Nor, through the war, do I see any way out of our difficulties. The devil of militarism cannot be driven out by the power of militarism without the successful nations themselves becoming militarized. Permanent peace can only come through the development of good-will. There is no redemptive power in physical force.

This brings me to the Christian point of view. For me, the teachings and spirit of Jesus are absolutely irreconcilable with the advocacy of war. Christianity may be an impossible idealism, but so long as I hold to it, ever so unworthily, I must refuse, as far as may be, to participate in or to influence others to participate in war. When the policy of the State—whether that state be nominally Christian or not—conflicts with my conception of right and wrong, then I must obey God rather than man. As a minister I must proclaim the truth as it is revealed to me. I am not a pro-German; I am not lacking, I think, in patriotism; I trust that I am not a slacker or a coward. I had thought that as a Christian minister I was a messenger of the Prince of Peace.

The vast majority of ministers and other church leaders seem to see things in an altogether different way. The churches have been turned into very effective recruiting agencies. A minister's success seems to be judged by the number of recruits in his church rather than the number of converts. The position of the church seems to be summed up in the words of a General Conference Officer—"We must win the war—nothing else matters." There is little dependence on spiritual forces. The so-called Prussian morality that might makes right, and that the end justifies the means, is preached in its application, if not in theory. "Military necessity" is considered to cover a multitude of sins. Retaliation, specifically repudiated by Jesus, is advocated. Private murder, under certain conditions, is lauded. Pacifism is denounced as a vice. Love is tempered by hatred.

Holding the convictions that I do, what is my duty under such circumstances? The Christian Guardian, presumably voicing the thought of the church, discusses the case in its issue of May 1st: "And if he be a preacher, we presume that he may feel that it is cowardly to keep silence, and that truth demands that he testify to what he believes to be the truth. Consistency demands that we recognize this fact.

"But in time of war the State has something at stake, and it rightly refuses to allow a peace propaganda to be carried on in its midst. Not only so but the church has a duty in the matter and that is to prevent unpatriotic speeches in her pulpits. And if the minister who is a confirmed pacifist has a right to speak his mind freely the church which he serves reserves the right to see that he does not use her pulpits nor her authority to damage or defeat the efforts of patriots who are trying to win a righteous war. In every such case the country and the church have a right to insist not only on the absence of seditious or disloyal speech and action, but also on truest patriotic utterances, and if a man cannot conscientiously declare himself a patriot he has no business in any church which prides itself upon its patriotism."

Apparently the church feels that I do not belong and reluctantly I have been forced to the same conclusion. This decision means a crisis in my life. My associations, my education, my friends, my work, my ambitions have all been connected with the church. After twenty-two years it is hard to get out, not knowing whither I go. In taking this step, I have no sense of disloyalty to my honored father or the upbringing of my widowed mother. On the other hand I have a growing sense of fellowship with the "Master" and

the goodly company of those who, throughout the ages, have endeavoured
to "follow the gleam." I still feel the call of service and trust that I may have
some share in the work of bringing in the Kingdom.

Yours sincerely,
J. S. WOODSWORTH

It is not an easy letter to analyse. The product of a long experience
inside the church and of much work outside the church, it was by no
means a simple statement of religious pacifism. This was understood
by Norman Thomas, the American socialist, who had received a copy
of the letter through a mutual friend. He wrote (Nov. 1, 1918), "to
extend my appreciation of the stand you took in your letter of resignation and of your reasons for your act . . ." and enclosed some literature
of the Fellowship of Reconciliation; he only refrained from sending
copies of *The World Tomorrow* because that journal had been banned
from the Canadian mails.

Indeed, one might hesitate before underlining Christian pacifism, in
the religious sense, as the letter's central theme. There was a definite
rejection of force on moral grounds, and acceptance of the "teachings
of Jesus." Yet the teachings were seen not as revelation but as supreme
human philosophy. Most important was the rejection of the church as
a reactionary institution and the instrument of vested interests within
the state. The rejection of capitalism as the author both of imperialism
and of war was clear. Perhaps the most characteristic parts of the
letter were the emphasis upon freedom of speech, freedom to work
along lines selected by the individual, and the very real reluctance,
though tempered since 1907, actually to make the break with his
church.

A more intimate view of this final resignation is found in a letter
which Woodsworth wrote to his mother two days after sending off his
letter to the Manitoba Conference. He noted that the people of
Gibson's Landing had resented the refusal of the British Columbia
Conference to reappoint him to the mission, and had subscribed a sum
of money which more than made up the portion of his salary that had
remained unpaid, accompanying this gift with a testimonial to him and
his wife: "We the people of Gibson's Landing and Robert's Creek wish
to show our grateful appreciation to you for all your labours and to
show the high esteem in which you have been held by us since coming
into our midst. . . ." When the presentation was made, he was carefully
informed that it was in no sense to represent his back salary but was
simply a gift from the people. Woodsworth wrote:

The people are all right. More than ever I feel that we shall have to work for
the people. Last night I spoke at a meeting held in the Rex theatre (Van-

couver) under the auspices of the Federated Labour Party. It took one back to the Winnipeg Forum days. . . . I used to think it would be fine to live in a time of great crisis, but really it isn't so exhilarating as one would imagine. None of us can escape it, so if one cannot exactly play the hero he must at least try to "put on a cheerful courage." . . . The thing that more than anything else has made me hesitate to take this step has been the dread of the distress it might cause you. . . . I have criticized the church but I have stayed with it all these years and this year I thought would be another trial of actual pastoral work. I think you were glad I took the position. Well, the year's work has not been unappreciated and yet I was given no appointment. Now, of course, I might return to my own Conference, but there I would have the fight that Ivens seems to be having, with the outcome doubtful. Looking to the future I cannot think I would be happy in the church. I have lost confidence in her leadership. . . . I'm willing to risk my future and the future of my family. Now I am not untrue in this to the training which you and father have given me. I was asked to admire Luther as he went out of the church of his day, and Wesley as he went out of the church of a later day. Don't be too much grieved if I catch a wee bit of the spirit of Luther and Wesley. . . . Yes, Lucy and I are a queer pair! If only we would settle down comfortably like well-behaved children. . . .[5]

Throughout the parting from the church there was little, if any, bitterness—and that is probably true of both sides of the case. A letter from a member of the Manitoba Conference indicates this:

When your resignation came before the stationing committee, it was received with regret. It was felt that in view of the fact that you had been minded to take this course more than once before, that nothing would be gained by any action contrary to your request. I think, though, that the feeling of necessity is more insistent in your mind than in ours. There were men on the committee who are pronounced in their support of the present war, though they would not desire to be called militarists, and some of them spoke rather strongly in the matter of Mr. Ivens' position, but I am glad to say that while, after their own consideration of the problems they were constrained to take a position different from yours, there was a very real and sincere regret that you felt you must separate yourself from the Methodist ministry. . . . I think that temperament accounts in some measure for mental and moral judgments; you would scarcely understand any sense of a majority judgment with a minority protest. But this letter is simply intended to declare a sense of brotherhood that subsists beneath any difference of opinion or conviction. . . .

"Temperament" has a very general meaning, but undoubtedly the author of this letter possessed a considerable understanding of Woodsworth's persistent refusal to let go a principle once it had been

[5]As before, his mother sorrowed, but was understanding: "Your letter leads me to trust that if you should be wrong in your judgment in looking at some of these matters that have given you such struggles through life they will be overruled in some way for your good. . . ."

accepted. He also understood Woodsworth's ability to sympathize with those "successful" individuals who can easily work within an institutional framework and the difficulty he experienced in assessing their virtues. This aspect of Woodsworth was the measure of his individualism.

As another light on his pacifism, an article written at Christmas, 1914, is significant. Among other things it clearly indicates that he did not formulate any clear-cut dogmatic or theological argument for his belief. The article was submitted to a journal (possibly the *Christian Guardian*) and rejected. The editor defended his decision on the ground that, "even if we were inclined to accept its teachings as true, the time for expressing such an opinion does not seem to be now." The article was headed "Out of the Night the Angel's Song," and was later published by Woodsworth in *Following The Gleam*.

The dream [of peace] haunts even those who are more directly responsible for the war. They justify war on the ground that it is necessary in order that there may be a permanent peace. We may doubt the logic or the spiritual insight, or in some cases, the sincerity of such protestations; but their utterance is most significant. Even hypocrisy is a tribute to virtue, and truth once recognized will ultimately draw the most wayward to herself. . . .

Even in the midst of this awful carnage there is a tenderness hitherto unknown. Indeed, the sense of shock—the unthinkableness—of the war is the best indication that a new conscience has developed. The night is blacker because we have seen the light. And still in the darkness we hear the angels' song!

What is our duty in this crisis—what can we do? Each must answer for himself—each must be true to the light given him!

Many are going to the front or are supporting the war in the belief that in this way they may help to bring about the triumph of right and the reign of peace. Some of us have not so learned Christ, yet we dare not dogmatise. We confess that we walk with uncertain steps. We plead that no one demand of us absolute consistency—and yet we must bear witness to the truth as it is coming to us. To overcome militarism by physical force seems like attempting to cast out Beelzebub by the power of Beelzebub. To secure his own victory, Jesus refused to call out even the legion of angels that awaited his bidding. He, true to his teaching, could save his life only by losing it. Is the disciple above his Lord? . . .

But, however we may differ in our interpretation of the teaching of Jesus, or in our convictions as to personal duty, there are some things, it would seem that we should all do.

We should keep our heads; we should try to be fair, even—if possible—in the midst of prejudice and passion. . . . More and more we must think not so much of the persons engaged in the war as the causes that led to the war—the great social and moral wrongs that inevitably led to disaster.

These are our real foes rather than the Germans and the Austrians, and they are found not alone in the enemy's camp. . . .

7

THE PLUNGE

IN THE SPRING AND SUMMER of 1918 Canadian domestic affairs were headed toward crisis. The accumulated grievances of the years of war had sharpened class and sectional divisions in the country; these now pointed toward major political and social disturbance. The term "union government" did not conceal either the exceedingly conservative nature of Sir Robert Borden's administration nor the economic and social discontent. In the cautious words of the Sirois Report, "Differences in the relative position [of economic groups] were extended, and contrasts were emphasized by the war. Canada's participation in it brought rewards as well as sacrifices and both were unequally distributed among the population. Inflation held down the real income of large sections of the labouring and white-collar groups. Although agriculture had prospered where crops were good, there were large areas in the West where crops were poor or had failed, in the later years of the war period."[1]

The Commissioners might have added that inflation and high prices struck the rural areas almost as hard as they did the working and white-collar groups. The lure of the city and the armed forces sent farm labour costs soaring and the prices which the farmers were required to pay for the goods they bought meant that their real income remained low.[2] The farmers were perhaps better prepared for a revolt against "the new feudalism" than were the urban workers. Certainly those amongst them who had been reading such papers as the *Grain Growers' Guide* since its inception in 1908 were ready for action, for it and the American publication *Nonpartisan Leader*

[1]*Report of the Royal Commission on Dominion-Provincial Relations* (Ottawa, 1939), p. 109.

[2]*Canadian Annual Review*, 1919, p. 321.

"preached a gospel that urged the wheat belt to revolt."[3] Both worker
and farmer were asking "who owns Canada?" and the labour movement in the West in these years was closely associated at some points
with the growing revolt of the farmers.[4] There were suspicions on
both sides, but both agreed that the old two-party system worked to
their disadvantage, and both wanted checks and controls upon the
new industrialism. Men such as F. J. Dixon, William Irvine, Salem
Bland, or R. A. Hoey could move back and forth between farm and
labour groups with relative ease, and the growth of the Non-Partisan
League did much to integrate the political thought of the two groups.

Although the Non-Partisan League was formally a revolt against
party it proclaimed a platform which differed in no material point
from that later devised by the Co-operative Commonwealth Federation. Indeed, had it not been for the uncompromising agrarianism of
Henry Wise Wood at the end of 1918 and early in 1919, the League
would probably have established a farmers' party capable of coalescing
with an urban labour party when the time came, instead of having its
strength dissipated in a loose Progressive movement which destroyed
itself in internal conflicts between left wing liberals and advocates of
group government.[5]

It is not surprising to discover that Woodsworth, in the summer of
1918, left British Columbia to associate himself with the work of the
Non-Partisan League. He was appointed secretary of the League (a
position previously held by William Irvine), and began an organizing
tour in northern Alberta. It was an unpropitious time for his new
undertaking. The controversy between Irvine and Wood on the continuance of the League as a political organization separate from the
United Farmers of Alberta was coming to a head, and Wood's strength
was great. In addition, crops in the province were poor and the farmers
reluctant to make commitments. In the north, frost had ruined a
promising crop and in the south there was drought.[6] As a result

[3]Paul F. Sharp, *The Agrarian Revolt in Western Canada* (Minneapolis, 1948),
p. 37.

[4]*Ibid.*, p. 62. The western labour movement was "in league with the farmers
during these years until the violence of the Winnipeg strike" alienated them.

[5]See *ibid.*, chap. VI; and W. K. Rolph, *Henry Wise Wood of Alberta* (Toronto,
1950), chap. IV. The conclusions drawn in this biography do not represent the
opinions of the above two authors. Perhaps Wood feared the political programme
of the Non-Partisan League as much as he did the actual machinery of its
organization. He objected strenuously to the government ownership planks, and
Rolph comments (chap. I) that the most notable aspect of Wood's character was
caution toward new ideas.

[6]*Alberta Non-Partisan*, Aug. 12, 1918.

organizing activity was discontinued and Woodsworth returned to the coast.

All doors to "respectable" work, at which he might earlier have knocked with assurance, were now closed to him. He was again compelled to leave his family at Gibson's Landing, and look for any kind of employment that might offer itself in Vancouver. On the docks he sought membership in the longshoremen's union, only to be told that the union's books were closed. He found himself waiting day after day in the rain, outside the union hall, for odd jobs for which union men were not available. The secretary of the union, E. E. Winch, admired the stand Woodsworth was taking and gave him a room in his house. Mr. Winch recalls that from the outset Woodsworth was anxious to participate in the union's educational work and that he resented working on Sundays, not on religious grounds but because it frequently interfered with the classes which he organized.[7]

When the influenza epidemic struck Vancouver, one of the victims was the business agent of the union. This man's wife was unable to obtain a nurse and she herself was physically exhausted. The secretary appealed to the members in the hall for a volunteer to assist the stricken family but none responded. Woodsworth, when asked later, agreed to stay with the sick man while the wife obtained much needed rest. The man was far gone with the sickness and he died that night; but the union showed its appreciation of Woodsworth's service by accepting him as a full member. It was a significant event in his life— one which helped to straighten the path to Parliament Hill.

As a union member he concentrated on the educational work of the labour movement and on the problem of gaining support for a social democratic party—the Federated Labour party.[8] Woodsworth's work with this group forms the background against which he developed his socialist ideas. In British Columbia labour groups at the time, there was a strong flavour of direct action—a revolutionary feeling based upon a semi-digested Marxism and an immense approval of the Russian revolutionary experiment. With this were mixed some syndicalist ideas coming from the United States through the miners' and lumbermen's unions in British Columbia and Alberta, some of which were influenced by the Industrial Workers of the World (I.W.W.). Out of the amalgam was to spring the One Big Union

[7]E. E. Winch to the author, June 16, 1948.

[8]The F.L.P. was founded in 1916. See R. G. Grantham, "Some Aspects of the Socialist Movement in B.C., 1898–1933" (unpublished M.A. thesis, U.B.C., 1935), p. 3.

movement.[9] Associated with this economic aspect of labour organization was the Socialist Party of Canada which had been formally established in 1904.[10] Many locals of the Western Federation of Miners and of other unions were affiliated with the S.P.C., and the leaders of the party were particularly dogmatic.

Strongly influenced by E. T. Kingsley and W. A. Pritchard, the S.P.C. took a strong stand against "palliative" measures, expounded what it believed to be pure Marxian doctrine, and asserted that the sole electoral aim of the party was to use elections as media for revolutionary propaganda. To obtain representatives in the legislature for the purpose of securing reforming legislation was considered an entirely useless ambition.[11] Whether the party actually advocated armed revolution (or whether it believed such revolution possible) is doubtful. But at least intellectually it understood that the revolution for which it called could not be peaceful.[12] For this kind of policy, Woodsworth had a deep aversion. In his lectures for the union and in his work for the F.L.P. he hammered consistently at the points which would, by a European socialist, be termed "revisionist."

Indeed, "revisionist" is perhaps the best word to describe his intellectual method and political thought—for it implies his refusal to accept uncritically the old norms and at the same time his appreciation of a cultural heritage. He condemned absolutes, thought always in terms of relatives, and distrusted self-contained systems in favour of "commonsense" and experience. This made him unpopular in the eyes of extremists, but formed his chief source of strength in an essentially moderate country.

On the docks and in the union halls this habit of mind did not go unnoticed. On one occasion, when he asked a sign-writing member of the S.P.C. to enlarge a lecture chart for him, the man refused on the ground that the chart was "absolutely haywire from the standpoint of socialist economics."[13] Even those who were sceptical about his economics, however, were forced to concede his sincerity. Of twelve hundred longshoremen on the Vancouver docks, he was the only one to refuse to load munitions destined for the use of the expeditionary

[9]The Canadian O.B.U. movement was stimulated, also, by the similar development in Australia. See files of the B.C. Federationist, 1918–19.

[10]Grantham, "The Socialist Movement in B.C.," p. 14.

[11]Ibid. The S.P.C. did elect several men to the B.C. legislature, and they had an influence on labour legislation, but the party continued to deny that this was a desirable purpose.

[12]Ibid., p. 88.

[13]E. E. Winch to the author, June 16, 1948.

force sent against the Russian government—in spite of the double pay offered for the job and his own pressing need of money.

In Vancouver he lost none of his enthusiasm for lecturing. At one point it became necessary to reconvert the large lecture charts, which were painted on old bed sheets, back to their original purpose. Shortly after their arrival in Vancouver, Mrs. Woodsworth washed these sheets and hung them out to dry. Soon the family was baffled by a story which circulated in the neighbourhood that Woodsworth was an undertaker. The story had started when a sheet had been hung out which had been a chart illustrating housing and health conditions in Winnipeg. In large black lettering the neighbours had read, "In 1915 we buried 279 babies."

In thinking through the problem of social reconstruction, Woodsworth agreed completely with the principles then being expounded by the British Labour party. In preparing his lectures and articles for the F.L.P. Sunday meetings and the B.C. Federationist, he read a good deal of the contemporary writing of the British socialists.[14] All of this strengthened his conviction that a just social order, in the final analysis, could only be achieved through political action. Immediate defence of the workers' position and improvement in their conditions of labour required an expanding unionism, but that unionism should also be used to support labour political activity. And, although the political party of labour in Canada must be militant, it must also work within the framework of British constitutionalism.

During the work on the docks and in the lecture meetings of the F.L.P. this double requirement became steadily clearer. On the one hand Woodsworth's sympathy with the underdog became a passion as he came to know the myriad shades of feeling upon which resentment against the economic order was based. On the other, he perceived the futility of "scientific socialism" as applied in a Canadian context, and he developed, as a result, his Canadian version of British gradualist socialism to meet the problem. On the waterfront he conceived a new appreciation of William Morris, and wrote about the bitter monotony of modern labour: " 'Variety in work!' What variety in the weary march trucking salmon cases—or doing the single-piece monotonous work that is the day's work for so many? . . . Is it any wonder that the worker dreams of a six hour day—and beyond that of a new social order when he can live a man's life and do a man's work?"[15] Some of

[14]Including J. A. Hobson, Democracy After the War; Labour and the New Social Order; and the socialist newspapers and Labour party pamphlets which he obtained through the B.C. Federationist and the F.L.P.
[15]B.C. Federationist, Oct. 18, 1918.

his writing on the conditions of wage labour was couched in very vigorous English as, for example, "A Sabbath Day's Meditation," which he wrote in the winter of 1919.[16]

. . . But there are other and less pleasant experiences that lead to meditation. To reluctantly race out of bed before daybreak on a winter's morning, to snatch a bite of breakfast, to walk a mile to work because the cars do not run early on Sunday, to stand all day long "on the slings," or with stiff hands wheel a heavy truck back and forward for hours over an uneven floor, to eat with unwashed hands at a cheap restaurant—then is the time to meditate. In fact such circumstances make one think furiously.

Why work on Sunday? Because the work during the week has not brought in sufficient money to support the family for a week. Sunday work is paid as "time and a half." But one should not work on Sunday—Oh, so the boss believes. He will not even walk to church; he rides in his private car— "Remember the Sabbath day to keep it holy." He joins in the response, "Lord have mercy upon us and incline our hearts to keep thy law." But his firm keeps its plant in operation every day in the week. He drops a coin in the collection for the poor. Whose coin? Do I receive all that I produce? Surely it pays someone to keep me working on Sundays even at time and a half rates! He goes home to wife and family and music and friends. I work on in the rain out of hearing even of the church bells.

From such feeling sprang a genuine militancy—and from that militancy an enthusiasm and tempered joy in the struggle for social reform. One of the most striking articles of this period he entitled, "Come On In, The Water's Fine!"[17]

My Winnipeg friends who knew me in connection with church work or social service activities would probably hardly recognize a longshoreman in grey flannel shirt, overalls and slicker, who lines up with the gang alongside a ship or stands waiting in line for his money at the office of the stevedoring company. Yet it is the same J.S.W. who, though declared to be down and out, is, in reality, feeling fairly fit and looking forward to the fight. . . . There is a certain exhilaration in having broken through artificial distinctions—in meeting men as men irrespective of nationality, or creed, or opinions—in being one of them. At lunchtime a big motor dray started down the street; half a dozen workmen, like so many youngsters, climbed on for a ride. The driver wore the button of the teamsters' union; we were one—members of the glorious army of workers! . . . How often have I thought of that phrase used concerning the Nazarene: "He became like unto His brethren." So much of our time seems to be spent in distinguishing ourselves from our brethren. Wealth, social position, academic titles, dress— all are used to set one above his brethren. Verily, that kind of thing has its reward! But life has other and more satisfying rewards.

---

[16]*Western Labor News*, March 7, 1919. Reprinted from the *B.C. Federationist*.
[17]*Western Labor News*, Feb. 28, 1919.

At present the odds seem against us. A minister in a Christian church is forced out of his church because he tries to be true to what seems to him the teaching of Jesus. A social service worker who has spent years in what he thought patriotic work is dubbed unpatriotic, pro-German, Bolshevist. Possibly, as some of our friends tell us, we may have made a big blunder. Possibly we may yet be forced to yield. "The flesh is weak." But though muscles often ache and the back is tired and much is uncongenial, there is more than compensation in being as yet no man's slave. And what if, as we believe, we are right!

So after the first shock I have got my breath and shout back my message of good cheer: "Come on in—the water's fine!"

Woodsworth was not led into hasty or ill-considered conclusions. He was by temperament averse to easy answers. Even in his work as a labour political organizer he devoted much of his time to refuting the absolutism of communist theory. In an article written shortly after he obtained work on the docks he drove home his pragmatist argument. Forget the precise phrases used by Marx, he wrote, and let us solve our own problems. Every dogmatist, whether Catholic, Protestant, or socialist, exhibits the same mental weakness. "It is the same type of mind that always looks for some extreme authority, and once having accepted that authority never feels quite sure of its ground unless it can quote chapter and verse, and if it can cite such authority seems willing to accept any statement, however unreasonable or far from the facts."[18] "No man's slave" was more than a catch phrase for Woodsworth; and the sceptical individualism it expressed remained a major element in the Canadian socialism Woodsworth helped to define. It is a tradition, with its long background in British thought, which is not so likely to expire as modern critics of collectivism fear. Fortunately its roots lie deeper than the North American frontier.

Opposing the direct-action arguments of the Marxists Woodsworth declared that evolution could be assisted: "The far-reaching effects of the war are manifest in every direction. Old ideas and systems have been found wanting and ruthlessly thrown on the scrap-heap. . . . 'The Britisher will never surrender his political freedom' and yet he meekly submits to conscription and rationing and censorship. The impossible has taken place. Every institution has been affected—government has assumed new functions. . . ."[19] He believed firmly in the possibility of a worker-farmer alliance in Canada and quoted the platform of the Non-Partisan League to show the growing agrarian awareness of the nature of the capitalist system. "Surely," he wrote, "the farmers must

[18]B.C. Federationist, Oct. 18, 1918.
[19]Ibid., Sept. 6, 1918.

have been studying the programme of the British Labour Party."[20] His dislike of the S.P.C. policies increased because they could apparently find no place in their system for the unclassifiable Canadian farmer.

While the Vancouver labour paper was moving steadily toward the advocacy of direct action, stimulated by the storm that centred in the problem of Trades and Labour Congress policy and control,[21] Woodsworth wrote a series of articles expounding the main points of the British labour programme. He specifically praised the British position for opening the party door to all producers by hand and brain and thus breaking away from the old trade union limitations and escaping "the weaknesses of those economic schools which restrict the clear 'producers' to manual laborers."[22] At the same time he believed that British labour aimed at revolution. Reviewing Hobson's book, *Democracy after the War*, he wrote,[23] "that whether the revolution will be bloodless or not depends really on the attitude of the small propertied class in control of the government." In Canada he saw danger in the government's suggestion that the Dominion police be expanded. The government was tempting fate, he suggested, when it claimed that revolutionary agitation was confined to the foreign-born population and then proposed measures against *all* the workers in fear of a crisis of unemployment.

Despite divided labour opinion Woodsworth asserted that "the British Labor Programme will become the peoples' Charter."[24] He could sympathize with the class bitterness expressed by a man like Haywood in the United States, or by S.P.C. and O.B.U. leaders in Canada, but he retained his belief that society cannot be reconstructed "at one fell swoop."[25] Thus the kind of class struggle which consciously aimed at revolution by force would frustrate its own ends. Painstaking preparation, education, and planning of the kind advocated by the

[20]*Ibid.* In the issue of Jan. 24, 1919, he wrote: "For years to come elections in Canada will be determined by the vote of the rural population." He also underlined the importance of the Canadian Council of Agriculture's platform and the spread of the co-operative movement in the West.

[21]For a brief account of the failure of the radical western delegates to get their resolutions on reconstruction accepted by the Quebec meeting of the Trades and Labour Congress in 1918, see H. A. Logan, *Trade Unions in Canada* (Toronto, 1948), p. 515.   [22]*B.C. Federationist*, Jan. 2, 1918.

[23]*Ibid.*, Nov. 18, 1918.   [24]*Ibid.*, Jan. 2, 1919.

[25]The *B.C. Federationist*, in expounding the idea of a revolutionary unionism continued its Marxian line: "These fantastic schemes such as 'State Socialism,' 'Municipal Socialism,' 'National Guilds,' 'Fabian' free thought Socialism and the many more or less step by step fallacies are completely out of joint with the evolutionary process that, in our present society, as in all those of the past, is controlled by the economic forces of production . . ." (Jan. 10, 1919).

British gradualists was the only commonsense approach; he was sufficiently percipient to write in 1919, "Revolution may appear to come more slowly [in Britain than in Russia] but there will be no counter-revolution. . . . It may take a few years to work out, but when it's done it's done for good."[26] Unquestionably there was an intimate relation between his pacifist position on war and his advocacy of democratic socialism—force could not settle social issues in either the national or the international field. While some of his Vancouver friends were critical of this moderate political stand, it was simply impossible to pillory a man as a traitor to the working class who had so obviously and completely foresworn the privileges of membership in the "bourgeoisie."

As the struggle of western labour leaders to overthrow conservative eastern control of the Trades and Labour Council was coming to a climax in the Western Labour Conference at Calgary (March, 1919), Woodsworth showed a marked sympathy with the cause of industrial unionism. He spoke and wrote as bitingly about Gomperism and the debilitating effects of organization by crafts as did any O.B.U. organizer. But he stopped short at the dogmatic implications of direct action in the O.B.U. programme:

The Federated Labor Party is remarkable not merely for what it says, but for what it does not say. There is no mention of "surplus value", of "materialistic interpretation of history", of "class-conscious wage-slaves", and the other well-worn phrases so familiar to us all. The Labor Party leaves the "scientific orthodox" group and the "revisionist" groups to fight out their theories, but takes the great underlying principle stressed by Marx, viz., the collective ownership and democratic control of the means of wealth production. Men may differ widely in theory and yet unite to fight a common foe.[27]

---

[26]*B.C. Federationist*, Jan. 2, 1919.

[27]*Western Labor News*, Oct. 11, 1918. Although Woodsworth did not exhibit the ungovernable rhetoric of Eugene Debs, his position with respect to the O.B.U. was comparable to that of Debs with respect to the I.W.W. (at least as the latter organization developed). See Debs's article "A Plea for Solidarity," written in March, 1914: ". . . like causes produce like results. Opponents of political action split the I.W.W. and they will split any union that is not composed wholly of anti-political actionists, or in which they are not in a hopeless minority. I say this in no hostile spirit. They are entitled to their opinion the same as the rest of us.

"At bottom, all anti-political actionists are to all intents and purposes anarchists, and anarchists and socialists have never yet pulled together and probably never will.

"Now, the industrial organization that ignores or rejects political action is as certain to fail as is the political party that ignores or rejects industrial action. Upon the mutually recognized unity and co-operation of the industrial and political powers of the working class will both the union and the party have to be built if real solidarity is to be achieved."

Reprinted in *Writings and Speeches of Eugene V. Debs* (New York, 1948), p. 370.

By the spring of 1919, then, Woodsworth had a fairly well defined policy of social democracy, and had been further inspired by his own entry into the working class. He had also a very distinct suspicion of direct action, particularly if that action was to be aggressive in the revolutionary sense rather than defensive of whatever positions might be attained through political and economic methods.

In that spring, work on the Vancouver docks was slack, and he accepted an invitation from Rev. William Ivens of Winnipeg to undertake a prairie speaking tour in the interest of labour political organization. Woodsworth was especially interested in Ivens, because Ivens had also lost his position for preaching too clearly certain aspects of the social gospel, and he had then become editor of the Winnipeg labour paper in August, 1918 (at which time the name of the paper was changed from the *Voice* to the *Western Labor News*).

The case of Ivens raises again the question of the attitude of official Manitoba Methodism to unorthodox ministers. Ivens had been removed by the Manitoba Methodist Conference in 1918 from his position as pastor of McDougall Church in Winnipeg. This action had been taken at the request of the board of McDougall Church and there is some doubt as to whether it represented the majority opinion of the church membership (not that a majority opinion was required). In the Victoria University Archives there is, under the title "Attitude of the Methodist Church to the War," a considerable collection of letters and petitions from church members deprecating the action of the Board and the Conference and requesting the reinstatement of Ivens. Rev. A. E. Smith, who was a member of the Wesley College Board when Bland was dismissed, and was president of the Manitoba Conference of 1918 which received Woodsworth's resignation and refused to keep Ivens at McDougall Church, was also a social gospeler. In June, 1919, Smith also resigned from the church.

One cannot refrain from the comment that the Manitoba Conference was even more cautious and conservative than the Methodist Church as a whole. The General Conference of the church, having been compelled through wartime necessity to acquiesce in certain developments of which many ministers did not approve, produced at Hamilton in 1918 a remarkable resolution declaring the need "for nothing less than a transference of the whole economic life from a basis of competition and profits to one of co-operation and service."[28] In arguing the case of William Ivens before the Court of Appeal of the Methodist Church of Canada in 1919, Rev. John A. Haw suggested that Ivens should have

[28]Quoted in M. V. Royce, "The Contribution of the Methodist Church in Canada to Social Welfare" (unpublished Ph.D. thesis, Toronto, 1938), p. 105.

been allowed to remain "without station" and free to pursue what he considered to be a mission amongst the working class. The Manitoba Conference had insisted upon his accepting a specific charge and when he refused, the Conference "located" him (and finally expelled him from the ministry). During the case Haw remarked, "William Ivens is not on trial. But the Manitoba Conference is on trial; and the whole character of Methodism is on trial; and the genuineness of our desire to readjust ourselves to the people we have lost is on trial. For here is the first case [sic] of a minister risking his position to carry the gospel to a class who, owing to social position, are disinherited and despoiled."[29]

The General Conference resolution of 1918 was a resolution; the actions of the Manitoba Conference and the Court of Appeal were actions. When A. R. M. Lower suggests that Methodism fathered a large proportion of Canada's radicals[30] perhaps he should have written "expelled" rather than "fathered."

On May 9, 1919, the *Western Labor News* carried a notice of Woodsworth's projected speaking tour, asking any local labour groups or rural districts that desired to hear him to communicate with Ivens. This speaking tour was completed and Woodsworth arrived in Winnipeg on June 8, three weeks after the commencement of the general strike in that city. His experience in Winnipeg during the remainder of the strike period, and throughout the strike trials, was to strengthen him in the basic political, economic, and religious positions which he had adopted.

[29]The record of the Court of Appeal is in the Victoria University Archives.
[30]A. R. M. Lower, *Colony to Nation* (Toronto, 1946), p. 499n.

8

THE WINNIPEG STRIKE

Woe unto them that decree unrighteous decrees, and that write grievous-
ness which they have prescribed; to turn aside the needy from judgment,
and to take away the right from the poor of my people, that widows may be
their prey, and that they may rob the fatherless! (Isa. 10: 1–2)
And they shall build houses, and inhabit them; and they shall plant
vineyards, and eat the fruit of them. They shall not build, and another
inhabit; they shall not plant, and another eat; for as the days of a tree are
the days of my people, and mine elect shall long enjoy the work of their
hands. (Isa. 65: 21–2)

ALTHOUGH MANY OF THE OLDER CITIZENS of Winnipeg today prefer to
forget the events of the spring of 1919, the Winnipeg strike was a most
significant occurrence in Canadian history, if for no other reason than
that it was the first and only time in Canadian history that a major
city was split clearly into two opposing classes. The strike was of
particular importance in the life of Woodsworth, not, as one might
assume, because it altered any of his convictions or left him embittered,
but because it served as a searchlight focused on the facts which he
was already fitting into a socialist analysis of Canadian life. Woodsworth emerged from the strike period more determined than ever to
pursue the course upon which he had embarked.

From the time of his first contact with the strike, three weeks after
its beginning on May 15, to the time of his arrest a few days before
its collapse on June 26, and on through the sedition trials of 1920, he
was prominent in the advocacy of the strikers' cause. It is necessary,
therefore, to look at some of the basic evidence of the strike period,
and give in some detail a picture of the problems and attitudes
created, in order to understand the part played by Woodsworth.

The selection of facts to describe the causes and course of the
Winnipeg general strike will inevitably influence the conclusion as to

its merits and shortcomings. Various interpretations have been advanced. One view originated with the Citizens' Committee of One Thousand, and was carried on through the government prosecution in the strike trials, the *Canadian Annual Review* and the *Cambridge History of the British Empire* (vol. VI). This view sees the real aim of the strike as the establishment of a Canadian soviet government which would spread forth its power from the banks of the Red River.

An opposing interpretation finds its origin in the strike newspaper, the strikers' defence committee established to fight the government indictments, and in the *Report* of the Robson Commission of July, 1919, which was appointed by the Manitoba Government to investigate the causes of the strike. According to this view there were no basic aims other than the improvement of wages, working conditions, and labour's bargaining position. This argument sees the high cost of living, threatened unemployment, and the employers' attitude toward collective bargaining as the real causes. Additional support for this view can be seen in the comments of General Ketchen, the officer commanding in Winnipeg, who appears to have anticipated the conclusions of the *Robson Report*. As the evidence of unrest accumulated in the early days of June he wired to Ottawa suggesting that the federal government should deal with the cost of living problem under the War Measures Act, if not by price-fixing, then by a prices board to investigate complaints and with power to prosecute. Such action, he argued, ". . . would allay universal indignation and unrest and go far to solve the situation."[1]

A third interpretation of the strike sought a compromise position. This can be seen in A. R. M. Lower's *Colony to Nation*, and Edgar McInnis', *Canada, a Political and Social History*, which lean slightly toward the strikers' interpretation; and H. A. Logan's, *Trade Unions in Canada*, which tilts almost imperceptibly the other way. Finally, D. C. Masters' monograph, *The Winnipeg General Strike*, vacillates between the two basic views and concludes, almost reluctantly, that the strike was not an abortive revolution.

Since the governments which were directly involved (those of Winnipeg, Manitoba, and the Dominion) exhibited a remarkable unanimity in accepting the first of these three interpretations, and based their vigorous action upon this analysis, it is worth further examination. Their point of view, at least in part, was the result of a

[1]See P.A.C., Borden Papers, Box 113, O.C. 564 (1), No. 61751. The author is indebted to Professor William Smith of Brandon College for drawing his attention to the evidence of General Ketchen.

general hysteria affecting most governments in North America, and the majority of business men, at the end of the First World War. The Russian Revolution was an accomplished fact. This increased, in many minds, the significance of leftist propaganda and organization in the New World. In the United States in the year 1919 the Red Scare rose to a crescendo, while in Canada there was prevalent the belief that I.W.W. forces were planning to combine with socialists and radical trade unionists, through the One Big Union, to overthrow constituted authority. There had been a series of strikes during the war period, culminating in a Winnipeg railway strike in 1918 which had threatened to become general in that city. Orders-in-council had been passed to suppress "dangerous" organizations and literature, and these regulations remained in effect after the close of the war.

It will always be difficult to understand fully the anatomy of a national "scare," but to be candid, one must recognize some degree of ulterior motivation in the development of such a phenomenon. In this case, there was the fear that unionization would get out of hand and kill the golden prospects of profit in a country newly equipped with industrial resources. Demobilization, and the reorganization of production, were bound to produce serious, if temporary unemployment, at least in this pre-Keynesian period. If the country could be convinced that aggressive demands on the part of labour were invariably to be taken as evidence of Bolshevist agitation, the position of the employer of labour in this difficult period would be a good deal more secure.

That this kind of reasoning was behind the Red Scare of 1919 in this country was pointedly suggested in speeches in the House of Commons, particularly by Ernest Lapointe[2] and C. G. Power.[3] Mr. Lapointe asserted that the high cost of living and the conspicuous consumption of war profiteers had much to do with the grave situation in the West. He suggested that the deliberations of the Mathers Commission on industrial conditions were too sluggish and had come too late. He further intimated that the government was trying to "mystify the public by acting a Bolshevist melodrama to cover administrative and governmental negligence." He believed that the government was backing the Winnipeg employers in an untenable position behind the facade of constitutional government. Industrial unionism on a wide scale was inevitable because "the various trades of an industry are all links in one chain. If one fails the others are worthless. . . . The

[2]Canada, House of Commons, *Debates* (hereafter cited as Hansard), 1919, pp. 3010 *et seq.*
[3]*Ibid.*, pp. 3029 *et seq.*

organization of capital has been unlimited. . . . It is only natural that there should be a similar evolution on the other side." Mr. Power repeated these sentiments and stated specifically that the principle of the general strike must be granted and not subverted because of the possible presence of a small number of "Bolsheviki." Major G. W. Andrews, of Centre Winnipeg, also entered this debate to decry the attempt to label the strikers Bolshevists, declaring, "if you apply the term to those men you apply it to me, because they are my friends."[4]

Ignoring the charges of partisanship and of attempting to falsify the issue, the governments concerned, the employers and the daily newspapers of Winnipeg asserted their conviction that the strike was part of a grand revolutionary plan. In the early days of the strike this position was most succinctly stated in the Commons by M. R. Blake (North Winnipeg). He quoted the *ad hoc* Winnipeg newspaper, the *Citizen*, to the effect that the strike was plain, ugly revolution, and said, "The trouble with labour is that it is being misled in the West. The revolutionary and socialist elements seem to be in control." The sedition act, he thought, should have been amended long ago. "Radical Socialist leaders must be interned or deported. . . . Sympathetic strikes must be abandoned. . . . The Criminal Code should be amended to prevent civic, provincial and federal employees joining in any sympathetic strike. . . . I speak as a neutral."[5]

The key argument of this "official" interpretation, based upon scattered allegations concerning individual labour leaders, rested upon the debates and resolutions of a peculiar assembly known as the Western Labour Conference which had been held at Calgary in March, 1919. Senator Robertson, the Minister of Labour, apparently believed throughout the strike that "the whole revolutionary scheme" had been hatched at that conference in Calgary. The senator was quoted by his colleague, Senator A. N. Maclean, as saying that the "play" had been written at the Calgary Conference and that the Winnipeg strike was the first rehearsal, with the main performance promised for a later date.[6] Even the *Toronto Star*, which afterwards carried the most impartial of all the contemporary accounts of the Winnipeg strike, accepted in the first few days the official version, and printed an article (May 17) claiming that the true source of the strike was the Calgary Conference.

It is undoubtedly true that there were many hotheads at that conference, and that it was, indeed, the preliminary meeting for the One

[4]*Ibid.*, p. 3020.
[5]*Ibid.*, pp. 3008 *et seq.*   [6]*Ibid.*, p. 3044.

Big Union drive. It is, however, highly debatable whether the Winnipeg strike was planned by the conference, or even whether the leaders at Calgary constituted an organized revolutionary body. Both the One Big Union conference and the Winnipeg strike were products of general conditions affecting labour throughout the country—conditions particularly resented by the volatile westerners.

The Western Labour Conference was called by the secretary of a temporary committee established during the Quebec meeting of the Trades and Labour Congress in 1918.[7] The committee was elected by a caucus of western delegates who had been frustrated during the Quebec meeting by the defeat of their resolutions calling for the release of wartime political prisoners, the prohibiting of labour leaders' holding trade union positions while enjoying government patronage, reorganization of the Trades and Labour Congress along industrial lines, and the proclamation of a six-hour day and five-day week in order to absorb returned soldiers.

There is little doubt that the western labour leaders who brought about and controlled the Calgary Conference were all either syndicalist, communist, or socialist in their general views—just as it is clear that the eastern controllers of the Trades and Labour Congress were primarily staunch defenders of craft unionism and the Gompers tradition. But even a casual reading of the proceedings and resolutions of the conference at Calgary will show that most of the leaders were far from understanding the intricacies of their own general theories, that the whole conference was essentially the product of anger at conservative eastern leaders coupled with the sincere desire to establish some effective form of industrial unionism.

The key resolution at the conference, and the one upon which future action was based, was number 3: "Resolved that this convention recommend to its affiliated membership the severance of their affiliation with their international organizations, and that steps be taken to form an industrial organization of all workers."[8] There were a number of other wordy resolutions calling for a general strike on June 1 if the censorship of radical literature were not relaxed, if political prisoners were not released, if the Allied troops were not withdrawn from Russia, and if the six-hour day and five-day week were not implemented. There were resolutions declaring the acceptance of the

[7]See *The Origin of the One Big Union: A Verbatim Account of the Calgary Conference, 1919* (Winnipeg, n.d.). For a discussion of the One Big Union see H. A. Logan, *Trade Unions in Canada* (Toronto, 1948), pp. 301 *et seq.*
[8]*The Origin of the One Big Union*, p. 11.

principle of the dictatorship of the proletariat for the transition to socialism, and resolutions sending fraternal greetings to "the Russian Soviet Government, the Spartacans [sic] in Germany, and all definite working class movements in Europe and the world."[9] The essential point, however, whether or not one agrees that there was no real understanding of political possibilities apart from the idea of industrial unionism, was that the origins of the strike in Winnipeg were apparently unconnected with the debates of the Calgary Conference. This seems clear even in the light of simple chronology, for the Winnipeg strike broke out first on May 1, and became general on May 15. At that time the One Big Union was not organized and, indeed, its organizational meeting was delayed because of the strike itself.[10]

One piece of recent evidence concerning the purposes and leadership of the strike is contained in A. E. Smith, *All My Life*. Smith became a communist in the 1920's and his posthumously published autobiography hews closely to the party line. Had the strike been a communist struggle it is probable that Canadian communists would now look upon it as their European comrades look upon the Paris Commune. Instead:

The mighty power of the working class was immediately evident. This was not a revolutionary struggle for power. As I look back now I know that the leadership from the beginning was afraid of the great power of the strike. There was no working class party with a conscious understanding of this power and what should be done. The strike leaders in Winnipeg told the workers to stay home. They tried to keep the struggle on a purely economic plane. And in the end they called off the strike without consulting the workers. Yet objectively here was revealed more clearly than by any other event in Canadian labour history the elemental factors of working class power. . . . Under conditions of a nation-wide political crisis the Winnipeg strike Committee would have become an organ of truly democratic power. (p. 30)

---

[9]*Ibid.*, p. 30.

[10]Logan, *Trade Unions in Canada*, p. 313. H. A. Logan states that the Winnipeg Trades and Labour Council, which led in organizing the Winnipeg strike, was dominated by the men who had led the Manitoba delegation at the Calgary Conference (p. 317). The evidence does not agree with this statement. The *Robson Report* (*Report of the Royal Commission to Enquire into and Report upon the Causes and Effects of the General Strike . . . in the City of Winnipeg . . .* ; H. A. Robson, K.C., Commissioner, Winnipeg, 1919), indicates the near unanimity with which the Council adopted the method of a general strike; D. C. Masters, *The Winnipeg General Strike* (Toronto, 1950), especially p. 132, shows clearly that R. B. Russell was the only direct connection between the Calgary Conference and the Council's Strike Committee. Russell himself, in an interview with the present writer, declared that he advised the Council against calling the strike at that time.

There is, then, little question that the Winnipeg strike grew spontaneously. At the first of May, after negotiations with their employers had broken down, the workers in the building and metal trades in Winnipeg came out on strike. The cause of the former was primarily that of a living wage, that of the latter the double question of wages and union recognition.[11] The employers of the building trades agreed that the average wage was inadequate but claimed they were unable to do any better.[12] The iron masters not only refused the wage demands but also declined to deal with the Metal Trades Council, the common bargaining agent of the metal trades unions. They asserted that collective bargaining applied only to the group of men employed by any one firm (or type of firms), and in this, as previously noted, they were supported by the governments.

The Building Trades Council and the Metal Trades Council then took their case to the Winnipeg Trades and Labour Council and the latter ordered a vote in all its affiliates on the question of a general strike—primarily to secure the principle of collective bargaining, and secondly as a demand for general wage increases to meet the soaring cost of living. The result of the vote was an overwhelming majority in favour of a general strike, and on May 15 approximately thirty thousand workers left their jobs (including, significantly, about twelve thousand who were not members of unions).[13]

The strike, which lasted until June 26, involved everyone in Winnipeg deeply, produced a spasm of fear throughout the "great middle class" of the city which led some of the people of Fort Rouge to sleep in churches for fear of being murdered in their beds, and yet was characterized primarily by its almost absolute lack of violence. Indeed, as already observed, the present communist criticism of the strike

[11]*Robson Report; The Winnipeg General Sympathetic Strike*, prepared by the strikers' defence committee; Logan, *Trade Unions in Canada*, p. 318.

[12]The strikers' defence committee maintained that after the strike was crushed the builders agreed to pay wages in excess of the schedule which had been demanded by the Building Trades Council (*The Winnipeg General Sympathetic Strike*, p. 30). A. E. Smith asserts that "the bankers" were basically responsible for rendering the class decision to refuse the labour demands of 1919: "The Builders' Exchange admitted the demands of the workers to be reasonable, yet said: 'We cannot pay the increase.' This was a class decision, not a mere local attitude of the Builders' Exchange. They said: 'The bankers refuse to do business on the new basis.' . . . In my own city [Brandon] the five hundred civic employees demanding higher wages, seniority and union recognition, met the same stubborn refusal. The city fathers were told by the bankers not to agree to the requests." (*All My Life*, pp. 47–8.)

[13]*Canadian Annual Review*, 1919, p. 466; *Robson Report*, p. 4; Logan, *Trade Unions in Canada*, 317–18. The idea of a general strike was in the air from Belfast to Seattle.

holds that the policy of telling the workers to stay at home was its greatest weakness.

At the very outset were established the two organizations which give the strike the aspect of a class conflict: the Central Strike Committee and the Citizens' Committee of One Thousand. These two bodies quite clearly represented the opposing classes in the strike. The Central Strike Committee was elected by the General Strike Committee which was composed of delegates from each of the unions affiliated with the Trades and Labour Council. The Citizens' Committee was an *ad hoc* group of business leaders whose chairman was A. L. Crossin, and which included A. J. Andrews, Isaac Pitblado, and others prominent in the city's legal and business life. One comment by a liberal lawyer who obtained an interview with the executive of the Citizens' Committee is rather disparaging. "I sized up the personnel. There was not a returned soldier there. Newspaper editors, bankers, manufacturers and capitalists abounded."[14] On the other hand, Mr. S. J. Farmer in an interview with the author said that at the meeting of the Trades and Labour Council which declared for the general strike there were one or two hotheads who saw the revolution around the corner.

The actual statistics of the strike tend to minimize the significance of the divisions in Winnipeg in 1919. The Citizens' Committee claimed to represent the great mass of neutral citizenry, but a contemporary article by an excellent news reporter, W. R. Plewman of the *Toronto Star*, observed that "it must be remembered that this [Winnipeg] is a city of only 200,000, and that 35,000 persons are on strike. Thus it will be seen that the strikers and their relatives must represent at least fifty per cent. of the population. In the numerical sense, therefore, it cannot be said that the average citizen is against the strike . . . there is no soviet. There is little or no terrorism."[15] That was the great trouble. The lawyers and business leaders of the Citizens' Committee, realizing the great mass of inertia that was the strike, were compelled to characterize it as positive, revolutionary, and the work of a small group of Reds, if they were to suppress the movement and re-establish business as usual.

In order to suggest further the attitudes of business, church, government, and labour leaders, something must be said about the course of

14J. W. Wilton, "Any Man" (unpublished manuscript, estate of J. W. Wilton, Toronto), p. 352.
15*Toronto Star*, May 23, 1919.

the strike. The original walk-out included not only most of the industrial workers, but also the employees of all the public utilities and services. This posed a difficult question for the Strike Committee. Basic services must be carried on because they did not propose an all-out war, contrary to the charges of their opponents. But this meant that it was necessary also to protect whatever workers remained at their jobs from facing the charge of being scabs. Thus the famous placards that appeared everywhere in the city explaining that the service being operated was "By Permission of the Strike Committee." These signs were taken by some to imply that government powers had actually been seized by the strikers; actually it was the head of the Crescent Creamery Company who suggested the use of the placards as protection for milk deliveries.[16] The police force voted in favour of the strike but at the request of the Strike Committee remained on duty and under orders of the municipal government. Water was kept at a pressure sufficient for domestic purposes, and the distribution of bread and milk was arranged by joint action of the Strike Committee and representatives of the Citizens' Committee and the City Council.

In the first days of the strike there appeared to be a steadily growing support for the workers' cause—a support which would compel the iron masters and the builders to concede the unions' demands. This appearance was heightened by the failure of the daily press to replace its staff immediately the strike began, while the *Western Labor News* issued daily Strike Bulletins. The middle-class dismay at being deprived of its own source of news is illustrated in the contemporary diary of a Methodist minister. When the *Free Press* finally was sold again on the streets on May 23, he wrote, "The *Free Press* has installed a wireless on the roof of its building so now we are all right, and the strike is practically broken, as the working folks have no money, and they are sick of the strike. . . ."[17] Further fear of a strike victory was stimulated by the fact that the majority of the city's returned soldiers were in support of the strike. This was undoubtedly one of the most disturbing features from the point of view of the Citizens' Committee. The day the strike started a great meeting of returned soldiers was called by the executives of the Great War Veterans' Association, the Army and Navy Veterans' Association and the Imperial Veterans of Canada. The purpose of the executives of these organizations was to obtain passage of a resolution condemning the general strike. How-

[16]*The Winnipeg General Sympathetic Strike*, p. 50.
[17]Diary of Rev. Dr. John Maclean (in Victoria University Archives).

ever, the executive resolution was defeated and another, strongly in favour of the strikers, was passed.[18]

As it turned out, the Citizens' Committee had no more cause to fear violence from the returned soldiers than it had from the strikers themselves. There were two noisy but peaceful mass interviews with Premier Norris and Mayor Gray, neither of which produced startling results.[19] At this point (June 5) a report from Winnipeg was received by the Adjutant General in Ottawa. It was from a competent observer, O. M. Biggar, and is very revealing.

Pitblado was in a highly nervous and excited condition and was very much afraid of an immediate attack upon the Industrial Bureau where the Citizens' Committee has its headquarters. The G.O.C. [Ketchen] refused to be stampeded, and in this he was supported by the Mayor, whom I met and who struck me as having both courage and sanity. . . . The Provincial Government was continuing to adopt a somewhat hesitant position except on the one point that no further mediation would be attempted by the Premier until the Strike Committee withdrew its claim to direct the activities of the citizens. . . . I understand that, within the two or three preceding days, General Ketchen's attitude had been to recommend the immediate settlement of the strike but the Provincial Government was not inclined to recede from the position they had taken. . . . Mr. Dafoe thought the existing crisis would come to an end with but slight outbreaks, if any, but he looked forward to a long period of unrest.

According to J. W. Wilton, a supporter of the Norris government in the legislature at that time, the Premier refused to consider that the provincial government had any positive responsibility with respect to the strike. When Wilton urged the Premier to announce legislation to enforce collective bargaining he received the reply, "No, I can't see my way clear to do that. I think we had better keep out of the fight."[20] Indeed, one is tempted to conclude that the real story of the strike lies in the singularly vigorous efforts of the Citizens' Committee to break it—or even to provoke an outbreak of violence which would justify the growing reserves of Mounted Police and militia.

[18]*Western Labor News*, May 17, 1919; *Toronto Star*, May 22, 1919. News of the veterans' action encouraged the *Star* to print a careful editorial warning against misuse of words like "bolshevism." "The Winnipeg citizens' papers says that this dispute has gone beyond the point of bargaining with trade unions—that the city is not facing a strike but a revolution. Yet it says also that 'the returned soldiers are unanimously behind the strikers.' This sounds like the language of despair for which we sincerely hope there is no warrant."

[19]Borden Papers, Box 113, O.C. 564 (1), Nos. 61801–3. That the leaders of the Citizens' Committee made continual demands for immediate arrest of all strike leaders and for deportation of as many as possible is abundantly clear from the evidence of the Borden Papers.

[20]Wilton, "Any Man," p. 355.

The policy of the strikers and the published directions in the *Western Labor News* indicate a consistently passive technique and a peculiarly cautious regard for "law and order." The editorials of the Winnipeg dailies, the actions of the Citizens' Committee and the three governments concerned, all seem to exhibit a determination to suppress the claim of the working class of the city that it need not work under conditions which it regarded as oppressive. This is not to paint the picture in black and white, but rather to emphasize again the hysteria that reigned almost supreme in 1919 amongst the middle and upper classes controlling the governments and economic life of the nation. There was undoubtedly a deep-seated belief that overthrow of all established institutions was imminent as a result of the spread of communist thought following the Russian Revolution, and that even if the Winnipeg strike was not designed as such a revolution the principle of the general strike should be effectively denied. Fear that the traditional bonds of society might break was widespread. In the Commons, M. R. Blake, representative of North Winnipeg, stated his belief that "the tired feeling is abroad in this land" and that the workers had ceased to appreciate "their responsibility to capital and the state."[21]

When the Citizens' Committee established its newspaper, the *Citizen*, it clearly enunciated its own views of the strike. It is worth reproducing some of this editorial because the Citizens' Committee spoke clearly for the "middle class" and the governments controlled by that class.

It is to the general public of Winnipeg that we speak in stating without equivocation that this is not a strike at all, in the ordinary sense of the term—it is revolution.

It is a serious attempt to overturn British institutions in this western country and to supplant them with the Russian Bolshevik system of Soviet rule. . . . Why is it that one finds many thousands of men and women among the strikers who state quite frankly that they had no wish to strike—that they did not want to strike, and yet, paradoxically, they are on strike?

It is because the "Red" element in Winnipeg has assumed the ascendency in the labor movement, dominating and influencing—or stampeding—the decent element of that movement, which desires the preservation of British institutions, yet is now striking unconsciously against them. . . . It is seriously to be feared that the strike cannot much longer be controlled and lawlessness averted. . . . The only way to defeat Bolshevism is for the people, the injured, the sufferers, those who are put to hardship through this strike, those who stand in the position of the proverbially "innocent bystander" who always gets shot in a riot, to organize. . . .

[21]Hansard, 1919, p. 3005.

Law and order? Yes—in a way, law and order has prevailed, to the extent that rioting has not occurred. Law and order to this extent has been kept, solely because the industries and commercial houses have submitted to the strike dictum and suspended operations. Why should not business be carried on so far as possible by men whose legitimate right it is to do business in this city?[22]

The endeavour to depict the strike as the work of a few radicals, and the continual reiteration of the theme that violence was just around the corner, were enthusiastically followed up by the *Telegram*, the *Tribune*, and the *Free Press*. To this was added the claim that the real danger was the alien element (referred to in the *Citizen* on June 12 as "alien scum"); exploitation of the traditional Winnipeg fear of its north-enders was intensive. The dailies could find no labour voice calling for direct action and were compelled to create the idea that the huge mass of foreign-born was about to rise in all its might. The editorial in number 1 of the *Western Labor News* Strike Bulletin (May 17) established the labour view on this subject. "There is great cause for congratulation during this struggle, in that until the present moment the participants are more orderly than a crowd of spectators at a baseball game. . . . There has been evolved a weapon of great power—orderliness." In the same issue a specific warning was sounded against *agents provocateurs*. These attitudes remained constant throughout the strike.

The several attempts at conciliation were blocked by the fundamental problem of recognizing the collective bargaining principle.[28] As the strike progressed, the employers and the representatives of the governments insisted that at the very least all public utilities should be "returned to normal" before the issues of the strike were discussed, and, when an attempt to mediate was made by a committee of the Canadian Railway Brotherhoods, again refused to deal with the Metal Trades Council on any grounds. The familiar employer's insistence broke all the mediation efforts; "give up the strike, then bargain on our terms."

By May 22 there was apparently a deadlock, and the necessity of breaking it appeared to many minds to be very great indeed. Not only had organized labour exhibited a colossal strength in Winnipeg,

[22]Winnipeg *Citizen*, May 10, 1919.
[28]Logan, *Trade Unions in Canada*, p. 318; *Canadian Annual Review*, 1919, p. 471; Masters, *The Winnipeg General Strike*, pp. 72 *et seq.* Masters' evidence shows the obstacle to a settlement in the employers' refusal (*a*) to bargain while a strike continued, and (*b*) to concede the principle of industrial collective bargaining.

but the idea was spreading. There were contemporaneous strikes of varying size and importance right across the country and labour leaders in Winnipeg and some other western cities were beginning to call for a Dominion strike committee.[24]

At this point the concerted offensive which finally resulted in the collapse of the strike was begun. On May 22 there arrived in Winnipeg from Ottawa two emissaries of the central government—Senator Gideon Robertson, Minister of Labour, and Hon. Arthur Meighen, Minister of the Interior (and acting Minister of Justice). On May 23 Sir Thomas White gave to a nervous House of Commons what he considered to be a reassuring statement.[25] He said he was hopeful of an early settlement, that he was in constant communication with General Ketchen, commanding officer of the Winnipeg military district, and that Ketchen had minute and definite instructions. The militia units in Winnipeg, he observed, "are completely filled up with volunteers, with plenty of reserves available in case of trouble. In addition to that the Royal North-West Mounted Police are on duty in Winnipeg. . . ."

The sense of an assembling force was, indeed, widespread in the city itself. In south Winnipeg this was felt to be right and proper. In this connection the contemporary diary of Dr. Maclean is revealing. On May 17 he noted, "The labour men have the upper hand, and so far as they can are showing Bolshevik methods. . . . Mounted Police have come to the city, several thousand men are drilling and in readiness for any riots. . . ." On May 20 he wrote, "We are under the sway of Bolshevism in the city. Everything is quiet, but there are some ugly rumours floating around, and the Home Defence Guards are all ready for action at a given signal. . . ." On May 26, "There is a battalion for every district of the city, soldiers are sleeping at Post Office and public buildings, and military ready for anything at a given signal." Not all of the middle class were quite so convinced about the need or the potential usefulness of the "home guard" organized by the Citizens' Committee. J. W. Wilton, a returned officer, had been given the call to report for duty and refused. He considered the Citizens' Committee had distorted the picture and that few of them had sacrificed their

[24]Logan, *Trade Unions in Canada*, p. 319. Cities affected included Vancouver, Calgary, Edmonton, Prince Albert, Regina, Toronto, and Sydney. In some of these the Trades Councils were actively considering general strikes in sympathy with the Winnipeggers and as an effort to break through the spiral of the cost of living in their own communities. See reports of negotiations involving the Metal Trades Council, in the *Toronto Star*, May 27, 1919, *et seq*. On May 31 the *Star* reported 12,000 workers out in the "general strike."

[25]Hansard, 1919, p. 2753.

interests during the war as had many of the strikers. Commenting on the Committee's trainees he described them as "rather corpulent gentlemen handling rifles as if they were sticks of dynamite."[26] No one, however, questioned the efficiency either of the R.N.W.M.P. or of the militia units. And the Commissioner of the Mounties had declared himself just as clearly as had the Citizens' Committee and the three governments. He even undertook to align the farmers against the strike by going out amongst them and declaring that it was revolutionary and aimed at the confiscation of property and the establishment of a communist form of government.

When the two cabinet ministers from Ottawa neared the city on May 22, they were met on their train by representatives of the Citizens' Committee, and it was with these men and the chiefs of the municipal and provincial governments that Robertson and Meighen associated during their inspection of the strike.[27] Such open partisanship induced Ernest Lapointe to observe in the Commons that "Senator Robertson seems to have sided with one party to the struggle, and obviously his usefulness as a mediator is gone, and I do not wonder that he is on his way back to Ottawa. . . ." Lapointe referred to Robertson's action in asking Gompers to order the A.F. of L. to stop their unions from supporting the Winnipeg strike as "a humiliating appeal by a responsible minister to a foreign labour leader." Mr. Meighen, he added, was the last man in the world to be selected as a mediator or conciliator. "He stands in Canada as the apostle of arbitrary enactments and despotic legislation."[28] The strike leaders asserted that the activities of Meighen and Robertson were "completely unknown" to them, and that they apparently worked exclusively with the Citizens' Committee.[29]

The preliminary consultation between the Ottawa ministers and the Citizens' Committee certainly served to alienate labour leaders and also enabled the *Citizen* to print a scoop on May 24:

"It is up to the citizens of Winnipeg to stand firm and resist the efforts made here to overturn proper authority." This statement was made yesterday by Hon. Arthur Meighen, Minister of the Interior, who, with Senator the Hon. Gideon D. Robertson, Minister of Labour, is in the city in connection with the strike situation. The two ministers have let it be known, authoritatively, that they regard the so-called strike as a cloak for something far deeper—a cloak for an effort "to overthrow proper authority". The same spirit, they say, has been noticeable in other parts of Canada, and Winnipeg seems to

26Wilton, "Any Man," p. 350.
27Masters, *The Winnipeg General Strike*, p. 71.
28Hansard, 1919, p. 3015.
29*The Winnipeg General Sympathetic Strike*, p. 98.

have been chosen as the starting point of the campaign. This is a statement of the views of the two ministers as expressed by themselves. . . . "There is absolutely no justification for the general strike called by the strike committee in this city," said Hon. Arthur Meighen. . . .

Senator Robertson's first action was to call a meeting of the postal employees (May 25). To them he issued an ultimatum. Unless they returned to work on the following day, and signed agreements never to support a sympathetic strike, and to sever their relations with the Winnipeg Trades and Labour Council, they would be discharged with loss of pension rights, and the assurance of no future federal employment.[30] The Norris government served a similar notice on its telephone workers, and the city council by a vote of nine to five passed a resolution against the principle of the general strike. It also authorized the dismissal of all civic employees who remained on strike. If any of these decided to return, they too must sign a "yellow-dog" contract.[31] This triple action obtained the general support of the middle class, and the city council under Mayor Gray upheld their part in it.

In the House of Commons on May 27, 1919, Sir Robert Borden delivered a statement on the labour situation in western Canada which, despite its superficial impartiality, clearly placed Ottawa on the side of the Citizens' Committee.[32] The industrial "unrest" was, he suggested, an integral part of the critical labour conditions throughout the world, and he appealed to everyone in the country to be moderate in that time of unusual strain. He indicated that his government had not been taken unawares by the labour problem inherent in demobilization, and that in April, 1918, the Mathers Commission on Industrial Relations had been given the task of illuminating the entire problem—a task which at the time of the Prime Minister's speech remained unfinished. The Prime Minister went on to calm the fears of labour by announcing his conviction that the nation's employers would not overlook the principles adopted by all the nations in the Paris Peace Conference—that they would cease to regard labour as an article of commerce, would respect the right of association and the right to a

[30]Ibid.; Canadian Annual Review, 1919, p. 469.

[31]Canadian Annual Review, 1919, p. 469; Logan, Trade Unions in Canada, p. 318. The city employees were required to state that they would remain free from "any union which is directly or indirectly in affiliation with any other organization, to whose orders, directions or recommendations such union or association, or its workers are obliged to conform, or act in concert with." They had to pledge that they would "not take part in, or support, or favour what is known as a sympathetic strike."

[32]Hansard, 1919, pp. 2851 et seq.

living wage, and would strive for an eight hour day and a forty-eight hour week.

As for the general strike in Winnipeg, which had then been in progress a little less than two weeks, Sir Robert stated that "the government has taken no sides in that dispute." But he also observed that the government occupied a position different from that of the private employer. He asserted that "if the needs of the people as a whole are to be regarded we cannot have in this country a complete dislocation of public services founded upon such reasons as have been put forward by the postal employees of Winnipeg," and he announced with some satisfaction at the close of his speech that "seventy of the postal employees have returned to work and no difficulty has been experienced in filling the places of those who have not returned." He made no mention of the cost of living as a cause of the strike but did recognize the necessity of arriving at a definition of collective bargaining acceptable both to capital and labour. The attitude of the central government on this subject is of great importance, as it meant that Ottawa gave wholehearted support to the employers and governments at Winnipeg.

To clarify the federal government's position on the question of collective bargaining Sir Robert read a statement prepared by the Minister of Labour, Senator Gideon Robertson. This declared that the employers of Winnipeg, and of Canada, admitted "the right of the employees to bargain with their employers concerning matters affecting any individual plant or industry." The statement then made clear the fact that the minister defined the terms "plant" and "industry" very closely by giving his view of the claims presented by the Winnipeg unions involved in the strike.

The central strike committee interprets the right of collective bargaining to mean that the central body shall have the power to approve or reject any agreement that may be satisfactory to the employer or classes of employer and their employees, which, if granted, would have the result of enabling any central committee entirely outside the industry or craft affected to dictate the acceptance or rejection of any agreement. Instead of giving to the workmen in any individual plant or industry the right of collective bargaining with their employers, the present plan deprives them of the right and places them entirely in the hands of a central body, which principle the Citizens' Committee of Winnipeg, Provincial and Federal Governments agree cannot be accepted.

With this statement of the issue by his colleague the Prime Minister specifically agreed, and by implication set his government the task of

protecting the workers of Winnipeg and the West from the dictatorship of their democratically elected trade union leaders. The gauntlet
was down, the issues defined, and the class alignment made clear. But
there was one important factor: one side in the struggle was prepared
to use force, the other was not.

On June 6, although there had been no serious violence, Mayor
Gray banned all parades and forbade the congregation of crowds. On
the same day the Dominion Parliament passed, with a remarkable
economy of time, an amendment to the Immigration Act, which
extended to British-born subjects the Act's provisions concerning deportation by executive order. This amendment, which was the cause
of considerable resentment in organized labour groups across the
country, passed all three readings in both Houses and received the
royal assent in less than an hour.[33] Its significance lay in the fact that
it implied that the leadership of the strike was not in the hands of
European-born aliens—an implication now definitely proven correct.[34]

This was the stage reached in the development of the strike when
Woodsworth arrived in Winnipeg on June 8. As he approached the
city across the prairies, stopping frequently to fulfil his speaking
engagements, he kept himself as well informed about the strike as was
possible from outside. He was anxious to use whatever influence he
might possess in the city to further a conciliation move, but discovered
that there was, by that time, practically no chance of success, chiefly
because of the insistence upon cessation of the strike before further
negotiations, and the blunt refusal to admit the right of a general strike
on principle. Almost immediately upon his arrival, Woodsworth wrote
a letter which was published in the *Western Labor News*,[35] stating
his own position and attempting to define the situation. In this statement he returned with great emphasis to one of his earliest established
concepts, the "sin of indifference."

Some at least of those who knew me for the past thirty years, in old college
days, in Grace Church, in All Peoples' Mission, at the Forum, or in various
social welfare activities, will not think that I am an irresponsible fanatic.
I appeal to such.

First of all let me say that I have no official connection with the strike.
I had arranged to visit Winnipeg weeks ago before the strike was called. . . .

He went on to condemn those who cried revolution.

The general public is up in arms. They have suffered inconvenience and

---

[33]*Toronto Star*, June 7, 1919.
[34]Masters, *The Winnipeg General Strike*, p. 129 and *passim*.
[35]*Western Labor News*, June 12, 1919.

loss. "Why should innocent non-combatants suffer?" The general public has not been innocent. It has been guilty of the greatest sin—the sin of indifference. Thousands have suffered through the years under the industrial system. The general public have not realized. It did not touch them. Now it is coming home to them. They blame the strikers. Why not blame the employers whose arrogant determination has provoked the strike. Why not, rather, quit the unprofitable business of trying to place blame and attempt to discover and remove causes that have produced this strike and will produce, if not removed, further and more disastrous strikes? . . . The crisis calls for extraordinary measures. Troops and more troops will not settle the question. Constructive radical action must come some time. Why not now?

Learning in more detail the preceding developments of the strike, Woodsworth concluded that the "general public," or at least that part represented by the Citizens' Committee and the three governments, was not prepared to concede any of the strikers' claims. Thus there appeared to be no alternative save for the workers to refrain from work to the limit of their resources, and to educate as many of the people on the sidelines as possible. The governments, he considered, were pursuing a course perfectly incompatible with the traditions of British liberty and, to add to his reasons for supporting the strikers, he was fully in sympathy with the goal of industrial collective bargaining.

He immediately threw himself into the fray, appearing with strike leaders (and outside sympathizers like A. E. Smith of Brandon and Canon Scott of Quebec), to address mass meetings in Victoria Park, and helping to raise funds for strikers' families. As he observed at close quarters the evolution of the strike he became increasingly convinced that the real plot was not the revolution allegedly sponsored by the One Big Union advocates, but the concerted actions of the Citizens' Committee and the three governments to suppress the whole idea of industrial unionism and the sympathetic strike. In a letter reviewing the strike for missionary relatives in China,[36] he wrote,

That strike has been entirely misrepresented. I know the inside details intimately. Without hesitation I say that there was not a single foreigner in a position of leadership, though foreigners were falsely arrested to give color to this charge. . . . In short, it was the biggest hoax that was ever "put over" any people! Government officials and the press were largely responsible. Of course some of them were quite sincere but absolutely hysterical. In the South End where Mother lived, people were guarding their homes with rifles against imaginary monsters, while the flesh and blood strikers were some of them holding what can best be described as great revival meetings, and praying for the strength to hold out for another week for what they believed were their rights. . . .

[36]Aug. 25, 1921.

Apart from the more abstract rights or wrongs of the situation he was deeply pained by the sight of the severe suffering and want which increased markedly amongst the strikers as the third week was passed, and by the obvious want of balance between the forces arrayed against each other. At every fresh move by the government to overwhelm the strike, his devotion to the cause of the underdog expanded.

That he was correct concerning the grave misapprehension under which the middle class were labouring is again confirmed by the diary of Dr. Maclean, who wrote on June 9:

Rev. [sic] J. S. Woodsworth, son of Dr. James Woodsworth came all the way from Vancouver and addressed the Bolsheviks last night at the Labor Temple. His mother and his brothers, sisters and family are feeling keenly his attitude. It is a sad thing that the Bolsheviks are supported by three Methodist ministers. . . . I expect that the strike will be over this week and the street cars running again. We may have a small riot or two before that, but these will end very quickly, as we are ready for them. . . . Every man and woman at the Mission [of which Maclean was the head] is out on strike, and all of them were ordered out by the Strikers' Committee at the Labor Temple. Any impartial observer studying the whole situation would naturally come to the conclusion that a revolution was contemplated for the whole Dominion and that it was to begin at Winnipeg. . . . Thank God our civic, Provincial and Dominion Governments have stood firm and the citizens, except aliens and Bolsheviks with a few strikers have stood by them. . . .

Dr. Maclean was right about the possibility of a "few riots." On the same day that the above reflections were penned, the police commission dismissed the entire police force, save a few top officers and two constables. The reason given was that the men had refused to sign a "yellow-dog" contract. Special constables were immediately enrolled at six dollars a day each, mounted on horses donated by the T. Eaton Company, provided with various equipment including baseball bats, and instructed by their new chief, Major Lyle, to patrol the streets. The inexperience and the point of view of the new force seem to have been the prime cause of several disturbances, the chief of which was a *mêlée* at the main business intersection of the city. The accounts of this event vary widely, and some extra heat was engendered since the sole casualty was a Sergeant Coppin, a returned man who had won the Victoria Cross and had enlisted as a special constable. The view of the *Citizen* was that the "riot" had "proved more emphatically than ever the necessity of ridding Canada of this alien element [which in its view was the cause of the disturbance]. Were it not for their presence there might be some chance of law and order in Winnipeg."[37] The Liberal J. W. Dafoe permitted the *Free Press* to assert that the "beating" of Sergeant Coppin was accomplished by "bohunks," "aliens," and "foreigners,"[38] and to join in the cry, "deport the aliens."[39]

The *Toronto Star* report of the congestion at Portage and Main emphasized the inability of the untrained mounted police to handle a crowd and observed that the sons of prominent Winnipeg families were doing point duty when the jostling started. This report also noted that calm descended on the broad intersection when Mayor Gray ordered the specials to withdraw.[40] The labour account[41] stated that there was a traffic snarl and that the specials attempted to break it by charging with bats swinging. Sergeant Coppin, who was graphically depicted by the dailies as being dragged from his horse and beaten insensible by Austrians and other varieties of foreigners, had, according to the same labour source, sworn that he had never been off his horse and that what minor injuries he had suffered were inflicted by returned men.

Woodsworth was revolted by what he considered an inflammatory distortion of the news on the part of a kept press, just as he was deeply disturbed by the unwise action of the municipal government against its employees and especially against its police force which had volunteered to remain on duty. It appeared to him that his reading of the socialist writers and his own analysis of the nature of capitalist society were being confirmed in the most violent fashion before his own eyes. Further support was given this conclusion as he heard the strikers condemned from the great city pulpits and then put under ban by the Superintendent of the Methodist Church himself. At a meeting of the Methodist Conference at Toronto, Dr. S. D. Chown, the Superintendent, condemned the strike as aimed at consolidating a force "not amenable to, and which does not aim at any constitutional settlement. . . ."[42]

Woodsworth continued to support the strike vigorously, speaking both at the Labour Church meetings and those of the "soldiers parliament." He had completely identified himself with the movement a week after his arrival. Probably Woodsworth sensed the turn that events were about to take and yet was prepared to maintain his stand,

[37]Winnipeg *Citizen*, June 12, 1919.
[38]*Manitoba Free Press*, June 11, 1919.
[39]*Ibid.*, June 7, 1919.
[40]*Toronto Star*, June 11, 1919.
[41]*The Winnipeg General Sympathetic Strike*, pp. 126 *et seq.*
[42]*Toronto Star*, June 12, 1919.

since the conduct of the strike itself was distinctly non-violent. Although startled, he was not bewildered by the sudden descent of the full force of government power upon the strike leaders.

In the early hours of June 17, the Royal North-West Mounted Police raided various homes in Winnipeg and made ten arrests. The men thus apprehended were hustled away in motor cars to Stony Mountain Penitentiary, and the books, records, and "seditious documents" discovered in their homes or at the Labor Temple were stored away for use at the trials. Four of the men arrested were "foreigners" who were later dealt with summarily by the Immigration Board, and who apparently had no intimate connection with the strike leadership. One of the "foreigners," Verenchuk, was unfortunate enough to be looking after a friend's house when the raid occurred. His name was not on the warrant but he was hauled out of bed at gunpoint and taken to prison where, thirty-six hours later, his name appeared on the warrant. He had served overseas with the Canadian Army, was twice wounded and honourably discharged in 1917. He was finally released after a sanity test.[48] William Ivens, editor of the *Western Labor News*, and Alderman John Queen, advertising manager of the same paper, were also arrested, as were R. B. Russell, secretary of the Metal Trades Council, Alderman A. A. Heaps, A. E. Bray, leader of the pro-strike veterans, and G. Armstrong, a member of the Socialist Party of Canada. All these were members of the Central Strike Committee; R. J. Johns was included in the arrests although he spent the strike period in Montreal as representative of District 2 Machinists before the War Railway Board. Ivens was "located" by the Manitoba Methodist Conference two days after his arrest on the basis of his connection with the alleged seditious conspiracy.

The arrests constituted a very heavy blow at the strike, robbing it of its most vigorous leadership and depriving it of the directors of its chief source of news and exhortation. On the day of the arrests the *Manitoba Free Press* printed the announced intention of the federal government to employ the newly amended Immigration Act to deport the British-born leaders without jury trial. The paper showed some nervousness at this sudden government action, although both before and after the arrests it was unqualifiedly opposed to the strike and interpreted it in the official manner. Commenting on the arrest of the ten men the *Free Press* wrote, "Their arrest will enable them to pose as martyrs in the cause of the workingman and will also supply them with a plausible excuse for failure. . . . The Dominion authorities have

[48]*The Winnipeg General Sympathetic Strike*, p. 200.

presumably considered these objections and deemed them less conclusive than the reasons known in the fullest degree only to themselves, which call for the drastic action which has been taken. . . .
Theirs is the responsibility and it must be left to events to vindicate
their sagacity or to confirm the apprehensions of the doubters."

The *Free Press* was correct in its thought that the Ottawa government was giving full attention to the situation; but it was too charitable
when it suggested that the Borden ministry really "considered the
objections" to a policy of force. The telegrams between the government
and its Winnipeg agents are interesting in this connection. Two days
after the arrests A. J. Andrews, who enjoyed the double distinction of
being a leader of the Citizens' Committee and special agent of the
federal Department of Justice (and who was to be Crown prosecutor
in the strike trials) wired to Meighen in Ottawa: "Everything I have
done has been at the suggestion of Senator Robertson, but because it
might weaken his position with Labour I have taken the full responsibility for the Justice Department." On the same day Borden wired to
Robertson in Winnipeg: "Pray accept warmest congratulations upon
your masterly handling of a very difficult and complicated situation."
One need not wonder that the strikers sensed a certain absence of
impartiality on the part of the federal ministers who visited Winnipeg.
Certainly Meighen himself gave a green light to the Citizens' Committee when he wired to Andrews on the day of the arrests: "Notwithstanding any doubt I have as to the technical legality of the arrests
and the detention at Stony Mountain, I feel that rapid deportation is
the best course now that the arrests are made, and later we can
consider ratification."[44]

As soon as Woodsworth heard of the arrests he conferred with his
close friend Fred J. Dixon and the two men decided to undo at least
part of the threatened disaster by carrying on the labour newspaper
themselves. Woodsworth had been associated with Dixon with increasing intimacy since 1910. In that year he had supported Dixon's
first attempt at election to the Legislature in which defeat came in
the form of only 53 votes. In 1914 Dixon was elected to the Manitoba
Legislature by a large majority. In 1915 (after the accession of the
Norris government) he increased his majority still further, and in 1916
took a very outspoken stand against registration and conscription. As
with Woodsworth, many of his friends criticized this stand to no avail.

[44]These telegrams were read into Hansard by Peter Heenan in 1926 during a
debate on Mackenzie King's policy of sending troops into strike areas (Hansard,
1926, pp. 4004 *et seq.*).

Dixon, like most of the other labour leaders of the strike period, had come to Canada from England. It is probably correct to say that Woodsworth valued Dixon's friendship above that of any other of his political associates, and was very close to him until a tragic death by cancer terminated Dixon's career in 1931. In their newspaper plunge in 1919, Woodsworth was nominally the editor, and together they managed to produce the labour paper without any break in its regular sequence of issues. Both men were aware that they would, sooner or later, face arrest,[45] but were convinced that this clear-cut issue of freedom of the press was one which they could not ignore. Nor did either consider the inevitable outcome from the point of view of his own safety. Both had already achieved an enviable reputation in the defence of free speech and the advocacy of social justice.

Under Woodsworth's editorship the *Western Labor News* continued to call for a policy of peaceful idleness in the face of increasing force. He observed that the execution of the government's policy had apparently been handed over to A. J. Andrews of the Citizens' Committee, who was now, as legal agent of the federal Minister of Justice, in charge of the prosecution of the arrested men. Andrews, it might be noted in passing, had been mayor of Winnipeg and also came from a Wesleyan Methodist missionary home. He was, in 1919, a corporation lawyer.

It was increasingly apparent that the direction of the anti-strike forces had passed into federal hands, and on June 18 Sir Robert Borden told the House of Commons, "The counsel at Winnipeg who had charge of the matter were selected with great care and were instructed that they should not take any proceedings for the arrest or prosecution of any person except under direction and with the approval of the Minister of Labour. That instruction, I understand, has been carried out."[46] And the fact that the anti-strike operations were closely supervised by the central government merely emphasized the importance of that government's interpretation of the strike itself.

When Mr. Meighen returned to Ottawa he gave a full account of the government's position in the matter. He stated that the Central Strike Committee had usurped the powers of civil government. The consequence of their actions, he said, "inevitably led to the establish-

[45]In a letter of Aug. 26, 1921, Woodsworth reviewed the incident thus: "When Ivens was arrested, in order to suppress the paper of which he was editor, Mr. F. J. Dixon, member of the Provincial legislature, and I felt it our duty to carry on the paper." Since Woodsworth viewed A. J. Andrews as an unscrupulous lawyer vested with almost unlimited powers he expected the worst.
[46]Hansard, 1919, p. 3857.

ment of a separate government—or better, assertion of governmental functions on the part of those in charge of the strike itself. . . ." One of his arguments was that nothing could justify a sympathetic strike since it involved "the breach of a bargain." The strikers wondered if that argument could not be applied to most strikes. The citizens of Winnipeg, remarked the Minister of the Interior, had set an example for the rest of "sensible opinion in Canada." The assumption in his speech that government powers had been seized (although no institution of government had been attacked and the police force had been requested to remain on duty) was particularly irritating to the Strike Committee since no facts were elicited to prove the point.

It was essential that the greater issue raised by the assumption of Soviet authority—and it was nothing less on the part of those in control of the strike in Winnipeg—should be once and for all decided and be decisively beaten down before they should concern themselves with the smaller and much less important issue upon which certain men had originally gone on strike. That is the stand the citizens of Winnipeg took. That is the stand the Minister of Labour took. . . .

He went on to admit that there was a high degree of organization amongst the country's employers but insisted that this must not be duplicated in the ranks of labour. "Can anyone contemplate such an event? . . . Are we to have on the one hand a concentration of employers, and on the other a concentration of all the labour interests of the Dominion, fighting it out for the supremacy?"[47] Other government speakers confirmed that this line of reasoning had been completely accepted by the administration at Ottawa. In the midst of a supply debate on June 12, Hon. N. W. Rowell took occasion to analyse the Winnipeg strike.

They went West [after the 1918 Quebec meeting of the Trades and Labour Congress] and organized this One Big Union movement to cut adrift from the sober leaders of organized labour in the United States. Why did they cut adrift? Because they knew that under the serious and judicious leadership of the men who made the labour movement what it is in Canada and the United States they could not advocate the overthrow of constituted authority without incurring the hostility of those men.[48]

Another debate was proceeding at the same time in the Commons upon a bill which obtained its first reading on June 18, the day preceding the arrest of the strike leaders. This bill provided for a

[47]*Ibid.*, pp. 3085 *et seq.*
[48]*Ibid.*, pp. 3411 *et seq.*

doubling of the strength of the militia. General Mewburn, the Minister of Militia, observed that as a result of the Winnipeg strike a system of temporary enrolments at Winnipeg had been necessary. This, he said, worked a hardship on the citizens of that city. The increased force, he argued, would be valuable in the first stages of a war, and, "in addition to that, a permanent force is absolutely necessary for the preservation of law and order in every country."[49] Mr. McMaster, of Brome, remarked that "what the minister has said shows the intention of the department. I say to this House that force is no remedy."[50]

Already, on June 10, the Solicitor General of the Borden government had recommended the adoption of the report of the Committee on Sedition and Seditious Propaganda.[51] The recommendations of the committee, which were adopted in their essence as an amendment to the Criminal Code (as section 98), provided for a very broad definition of seditious intent and increased the maximum penalty upon conviction from two to twenty years.

These transactions at Ottawa, together with the amendment to the Immigration Act mentioned above, built up the sense of tension at Winnipeg. When the objections taken to the militia bill by such a stout defender of constituted authority as T. A. Crerar[52] were ignored by the government, and when the arrests of June 17 had occurred, there could be little doubt that the immediate future of the strike movement would be unhappy.

June 21 was the "Bloody Saturday" which the Citizens' Committee had been predicting. It was occasioned by an illegal parade of returned soldiers organized as a result of Senator Robertson's alleged conspiracy with the leaders of the Citizens' Committee. The returned soldier supporters of the strike called a parade to form up near the city hall in order to march to the Royal Alexandra Hotel where Senator Robertson was ensconced. Their purpose was to request, through this mass demonstration, an account of the minister's plans with regard to the strike and of his actions since arriving in Winnipeg.[53] They asserted their purpose to be justified by Robertson's almost exclusive association with their opponents in the strike, and were no doubt spurred on by the fear of further governmental action to follow

49*Ibid.*, p. 3968.
50*Ibid.*, p. 3969.
51*Ibid.*, pp. 3285 *et seq.*
52*Ibid.*, p. 3973. Crerar put forward against the militia bill the double argument of economy and trust in the people's good sense.
53*The Winnipeg General Sympathetic Strike*, p. 190.

the arrests of June 17.[54] The city was alive with Mounted Police and all were aware that General Ketchen had alerted the militia units, and that a large number of machine-guns had been shipped in to Winnipeg.

But the parade was illegal since the mayor had earlier promulgated his order banning such demonstrations. The leaders maintained that the ban was an unconstitutional denial of the civil liberties for which they had recently fought, and was unjustified by previous mass violence; with this attitude Woodsworth expressed his agreement.

On the morning of the parade Mayor Gray issued a proclamation warning that anyone taking part in it would do so at his own risk. As the parade itself was forming up the Mayor read the Riot Act.[55] After that the machinery by which the parade was stopped was put into action. The procedure followed and the results obtained were outlined by Hon. N. W. Rowell, the President of the Privy Council and minister responsible for the Royal North-West Mounted Police.[56] Rowell said he had received "in May" a telegram from the Attorney General of Manitoba asking if the R.N.W.M.P. could co-operate with the provincial authorities. The minister then sent a wire to the Commissioner of the R.N.W.M.P. asking him to "kindly instruct local officer Mounted Police to co-operate with Attorney-General if asked by him." He also sent communications to the Attorney General of Manitoba and other western provinces assuring them of federal aid, both police and military, in the maintenance of order. His account of the "silent parade" in Winnipeg stated that "the first shots were fired by the paraders, or those associated with them, and the Mounted Police fired only in self-defence. The information that we have is that the police acted with great coolness, great courage, and great patience, as is characteristic of the men of the Royal North-West Mounted Police." He concluded this statement to the Commons with the remark that "the sooner all classes fully recognize that it is the intention of the federal government and of the provincial and various municipal

[54]It is difficult to understand why D. C. Masters in his study of the strike altered the chronological order by describing the events of Bloody Saturday ahead of his account of the arrests of the strike leaders. The obvious causal relationship is, by his procedure, somewhat obscured. See Masters, *The Winnipeg General Strike*, pp. 83 *et seq.*

[55]*Manitoba Free Press*, June 23, 1919; *Canadian Annual Review*, 1919, p. 475; Masters, *The Winnipeg General Strike*, p. 85; *Western Labor News*, June 23, 1919. The *Free Press* wrote, with heroic disregard for the facts, that the parade was "the inevitable outcome of the spirit of contempt for the regularly constituted authorities which has been preached and practised for the past five weeks in this city."

[56]Hansard, 1919, pp. 3843 *et seq.*

governments in Canada to maintain law and order and to protect life and property, the more speedily we shall reach common understanding in relation to all matters affecting the public interest."

When the Mounted Police broke the parade by an armed charge,[57] when soldiers appeared on the streets with rifles and machine-guns and the city seemed to be under military rule, Woodsworth arranged for a full report of the police-military action. There also appeared in the *Western Labor News* several editorial comments upon these events. Since these represent Woodsworth's immediate reaction to the blaze of federal force, and since they became instantly the basis of a charge of seditious libel,[58] they are worth close examination. Of the six items in the charge, one consisted of the two verses from Isaiah which appear at the head of this chapter, one was a news story of the "silent parade," and the remaining four were editorials. The news report presents a different and fuller version of "Bloody Saturday" than that given in the Commons. This report stated:

Apparently the bloody business was carefully planned, for Mayor Gray issued a proclamation in the morning stating that "any women taking part in the parade do so at their own risk." Nevertheless a vast crowd of men, women and children assembled to witness the "silent parade". . . . No attempt was made to use the special city police to prevent the parade. On a previous occasion a dozen regular city police had persuaded the returned men to abandon a parade which had begun to move.

On Saturday about 2.30 p.m., just the time when the parade was scheduled to start, some fifty mounted men swinging baseball bats rode down Main Street. Half were red-coated Royal North-West Mounted Police, the others wore khaki. They quickened their pace as they passed the Union Bank. The crowd opened, let them through and closed in behind them. They turned and charged through the crowd again, greeted by hisses and boos, and some stones. There were two riderless horses with the squad when it emerged and galloped up Main Street. The men in khaki disappeared at this juncture, but the red-coats reined their horses and reformed opposite the old post-office.

---

[57]In this charge by the R.N.W.M.P. there were about thirty casualties, including one death. Sixteen of the casualties were police. (Hansard, 1919, p. 3845.)
[58]Manitoba Court of King's Bench, Fall Assizes, 1919, Suit no. 2170/3. A second charge was laid against Woodsworth in November (King's Bench, Suit no. 2168/3), on which he was indicted for "speaking seditious words." While the strike trials were pending he addressed a meeting of the Labour Church in Winnipeg, Nov. 16, 1919, at which he was reported as saying: "If we get a penitentiary sentence we will carry with us the picture of this gathering of 5,000 people who are behind us. Indeed a sentence for us might cause a great triumph on the part of the people. I cannot conceive of this 5,000 people leaving us or the others there for very long. They say we are trying to stir up revolution. If there are any government officials here I want to say that if they want to stir up revolution let them go on as they are doing."

Then, with revolvers drawn, they galloped down Main Street, and charged into the crowd on William Avenue, firing as they charged. One man, standing on the sidewalk, thought the mounties were firing blank cartridges until a spectator standing beside him dropped with a bullet through his breast. Another, standing nearby, was shot through the head. . . . The crowd dispersed as quickly as possible when the shooting began. When the mounties rode back to Portage and Main, after the fray, at least two of them were twirling their reeking tubes high in the air. . . . Lines of special police, swinging their big clubs, were thrown across Main Street and the intersecting thoroughfares. Dismounted red-coats lined up across Portage and Main declaring the city under military control. Khaki-clad men with rifles were stationed on the street corners.

The report noted that open-air strike meetings would be abandoned but that the strike was by no means broken. The returned men were said to be incensed at this "infringement of their human rights" and the "murderous assault of the mounties." They "assumed full responsibility for the 'silent parade' proposition, making a special request that the strikers should not join them. 'This is our affair,' they declared. Had they intended violence they would hardly have invited their wives to join the parade."

This report, full as it is of editorial comment, is a measure of Woodsworth's horror occasioned by the ruthless action. The strikers who had, he knew, been conducting their meetings peacefully during the warm spring evenings, were now face to face with an unleashed strength which openly challenged them to use the forceful methods to which they were utterly averse. The significant features of the news report, as well as of the editorials, are their moderation and their note of hope.

One of the editorials accused the government of introducing Kaiserism into Canada, and canvassed the future of the strike in these terms:

But they must not be allowed even temporary satisfaction. Organized labor must continue the magnificent fight of the last five weeks until its just and moderate demands are granted. It were better that the whole 35,000 strikers languished in jail; better, even, that we all rested beside the men who were slain on Saturday than that the forces of Kaiserism shall prevail. . . . The Committee of 1,000 has, however, many lessons to learn— among other things the members of that committee must be taught that ideas are more powerful than bullets. . . .

A clear emphasis was given in the editorials to the programme of social reconstruction of the British socialists, and the contrast was drawn between the attitude of the British and Canadian governments.

The business men who controlled society were portrayed as blind to the great forces at work in the world and unable to consider a reformer as anything but dangerous. " 'Anarchist, Internationalist, Pacifist, Pro-German, off with them to the penitentiary. He would subvert constituted authority.' In England he is called into the councils of government." A quotation from Rt. Hon. Arthur Henderson was printed, to the effect that if barricades became necessary, they would be manned by those trained in the use of weapons. "That is not incendiary writing. It comes from Rt. Hon. Arthur Henderson who sees some of the dangers ahead if the legitimate aims of labour are balked."

This became Woodsworth's most powerful motivation during the strike. He had seen the difficulty of preventing the use of force, and he recognized the necessity of obtaining by peaceful means the basic demands of the dispossed.

Do our Canadian businessmen suppose that with revolutions going on all over Europe, and with this programme offered in England as a substitute for sudden and perhaps violent revolution, that we in Canada are going to be permitted to go with undisturbed step along the accustomed ways? . . . Whether the radical changes that are inevitable may be brought about peaceably, largely depends upon the good sense of the Canadian businessmen who now largely control both the industry and the government of this country. We confess the prospects are not very bright.

The final important theme of the editorials was entitled "Is There A Way Out?" The determination on both sides of the strike was noted.

The City Council, the Provincial Government or the Federal Government have adopted no constructive policy. They stand prepared only for oppressive measures. In the meantime the returned soldiers are becoming restless and threatening to take things into their own hands. They are tired of the policy of "Do Nothing—Keep Order" so consistently followed by the strike leaders. . . . But all thoughtful men must think of the terrific cost. Then, when one side is brought to its knees, what will be done? . . . Why could not our government boldly face the situation as the British government has done? Let the state take the responsibility of finding a suitable job for every man at a living wage. If this were done, the question of whether or not a man should be reinstated in his particular job would not be a vital one. It would become a matter of readjustment. . . . Behind the whole question of collective bargaining and the sympathetic strike lies the question of the democratic control of industry. The British government is attempting to solve this most important problem by creating new machinery in the form of industrial councils. These are not the solutions proposed by the workers, but apparently they have been successful in forming a sort of modus vivendi. That, after all, is the British way. . . . Why not the appointment of a strong commission with wide powers. When, during the war, there was trouble with the miners in the Crow's Nest, the government appointed a commission to operate the mines. The academic right of the operators to run their own mines was a secondary consideration. . . . So we need a commission with extraordinary powers to make full investigations; powers to suggest and enforce radical and far-reaching policies; powers, if found necessary, to actually keep the business of the country running. . . .

These ideas, however, proved unacceptable to the federal government. Its special agent at Winnipeg, A. J. Andrews, paid a personal visit to the office of the *Western Labor News*, where he arrested Woodsworth, charging him with seditious libel.[59] At the same time, the *Western Labor News* was ordered to cease publication. Fortunately, from the viewpoint of the labour paper, F. J. Dixon was with Woodsworth when the latter was whisked away to disappear through the fortress iron gates of the Rupert Street Jail. Dixon informed the Strike Committee of the occurrence, and himself carried on the paper. In a letter, Woodsworth told his wife of how the newspaper was kept going after his arrest.[60]

It seems that a warrant was out for him [Dixon] on Tuesday. Probably when they seized our press and manuscripts they found some of Dixon's stuff. He had warning and went to the house of a friend. They got another press to print a paper, "The Western Star." Dixon sat up till two o'clock writing new articles which were sent by a roundabout way through various hands to the press. So next morning, to the surprise of all, the paper appeared as usual though in a new form. The publishers had used the name of a Liberal paper. The other members of the firm not sympathetic to labor refused to allow this to be used. So next day the labor boys worked the starting of a new paper without permission, and issued "The Enlightener." They hadn't big enough type, so they "borrowed" some from another newspaper office in the same building. Those interested in stopping the paper got out a warrant to hold the type, but it seems they couldn't, on a technicality, stop the press. So, with a bailiff and three special police looking on helplessly, the new paper was run off! All this time Dixon was in hiding, writing for dear life. Fearing discovery, he shifted at midnight to the home of another friend. Then when Ivens got back on his paper (how, I do not yet know), and hearing that Pritchard and I were out on bail (Pritchard *is* out; I'm not), Dixon walked down to the police station and gave himself up. . . .

And so the elimination of the strike leadership appeared to have reached the detail stage of rounding up and attempting to silence even the second rank. Woodsworth learned of these events from

[59]J. S. Woodsworth to his wife, June 27, 1919.
[60]*Ibid.*

Dixon, who, on June 26, arrived at the provincial jail and was placed in a neighbouring cell. Writing from prison to his wife he reflected in the same letter,

If the world is divided into the sinning and those sinned against, I fancy the jailed will come into the latter class and I must take my place with them. As Debs says, "while there is a soul in prison I am not free." . . . Well, this surely about finishes the old conventional ideals. To be in jail is no longer the most terrible thing. "Justice" is no longer enthroned. In practice it depends upon a dozen conflicting interests, political and commercial. But one is committed as never before to the cause of the poor and the helpless, particularly the foreigner. This is only the first round! . . .

On June 25 Premier Norris received a message from the secretary of the Central Strike Committee advising that the Committee had decided to terminate the strike on the following day. This decision was resented by many of the rank and file strikers, but the Committee argued that with public meetings banned, revenue petering out, many working class families on the verge of starvation, and abundant evidence of the federal government's determination to suppress the movement, continuance of the strike seemed worse than futile. The Committee also referred to the qualified success represented in an acceptance by the iron masters of the "principle of collective bargaining," and in the pledge of the provincial government to appoint a commission to investigate the causes and course of the strike.[61]

Although the *Report* of the Robson Committee had no influence on the strike trials, it was a most interesting document. The *Report* goes further than the immediate causes and notes the general concentration upon domestic grievances, with the cessation of the war, and the resentment of the working class in the face of "undue war profiteering." The Commissioner gives his blessing to a statement by President Winning of the Winnipeg Trades and Labour Council, which asserted that the high cost of living, long hours, low wages, poor working conditions, profiteering, the growing "intelligence" of the working class concerning the inequalities of modern society, and the refusal of the employers to recognize labour's right to bargain collectively, were the causes of the strike. The *Report* observes that Winning's statement was published in the press and that "no one sought to challenge this evidence" (p. 19). Other comments by the Commissioner concerning the motives of the strike are interesting: ". . . it is too much for me to say that the vast number of intelligent residents who went on strike were seditious or that they were either dull enough or weak enough

[61]Winnipeg *Enlightener*, June 25, 1919.

to allow themselves to be led by seditionaries" (p. 13); "It should be said that the leaders who brought about the general strike were not responsible for the parades or riots which took place, and, in fact, tried to prevent them. The leaders' policy was peaceful idleness . . ." (p. 17). The *Report* concludes with tentative suggestions for reform along educational, medical, and economic lines: "There should be no difficulty in deriving the means for the carrying out of the specific objects above mentioned. It is submitted that there should be a scheme of taxation of those who can afford it, and application of wealth to the reasonable needs of others in the community whose lot in life has not been favoured." A leading member of the Manitoba bench who was asked in 1957 why the *Robson Report* did not have more influence than was apparently the case, replied: "Well, you know, Robson was always a socialist."

By June 25, when the strike was abandoned, some at least of the workers felt that the threatened arrest of leaders who might vigorously replace those already apprehended had played too strong a part in this capitulation. Certainly all were disappointed with the outcome, particularly since there was no guarantee that strikers would be reinstated or that the Citizens' Committee's interpretation of the "principle" of collective bargaining would be at all satisfactory.

For Woodsworth, the collapse of the strike steeled a resolution already formed to work for the prevention of another such social catastrophe. If the utmost effort and self-denial on the part of the workers, expressed through exclusively economic action, could not achieve even their minimum demands it was more than ever evident that political action was essential. He knew that the purpose and conduct of the strike had been non-violent and was much impressed with the fact that in the federal police raids of the first and second of July (as well as in the local arrests of June) not a single firearm had been uncovered from one end of Canada to the other. Much more vigour, he was now convinced, must be put into the attempt to capture control of the governmental machinery which, in the hands exclusively of business men and their representatives, could be used to such disastrous effect. The story of his activities and thought from the end of the strike until his election to the House of Commons is one of constant organizational work. His purpose was to establish a strong working-class political party on the British model.

In great part this work was made possible by the willing participation of his family—a participation the more impressive since it was achieved, much of the time, from a distant isolation. Mrs. Woodsworth had remained throughout this period with their six children at Gibson's Landing in British Columbia and had begun teaching in the village school. The same person who had helped bring about the refusal of the British Columbia Methodist Conference to renew her husband's mission appointment had tried to have her ousted from her position. The attempt, however, ended in a forced apology from the merchant, and the Woodsworth family had its spirit lifted by the open under-standing and support it received from the fairly radical little com-munity. To the absent head of the family came a steady flow of letters assuring him of support and confidence. One letter, written by Mrs. Woodsworth to her sister-in-law in Winnipeg, is a lucid explanation of her thorough acceptance of her husband's position.[62]

I am sure there is no need to go into our position. With James, I have entirely ceased to wish for luxury, ease, comfort or advantage for us, yes, or for our children, while countless thousands never do and never will, under the present system, get a chance for ordinary decent living. You see, since James has been a longshoreman, I have seen that those who work with him can never get enough money to clothe and nourish their children and to provide for dentistry, surgery, high-school or university education, music, travel, or indeed, the delights of a few hours every day of care-free leisure. We like all these things intensely. The only reason we have not been actively in the conflict to help make them general for the human race, is that because others have never had them, it has taken us this long time to realize how clear-cut is the issue as to whether or not they shall get them. . . .

[62]Mrs. J. S. Woodsworth to Miss Mary Woodsworth, June 30, 1919.

9

ELECTORAL VERDICT

DIXON AND WOODSWORTH WERE RELEASED from jail on June 28 on two sureties of fifteen hundred dollars each. Their cases were remanded several times thereafter until, in November, the indictments were found to be true bills. Before Judge Galt in the assize court, on December 3, both men pleaded not guilty of publishing seditious libel. The trial was postponed at the request of the Crown counsel and did not actually begin until January 29, 1920.

While the legal machinery was being put in readiness all of the arrested strike leaders joined in the work of the Labour Defence Committee and organized speaking tours to gain support and financial assistance across the country. On its side the Crown published some of the evidence of seditious intent and the general atmosphere created was far from judicial.

Woodsworth entered into his work with a will, making speaking tours as far east as Montreal and west to Vancouver and Victoria. His reception in most places was enthusiastic and an added flavour was given his meetings by the ubiquitous official reporter. Woodsworth believed he could sense a great demand for social reform. The prairies in particular, he felt, were catching fire. "On the trains, in the hotels, everywhere people are thinking, thinking, planning and dreaming of the days that are to be. We have already entered a new period in our Canadian life. . . ."[1]

In traditionally staid Toronto he was welcomed by a great meeting at the Open Forum, and, after the meeting, was honoured at a tea attended by leading University figures, many of whom contributed to the strikers' defence fund. Similar experiences in cities both east and west encouraged his belief that a genuine and widespread desire for

[1]*Western Labor News,* July 18, 1919.

political and social reform did exist. As part of the defence campaign he endeavoured to secure help also from earlier friends in the Methodist organization, and in some cases received encouragement. To one official in the Department of Evangelism and Social Service at Toronto he sent a copy of the grand jury's indictment of the eight men charged with seditious conspiracy. The letter in reply read:

I am doing all in my power to give full publicity to the document but it is almost impossible to penetrate the veil of ignorant prejudice which prevails here. Even our warmest sympathisers agree that an angel from heaven armed with any amount of evidence could not make the slightest impression on the average business man of Toronto on the matter of the Winnipeg strike and the consequent trials. . . . Rest assured that I, and those for whom I can speak, will lose no opportunity of awakening the people to a sense of responsibility for what is being done in their name and to lead them to an enlightened judgment. . . . Of course the trial judge is acting according to his lights, but it is hard to think that he has escaped the influence of the fierce press campaign of the last six months. . . .[2]

Woodsworth's optimism concerning a widespread reform sentiment was increased by the vast movement of political discontent represented in Ontario by the Drury victory and the United Farmers' movement, and in the West by the gathering of populist forces under the banner of the Canadian Council of Agriculture. He retained his earlier belief that the progressive forces of farm and city could form an effective alliance, and saw in the "New National Policy" advanced by the farm organizations a continuance of the purposes of the Non-Partisan League. The seriousness of the division between H. W. Wood and T. A. Crerar was not at that time entirely apparent and Woodsworth seems to have attached more importance to the inclusion of an unemployment relief plank in the farmers' platform than he did to Wood's insistence on the class basis of the farmers' movement.

Because he was optimistic about the potential strength of a Canadian social democracy Woodsworth exhibited no deep bitterness following his experiences in the strike. More and more he became convinced that the whole episode was the outcome of an economic system. The rapid development of industrial and financial capitalism in Canada meant that many individuals had become the almost unconscious dupes of the system. The ideas about capitalists entertained by many Canadian socialists, he felt, had been drawn from out-of-date European books and not from close observation of the Canadian scene. Our middle class, he suggested in an article entitled "Business Man's

[2]Feb. 18, 1920.

Psychology,"[3] is very different from its European counterpart. Most of our wealthy men had not inherited their wealth and they lived by no means a life of self-indulgent leisure. Behind most of them lay an old eastern homestead and their concept of labour relations was based on their ideas about the "hired man." With the sudden divorce of the *entrepreneurs* from personal contact with the workers a gap had been created which no one had bothered to think about and which the business man believed could be overlooked as long as he supported private charities.

Woodsworth's ideas were further developed in a series of articles under the title "What Next?" and published in the *Western Labor News* during July and August of 1919. Here again he concentrated upon the question of a working-class political party. The ideology was strongly reminiscent of the British Labour party's post-war programme and was designed to include all classes of producers.

Our ultimate objective must be a complete turnover of the present economic and social system. In this we recognize our solidarity with the workers the world over. . . . Such a revolution is that contemplated by the British Labor party, now the Opposition in the British House of Commons, and likely within a short time to be the Government. . . . Such a change, we hope, will be accomplished in this country by means of education, organization and the securing by the workers of the machinery of government. We look forward to the formation of a Canadian organization broad enough to include all producers.[4]

The desire to accomplish the social democratic programme by peaceful means had undoubtedly been strengthened by his strike experience and he heavily underlined this feature of the argument.

If those in authority harden their hearts and refuse to let the people go, the people may, in desperation, resort to violent methods to attain their rights. But physical force provokes reaction. It is negative in character. It is an attempted short cut that delays rather than hastens permanent reform. We believe that moral ends can be attained only by the use of moral means. . . . The fight is not between hand workers and brain workers. It is not between industrial workers and agricultural workers. The fight is essentially between the producers and the parasites. . . .[5]

Succeeding articles developed a programme of specific proposals including the progressive socialization of all transportation and communication facilities and other public utilities, natural resources, banks, and insurance. Quoting freely from the programme of British Labour, Woodsworth suggested that the path of socialization would

[3]*Western Labor News*, July 18, 1919.
[4]*Ibid.*   [5]*Ibid.*, July 25, 1919

not stop short of basic large-scale manufacturing and commercial institutions and that public industry must eventually be directed through joint management-worker committees. He displayed his close acquaintanceship with the contemporary British debate upon these topics when he wrote: "Within each political district, delegates to the administrative body should be chosen through vocational organization rather than as at present according to geographic residence." On these questions he seems to have adopted a compromise between Fabian ideas and Guild socialism.

This social democratic programme was the basis of the political discussion of the middle group of labour leaders—men like S. J. Farmer, F. J. Dixon, A. A. Heaps, John Queen and W. D. Bayley— who had little respect for the Gompers tradition of non-partisan trade unionism, and who saw no answer either in an industrial unionism divorced from the party method or in revolutionary dogma.

While carrying on the double campaign of political education and fund-raising for the strikers' defence, Dixon and Woodsworth had also to pay attention to the problem of their own defence. Dixon's case was to be tried first, and he decided to defend himself. His trial opened on January 29, 1920, with Woodsworth's scheduled to follow immediately after. Dixon's defence developed into a sixteen-day single-handed battle in which he propounded one of the finest arguments for the freedom of the press ever heard in Canada.[6] Despite the alleged partiality of the bench and the potential hostility of a carefully selected farmers' jury, he won an acquittal. Immediately following the conclusion of Dixon's trial the court announced that the charges against Woodsworth would not be prosecuted. The Crown entered a *nolle prosequi* on the seditious libel charge on February 16, 1920. The charge of speaking seditious words remained unaltered until March 7, 1920, when the Crown entered a "stay of proceedings." On March 13 Woodsworth received a telegram from the Deputy Attorney General informing him that he need not "appear" in Winnipeg again unless advised. He was never formally notified that the charge had been dropped, and, technically, he could have been summoned to stand trial at any later time.

There are several possible reasons why the Woodsworth case was not pressed. Earlier in the month, R. B. Russell had stood trial separately on the seditious conspiracy charge, had been convicted and sentenced to two years' imprisonment. Then came the acquittal of Dixon which left the score even. It is likely that the government

[6]See *Dixon's Address to the Jury*, published by the Defence Committee.

lawyers wished to avoid the strong possibility of two successive acquittals before the remaining seven men came up for trial. It was also painfully apparent that the inclusion of the two verses from Isaiah prejudiced the Crown's whole case against Woodsworth. People in Winnipeg were already quoting the London *Daily Herald* which had said that Isaiah was lucky to be dead.[7]

Satisfaction with the outcome of their own entanglement was, however, modified for Dixon and Woodsworth by the earlier conviction of R. B. Russell and again by the conviction in April of six of the other arrested strike leaders. In the third trial only A. A. Heaps won an acquittal. Bray, the veterans' leader, was sentenced to six months (on the charge of being a common nuisance), while Ivens, Johns, Pritchard, Queen, and Armstrong were each sentenced to one year in prison.

In the midst of this flurry of legal activity, immediately after the dropping of his own case, Woodsworth undertook another speaking tour which carried him as far as the Pacific coast, and Gibson's Landing. He also participated in the preparations for the 1920 Manitoba provincial election and campaigned vigorously on behalf of the labour candidates in Winnipeg. The entry of socialist candidates in this election he considered of particular importance, for the more conservative leaders of the international unions were pressing hard to regain control of the Trades and Labour Council. During 1920, led by men like R. A. Rigg, who had apparently dropped his socialist proclivity and who worked in close association with representatives of the Dominion Department of Labour, the Trades and Labour Council came back under the control of the non-socialist craft unionists. This group also managed to oust Ivens from the editorship of the *Western Labor News*. At the same time there was evidence of the formation of a labour group even to the left of the Socialist Party of Canada, the Workers' Alliance, which was a predecessor of the Canadian Communist party. The middle way was in danger, and Woodsworth bent every effort to support those who would pursue it. He spent much of his time helping to organize, and speaking for the Dominion Labour party which the social democratic group had established in Winnipeg as its political organization. He worked also for the Labour Church, conducting classes in economic history and holding public meetings.

This "church," established by William Ivens after his expulsion in 1918 from McDougall Church, was creedless, "founded on the Fatherhood of God and the Brotherhood of man." It was the carrying through

[7]This was mentioned in the *B.C. Federationist*, Oct. 1, 1920.

of the social gospel to one of its logical conclusions—the beginning of a new religious sect. Undoubtedly the Labour Church possessed a political character just as evident as was its religious, but that was inherent in its particular application of the social gospel. The political side of the Labour Church was not admirable in the eyes of the chief Crown prosecutor of the strike trials. A. J. Andrews said, "I maintain that this so-called Labour Church is merely a camouflage for the preaching of sedition and for fanning the flames of unrest. . . . Their doctrines were intended to make you forget all you ever were taught at your mother's knee. Their aim is to remove the word duty from the dictionary and substitute pleasure for vice. The whole vile doctrine preaches duty to class, self before country."[8]

Woodsworth's work with this sect was part of his wish to "secularize" religion—to make it part and parcel of everyday living. But there was also a touch of revivalism in the new movement which seemed to bring back for him his early, unclouded acceptance of the Methodist faith. His own account of the "history" of the Labour Church is interesting from that point of view, and also in its integration of social and religious elements:

I remember my first Labour Church meeting. It was the third week of the strike. The vast congregation, estimated at 10,000, filled Victoria Park. For nearly two hours I talked—could not but talk! Dixon talked, Canon Scott talked, Robinson talked, Ivens talked. The people stood it—in a double sense of the word, and then gave a collection of $1,500 for the relief of the girls on strike. The police detectives reported us as Bolshevist spellbinders and a dangerous crowd of illiterate foreigners. Some of us thought we felt the spirit of a great religious revival. . . .[9]

His confirmed opposition to the old church organization was, at the time, made abundantly clear.

This movement became solidified by the opposition of the ministers and the churches to the strikers. Staid old Presbyterian elders refused to darken the doors of the kirk. Wesleyan local preachers could no longer be restrained. Anglican Sunday School teachers resigned their classes. Class lines became clearly drawn and the "regular" churches stood out as middle class institutions.[10]

---

[8]Winnipeg *Tribune*, March 15, 1920.

[9]J. S. Woodsworth, *The First Story of the Labour Church* (Winnipeg, n.d.), p. 8.

[10]*Ibid.*, p. 9. In a series of "Unconventional Sermons" published in the *Western Labor News* in September and October of 1920, he gave high praise to Upton Sinclair's *The Profits of Religion*, and continued the attack upon hypocrisy in the churches: "Only the other day at the Annual Fair in Vancouver, Bishop de Pencier, accompanied by the Mounted Police solemnly blessed a captured German gun. Think of this in the name of Jesus!" (*Western Labor News*, Oct. 15, 1920.)

He pointed out that the movement had grown rapidly, that it had organized its own Sunday schools, young people's societies, economics classes, and other activities; that it was feeling its way toward a new constitution which would itself contain an open door to change. Typical of the altered forms was the "Grace before Meat" suggested by Woodsworth while visiting the house of a Labour Church family:

We are thankful for these and all the good things of life. We recognize that they are a part of our common heritage and come to us through the efforts of our brothers and sisters the world over. What we desire for ourselves we wish for all. To this end may we take our share in the world's work and the world's struggles.[11]

A form of prayer, this, which would have warmed the heart of such a person as George Lansbury. Again,

The movement is born of a social age. Its viewpoint is social, not merely individualistic, its aims are social, not merely individualistic; that means that it stands for replacing the present selfish scramble for existence by a co-operative commonwealth in which each will have a chance.[12]

The most interesting sections of his analysis of the Labour Church are those in which he deals with the nature of religion and the idea of God:

While the Labour Church refuses to be bound by dogmas, we believe that it is essentially in line with the teachings and spirit of Jesus of Nazareth. Most of us gladly, if humbly, acknowledge his leadership and inspiration. . . . Religion, insofar as it is vital, changes and grows. That is true of the individual. When I was a child I thought as a child, spoke as a child, understood as a child; but when I became a man I put away childish things. Some people never grow up spiritually—and pride themselves on their childishness! . . . Religion in this broad sense is simply the utmost reach of man—his highest thinking about the deepest things in life; his response to the wireless messages that come to him out of the infinite; his planting of the flag of justice and brotherhood on a new and higher level of human attainment and purpose. . . .[13]

With changing forms of society, he wrote, came varying ideas of God. What then is the modern worker's idea of God?

He is becoming conscious of a determination to understand and control the machine and to determine his destiny. This great new Life Force that is pulsating in his own veins and through society—is this not his idea of God? . . . The Labour Church, born of the class struggle, at present limited in its activities, "Protestant" in its attitude rather than "Catholic" in its spirit, nevertheless reaches out to the religion of the future. . . .[14]

---

[11]Woodsworth, *Story of the Labour Church*, p. 11.
[12]*Ibid.*, p. 12.   [13]*Ibid.*, p. 14.   [14]*Ibid.*, p. 15.

Although the Labour Church did not last long, and although Woodsworth himself soon turned almost exclusively to political avenues, this statement of his religious views was to need little change until the end of his life. The loyalty which he inspired was to no small degree based upon his continuing presentation of such a synthesis of ideas. A combination of the vibrant zeal of the revival with the cool rationalist faith in the perfectibility of man; the idea of class struggle with that of social interdependence and universal co-operation; some of the features of Marxian economics with the incessant pressure for immediate reforms; the functions of the preacher and the teacher with those of the practical politician; and an unbounded sympathy with the under-privileged leavening the whole—constancy to this amalgam of ideas and emotions was to enable him in 1939 to stand alone against the otherwise unanimous opinion of the Canadian House of Commons and still retain the deep respect and affection of all its members.

The importance of the social gospel both in shaping Woodsworth's own ideas and in preparing a favourable reception for those ideas is difficult to exaggerate. In the light of recent neo-orthodox criticism it is easy to say that the liberal theology and the social gospel of the late nineteenth and early twentieth centuries were weak and amorphous. It has been argued that the religious liberals secularized their theology and accepted uncritically the rationalist doctrine of the perfectibility of man in this world. Yet while we may agree with twentieth-century restatements of orthodoxy, with their frightening emphasis on the doctrine of original sin, and their reflections on the inadequacy of liberalism, we must see these religious tendencies in their historic contexts.

Both the social gospel and neo-orthodoxy were worried about the influence upon churches of great secular forces. Both were concerned fundamentally with man's salvation. The social gospel tried to face the problem of unfettered private wealth and the evil social results of an unqualified acceptance of individualism. Neo-orthodoxy tries to face the problems of leviathan government and the nature of the sin which permits mass war—and it returns naturally to a re-emphasis of the individual's relationship to God. The social gospel was more "secular" than neo-orthodoxy because it had to call for social action through government. Neo-orthodoxy is less "secular" because it has observed that mere increase of government and material welfare does not guarantee man's salvation now or in the future. For our purpose, then, it is useful to note that both movements arose in direct response to historic conditions—and that just as in the sixteenth century the aspects of Christianity that each movement stressed reflected the origin of the movement.

Woodsworth's efforts on behalf of the Labour Church were carried on simultaneously with his more purely political activities in the Dominion Labour party. Although there were doctrinal differences within the left wing of the Winnipeg labour movement, there was considerable co-operation in the provincial election of 1920. The Dominion Labour Party nominated Dixon, Ivens, James, and Tipping; the Socialist Party of Canada, Armstrong, Pritchard, Johns, and Russell; and the Social Democratic party, Queen. All these men had been more or less closely associated with the leadership of the strike. The results of the provincial election in the late spring of 1920 showed that the concentrated educational campaign conducted by the labour leaders, together with a public reaction against the methods employed to break the strike, had produced a definite leftward swing in Winnipeg. Ivens, Queen, and Armstrong, although serving jail terms, were all elected, and Dixon headed the polls with a spectacular majority. It was estimated that in the Winnipeg constituency (under a system of proportional representation) over 80 per cent of the voters put Dixon's name on their ballots, and that the labour vote was 42.5 per cent of the total.[15]

Woodsworth found his own opinions expressed in the newly established journal, the *Canadian Forum*, when it wrote, "Never in Canada have the devotees of law and order received a ruder shock. . . . The lesson is obvious yet it should be stated. Any government which attempts to throttle free men in Canada or elsewhere will fall of its own weight and be fortunate if it does not bring crashing in ruins the structure which with clumsy hands it seeks to buttress.[16] Indeed, the very appearance of this new journal, with its ready defence of the Left in Canada, was one more support for Woodsworth's growing optimism about, and enthusiasm for the political method.

After the success of the Manitoba election, he felt free to turn his mind to the problem of reuniting his family. Although his assistance had seemed necessary in the election struggle, the strain of an extended absence from his wife and children was not easy to bear. And although life at Gibson's Landing had its attractions for them it was

15*Canadian Forum*, Dec., 1920.
16*Ibid.*, Oct., 1920. The *Forum* was established in the autumn of 1920 by a liberal-progressive group in Toronto. G. E. Jackson was chairman of the editorial board, C. B. Sissons, political editor, and Barker Fairley, literary editor.

necessary to move the family closer to high schools and a university. Also, while the immediate crisis in the Manitoba political scene had passed, in British Columbia there was an impending provincial election. It was important, too, that Vancouver could provide a more attractive climate for one who was never robust in health. In a letter to his family concerning these problems he wrote, "I think the next move must be for us to try to get together and get into a home. Many would like me to stay here. But although that would be an immediate solution, I think even for health's sake we would have to move sooner or later, and it might be better to have a strenuous time now rather than later in the life of Mother and myself. I can't like this climate and there's no 'scenery'. One would become 'spiritually' barren here. . . ."[17] The last sentence appears out of character, perhaps, in view of Woodsworth's life-long association with Winnipeg; but he was not the first Winnipegger to express privately an aversion to the great spaces and the dry cold.

Toward the end of August, 1920, Woodsworth left for the coast. In Vancouver he purchased a house in Kitsilano and the family moved into the city from Gibson's Landing. Financial problems were pressing but from several small sources of income he was able to carry on and devote his entire energy to the cause of labour education and political organization. Indeed, the way in which the immediate financial obstacle was overcome was another indication to him of the widespread faith not only in his own sincerity but in the whole idea of a social democratic movement. A portion of the small but cheerfully made donations from labour meetings and classes and from the Labour Church helped. Contributions came from friends across Canada, and even in the United States, and these were received gratefully as help in the struggle against social injustice.[18] From those who could not contribute financially he received equally important support. In his papers is a letter from a group in the Labour Church on the occasion of his departure for Vancouver. "You know how to do it, Jim. Make their faces shine as you made ours shine with the beauty of that better day; and we have no fear but that in saving the world for others they will have the best kind of a time and in the best possible way save themselves. . . ."

In Vancouver Woodsworth worked again with the Federated Labour

[17]April 11, 1920.

[18]In his commonplace book, for example, Woodsworth noted amongst other gifts one of fifty dollars from "a group of Toronto friends." His work on the Vancouver docks in 1919 before he left for the prairie speaking tour had brought in only $289.

party, which still occupied the centre position in the labour movement on the coast. As in Winnipeg he discovered a left wing of labour consisting of the Socialist Party of Canada, One Big Union supporters, and a nascent communist group; and a right wing adhering strictly to the international craft unions. During 1919 and 1920 there had been a considerable intensification of activity on the far Left and the main labour paper was flirting alternately with syndicalist industrial unionism and communism. Thus Woodsworth's articles and reports of his speeches in the *B.C. Federationist* were sandwiched in between glowing accounts of communist gains in England, editorials insisting that the nomination of labour political candidates could serve only as a propaganda medium, and flat statements that the function of a labour ministry "is to carry on a capitalist government."[19]

Busy participation in the educational work of the Federated Labour party brought about Woodsworth's nomination as one of the three party candidates to contest the provincial election in the Vancouver constituency. A full manifesto was issued, bearing Woodsworth's name and those of the other two candidates, T. Richardson and W. R. Trotter.[20] Woodsworth's influence was predominant in the formulation of the manifesto which adopted completely the revisionist or Fabian position. The F.L.P. accepted the challenge of the far Left and plunged forward along the path of constitutional revolution. Kautsky, Bernstein, and Jaures were hurled at them, but they fought the election on specific issues as well as on their general, loosely devised manifesto.

In his own campaign speeches Woodsworth focused discussion upon the specific points particularly, and laid stress upon the immediate benefits obtainable through the election of labour representatives. The main defence of this policy he stated clearly as being the prevention of forceful revolution. Simultaneously, in an article for the *B.C. Federationist*,[21] he integrated his pacifist convictions with the general social democratic platform, as he had done earlier with respect to the social gospel. Here, Hobsonian ideas concerning the deep-reaching tentacles of imperialist propaganda were developed at some length and particular emphasis laid upon the necessity of preventing imperialist indoctrination through Canadian schools.

The electoral verdict in Vancouver was a real satisfaction to the three F.L.P. candidates. Each of them polled between 7,000 and 7,500

[19]*B.C. Federationist*, Oct. 20, 1920.
[20]Federated Labour party "Manifesto in connection with the British Columbia Provincial Election to be held December 1st., 1920."
[21]Nov. 26, 1920.

votes.[22] Although the Liberals carried the day, the F.L.P. accumulated a considerable voting strength and its three candidates were far ahead of the six candidates of the more radical and doctrinaire Socialist Party of Canada. Again Woodsworth experienced the feeling that the forces of constitutional socialism were the really significant power in Canadian politics—the power of a not distant future.

For the remainder of the winter of 1920–1 he busied himself with the educational work of the labour movement, conducting classes in economics, speaking regularly at Sunday meetings, and contributing articles to the labour paper. One of his children was already about to enter university and two more preparing to enter high school. His wife was a leader in the newly organized Women's International League for Peace and Freedom and sometimes spoke at his political meetings. Life may have been hard, but it was very full. Woodsworth felt pride in achieving the position of "professional politician" without the backing of wealthy supporters or the rewards of office. He always accepted the designation of professional politician (after defining the term) as a compliment, and while in Parliament considered that a "part-time" as opposed to a "professional" politician was the less admirable. Having given his own career completely to the political cause of the dispossessed he could see clearly some of the damaging shortcomings of politicians whose private business remained their primary concern or whose independence came too easily from the private wealth of sponsors. At least until his election to the federal House, personal financial problems loomed large. In the spring of 1921 he was again forced to leave his family for a while.

In British Columbia, the political climate had moderated, while in other parts of the West a greater opportunity to assist the socialist political cause seemed to exist. In Winnipeg, particularly, a chance was offered to combine the answer to his own financial plight with the best political opportunity. When William Ivens wrote suggesting that Woodsworth return to Winnipeg as secretary of the Labour Church, Woodsworth was pleased, for several reasons. He wrote back,

I shall be glad indeed to meet the Winnipeg group again. That strike experience in common did more than you can understand to create a certain solidarity and enthusiasm which it will take more than the later divisions to abolish. You ought to live at the coast for a while and you would think that the Labour Movement in Winnipeg wasn't so slow after all. Of course we are all very "advanced" scientifically but we don't seem to stand up to a situation!

---

[22]This placed Woodsworth fifteenth in the competition for the six seats allotted the Vancouver constituency (*B.C. Federationist*, Dec. 3, 1920).

You ask how I'm earning a living. Well, I'm not. That's one reason I have to get out. . . . Now the "season" is about over anyway and the workers are in their gardens or at picnics, I feel that a good deal has been done in preparing the way for future work but there is, outside of New Westminster, no definite organization to show for the winter's work. . . . I hate to think of leaving the family again. But they will be more comfortably located than before—that is the children are at school, and so suffer no privations that way.[23]

Disappointment with the temporary apathy in Vancouver was soon dispelled by another prairie trip. The events of the spring and summer of 1921 are briefly told in another letter of that year.

Then, finances being exhausted, I took to the road again. Spent a month lecturing in Calgary. Fired the opening shot in the Medicine Hat election, in which Labour backed the farmers and overwhelmingly defeated the Government candidate. Then on to Winnipeg where I am working in connection with the Labour Church. We have a central theatre meeting and half a dozen suburban branches. During the week I conduct six group study classes in industrial history and economics. . . . Our plans are very indefinite. I am "blacklisted" and must take whatever work offers for the time. It's not easy financially, and anything but pleasant to be separated from the family; but will not give up the fight before we are forced to do so. To an outsider my course may seem erratic, but it is really right in line with the work of all the previous years. The idealism of today has largely passed from the churches—at least so we think. We are confident that time will vindicate our position. . . .[24]

Participation in the Medicine Hat election stimulated Woodsworth's enthusiasm for the political development in Alberta. He seems to have ignored the stumbling block of the United Farmers of Alberta's leadership. Perhaps this is more understandable when one considers the rapid shifting from one political stand to another by William Irvine and others who had earlier supported the Non-Partisan League. In 1918 and 1919 that group had held steadfastly to the idea of a farmer-labour political party, separate from the administration of the U.F.A. This idea was defeated in the U.F.A. convention of 1919, and in 1920 Irvine published his book *The Farmers in Politics*. This work argued the doctrines of Henry Wise Wood; doctrines advocating co-operation economically and group government politically. The implication was clear that the farmers must go into politics as a class, and that if they were to co-operate with labour it should be after and not during elections. Simultaneous with this shifting position there occurred other divisions within the Progressive movement. T. A. Crerar, with the

[23]Woodsworth to William Ivens, April 24, 1921.
[24]Woodsworth to relatives in China, Aug. 25, 1921.

"Manitoba Idea" of co-operation with any other low-tariff group, was doing battle with H. W. Wood, J. J. Morison, and the economic class concept of the farmers' political effort. To add to the confusion, by 1921 Irvine again appeared to be shifting his stand, and by the time of the federal election of December was prepared to campaign as a labour-farmer candidate in Calgary.

All this made it difficult for Woodsworth (as it did for the country's political journalists) to discover the precise possibilities of planned co-operation between labour and the farmers toward the end of a national party. The actual course taken by the Progressive movement and the fact that Woodsworth's federal constituency was to be purely urban rendered the problem temporarily academic from his point of view. This is not to say that he ceased to interest himself in agrarian affairs—as his participation in the Medicine Hat election indicates— and, indeed, he continued to look forward with great hope to the establishment of a genuine farmer-labour party. He took particular satisfaction in the U.F.A. victory in Alberta in the summer of 1921 and commented upon Mrs. Nellie McClung's failure to support the agrarian candidates: "too bad she couldn't see the signs of the times."[25] Perhaps, too, his disapproval of the purely geographical basis of parliamentary representation led him to minimize the obstacle to a farmer-labour party inherent in the Wood dogma of group government, and to see the U.F.A. policy as a step toward a representative system that would recognize economic groups.

Despite this nebulous political situation Woodsworth continued to hammer at obvious cracks in the capitalist system. In particular the recurring problem of unemployment, the unnecessary suffering and human wastage it involved, absorbed his attention. Shortly before he left Vancouver he wrote an article for the *Canadian Forum* on the question. "In a small city (Vancouver) ten thousand unemployed. What an economic loss! If these men were on strike what volumes of righteous indignation would be poured forth from the disinterested citizens! These citizens now content themselves with grumbling about giving relief to men who, no doubt, wasted their earnings in riotous living. . . ." From neither of the old parties could an effective solution be expected, and the workers were beginning to drift toward the fallacy of forceful revolution. In them could be perceived

a feeling akin to that of the religious enthusiast who was convinced that the "Day of the Lord was at hand." With many, belief in the inevitableness of the revolution has led to a sort of fatalism. They can do little to hasten the

[25]Woodsworth to his daughter, Grace, July 20, 1921.

event. Or again, ameliorative measures are not to be encouraged as they may somewhat retard the approaching climax. Eagerly they scan the newspapers for news from Soviet Russia, for signs of a break-up in Middle Europe, for a more aggressive movement in Great Britain. In their halls all day long they debate the merits of "direct action," "the dictatorship of the proletariat" or speculate as to whether there is any possibility in this country that change might be brought about without violence. . . .[26]

The conclusions from such observations seemed obvious. If the co-operative commonwealth were to be achieved through recognition of the brotherhood of man, and if the evils inherent in violent change were to be avoided, the government had certain immediate responsibilities with regard to the social threat of unemployment. The article presented five principles for consideration. Most unemployment is involuntary; when private enterprise fails to maintain full employment the state should provide adequate maintenance; the state should provide work when private enterprise fails to do so; that work should be productive; financing it should be considered a first charge on the national resources and credit of the country.

Imploring the public to realize the seriousness of the industrial problem, Woodsworth obtained more than a formal support from the *Forum* itself. In April it commented that many people would question the claim that the state itself should provide work, but none, it said, would deny that sweeping reforms were necessary to curtail the periodical recurrence of unemployment. In May, noting that one out of every five workingmen in Canada was idle, it wrote, "We are face to face with the realization that before things can be better they must be worse. . . . It is a trite but true saying that a desperate situation demands desperate remedies. . . ." It agreed with Woodsworth that unless adequate maintenance were provided violence would be inevitable. And in September it printed an editorial urging the need for immediate and serious planning for a national system of unemployment insurance. Faith in the Liberal plank of 1919 guttered early.

The support offered by this new national journal for immediate reforms, although its readership was rather limited, was encouraging, and his faith was also bolstered by the steady flow of letters from old and new friends. Typical of these was one (March 16, 1921) from a Superior Court judge in Montreal whom Woodsworth had known in the days of the Canadian Welfare League. ". . . I had followed your brave fight in Winnipeg with much interest and sympathy; though, frankly, I have often asked myself then and since: Was it worth while?

[26]*Canadian Forum*, April, 1921.

The lack of cohesion and leadership in the ranks of labour throughout the country and the continent; treason to the common principles through self-seeking desires; the apathy of the masses and the prevailing unreason you speak of, at times make one feel that the heroic effort was in vain. And again, I check myself and say that no noble deed is ever without effect. . . ."

Woodsworth arrived in Winnipeg early in June, 1921, and resumed his activities in the Labour Church of which he was secretary from June to December.[27] The temper of the city was increasingly favourable to a labour political effort, and although his immediate personal situation was not very happy he wrote to his family on the coast, "Rumour has it that there may be a Federal election this Fall. It will likely come within six months anyway. I suppose we ought to hang on till then so as to be in the fight. But these days I would be quite content to find a little corner somewhere. . . ."[28] Soon he was completely absorbed by the intricate pattern of the labour Left in the prairie capital and was himself actively engaged in the struggle to achieve a strong social democratic party.

As suggested above, the Winnipeg Trades and Labour Council had, during 1920, passed out of the control of socialist leaders and into the hands of A.F. of L. representatives. Then, during the early months of 1921, a similar shift occurred within the Dominion Labour party, the Winnipeg organization that had achieved considerable success as the social democratic vehicle in the 1920 provincial election. Within this party the social democrats found themselves engaged in a constant struggle to prevent the emasculation of the party platform and even the supporting of anti-labour men in civic elections.[29] By March of 1921 the original leaders of the party had bowed out in the face of a steady infiltration of more conservative craft unionists. Concerning this development Woodsworth wrote, "In Winnipeg, owing, it is alleged, to an attempt of the A.F. of L. section to dominate the political organization, there has been formed the Independent Labour party. . . ."[30] The final break with the Dominion Labour party came in March, 1921,[31] while Woodsworth was still in Vancouver, and the Independent Labour party was established by a group which included

[27]The salary for the job, he observed, was $50 a week, "the amount of an O.B.U. organizer, that is about at the rate of a skilled mechanic."
[28]July 20, 1921.
[29]B.C. Federationist, March 11, 1921.
[30]Clipping in Woodsworth papers from the journal Canadian Brotherhood of Railway Employees.
[31]B.C. Federationist, March 11, 1921.

F. J. Dixon (M.L.A.), S. J. Farmer, W. D. Bayley (M.L.A.), and William Ivens (M.L.A.). The *Western Labor News*, by then also under A.F. of L. control, censured this group for bolting, but the other labour members of the Manitoba legislature sympathized with their action.

The rift between the conservative and the socialist labour leaders widened perceptibly. According to S. J. Farmer,[32] the main reason for the establishment of the new party was the policy adopted in the D.L.P., over the opposition of the social democrats, of encouraging trade union affiliation as opposed to individual membership. This procedure gave a superior strength to the anti-socialist A.F. of L. spokesmen in the party meetings and was the technique used to lead the D.L.P. away from a socialist policy. Discussing the origin of the I.L.P. the *Manitoba Free Press*[33] noted that its leaders had been the chief officials of the party they rejected. "The membership [of the D.L.P.] repudiated them, reorganized the party and tightened up the trade union affiliations." In the eyes of the Sifton paper the I.L.P. was merely "a group of nondescripts" and the *Free Press* recognized the D.L.P. as "the official party of organized labour in Winnipeg."

In August of 1921 a further element of confusion was introduced through the revival of the Canadian Labour party, originally established in 1906. James Simpson of Toronto, himself a social democrat, had been the most consistent spokesman of this party, but he had failed to get any clear endorsation of his party through the Trades and Labour Congress.[34] Now, however, apparently because of the increasing political unrest in the country, the local Trades and Labour Councils, with the tacit blessing of the Trades and Labour Congress, seemed prepared to extend encouragement to the Canadian Labour party in order to prevent the evolution of a more radical national movement. At first it was not quite apparent what line the revived national party would take. Its secretary, Simpson, was a socialist and its platform contained many of the socialist planks. Some of the Winnipeg socialists, including A. E. Smith,[35] agreed to accept it, but most were sceptical of its leadership and especially of the fact that it seemed to have grown out of the Winnipeg meeting of the Trades and Labour Congress in August. In September the Dominion Labour party joined the new national organization. The I.L.P., after sending delegates,

[32]Interview with the author, June, 1948.
[33]Oct. 21, 1921.
[34]See H. A. Logan, *Trade Unions in Canada* (Toronto, 1948), pp. 426 *et seq.*
[35]A. E. Smith, *All My Life* (Toronto, 1947), pp. 68 *et seq.*

withdrew from the local organizational meeting[36] and turned itself to the problem of electing an unqualifiedly social-democratic candidate to the federal Parliament from Winnipeg.

Woodsworth joined the I.L.P. almost automatically when he arrived in Winnipeg in June. In addition to the work of the Labour Church he entered fully into the I.L.P. discussions and preparations for the impending federal election. By the time of the dissolution of Parliament early in October he had helped to draft an election platform and was again feeling the excitement of a critical battle. This time the chances of success appeared greater than ever before. The question of a candidate to contest the constituency of Centre Winnipeg, where the party's strength was focused, was settled in September before the date of the election (December 6) was announced. Of the most likely candidates—Farmer, Dixon, Bayley,[37] and Woodsworth—Farmer was considered best for the municipal field as he had twice been a mayorality candidate, while Dixon and Bayley were already members of the provincial legislature. The names of Woodsworth and Farmer were both put forward at the nominating meeting and when it appeared that a majority favoured the former as a federal candidate Farmer moved a resolution that the nomination be made unanimous.[38]

The Trades and Labour Council through the *Western Labor News*, and the Winnipeg dailies continued their policies of belittling the I.L.P. Immediately following the first meeting of the Woodsworth election committee the *Western Labor News* wrote, "If he does not get endorsation from the official labor party then it is practically certain that he will not get the votes on polling day."[39] But this attitude seems to have lacked heart, as the D.L.P. failed even to nominate an "official labour candidate" in Centre Winnipeg. The Socialist Party of Canada nominated H. M. Bartholomew, but withdrew him well before the election date. Even the Workers' Alliance (communist), which nominated J. Penner to contest the North Winnipeg constituency in competition with the other labour candidate, R. B. Russell of the Socialist Party of Canada, did not run a man in Woodsworth's constituency.[40]

[36]*Western Labor News*, Oct. 14, 1921.
[37]W. D. Bayley was principal of King George V School in St. Boniface.
[38]*Independent*, Sept. 23, 1921. The *Free Press* (Sept. 22) professed to believe that the Woodsworth nomination came as a surprise in labour circles, but there is no evidence to support this; probably it was an attempt to create dissension within the new party.
[39]*Western Labor News*, Oct. 14, 1921.
[40]Penner polled just enough votes to rob Russell of victory over the Liberal E. J. McMurray in North Winnipeg.

It was soon apparent that the I.L.P. had selected an exceptionally strong candidate. Woodsworth's long history of support for the Winnipeg labour cause, together with an ability to convey his conviction to any audience, created deep concern amongst Liberals and Conservatives. The Liberals had nominated J. W. Wilton who had broken with the Norris government on the issues of the strike, but a strong minority group within the party was dissatisfied and nominated Mrs. John Dick as an independent.[41] A similar division of opinion occurred within the Tory ranks, and the official candidate, N. K. McIver, had to meet the competition of the independent G. W. Andrews. The reasons for the Conservative and the Liberal splits were exactly opposite. Andrews was the sitting member for the constituency, and had voiced criticism of the Borden government's handling of the strike. Thus, while the Liberals sought an official candidate with a pro-strike background, the Tories rejected one with such a history. J. W. Wilton summed up the situation thus: "The forces opposed to him (Woodsworth) were split four ways, while in his rank there was no split. Labor men had avenged 1919 in 1920 and were determined to avenge it still more completely in 1921."[42] Amongst his opposition there was much mutual denunciation, but all united in vilifying Woodsworth—which seemed only to convince the electorate of his authenticity as a working-class representative.

In September, 1921, the I.L.P., in order to obtain circulation for its platform and policy discussions, had established a new paper, the *Independent*.[43] Through this organ, and in scores of addresses, Woodsworth waged a lively campaign similar to that which he had undertaken for the Federated Labour party in Vancouver. The I.L.P. manifesto[44] bore a close resemblance to that of the F.L.P., just as the F.L.P. statement was very similar to the Woodsworth *Western Labor News* series, "What Next," of the previous summer. Again the predominant influence was that of Woodsworth, but the manifesto bore obvious traces of the thought of F. J. Dixon, the next most persuasive person in this group—who had not then accepted the socialist position fully, nor was ever to do so—in the planks demanding direct legislation and the land values tax. It also incorporated statements from the pacifist views of Woodsworth, Ivens, and Dixon. In the preamble the

[41]J. W. Wilton, "Any Man" (unpublished manuscript, estate of J. W. Wilton, Toronto), p. 375.
[42]*Ibid.*, p. 376.
[43]The editorial committee was composed of W. D. Bayley, S. J. Farmer, Thos. Brown, F. J. Dixon, Wm. Ivens, and G. A. Tanner.
[44]Reprinted in the *Independent*, Dec. 2, 1921.

manifesto attempted to skirt the issue of the struggle between the
A.F. of L. and O.B.U. groups, stating that the party was "formed for
the purpose of giving political expression to the aspirations of all
workers, regardless of industrial affiliation, who believe in the establishment of a co-operative commonwealth with production for use instead
of for profit as its economic basis."

The manifesto included a number of planks designed to meet
"immediate pressing needs," such as unemployment insurance. Similar
planks had been incorporated in the platform of the Liberal party in
1919, but Woodsworth dwelt continually upon the similarity between
the Tories and the Liberals in their relation to the business of the
country. Both, he insisted, had had ample opportunity to produce
reform, but both accepted the basis of private capital's control of the
economy and were thus incapable of producing serious reforming
effort. Whatever reform they did produce, he argued, would be
frustrated by their failure to recognize the principle of co-operation
as opposed to that of competition. On the subject of unemployment
insurance Woodsworth was to spend the years right up to his retirement in 1940 reminding Liberal governments of their 1919 plank
concerning the question.

In his speech accepting the nomination he traced the historical
development of Canada from pioneer days to its modern system of
special privilege. "The manufacturers group, which had secured
tariff protection, really dominates the government. . . . Private companies grab the fairer lands, mines, timber limits and other natural
resources. The fortunes thus amassed form the basis of the money
monopoly which now dominates the life of Canada. Interlocking
directorates have resulted in the consolidation of all these interests,
and in exploiting Canadian resources the future was lost sight of."[45]
As in the British Columbia election he stressed heavily the possibility
of immediate benefits through the election of a strong labour representation. He assailed Arthur Meighen for talking of the need for
tariff protection instead of suggesting a solution for the unemployment
problem, and for allowing the country's natural resources to fall into
the hands of American investors without even recognizing that the
development was taking place.[46]

While the Conservatives concentrated on the need for a strong man
(Meighen), and protection against revolutionary groups, and while
the Liberals emphasized the need for "a change," the I.L.P. adopted

[45]*Manitoba Free Press*, Oct. 19, 1921.
[46]*Ibid.*, Oct. 25, 1921.

as its slogan, "Human Needs before Property Rights." Although it
indicated the particular immediate reform legislation for which it
would press, it did not camouflage its socialist aims. It also stressed
the very particular need of working-class representation in order to
prevent a repetition of the abuse of federal military-police force such
as had characterized the later stages of the Winnipeg strike. Trade
unionism was not enough. In one of his campaign articles,[47] Woodsworth wrote,

Let us frankly realize that trade unionism has accomplished much—and
industrial unionism may accomplish more. We cannot afford to neglect this
field. That does not imply that we do not recognize its limitations. So with
Parliament. Through political action the workers have accomplished much—
leisure, educational opportunities, industrial safeguards, etc. They can
secure more.
    If parliamentary control were of no value, why should the Manufacturers'
Association and the Railroads and Banks be so deeply interested? You may
say that in the last analysis it is because Parliament controls the courts and
the military forces. Well, even on that ground, might it not be worthwhile
for the workers to have control? Suppose we admit that the parliamentary
machine is outgrown. It is there, nevertheless and must be reckoned with.
Or, it is suggested, you cannot beat the politicians at their own game or with
their own weapons. Look at Alberta! . . .

From that example, argued Woodsworth, the value of solidarity is
perfectly clear. "So when we are trying to elect a working class representative to parliament, should we insist on uniformity in economic
and sociological and philosophical views? Such insistence means failure
at the polls." The suggestion that uniformity of opinion in details was
not necessary was apparently an appeal for the support of members
of the Socialist Party of Canada and also for the vote of all progressive
trade unionists, whether O.B.U. or A.F. of L. It did not abandon the
aim of social revolution. In other articles and speeches Woodsworth
underlined the purely socialist demand for early expansion of public
ownership in transportation, public utilities, finance and industry.[48]
    Whether the policy was logical or not, it was distinctly successful.
On election day 7,774 voters favoured the I.L.P. candidate. The two
official candidates of the Conservatives and Liberals drew 4,034 and
4,032 votes respectively, while the independent Liberal received 2,314
and the independent Conservative 1,120.[49] Although Woodsworth's
vote was thus a minority of the total votes cast, it was greater than
either the combined Conservative or the combined Liberal vote. There

[47]*Independent*, Sept. 9, 1921.
[48]*Ibid.*, Sept. to Dec., 1921.   [49]*Ibid.*, Dec. 12, 1921.

was sufficient cause for rejoicing and his supporters provided a traditional victory march. The wedge had been entered and Woodsworth emerged as the first socialist representative of the working class in the Canadian Parliament.[50]

Much of his first electoral success depended upon the working-class reaction to its experiences of 1919. But the idea of the co-operative commonwealth, around which his election platform was built, was of undeniable importance. That platform, despite some literary shortcomings and its great generalities, represented a high goal which appealed strongly to the working class of Winnipeg. As Woodsworth was returned year after year to Parliament it became apparent that his election in 1921 was not simply the aftermath of the strike; increasingly, he became the spokesman of all those Canadians who found themselves on the political Left.

In 1926, after five years in the federal House, Woodsworth published a comment upon the festivities accompanying the formal opening of Parliament:

The light laughter rings through the corridors as I write. I am not a misanthrope, but I cannot keep out of my mind the pictures of plain homes, in some of which there is a desperate struggle for mere existence. What is Ottawa to them? In some way the Government has been removed too far away from the people, or was it ever thus? . . . No, I cannot get back to talking politics tonight! Before me lies a letter from a disheartened Cape Breton miner: "There are some 2,000 miners around Glace Bay, who are getting work from one to two days a week, and I suppose you know what that means—and that, after five months' strike. . . ."
    (Music floats up from the Senate Chamber)
". . . The stomachs of the men, women and children demand prompt action, and I thought the government might help."
Somehow the music and the miner's letter clash. I like music, but I wish the music would stop. Even my comfortable office is getting on my nerves! Hang it! I don't believe I was meant to be a politician![51]

It was as a politician that he was to wield his greatest influence.

[50]He had been preceded in Parliament by two other representatives of labour: A. W. Puttee of Winnipeg (1900–4), and Alphonse Verville of Montreal (1900–4; 1908–17). The former, however, did not possess an organized socialist party behind him, and the latter was more concerned with trade union affairs and such matters as the eight-hour day than with the achievement of socialism.

[51]Winnipeg *Tribune*, Jan. 23, 1926. Reprinted in J. S. Woodsworth, *Hours That Stand Apart* (Ottawa, 1927).

PART II: 1922-1927

10

OTTAWA

MANY PEOPLE IN 1922 BEGAN to take stock of the men in Canada's Fourteenth Parliament. The new cabinet was undistinguished, led by the cautious William Lyon Mackenzie King, who lacked almost completely the confidence of his own Liberal party managers. Arthur Meighen, leader of the opposition, and most of his colleagues, were already in some respects men of the past, identified with policies which had deeply divided the country and too openly favoured big business.

It was the new group of sixty-five Progressives from Ontario and the prairies, burning with reform zeal, and the two Labour representatives from Calgary and Winnipeg, who caught the public eye and provided interesting speculations about the future. With their doctrine of group government, their fierce hatred of eastern-controlled tariffs and financial institutions, and their "balance of power,"[1] the Progressives could be a determining factor at Ottawa. How many would hold out against the blandishments of official Liberalism and how many would move further left? A part of the answer to this political riddle depended upon the relationship between the Progressives and the two socialists, Woodsworth and William Irvine.

What were these men really like, asked the Ottawa Press Gallery? In Irvine, a native of the Shetland Isles, editor and clergyman, they discerned a man of mercurial brilliance, and a social gospeller who preached in the Unitarian Church in Ottawa. Irvine had flirted with socialism in the Non-Partisan League and had also written a book expounding the ideas of group government better than those ideas had ever been presented by Henry Wise Wood himself.[2] Furthermore, although his Calgary seat was held in the name of the Labour party

[1]Neither King nor Meighen controlled a majority of the House.
[2]*The Farmers in Politics* (Toronto, 1920).

of that city, his election had been made sure by the full support of Progressives in rural sections of the riding. If group government meant separate representation for each economic interest in the nation, apparently it did not preclude co-operation between two of those interests in the pursuit of common objectives. The attitude of Progressives like R. A. Hoey of Manitoba, E. J. Garland of Alberta, and Agnes Macphail of Ontario seemed to underline this potentially important alliance.

That Woodsworth himself held the co-operation of farmer and worker to be of great importance has already been shown, and his presence in the House attracted the immediate attention of the Ottawa reporters. When the session was only two months old, and before there were conclusive signs of the political path he would follow, the Montreal *Standard* published a profile by "D.C.L." which remarked, "Woodsworth is a small sized man of forty-eight with a short-cropped, tapering beard streaked with grey. He is thin and pale and ascetic, a little bit bald, built generally on delicate lines. . . . His countenance, while not dour, is rarely illumined with a smile. . . ." The author noted that Woodsworth spoke splendidly, with a clear-cut, easy delivery; that his voice was rather of the staccato pitch, not unpleasant, and accompanied with energetic gestures: "He hasn't at all the method of the preacher, no ponderous solemnity. . . . The House appears to think well of him."[3] Here was an accurate sketch, one which caught those features and characteristics which would be deeper etched and much better known to the House and to the country during the next twenty years. The persistence of that quiet, straight-ahead voice was to be both influential and irritating. The sincerity of the man who was no longer a minister, and the strength of one who appeared frail, would become part of the legend of Canadian politics.

In this second major period of his life, Woodsworth's personal religion came close to pantheism. His children no longer attended Sunday school (a break made at Gibson's Landing in 1918), they were not taught "Hymns of Adoration" but rather such poetry as these lines of Hartley Coleridge:

> So then believe that every bird that sings,
> And every flower that stars the fresh green sward,
> And every thought the happy summer brings,
> To the pure spirit, is a Word of God.

[3]Montreal *Standard*, April 15, 1922.

And Woodsworth, answering his own question as to whether the loss of an evangelical God carried with it a loss of incentive, wrote:

For myself I must say that I was never very keen on being an angel with a "crown upon my forehead" and "a harp within my hand." But the inner urge toward higher things is as strong as ever—yes, much stronger. No one who knows anything of the fierce joy of the conflict will worry very much about his "reward in heaven"... . Religion is for me not so much a personal relation between "me" and "God" as rather the identifying of myself with or perhaps the losing of myself in some larger whole... .[4]

Now his break with the past was complete. The "energetic gestures" were the outward expression of a fresh surge of creative zeal.

Is not the fear of breaking with old beliefs the most insidious kind of unbelief? Faith is a confident adventuring into the unknown.

> Haul out; cast off; shake out every sail;
> Steer for the deep waters only.
> For we are bound where mariner hath not yet dared to go,
> And we will risk the ship, ourselves and all.
> Oh daring joy—but safe!
> Are they not all the seas of God?
> Oh farther, farther, farther sail!

Woodsworth, attending his first Parliamentary session in 1922, had had to leave his family in Vancouver, where the family home remained for another year. The tall frame house he had purchased a few blocks from the waterfront in the Kitsilano district had been acquired at the peak of post-war prices—he had even borrowed on life insurance to make the down payment. Now, with his first adequate salary in some years, he faced the problem of paying off the mortgage in deflated dollars. When the Woodsworths moved into the Kitsilano house, it badly needed painting and the oldest boy, Charles, and his father did the job themselves. The long experience with tight budgets also led Woodsworth to make an experiment in his children's education. The eldest, Grace, was already entering her first year at the University of British Columbia. Woodsworth insisted, however, that Charles should go first to technical school, despite the fact that the boy's taste ran rather to literature and history than to mathematics and the sciences. From his own experience he knew what it was to be tossed into the working world without specialized training and he was determined that his children should learn some definite trade, both to protect them economically and to teach them the importance of manual and

[4]J. S. Woodsworth, "My Religion," scrapbook clipping, 1926.

skilled labour. The idea was, perhaps, plausible. In practice it did not work out very well, for although Charles enjoyed the carpentry and machine-shop work, he bogged down under the load of mathematics and science. When, in the following year, the family moved to Ottawa he enrolled in the regular high school course and everyone breathed more easily. Observing the results of his experiment, Woodsworth gave up the idea without remonstrance, and the rest of his children chose their own courses. But although he gave in on this question he could not relinquish his right to decide another. He steadily refused to permit his sons to take cadet training, and at least one of them felt a passing sense of shame as he was left sitting alone in the classroom meditating on the unkindness of fate in this respect.

Woodsworth's general ideas on education were broad. All six of his children went to a university and all except one had at least one trip to Europe either during or after the university course. The father's attitude to money, which made this possible, was a fundamental trait. Inherently frugal and disliking show or extravagance, he yet had no love for money as such but devoted such funds as he had to their most useful purpose. He never, even in his parliamentary days, received more than a modest income. Apart from his indemnity of $4,000 his extra income averaged about $400 from newspaper articles; the rent from the Vancouver house never offset the cost of living in Ottawa plus the Kitsilano mortgage. Yet by careful planning and the utmost of care in daily living he was able to achieve more than most men with several times his income. Following this rigorous domestic plan, he did more than his part, probably with some ill effect on his health, for by the end of the 1920's he was beginning to suffer from increasing blood pressure. While away from his home, which was the greater part of the time, he seldom ate in any but the cheapest restaurants. During boat or train trips he acted as his own porter, and in accommodation allowed himself only the minimum of comfort. But although his children were often refused pennies or nickels, they received money for bicycles; and none was denied instruction on violin or piano. Later, their father never asked for an accounting in their larger projects, knowing he could trust them to make the most of their opportunities.

If education and wide experience for his children were a continuing concern, Woodsworth never regarded his own education as complete. In the parliamentary period that was opening before him, he would always place high value on travel. If his taste in reading began to narrow down to his chosen field of left-wing politics and economics, his appetite for first-hand knowledge of Canada and the world grew proportionately. Probably travel was for him a legacy dating back to his father's missionary endeavour, with its prairie buckboard and the trips to England for recruits. He recalled vividly his own European and Middle Eastern trips, and in this later period Mrs. Woodsworth joined him in tours to Europe and Asia. Indeed his wife, with her fluent French and German, left him somewhat abashed when he found himself dependent upon her in the smallest transactions on the Continent.

In the development of the family relationship Mrs. Woodsworth's humour, her gentleness combined with very great strength, and her intelligent support of her husband through the most trying times was of fundamental importance. It would be difficult to exaggerate her rôle from the time she was first accepted by the Woodsworth clan as a slightly fey Irish girl, through her contributions at All Peoples' and Gibson's Landing, to her steady support during the parliamentary years and the final crisis of her husband's last illness. How much of her husband's achievement depended upon her will only be truly known by Lucy Woodsworth herself. Even though the household seemed always to revolve about father and husband, Woodsworth's insistence on the essential equality of man and woman must have sprung in large part from his knowledge of his wife's strength and wisdom.

Once in Parliament, Woodsworth took the new life with immense verve. Even after he had moved his family to Ottawa his office on Capitol Hill was the centre of his existence. In one sense, the new work was not so very different from that of his earlier plunges in welfare activities; the gathering and dissemination of social information was still important, and his parliamentary office reflected this. Fitted with books, pamphlets, and steel filing cabinets which contained a growing mass of correspondence with people all across Canada and in all walks of life, the office also became a centre for anyone visiting Ottawa who wished to learn something of labour politics, unemployment, civil liberties—or just to meet and talk with the country's most dramatic spokesman of the Left. The office also gave evidence of some of Woodsworth's chief characteristics. There were no samples of modern art, but there were several books of sentimental poetry and a number of souvenirs of his travels and his boyhood home.

On top of one of the filing cabinets reposed three huge scrapbooks (newspaper size) and two smaller ones, in which he had pasted every

printed item and many other documents concerning his activities from
the time of the Winnipeg mission days. These volumes he was to keep
up to date until 1939. The items on each side of each page were fitted
in half underneath each other so that each volume, when complete,
resembled a small barrel. They contain today valuable source material
for the student of Canadian labour and socialist history. Woodsworth
himself treasured these books (although during his last illness he unfortunately directed that many of his files be destroyed) and they
represent both his strong historical sense and his pride in the movement he was helping to shape. Unlike other little vanities, such as his
trim beard, his strong interest in publicity was more for the cause than
for himself. In this category, too, were the cartoons which decorated
one corner of his office—by Arch Dale, A. Racey, and Jack Boothe—
showing him variously as the troubled nursemaid of the U.F.O. and
Pink Labour, or as a Scottish clansman charging with fiery cross the
parliamentary bastions of capitalism—which shelter the huddled figures
of Bennett and King. Other office ornaments reminded him of his past:
the short steel bill hook of a Vancouver stevedore, the half neck yoke
used as a weapon by the Winnipeg specials of 1919, his grandfather's
sword dating from 1837.

It was in this office, Room 616 of the House of Commons, beneath
photographs of Keir Hardie, E. D. Morel, Eugene Debs, and Fred
Dixon, that plans were to be laid for Canada's first nation-wide socialist
party. And it was here that many of Canada's best political and social
thinkers drew inspiration and found a focus, particularly during the
long years of the great depression. Here, too, Woodsworth exchanged
ideas with Henri Bourassa and both men discovered that they had
much in common—Bourassa increasingly concerned about the growing
complexity of Montreal working-class problems, and Woodsworth
learning more of the Catholic approach to socialism. To Room 616
came also a stream of trade union officials, social workers, unemployed,
clergymen, immigrants, students—seeking advice, consideration of
their problems by Parliament, or simply encouragement. One wonders,
too, how many Liberal back-benchers found here a clear understanding of the force that was to urge their party toward new and unfamiliar
policies.

Woodsworth had a special weakness for newspaper men. He himself
had helped edit small papers such as the *Western Labor News*, and
throughout the twenties and thirties he was a steady contributor to
newspapers and magazines, especially the little labour weeklies across
the country, for which he wrote regular articles. He always felt himself

at home in the company of newspaper men and many of them fully
reciprocated his friendship. During these years in the House such
respect from the fourth estate grew rapidly.

He was at his prime physically, and threw himself into his work
with complete disregard for health. He rapidly established himself as a
skilful debater. Despite his running afoul of the sticky House rules
and the heavily weighted two-party tradition, there were soon many
members who would not readily cross swords with him on the floor of
the House and who contented themselves with quick interjections, not
always recorded in Hansard. Woodsworth's own principles, now well
established and, to himself at least, clear and simple, enabled him to
pick an almost unerring path through the misty cross-currents of the
struggle for parliamentary advantage. He was the more formidable
since, even while he was arguing pacifism, all recognized that there
was no element of fear in his character; that without regard for cost
he spoke his mind on the most perilous and unpopular matters.

Membership in a social class is an insidious matter. It is not just a
question of who owns what bonds, shares, stocks, mines, or timber
limits. It is also a question of how you think, where you live, whom
you know, what patronage you control, who were your parents and
thus, whether you know when to bow, scrape, or salute. It was this
multiple kind of class distinction that inspired amongst the 1921 Progressives the North American idea of constituency control of their
representatives. Suspicion of class feeling led them to use the "recall"
or signed resignation slip which they could present to their elected
representative should he ever exhibit signs of succumbing to the
protocol of life in provincial or federal capitals.

Woodsworth shared this fear fully, and was continually revolted by
the pomp and class display of official Ottawa—vestiges of British
feudalism, he thought, wedded to the harsh new-world consolidation
of economic power. He never failed to voice protest against "the great
occasions" as being worse than useless extravagance. The opening of
Parliament in 1922, in the midst of post-war depression, struck him
with particular force and his description of it was printed in farm and
labour papers across Canada. Resentment of Lord Byng's "stiff
acknowledgement" and the "gracious smile" of Lady Byng for each
person who passed the throne was mixed with a supreme distrust of
the society that could erect this façade:

Only now am I beginning to sense the fact that we have a governing
class. . . . as I saw Clifford Sifton and his wife who, during my boyhood
days in Brandon I had known as neighbours, I wondered whether, after all,

the majority of this grand assembly were not very ordinary folk. The whole affair appeared to me very false and superficial—an attempt to impress upon our young democracy the vestigial remains of the feudalism of Europe. Then something like anger took possession of me as I thought of a recent speech of Sir Clifford Sifton before the Toronto Board of Trade: "What he considered to be quality in immigration," Sir Clifford said, "was a sturdy peasant in a sheepskin coat with a big wife and four or five children—the union man who will not work more than eight hours a day, and not that if he can help it, who will not save his money and who comes to the city to be fed, is quantity not quality, I believe. Whether he is British or not, we do not want him. He is no good." Ah! Here we have stated with brutal frankness, almost with coarseness, the idea for the future of Canada held by Sir Clifford Sifton and his kind.

And here, in the crimsoned Senate Chamber with the court dress and uniforms beneath vast paintings of the war, Woodsworth saw "imperialism, militarism, capitalism, society, church, government—all inextricably mixed in a system that gives to the few the places of power and consigns the many to unrelieved drudgery and impotent longings. . . . In heaven's name, when you see me weakening, pull me off!"[5]

[5]*Alberta Labour News*, March 25, 1922.

11

THE NEW MEMBER

WOODSWORTH'S REACTION TO THE FORMALITIES of Ottawa was clear notice that he did not intend to water down the principles which he had enunciated over the preceding decade. Many contemporary journalists and later academic commentators professed to see an unwillingness in Woodsworth to use the term "socialism," or to press for the full socialist programme—and they suggest that he sailed under false colours. The evidence does not substantiate this charge. His persistent stand on all questions of civil liberties, and on the whole range of public ownership and planning, carried him far beyond the point where any non-socialist could possibly give him support. On civil liberty alone, his interpretation was wider than any that could be accepted save by the most liberal members, but was always guided by the assumptions of John Stuart Mill's great *Essay*. His insistence on the organic relationship between civil liberty and social good, when added to the specifically socialist elements in his thought, marked him indelibly with the British stamp.

The first House of Commons sally by the new labour member was on the Address in reply to the Speech from the Throne early in the 1922 session. His first speech was important because it served as a manifesto to his fellow members, particularly the Progressives. Before he rose, Woodsworth was already aware that he would have considerable Progressive support. The Progressive Whip had co-operated in securing a regular position in the debate for Woodsworth and Irvine. Also, Woodsworth had had several meetings with "certain Progressives who recognize their responsibility to the labour section of their constituencies."[1] There were some twelve or fifteen of these (who were to become in 1924 the "Ginger Group") and although they did

[1]J. S. Woodsworth in the *Independent*, March 24, 1922.

not call their meetings a caucus these meetings were really the earliest political origins of the C.C.F. at Ottawa. The fact that they were regularly held gave Woodsworth confidence that not all of the Progressive group would fall into the arms of Mackenzie King's Liberal party.

Woodsworth spoke after many Tories, Liberals, and Progressives had said whether they accepted the government's cautious Speech from the Throne. He left no doubt that he saw unemployment as more than the "misfortune" that the speech called it. The two hundred thousand unemployed called for more than temporary measures of grudging relief from an economy-minded government: "I claim that we have come to a period in the history of our country when we must decide once and for all which shall prevail, profits or human welfare. I feel confident that there is a group of men here, new members of the House if you will, who have clearly made up their minds that, insofar as they can decide it, human welfare is to be given the precedence."[2] Although Woodsworth could not know the details of King's difficult position between the Montreal wing of Sir Lomer Gouin and the former Unionist Progressive wing of Dafoe, A. B. Hudson, and T. A. Crerar, he believed that any reform zeal in King would take a back seat to the necessities of holding office for himself and for the Liberal party. Thus he laid down in his first speech the challenge to action that he was to present to the treasury benches on every possible occasion from 1922 to 1940. His suspicion that progressive legislation would lose precedence to political expediency seemed to be confirmed when it was seen that the first mild endeavour along this line came only after five years of Liberal government, and as a result of political extremity.

Woodsworth's first speech then continued with an analysis of the extent of unemployment and the statistics of Canadian social welfare. Unemployment and family hardship, he insisted, in industrial society, were largely involuntary:

... under these conditions the state is under obligation to provide work. I am not much concerned whether by the state we mean the municipality or the province or the Dominion. I would say, however, that whilst the speech from the throne would seek to evade, on the part of the Dominion, the responsibility for this problem of unemployment, in my judgment it is impossible to do so. The body that has to deal with great questions like immigration, the fiscal policy of this country and our external relations, cannot say that it has no responsibility toward unemployment, which is one of the consequences of, or intimately related to our fiscal policy and our rela-

[2]Hansard, 1922, pp. 86 *et seq.*

tions with other countries; and this House before it rises must deal with this question of unemployment. . . . I would say that the financing of any [unemployment insurance] scheme is a first charge on the natural resources and credit of the country. . . .

Here was the linking of various themes into a total pattern of responsibility—the voice of a conscience that would dog the cautious constitutionalists until Woodsworth's last days in the House. The insistence on accepting moral responsibility was to lead to bitter debates over the nature and purposes of the B.N.A. Act, the purposes of armaments, and Canadian foreign policy, as well as the functioning of class institutions and the profit motive. It was the opening gun in a campaign to inject real principles and real issues into the sham battle of Canadian politics. At other points in his speech Woodsworth called for the inclusion of all railways within the C.N.R. system, the breaking of the private monopoly of banking and credit, a capital levy to reduce the war debt, a steady refusal to maintain a large defence estimate, and planning of our productive capacities. "Mr. Speaker," he concluded, "we are too small a group to have very much effect in this House, I fear, but I would like to tell you that behind the divisions and often the crudities of the labour people who are the very foundation of the great industries of this country, there is an intense idealism, a looking forward to a period of world brotherhood. . . ." It was a fighting speech, and it revealed a great ambition.

When William Irvine rose to make his maiden speech in the debate on the Address, he presented clearly the idea of group government, as well as the suggestion that he and Woodsworth were in Parliament specifically to represent labour. When the Prime Minister offered Crerar and others a place in the cabinet, he said, it should not have been on the condition that the cabinet remain a purely Liberal ministry. This ignored the principle of development and progress, which demanded that each economic group be given a share in the government so that the government would really represent the opinion of the House. Both the old parties, he suggested, represent "big interests" despite their insistence that they represent everyone. A third group is that of the organized farmers, and a fourth, that of labour. ". . . I wish to state," he told the Speaker, "that the honourable Member for Centre Winnipeg is the leader of the labour group—and I am the group. But even if we are small, I should like to say, without any presumption whatsoever, that a small living seed, however small it may be, is greater than a dead trunk."[3] He went on to suggest that his group

[3]*Ibid.*, pp. 216 *et seq.*

government thesis would require that a government could only resign on a straight vote of confidence. The various groups could, under such circumstances, vote for or against different measures on their merits without the threat of resignations and elections. Later in his speech he expounded the "famous Douglas system of credit." On this second theme, Woodsworth was not at one with his colleague, although the concept of a managed currency in some form he accepted.

It seems clear that Woodsworth believed group government should be tried. Certainly he detested the strict two-party system with its implications of cabinet dictatorship and its limitations on "true representation" of the constituencies. But he viewed the Progressives' group government doctrine primarily as an interesting possible experiment. Sometimes he seemed to go beyond this, but it is likely that he was more interested in the fervour with which the United Farmers of Alberta clung to the idea than he was in the idea itself. In any event, by 1932, there is little reference to it in his speeches or letters.

Conservatives in any society stand for peace and order. But on occasions when they feel their position to be directly challenged, the cautious dignity which they normally exhibit may be replaced by a policy less cautious and certainly less dignified. Woodsworth was faced many times by the conservatives of Canada in their least dignified moments. When he introduced bills in 1922 and 1923 to curb the anti-labour activities of the Royal Canadian Mounted Police, *Saturday Night* dubbed him "one of those who desired to see a Soviet form of government established in Manitoba" in 1919, and implied that his desire to "weaken" the Mounties was intimately related to his underlying revolutionary purpose.[4] His bills to amend the Immigration Act and the Criminal Code were subject to much the same kind of inference. Yet these projects of his, although they took time to ripen, were a successful attempt to rid Canada of the 1919 amendments—amendments which had produced the incredible section 98 of the Criminal Code; denial of jury trial to people who were charged with sedition or with being "undesirable," and who were threatened with deportation under the Immigration Act; and the proven espionage activities of the R.C.M.P. within labour organizations. This legislation of the 1919 period had created conditions comparable to those existing in Britain at the time of Peterloo, or in the United States at the time of the Alien and Sedition Laws, or the McCarran-McCarthy period. It may be argued that as Canada pulled out of the post-war depression this legislation would have been repealed in any event. That may

[4]*Saturday Night*, March 24, 1923.

possibly be true, but it is certainly debatable. The significant point is that repeal was strongly opposed all along the line, while the changes in the labour policy of the R.C.M.P. were almost imperceptible despite the endeavours of Woodsworth to publicize the situation. The careers of some Mounties such as Corporal Zaneth or Sergeant Leopold were susceptible of an *agent-provocateur* interpretation.

Woodsworth's concern with the subject of civil liberty stemmed from a much more personal experience than could be claimed by members of the cabinet. This was apparent in the debate over one of the first measures of the new King government. The Minister of Militia and Defence, George P. Graham, introduced a resolution to create a Department of National Defence which would administer the Navy, Army, Royal Military College, Militia Pensions, and R.C.M.P. Such a proposal to put civilian police under a department whose purposes were essentially military brought questions from the Progressives and the labour men. Woodsworth argued that the R.C.M.P. should be reduced in size, confined to policing the territories and kept a civilian force. "I doubt very much," he said, "whether the honour that was once attached to that force is maintained today. . . . I believe there is no other organization that causes so much friction in our communities as the North-West Mounted Police. . . . To a very considerable extent they are reduced to the position of being a secret service department."[5]

Remarks of this kind struck showers of sparks in many quarters. Woodsworth put on the record the kind of evidence of which many members were unaware. Over $100,000 was noted in the Minister's report as being "spent on special agents and detectives"; spies regularly attended the meetings of organizations like the O.B.U. and the Labour Church; American detectives were hired for labour espionage; night raids on trade-union leaders' homes, with general warrants, were common, and usually resulted in the seizure of books and journals. The 1920 court evidence of Corporal Zaneth showed that he had joined the Socialist Party of Canada and other labour organizations, distributed literature and acted, in Woodsworth's words, as an *agent-provocateur*. The use of Mounties in the Winnipeg strike was certainly provocative, he argued, and then he showed that the police officers had purchased evidence for the Crown's case. Nor was the R.C.M.P. activity limited: "I should not like to suggest how many thousands of dollars I have cost Canada in having the police trail me around. I want to make that very clear; possibly I was worth watching. But the things

[5]Hansard, 1922, pp. 670 *et seq.*

I am saying today are the very things for which I was trailed, and my fellow citizens in Winnipeg have very clearly given their verdict as to what they think of this sort of business."

Understandably, Woodsworth spoke with some heat when he recalled the efforts of the Mounted Police to discover the content of a lecture he had given at the University of Saskatchewan, or the time he was taken to a police office and asked to promise not to repeat statements he had made at a public meeting. Mr. Meighen's interjection that "within the last few years" there had been good reason for maintaining a strong R.C.M.P. led directly to Woodsworth's formal resolution that the force be confined to the territories.[6] His argument that four million dollars was an extravagant federal police expenditure (when in the same year a quarter of a million went to unemployment relief) was of some weight with an economy-minded government; the Minister of Militia and Defence agreed to cut down this amount.

Once the issue was squarely joined the Progressives came to Woodsworth's support. When H. C. Hocken of Toronto called Woodsworth a "red revolutionary," T. W. Bird, O. R. Gould and John Morison brought their prairie voices to counter the charge and labelled it the same "propaganda" as that put out by the Tory government during the strike. When the Conservative John Baxter of Saint John called for a vote "to stand up either for the reds or against them" the party lines broke slightly. Although the motion was lost 47 to 108, Woodsworth had rallied a large section of the Progressives behind him (and a few Quebeckers who voted on the grounds of provincial rights). The stormy debate was widely reported in the press and the impression was left that Woodsworth's attack was given validity by the Minister's promise to reduce the amount spent on the force. A similar resolution in 1923 produced more attacks on Woodsworth's motives and a clarification of party lines. Robert Forke had by this time marshalled many wavering Progressives and only the dissident "Ginger Group" voted for the resolution.[7]

The case for a repeal of the 1919 amendments was even stronger. The Liberal Ernest Lapointe had prepared the ground for an Immigration Act amendment in 1920. The predominantly Conservative Senate had vetoed the repeal then, and in 1922 the government sent Woodsworth's new repeal bill to a special committee which watered it down. Even so, it did not get high enough on the order paper for discussion in the House in 1922, and his bill for the repeal of section 98 was also snowed under by the government programme.

[6]*Ibid.*, pp. 829 *et seq.*
[7]*Ibid.*, 1923, pp. 1139 *et seq.*

The most interesting aspect of the opposition side of this preliminary skirmish was Arthur Meighen's statement about the origins of the 1919 amendment.[8] It was passed, he said, "because we were then having difficulty with just that [British] class of immigrants and we felt that we had to take some summary and effective method of dealing with the difficulty. . . ." Sufficient support was mustered to pass an Immigration Act amendment in 1926[9] which restored jury trial to the immigrant classes affected by the 1919 legislation. At the same session the offensive sections of the Criminal Code were also amended,[10] although again the asperity of the debate induced several members to charge Soviet influence, and Woodsworth to remark "I do not know why in Canada, other than because we are so near to the hysterical United States—we have to become so excited about Russia." And the obstruction of the Senate served to keep the question open.

Further evidence of the methods of the defunct Union Government was procured when E. J. McMurray asked for all the records of the 1919 communications between Ottawa and A. J. Andrews, General Ketchen, and the other federal agents in Winnipeg.[11] Some letters were produced, and McMurray, Woodsworth and any others who wished were permitted to examine the "personal" files on the subject. Among other things it was revealed that the lawyers who had been retained by the government and who were all associated with the Citizens' Committee received payment amounting to $154,020.20. The strike issue was far from dead and would be fought over many times in succeeding debates.

While such issues as this were fairly clear, there were areas of the immigration problem subtle enough to baffle even the most stalwart labour representative and socialist. One of the stubborn facts of North American history is that whenever organized labour has expressed itself on the subject of immigration it has appeared to be either conservative or outright exclusionist. Canadian labour has been no exception, and Woodsworth himself had seen in Winnipeg what can happen when a non-selective immigration policy dumps thousands of foreign workers into the labour market. In addition, he adopted his socialism in the twentieth century at the very time when socialists everywhere were dropping some of their nineteenth-century internationalism in favour of a larger infusion of nationalism.[12] Certainly much of his

[8]Ibid., 1922, p. 3285.   [9]Ibid., 1926, p. 4120.   [10]Ibid., p. 4085.
[11]Ibid., 1922, pp. 1068, 1182. See also Woodsworth's question (p. 2042) and the reply of Hon. James Murdock.
[12]An excellent discussion of this question is found in Franz Borkenau, *Socialism: National or International* (London, 1942).

socialism was nationalist and protective. At times his desire to protect the productive classes of Canada against exploitation clashed with his internationalism which, in foreign policy debates, was to become increasingly pronounced. There is no attempt here to say that his total attitude was consistent—and he did recognize, as the twenties gave way to the thirties, that he faced a dilemma. It was a dilemma faced in one way or another by all socialists of the century.

Out of this background Woodsworth tried to select the most defensible policy on immigration. He voted for the King-supported "effective restriction" policy which grew out of British Columbian pressure in 1922. In a time of unemployment, he argued, temporary exclusion was a valid policy. The problem of oriental labour in British Columbia, he asserted, was started by the C.P.R. and other corporations who brought orientals in for cheap manageable labour. Now that some of the immigrants at the coast had made a little money and were competing with small retailers and in the fishing industry, the exclusion cry was heard more often. But even exclusion of orientals was no answer, he argued, to the problem of maintaining adequate wage standards, since cheap labour was being used on the other side of the Pacific increasingly in industrial growth. How was Canada to solve her share of this world problem?

First, he suggested, we should not underestimate oriental nations. "I want to protest that the civilization of China and Japan is not what we have sometimes called heathen, and that it is not a low type of civilization."[13] We should realize, he argued, that we must improve our own standards of education in order to understand the problems of Asia. While admitting temporary exclusion, we should legislate for certain minimum labour standards and also prevent anti-union activities so that the orientals can share in the efforts of Canadian unions. In the final analysis, he said, the modern world economy is too integrated to preserve one nation's standards by a policy of excluding immigrants of any kind.

On each occasion that the immigration question came up Woodsworth related it to the unsatisfactory employment, living, and educational conditions of the country—conditions that should be improved before large-scale immigration could be accepted. Today, in a period of relatively full employment, of partially effective unemployment insurance, and of generally improved trade-union status, this position on immigration may seem to have lacked imagination. In the 1920's and 1930's, however, the hesitant advances toward individual economic security had still to be made.

[13]Hansard, 1922, p. 1570 *et seq.*

Together with William Irvine, Woodsworth made certain that all matters of concern to labour received a thorough airing, and that the pertinent planks of the I.L.P. obtained a good share of publicity. In this period the most striking instance of unsatisfactory labour conditions was to be found in the Cape Breton properties of the British Empire Steel Corporation. The question arose sharply after the amalgamation of various companies in Nova Scotia to form the large unit—British Empire Steel Corporation (BESCO). In January 1922 the company announced a wage cut of 37½ per cent, affecting 12,000 workers, most of whom were organized in District 26 of the United Mine Workers of America. The wage reduction meant that Nova Scotia miners' salaries would average about 71 per cent lower than those of Alberta, although the Nova Scotia cost of living was 17 per cent higher than that of Alberta. James Murdock, the federal Minister of Labour, had granted the U.M.W. request for a conciliation board, but the chairman's casting vote had been on the company side to sanction a wage cut of 32½ per cent. This the men rejected bitterly and they sent, without result, a delegation to the company's Montreal headquarters.

Semi-famine conditions appeared in northern Cape Breton and the men became desperate. They "struck on the job," that is, they cut back production to "equal" the pay cut, pleaded unsuccessfully with the provincial Liberal government to intervene, and sent a large delegation to Ottawa. The delegation was a cross-section of the Nova Scotia mining communities and included the mayors of Glace Bay, New Waterford, Dominion, and Springhill. When the Prime Minister refused their request for a royal commission, yet suggested no other federal action, Irvine obtained the adjournment of the House to discuss this serious crisis.[14]

Irvine outlined the steps in the drama and pointed to the recent corporate amalgamation with its issuance of nineteen million dollars of "watered stock." "If it is necessary," he maintained, "to pay dividends upon that watered stock, surely it can only be done by reducing the wages of the producers. . . . Surely there is some constitutional authority which will face the situation. . . . Human nature can stand only so much; if it gets a little more than it can stand, what is going to happen?" The Winnipeg strike was still fresh in everyone's mind, and here the issue was again joined.

Donald M. Kennedy, a U.F.A. Progressive from Edmonton, followed Irvine in urging that the government accept the responsibility which followed from the annual federal subventions to the Nova Scotia coal

[14]Ibid., pp. 497 et seq.

and steel industry—payments which he might have noted were started by Sir John A. Macdonald in the late 1880's and which had been continued ever since as a matter of national policy. To this, W. F. Carroll, one of the Liberal Cape Breton members, suggested that if the miners would resume full production, then the Nova Scotia government would appoint a royal commission. The Minister of Labour, joining the debate, suggested only that red agitators were at the bottom of the trouble.

When Woodsworth entered the discussion he argued that "the workers' curtailment of output is a natural, recognized mode of procedure in the business world today. There are factories all over Canada which, so soon as their managers think that profits are not sufficiently high to warrant further operation, curtail their production or sometimes stop work altogether. . . ." If it was wrong for labour to do this it was wrong for capital—and the solution was to be found in the nationalization and economic planning of large-scale industry. In the existing situation the workers had no choice, he argued, but starvation. Why could not the government act, instead of sheltering behind the tattered barrier of provincial rights? "Again and again it has intervened in industrial disputes across the country. . . . The trouble in Winnipeg . . . went on week after week. The municipality seemed almost helpless; the province seemed almost helpless. The federal government took no action for quite a time; then at last they did take action with a club. . . ." The power and the right were there, he argued; why wait for violence? In Nova Scotia, he concluded, the corporation had the provincial government by the throat and the miners had taken the only possible non-violent, and therefore the correct course in coming to Ottawa.

Progressives E. J. Garland, T. W. Bird, H. J. Logan, Agnes Macphail, and T. A. Crerar all gave support to the call for federal mediation. Logan said: ". . . it seems to me that the sentiments of the Progressive party and the sentiments of labour are very near together at the root. The reason for this Progressive group being here is because of the widespread discontent, of which this labour trouble in Nova Scotia is a manifestation." Charges of sedition made against the labour group, such as those made by the Minister of Labour, "kindle the farmers' hearts." The appointment by the government of a federal royal commission "would make it easier for a good many of us from now on to give them that whole-hearted support that we have it in mind to give them so long as they array themselves with the forces in this country that are making for righteousness. . . ." Here was a very different note than that struck by the farmer members of the strike trial juries—yet it was the note of men who were almost painfully desirous of returning to a purified major party.

It remained for Mr. Meighen to provide the real surprise of the debate when he remarked that the government had a duty to intervene in the Nova Scotia "class war" and when he supported the right of the miners to give two-thirds of a day's work for two-thirds of a day's pay. This bombshell, together with Agnes Macphail's long quotation from the Prime Minister's book *Industry and Humanity*, nettled the Prime Minister very considerably. R. MacGregor Dawson's biography of King[15] has nothing to say on this whole subject. King, according to his diary, knew very little about most of the subjects debated in the House, but one might have thought that his background in the Department of Labour—if not his work for the Rockefellers—would have given him some enlightenment here.

Appealing, perhaps, to his own Presbyterianism rather than to his liberalism, King berated the opposition leader for condoning "loafing on the job" which he stated to be one of the worst kinds of industrial warfare known. Nevertheless, when Crerar suggested reconvening the federal conciliation board and reconsidering the award, the Prime Minister agreed that if any member of the board requested this action it would be taken. He appealed to the miners to try again to obtain relief from the provincial government—a defence of those provincial rights for which King never ceased to have the highest regard.

Finally a new federal conciliation board was appointed, and when, one year later, there was still no settlement, Woodsworth again raised the matter in the House.[16] He noted a developing sentiment among the miners for direct action and quoted from a speech of the president of BESCO, who threatened to "withdraw his capital" if the "bolshevists" were not driven from Cape Breton. It seemed to be the old circle of repression, the apparent breakdown of constitutional avenues for the redress of grievances, and a growing sentiment for violent measures. Whether or not the government controlled "property and civil rights," argued Woodsworth, "it has the protection of the citizens of this country in its charge and action ought to be taken to prevent this matter from developing further. . . ." Once more came the ministry's answer that the Department of Labour had no coercive power. The Nova Scotia government was really responsible because BESCO operated under a provincial charter.

[15]R. MacGregor Dawson, *William Lyon Mackenzie King: A Political Biography, 1874–1923*, I (Toronto, 1958).   [16]Hansard, 1923, pp. 1704 *et seq.*

By the time Parliament met in 1924 the federal government had decided after all that it did have coercive power—but again it was the power of the club. When the province poured police into the strike-bound mining towns the federal Minister of National Defence, on the advice of a judge and over the protest of the local mayors, ordered in the militia. A number of union leaders were arrested and later released, but J. B. McLachlan, secretary of the U.M.W.A., District 26, was held on a charge of sedition. In his speech on the Address,[17] Woodsworth outlined the evidence of several recent investigations of conditions in Cape Breton: "These enquiries and commissions have revealed wretched housing and sanitary conditions, abuses connected with the company's stores, unsatisfactory working conditions, low wages, irregular work, and in the case of the steel workers, long working days of 11- and 13-hour shifts with every other week 24 hours on end. These unsatisfactory conditions prevail notwithstanding the fact that Canada was a signatory of the peace treaty under which the workers were supposed to be given an eight-hour day." It was high time, he argued, to investigate the employers, and he urged the appointment of a parliamentary committee to review war profits, absentee management, concealment of real profits through subsidiary companies, watered stock, and other devices of company directorates.

Despite the offer of parole to McLachlan, he still stood as a convicted criminal, said Woodsworth. And why? Because he circulated a letter protesting the brutal actions of the provincial police in running down men, women, and children—statements later substantiated by statutory declarations. He noted that the last man charged with seditious libel in Nova Scotia was Joseph Howe. But, unlike Howe, McLachlan could not claim to have had a fair trial. He had been bundled off to Halifax to face judges who had been so closely connected with the coal companies that Nova Scotia labour considered the court a company department. (Woodsworth named the company connections of four of the six judges and remarked that the other two were not *known* to have such connections.) Further, he observed, the Minister of National Defence, who sent in the troops, "has been, if he is not still, the solicitor for the coal companies. . . . Now, Mr. Speaker, if anything more were needed to destroy the respect for the impartiality of the courts, it was supplied by the congratulatory telegram sent by BESCO to the Attorney General of Nova Scotia." The speech ended with a strong plea for the repeal of the 1919 sedition legislation, without which McLachlan would not be lying in Dorchester Penitentiary.

[17]*Ibid.*, 1924, pp. 62 *et seq.*

Whether or not Woodsworth knew that the U.M.W. secretary was a communist (or about to become one) is not certain. But it would have made no difference in his position, as it had made no difference in Vancouver in the debates over direct action, or later in the treatment of Tim Buck. The great questions remained of the danger of depriving anyone of the widest possible civil liberty, and of the fundamental responsibility of government in matters of social welfare.

In February of 1925 the Cape Breton situation was still acute. The old agreement with the company had run out and a new one was stalled over the company's campaign for a further 10 per cent cut. Woodsworth had visited the area in January and observed the absolute destitution of the mining communities, where many of the men had been idle for the previous six months. "I might," he said, "very readily have escaped responsibility by simply saying that it was not the policy of the government to give relief."[18] But a myopic interpretation of the B.N.A. Act would do no good, since "need of a serious character knows no boundaries, provincial or even national." Again he reminded the government of its powers for peace, order, and good government and of the action of the Judicial Committee of the Privy Council in declaring *ultra vires* the Industrial Disputes Investigation Act. Something would have to be done to cut through the constitutional morass since now even a federal conciliation board could have no authority and the provincial government appeared very reluctant to offend the coal and steel directors.

With this reiterated appeal the Minister of Labour declared his great sympathy, but asserted that the province had "jurisdiction." Nova Scotia, he said, was always looking for something from the central government; the companies had received from Ottawa nineteen million dollars over the years; the Nova Scotia government received annually $600,000 in coal royalties and was therefore the proper authority from which to seek relief. What he said about "better terms" for Nova Scotia, the coal-steel subventions and provincial royalties was all correct, but seemed to imply a further federal right to intervene in case of gross maladministration of these federally underwritten benefits.

As usual, Arthur Meighen saw the logical weakness and, like Woodsworth, charged the government with using the B.N.A. Act only as an excuse for inaction. T. L. Church, Toronto's professional ex-mayor and the leading Tory democrat, underlined the point that the government which provided these benefits and controlled such things as

18*Ibid.*, 1925, pp. 459 *et seq.* Woodsworth, like Irvine earlier, had obtained adjournment to discuss this as a "matter of urgent public importance."

tariffs and immigration could not evade all responsibility for the conditions of the BESCO towns. E. J. Garland, W. C. Good, and others of the Ginger Group entered the lengthy debate examining living standards, the company's attitude, the activities of labour spies, and uniting in the demand for a government relief measure.

When the Prime Minister entered the discussion it was to announce that Nova Scotia's Premier Armstrong had just agreed to appoint an investigating commission and to request the company not to make its cut until after the investigation.

During the debates in Ottawa, the eastern situation deteriorated rapidly. An outbreak of violence at New Waterford prompted Woodsworth's question: "How far must it go before the government will intervene?"[19] And again, Murdock's reply that Ottawa would act if requested by the Nova Scotia government. Action quickly followed— with revolvers drawn. A "Ginger Group" question put by Shaw[20] drew from E. M. Macdonald, the Minister of National Defence, the announcement that correct constitutional procedure had been adhered to. The Attorney General of Nova Scotia had requested the sending of troops, after petition from the mayors of Sydney and Sydney Mines. Murdock, the House was informed, had left, like Robertson and Meighen in 1919, to act as conciliator. Commenting on the continuing Cape Breton tragedy, the *Canadian Forum* remarked that "the argument for nationalization here is overwhelming."[21]

Out of the 1925 crisis came an unsatisfactory compromise which, by the beginning of 1926, was further bedevilled by curtailment of production by the company. A. A. Heaps[22] and Woodsworth argued that the over-capitalization of the company, its alleged inability to pay a living wage and to provide steady employment called for a federal royal commission.[23] Further, if the tariff-subsidy policy and the C.N.R. coal-purchasing policy were to be continued, the government now had full grounds for taking over the industry entirely. When questioned as to whether the federal government would provide relief for the impoverished Nova Scotian communities, Ernest Lapointe announced that the government would "ask for authority" to assist the provinces in unemployment relief when critical conditions actually existed.[24]

[19]*Ibid.*, p. 4125.
[20]*Ibid.*, p. 4242.
[21]April, 1925.
[22]Heaps was elected in North Winnipeg in 1925 after defeat there in a 1923 by-election. He was re-elected in 1926. Irvine lost his seat in 1925 but regained it in 1926. Both men accepted Woodsworth as leader of their "group" in the House.
[23]Hansard, 1926, pp. 424 *et seq.*   [24]*Ibid.*, p. 497.

To Woodsworth the position of the workers in the web of the Nova Scotian coal-steel economy was further stark illustration of the need for planning and vigorous federal policies. On the floor of the House he expounded the ideas he had adopted earlier. No longer was it the fault of the individual worker if unemployment struck him down, he argued in the 1922 session.[25] Where were the skilled workers of the Nova Scotia mines and mills, of the Winnipeg railway shops, to turn if their employers decided to curtail production? Economic dislocation usually started, he argued, with the decision of the Montreal bank directors to restrict credit and to accept periodic unemployment as a necessary corrective in the trade cycle. What, then, of the workers and their families? "Any administrative body in a country capable of producing as Canada can produce, which fails to provide for the primary needs of its people even to the extent of food and clothing and shelter, ceases to command the loyalty of those people. . . ." When the Prime Minister interrupted with a sharp question "Any concrete suggestions?" Woodsworth appealed for action at the current session to investigate the problem and establish a system of unemployment insurance, suggesting that this would lead into other necessary fields. King's emphatic answer was that unemployment relief was a municipal-provincial problem, and only in the last resort should it concern Ottawa.

Despite the perpetual frustration of the B.N.A. Act, Woodsworth campaigned to improve the legal position of Canadian workers. When the company town at Powell River in British Columbia implemented the instructions of its American directors to outlaw trade unions, Woodsworth was on his feet declaiming: "Surely here is one case in which there can be no conflict of authority; here is one instance in which the federal government can act. If the federal government is not in a position to assure civil rights to the people, I want to know for what we exist?"[26] Mr. Vien, of Lotbinière, speaking for the Liberal provincial rightists, chided Woodsworth: "You ought to know your B.N.A. Act." And Woodsworth replied, "I am not going to offer any threat. . . . But I should like to offer a little bit of advice, if I may, to the country and to the government. Some of us have been trying to urge that the labour people act through what are termed constitutional methods. . . . But how can we do so with any hope of success if the government admits that under present circumstances it is helpless to protect the men?" If, he argued, property and civil rights were

[25]*Ibid.*, 1922, p. 1071.
[26]*Ibid.*, 1923, pp. 2892 *et seq.*

entirely within the provincial sphere, why did the federal government send troops to Nova Scotia? What, indeed, was the meaning of residual powers in a federal constitution?

In 1925 he moved that the government limit the hours of work on federal public works to eight hours a day and forty-eight hours a week.[27] Were the labour provisions of the peace settlement to be a scrap of paper? "I ask that the government no longer continue to allow this question to be made a football, to be kicked or thrown backward and forward between the federal authorities, the workers being allowed to suffer in the meantime." He urged King to use the undoubted federal power to bring various works under Ottawa's jurisdiction by declaring them to be for the general advantage of the nation. There were many industrial, mining, and railway operations benefiting from tariff protection or federal assistance of other kinds that could be accurately named in this way.

Two members of the government replied to this request. The Minister of Labour argued that the different wage levels in different areas had to be recognized. The Prime Minister asked: "Do honourable members think that the friends of labour are going to assist the cause of labour by provoking that kind of controversy between the provinces and the dominion in these matters?" As for BESCO being declared a work for the general advantage of Canada, "They are doing work for large numbers of private industries, for the province of Nova Scotia and for other provinces and concerns with which this government has nothing whatever to do."

Neither of the government spokesmen answered directly the main questions of Woodsworth's motion: how was the international labour code of 1919 to be enforced by Canada, and how far were the major economic undertakings of the country to be left in isolated provincial pockets as far as social welfare was concerned? The answer given was a political one, based on the knowledge of a provincial rights movement and the Liberal tradition of safeguarding provincial jurisdiction.

After some rather sharp crossfire, Woodsworth withdrew his motion in order that Irvine could move for the eigh-hour day on all recognized Dominion works. This was declared out of order because Irvine had already spoken in the debate. Then E. J. Garland moved the same thing, only to be ruled out of order on a technicality. The incident was only one of many; the Ginger Group was testing the almost unlimited power at the disposal of a responsible ministry. But it was also helping to educate public opinion—a growing body of opinion

[27]Ibid., 1925, pp. 4750 et seq.

which would finally give support to a broader concept of national minimum standards of social welfare.

In the meantime the Prime Minister gave full confidence to Ernest Lapointe who continued to assert the extreme compact theory of Confederation. Heralding the approaching Dominion-provincial conference he said the meeting would be a second Quebec Conference, and that it was now realized that changes in the B.N.A. Act must have the prior consent of all the provinces.[28]

[28]*Canadian Forum*, March, 1925.

12

ASSESSING
"NATIONAL POLICIES"

THE ATTACK FROM THE LEFT, forceful considering the diminutive group that launched it, was perhaps even more penetrating during debate on such matters as fiscal policy and public ownership. Woodsworth's first speech on a Liberal budget showed that he had applied his socialist principles to Canadian history.[1] He observed that the government proposed to raise most of its revenue from tariff and indirect taxes—those methods which pressed hardest upon the common man and favoured the wealthy. Was this government, he asked, like previous Canadian governments, only concerned with giving a clear field to exploiters? Already the greater part of Canadian mining, lumber, and pulp resources was owned by Americans. Most of the country's natural resources, which should belong to the people, had been virtually given away in the preceding years. And now, with the exploitation of these resources and the growing industries based upon them, wealth was steadily being concentrated in the hands of a very small class. David Mills, the first serious advocate of public ownership of national railways, was quoted from the 1880's to illustrate "the reckless way in which our franchises were given away in those early days." Using the Drayton-Acworth report, Woodsworth stressed the tremendous assistance, amounting to nearly three hundred million dollars, that had been given to private railways and that now was largely foisted on the public as part of the C.N.R. debt load. For industry, he used the government's own statistics to show the consolidation of business holdings, which had resulted in control by the private banks of "the very

[1]Hansard, 1922, pp. 2242 et seq.

life of the people." And the culminating indictment, he argued, rested in the Liberal failure to redress any of the grievances of the war period.

This most recent form of exploitation, cried Woodsworth, was a magnificent opportunity for the profiteer. "We know the huge fortunes that were made during the wartime from the revelations of the committee on the high cost of living. . . . There has been no effort made by the incoming government, so far as I can see, to recover from the profiteers the blood money which they laid up during the time of war." Pointing to the low income taxes of Canada (11 per cent of the government revenue came from this source in 1917–18) he asked,

How did we do our war financing? We borrowed and we borrowed more instead of paying as we went. . . . The food and clothing and ammunition which were needed during the war were produced during the war. The high financing which we did at that time was, after all, a matter of bookkeeping by which a comparatively limited group of people obtained a stranglehold on the rest of the country. . . . We today have a right to say whether those people shall or shall not retain their ill-gotten gains.

Although he did not use names such as Flavelle, Pellatt or Mann, or any of the St. James Street contributors to the party campaign chests, the House knew the significance of the attack.

In one way, this kind of sustained analysis of the nature of exploitation harked back to the days when the Liberals' ancestors called themselves Clear Grits; or earlier to the onslaughts of a Mackenzie, a Gourlay, or a Bidwell. But there was a difference. The earlier Canadian criticism of the family compact or the Ottawa "boodlers" had been conducted by men and on behalf of men who, in their desire to break politico-economic monopoly, had as an aim the creation of a "free enterprise" competitive society which would give them "equal opportunity" with everyone else to become prosperous. Now the aim, after years of experience with the principle of competition, was modified by the broad concepts of co-operation and democratic planning. The two eras of radicalism had in common the essentially conservative desire of protecting national resources from prodigal exploitation, and the liberal one of rendering the common people independent economically and politically.

These aims compelled Woodsworth to go a long way in his analysis of the 1922 budget.

I think, of several hundreds of [unemployed returned soldiers] who are reported to be marching on Ottawa at the present time in the hope that they will be able to present their case to the House. Have those men no claim upon the resources of the country? . . . It seems to me, Mr. Speaker, that we shall have to face in the near future the ultimate and final solution of these huge debts which we have accumulated. Personally, I can see nothing for it but repudiation or a capital levy. . . . We do not call it repudiation when a man has stolen a large amount and the state comes along and takes it back.

The practical difficulty, created by the fact that some of the debt had changed hands, could be met by following Britain along the road of progressive direct taxation of those able to pay, and this was particularly just, he argued, as deflation proceeded to double the value of the bonds then held.

In the following year, 1923, Woodsworth seized the opportunity offered by the government's introduction of a new combines investigation bill to examine still further the problem of exploitation.[2] The Prime Minister had indicated that the purpose of the bill was to facilitate governmental inspection of combines, trusts, mergers, and monopolies. King had been responsible, while he was assistant to Labour Minister Lemieux in 1909, for the first act of this kind in Canada (apart from earlier clauses in the tariff laws and Criminal Code), and, like Theodore Roosevelt in the same period, he had insisted that it was essential to distinguish between "good trusts" and "bad trusts." The new bill was required because earlier legislation had been repealed by the Board of Commerce Act of 1919 which, in turn, had been ruled *ultra vires* by the Judicial Committee of the Privy Council, leaving no separate anti-trust legislation on the statute books of Canada.

The distinction between "good" and "bad" trusts the Prime Minister repeated in 1923 as justification for the secrecy which was to surround the investigation of big business under the new act. Secrecy was essential, he asserted, in order that "good trusts" would not be damaged by the public knowledge that they were being investigated. If such investigation showed a trust to be "bad" (detrimental to the public interest) the bill provided no enforcement machinery other than the full publicity of the commissioners' final report. Once it is known that a trust is bad, said King, "it is natural to expect that the public will speedily find some means to protect itself." He did not suggest the nature of the means that might be found, and the whole history of American anti-trust legislation since 1890, together with the unsolved dilemma of American progressivism, suggested that his assumptions were shaky at best. When Stevens and Hanson for the

[2]*Ibid.*, 1923, pp. 2551 *et seq.*

Conservatives had finished condemning the "inquisition" to be established by the legislation, and alleging that farmers' co-operatives were also combines, Woodsworth put the socialist case.

Observing that the Webbs in England and "most socialists" favoured combines as partial advances toward greater economic efficiency, he said, "it is impossible for us effectively to break up these combines. The only possible thing for us to do if we want really effective action is to take hold of them and carry them one step further until we have such a complete combine that the public, through its various organizations, co-operative, municipal, provincial and federal, will be able to use it for its own purposes. . . . This is essentially the age of combinations and insofar as we still have competition it is indication of incomplete development." Thorough regulation was impossible, he concluded, and in any case it was not even envisaged by this bill.

Following in the steps of David Mills, who had feared that the C.P.R. bargain of 1880 would make a corporation the proprietor of the Canadian government, Woodsworth declared that the people must decide whether the inevitable industrial and financial combinations would control the political authority or *vice versa*. "Let us have combines," he exclaimed, "and let us appoint officials to administer them who will decide their policies with a view to the public interest." When it came to deciding how he would vote on the bill, Woodsworth declared himself for it, but without enthusiasm. The publicity it would provide would be good and would perhaps lead to the time when the House would "begin in a democratic way to operate these larger units."

While most of the earlier radicals in Canadian history had not seriously contemplated the use of government to operate economic enterprise and had been content to attack monopoly, still there was a tradition of positive government in Canada which is not just one of our great historical myths. The United Empire Loyalists had been subsidized; the pioneers had petitioned for roads, bridges, post offices, and then canals and railways. Sometimes, as in Nova Scotia, governments had built railways and almost always they subsidized them heavily. The tariff itself smacked of government planning and then had come coal-iron subsidies, assisted immigrant passages, public health grants-in-aid to provincial governments, and the Wheat Board. In the provinces themselves there were such experiments as publicly owned telephones and hydro-electric power systems. Even some municipal governments had entered the utility field with organizations like the Toronto Transportation Commission. Most of these reflected

Conservative or Western Progressive rather than Liberal policies. They implied a recognition of two apparent facts: that the welfare of the individual could be advanced through collective action guided by political authority, and that the circumstances of Canadian geography and population dictated collective action. What Woodsworth was attempting was the application of socialist thought to a nebulous Canadian experience which pointed to political-economic conclusions similar to his own. He was bound to take exception not only to the Liberal budget speech of 1923 but also to the amendment offered by Robert Forke on behalf of the orthodox wing of the Progressives.

Forke had called for all-round tariff reductions and a heavy tax on unearned incomes. Although he agreed with the amendment as far as it went, said Woodsworth, free trade did not touch the root of the modern problem any more than did the King panacea of governmental economy.[3] Given the resources of the country and an industrious population, he argued, it was sheer nonsense to tolerate the unemployment that was afflicting the nation and being ignored by the government. What plan for our economic improvement did the government offer, he asked. "Well, they are taking a tax off candies and putting a little higher duty on raisins. Is that a proper solution?" Free trade, he asserted, might have been a useful measure in an earlier period when there was real competition between the trading classes. The desirable path to follow now, however, was that of increasing collective action which would find at least a focal point in the central government.

Woodsworth stuck to this central theme—that democracy must be broadened out from the political to the economic field. "We are producing," he said, "in a collective way, and yet our institutions, economic and political, are lagging behind our method of production." Planning and democratic control of the economy must come, he said, because "we have forgotten the primary reason for production." The radical nature of his argument in 1923 may best be estimated by comparing it to the remarks of the official Progressive leader, Robert Forke, in the same budget debate: ". . . The tariff is the great bone of contention and the cause of ill feeling, hatred, envy and jealousy and, in short, is responsible for the condition of the world today."

Apart from the major proposition of bringing under public or cooperative ownership the means of production and distribution, there were many specific and immediate questions of economic control on

[3]*Ibid.*, pp. 2718 *et seq.*

which Woodsworth and the more radical Progressives were in complete agreement. In 1923, Robert Gardiner, E. J. Garland, and Woodsworth led an attack on the government's policy of leasing water-power sites to private firms without adequate reservations.[4] And in a later debate Woodsworth argued that even the direction of the publicly owned C.N.R. had been allowed to drift too far away from direct control of the people's representatives. Such a great corporation, he argued, cannot be effectively kept out of politics, and the board of directors was still further independent in that it contained no representation of the railway workers.[5] The mere appointment of a board of directors by the government, he said, was an insufficient guarantee that the road would be operated in the public interest. The government, after all, was only a committee of the Liberal party, and since any amendments to government policy were considered as want of confidence motions, the government supporters were reduced to silence and the opposition to impotence.

Here Woodsworth showed that he was no mere doctrinaire. He would not be content with mere forms of public ownership but recognized the evolution of a problem which has disturbed British socialists much, especially since 1945: the question of safeguarding democracy in the administration of public enterprise. Certainly Woodsworth was never caught unawares by the argument that people should not look to the government for protection against economic forces beyond their own control. In 1927 he seized upon the government's decision to increase the salaries of the Supreme Court Judges, in order to examine this contention.[6] "It is a rather deplorable condition," he declared, "if such men [as judges] when needed for the service of their country refuse to render that service except in return for eight, ten or fifteen thousand dollars a year" while the average wage is under one thousand dollars and when the government answers the call for social legislation with the horrific term "paternalism." "That term 'paternalistic' always amuses me. If this proposal for judges' salaries and pensions is not paternalistic—the caring for these poor gentlemen who have to maintain social and other obligations—I do not know what it is. . . ."

Perhaps the chief beneficiaries of the old kind of paternalism were Canada's bankers. Under the Bank Act which came up for review decennially, they enjoyed a monopoly control of credit and currency value which was reflected in the steady amalgamation amongst the banks, and in the serious restrictions on the credit available to farmers

[4]*Ibid.*, pp. 3421 *et seq.*
[5]*Ibid.*, pp. 3635 *et seq.*　　　　　　[6]*Ibid.*, 1927, pp. 1558 *et seq.*

and workers who were considered by great bank presidents to be "poor risks." All this constituted Canada's sound banking system and was a focal point of the Progressive-socialist attack.

In 1923, a review year for the Bank Act, Woodsworth, Irvine, and several Progressives obtained seats on the House Banking and Commerce Committee. There they had an opportunity to question representatives of the banks and to air their own opinions on money and banking. It was the beginning of a long campaign to educate Parliament and the public in this complex field, a campaign which eventually produced Bennett's Bank of Canada and, in 1937, the King act giving full government ownership of the central Bank. This key instrument of economic control is one of the greatest achievements of the long and consistent pressure from the political Left on the federal Liberal party. While the financial theories of the Left ran through the spectrum from funny-money social credit to sober proposals for farm credits, their common denominator was both sensible and progressive; certainly they threw into stark relief the archaic and obscure doctrines of the bankers' government.

In 1923 the bill to extend the bank charters for another ten years was piloted by W. S. Fielding—the man who, in 1886, had headed the Nova Scotia legislature when it advocated secession from Confederation and who had entered the 1897 Laurier government to help Sir Wilfrid transform the Liberals into a protectionist party of big business. It came as no surprise when Fielding pooh-poohed the arguments advanced in committee by the Progressives, or when he countered Speakman's amendment, calling for a one-year renewal of the charters and further investigation of the banking system, with the statement that the farmers had not "established" their views.[7] "I am largely of the opinion," said Fielding, "that one good crop in the West—let us pray heaven that it come this year—will remove very much of the irritation that exists among our Western friends. . . ." Why not, he suggested amiably, let the bill slide through the committee stage without worrying about amendments?

Fielding's suave approach did not deflect the attack of the farmers or of labour. Woodsworth opened up the matter sharply when he described the implications of the bank monopoly. "It means," he declared, "the power to determine very largely what can be produced, where it can be produced and under what conditions it can be produced." With no provision for the establishment of small banks, no provision for long-term loans and "no provision for work and the

[7]Ibid., 1923, pp. 4014 et seq.

capacity to work being regarded as the basis upon which public loans may be obtained," the Bank Act was the worst kind of class legislation. He reviewed the proceedings of the House Banking Committee which had been rendered pyrotechnic by the recent failure of the Merchants' Bank in which many depositors had lost their savings. This fiasco, the high current interest rates, and the nature of the monopoly had led to certain amendments being proposed in the committee, such as the appointment of a government auditor, regular inspection of the banks and provision in the Act for small banks and co-operative banking credit institutions.

All the amendments had been turned down, but the evidence and discussion had convinced Woodsworth that the bankers themselves, while claiming that the gold standard must be retained, did not know what that standard was or what money and credit really represented. What they did understand, he said, was how to create and maintain an irresponsible monopoly. He then turned to statistics, to lay before the House some of the evidence proving the extent to which the banks were the control point of a monopolistic system of interlocking directorates. From the board of the Bank of Montreal the names of Sir William Meredith, Sir Charles Gordon, R. B. Angus, Lord Shaughnessy, H. R. Drummond, J. H. Ashdown, Lieut.-Col. H. Molson, D. F. Angus, and others were linked to the vast industrial-commercial-financial empire which, through their position on the boards of other companies, these men controlled. The result, he pointed out, was that "we have had the division of labour go on until the financial men form a group by themselves and the other people who actually do the manufacturing, whether the employees or the employers, the organizers and managers do not really own the factories." From the great American jurist, Louis Brandeis, he drew the opinion that both loss of liberty and intimidation were inherent in such a system. Further, the system itself tended to self-perpetuation, the establishment of an hereditary financial feudalism. "It is strange how some of the old family names crop up. I am reminded that some generations ago in this country a fight had to be made against what was known as the family compact. . . . There is today a far more serious menace to the welfare of this country than was the family compact in our grandfathers' days. . . ."

The whole nature of our society, claimed Woodsworth, was determined by the men at the top of this pyramid. Sir Arthur Currie of McGill, for example, was a point of contact with the universities, and J. H. Ashdown with the educational and religious policies of the West. Gouin, he implied, as Minister of Justice and the man responsible for the R.C.M.P., would surely be influenced by his pulp and paper holdings when he authorized use of the Mounties in the Powell River company town in British Columbia. The operations of this close-knit class, said Woodsworth, were displayed clearly to the Progressive members of the banking committee when even an amendment guaranteeing bank clerks the right to organize was killed by the Conservative-Liberal majority.

Other Progressive speakers opened up various aspects of this question in supporting the Speakman amendment, particularly complaining of the swarm of paid lobbyists who had descended upon Ottawa to ensure passage of the Bank Act. Speaker after speaker observed that the government seemed more anxious to "slam through the ten-year contract" than to bring the directors of the Merchants' Bank before the House to explain the reasons for its failure. E. W. Bird of Nelson noted the "very significant combination of forces brought about in this House to prevent us in this quarter securing what we consider to be a very reasonable delay in the revision of the Act." Agnes Macphail was sarcastic about "the undue haste of the bankers and their friends in this matter" while E. J. Garland and G. G. Coote derided the government for keeping the House late at night, leaving the matter till almost the end of the session and ruling out of order all discussion of the Merchants' Bank failure.

In essence, this was the old North American drama of attacking the "Monster" of banking—a monster which had not lost its grip since Andrew Jackson fought Nicholas Biddle or W. L. Mackenzie attacked the Bank of Upper Canada in the 1830's. But the nature of the monopoly was again fully exposed for those who cared to see, and many Progressives were moving through this debate to a position to the left of mere agrarian or sectional revolt. In the Bankers' Association they saw not only the monopoly of easterners but the centre of an economic-political system that embraced all the provinces equally. And the argument of the legal lobby that there was really brisk competition among Canadian banks they believed no more than did Mr. Graham Towers in 1953 when he told the bankers that in their league it was not "nearly as tough as it is in the cloak and suit trade."[8]

In the several votes taken at various stages of the debate, all amendments were cast aside over the combined Progressive-Labour vote—amendments attempting to limit the re-chartering to one year, to

[8]Toronto *Globe and Mail*, Feb. 5, 1953. Mr. Towers was answering the bankers who combined in vigorous opposition to the chartering in Canada of a Dutch bank.

establish a government audit of banks, to guarantee organizing rights to bank employees, to reduce the amount of capital required before a charter might be issued, to send the bill back to committee for evidence concerning the Merchants' Bank (which was by this time resting quietly in the arms of the Bank of Montreal) and to limit the legal interest rate on loans to 7 per cent or even 8 per cent.

In 1923, then, the bankers won; but the attack continued. In 1925 Woodsworth again used the House as a medium of public education when he moved "that . . . it is not in the interest of the country at large that the privilege of issuing currency and of controlling financial credit should be granted to private corporations."[9] The resolution, he said, was purposely negative in form because the "first step is to show the injustice and inefficiency of the existing system." He accused the bankers of not knowing the real nature of money, quoting from J. M. Keynes, F. W. Taussig, and others to build up his case for managed currency. It was the beginning of a very important education of the Liberal party. Woodsworth showed by reference to the 1924 meetings of the banking committee that Sir Frederic Williams Taylor "did not appear to have any scientific or economic knowledge of the money situation; in fact, he himself said that he was simply a practical banker." The fetish of the gold standard, Woodsworth showed, really meant nothing because the bankers themselves did not understand it or realize that gold was not an automatic regulator and that prices were set by a number of influences: the amount of money in circulation, the availability of credit, the state of the labour market, productive capacity, and so on.

Basically, argued Woodsworth, those who control credit control the price of all things. "Why," he asked, "should not the government democratically control this money situation rather than allow a group of a dozen men who are not responsible to the people to do so? . . . Thus we face the larger question as to whether or not the people are to be sovereign, as to whether we have not had our liberties filched from us without most of us having been aware of what has taken place."

The "debate" was adjourned without question put, and in the course of it the Speaker had to ask a noisy House for quiet. Already many members were both bored and annoyed with repetitive criticism of a system which they themselves enjoyed, or with analysis of money theories which they found obscure.

But neither the criticism nor the analysis would cease, and when the banks stayed high and dry in the depression while the "rags and

[9]Hansard, 1925, pp. 753 et seq.

ends of confederation" foundered in economic catastrophe, the audience finally gave ear. And along the route there was support for criticism of specific favours showered upon the "Monster" by government action—for example, when able members like S. W. Jacobs of Montreal (Liberal) and W. C. Good of Ontario (Progressive) backed Woodsworth's suggestion that the government policy of raising a one hundred million dollar loan through the Bank of Montreal, at a charge of five million dollars, should be reversed in favour of employing national credit directly.[10] And later in 1925 the government saw fit, under the bright light of banking criticism, to pay $5,450,000 for the relief of depositors in the Home Bank, which had followed the Merchants' Bank into oblivion. By the spring of 1926 Woodsworth was able to state in the House, while arguing his motion for a "national system of banking," that the Bankers' Association had thought it desirable to spend one hundred thousand dollars "in connection with the revision of the Bank Act."[11]

[10]*Ibid.*, p. 4020.
[11]*Ibid.*, 1926, p. 2417.

13

MILITARISM,

IMPERIALISM, AND NATIONALISM

WOODSWORTH WAS, PERHAPS SURPRISINGLY, held in high regard by many Quebeckers. For this the main reason was the prominence given to his speeches both inside and outside the Commons on militarism and Canada's external relations. In the 1925 election campaign, for example, the Winnipeg *Weekly News* (October 23) was able to quote N. K. Laflamme, a Montreal Liberal, who said of Woodsworth: ". . . a man of absolute sincerity, perhaps a little ahead of his time. But who can tell? Times are changing. We Quebec members were at first astonished and inclined to be suspicious of Mr. Woodsworth; I am glad to say that feeling has disappeared. Upon becoming acquainted with him we find that we like him very much."

But there were always those in Quebec who had their doubts about his position on the subjects of militarism and imperialism because it became increasingly evident that he viewed them as part of a total pattern of exploitation. Although he had much in common with Laurier in his desire to avoid Canadian entanglement in the vortex of European militarism, his conclusions were reached not only from observation of the European scene but also from his analysis of the nature of Canadian capitalism.

In a standing militia he saw not only the suggestion of imperial tribute but a threat to organized labour's right to strike. The immorality of the whole social system was the backdrop to his attitude to war and imperialism; thus he had more in common with a progressive thinker like Bourassa than with nineteenth-century Liberals like Laurier or Lapointe. But however this may be, there can be no question that Woodsworth did more than anyone else in the 1920's and 1930's to stimulate discussion of Canada's external relations. It may be that in his enthusiasm and in his willingness to experiment he sometimes arrived at dubious conclusions, but in the process of arriving at them he induced many Canadians to take a far broader view of political purposes than they would otherwise have done.

In 1922 Canada was not in any sense a strong military nation. Yet she had played a significant part in the war and her independent status was in process of recognition. There was a question, therefore, of whether that status should be clearly stated, and of what kind of international rôle Canada would seek to play. With respect to status, Woodsworth was strongly in favour of a clear statement rather than a vague understanding—just as he had earlier opposed the vague meaning of the Methodist Discipline which many had told him was implicit in its terminology. He was equally insistent that Canada should give an unequivocal lead in disarmament and therefore, he thought, toward world peace. Thus, although post-war economy had already pared the "defence budget" almost to the vanishing point, he fought it as a symbol of capitalist force in domestic affairs and co-operation with imperialism abroad. The immense carrying charges of the war debt supplied additional fuel to his argument.

In the first militia vote in 1922 he led such an attack, backed fully by a number of Progressives, that the Minister (Graham) offered to "follow the suggestion of the House" and reduce by $700,000 his proposed estimate of $1,100,000. "It seems," said Woodsworth, "to be taken for granted that we must follow the example of European nations and proceed to arm. . . . Now I should like to challenge the implication that in order that we may become a self-sufficient nation it is necessary for us to maintain a militia force."[1] While the nations of the world are discussing disarmament, he argued, "we in Canada are in a peculiarly good position to accomplish it. We have the Pacific on the West, the Atlantic on the East; we are bordered by a friendly nation to the South; why should we be prepared to resist aggression on any of these fronts? . . ." In the House we may argue about some unnamed enemy, he declared, but in the country there is a feeling that, having fought to end war, "we should try to get back to an absolute peace basis. . . . Now is the time when we should decide whether or not an armed force means or makes for peace. . . ."

He then recalled Graham's argument that the militia was necessary for defence against internal disturbance, and said that this plea might

[1]Hansard, 1922, pp. 1143 et seq.

be valid for European or imperial states faced with the problem of subject races, but it was preposterous as applied to Canada:

I do not think we have any classes that are particularly dangerous. A good many of our forefathers came here to escape the military burdens of Europe; why should we proceed to set up military forces in this country similar to those which they left in Europe? If we provide for the needs of the people there is no doubt that we shall have a loyal population. . . . Instead of being an insurance against trouble [the permanent militia] are rather, it seems to me, provocative of trouble.

Here was the core of his argument against military expenditures—even the dilemma of "the friendly nation to the South" which, far from avoiding in future years he would enter still more deeply. The details and implications of the position he elaborated on every possible occasion and he was sure, right down to 1939, of a heavy backing right across the country. For although few Canadians would go all the way with his pacifism, most of them were isolationist, with respect to both imperial politics and world problems, and many agreed with him about the relationship between military strength and the capitalist system.

In 1922, when the naval estimates were up, he reminded the Minister that national disarmament was not just his own personal recommendation. It was the hope "of the people who sent me here."[2] As far as any naval expenditure was concerned, he insisted, no action at all should be taken until after the next Imperial Conference (1923), "until it is decided what the status of Canada really is." Canada must not again fall into the trap which caught Laurier: that of undertaking an independent navy on the assumption that its use would be decided at home, and then finding that it was automatically committed to war as a result of policies, in the formation of which Canada had no voice. The mental attitudes of 1910 must be abandoned, he declared; "surely the war has taught us . . . that preparedness does not insure us against war, but that the surest way of creating or maintaining peace . . . is that we should indeed scrap our navies and our great armaments." In 1925 Woodsworth declared that it was then clear that the "war to end war" had been merely a skirmish. War, he insisted, was caused primarily by commercial interests and it was time to assert that Canada should tell her militarists that she proposed to obtain national defence "along other lines. . . . I recognize that the policy which I have advocated would involve risks, but the present policy involves not only risk but almost certain failure. Why not take those risks which are

[2]*Ibid.*, pp. 1854 *et seq.*

incident to the development of the new means of protecting our nation?"[3]

As the Conservatives entered the debate to demand heavier naval expenditure toward fulfilment of Canada's "imperial obligations," Woodsworth seized upon Guthrie's assumption that the navy should automatically grow as the nation grows. "That," he declared, "is precisely the militaristic point of view according to which militarism is an essential part of any nation's life." For Canada, as for himself, he desired the rôle of pioneer, and as a pioneer he had declared total war on militarism, capitalism, and imperialism. Thus when T. L. Church complained that the parsimonious Liberals had lopped one hundred thousand dollars off the grant for "cadet services" and would thereby eliminate the cadet summer camps, Woodsworth agreed that physical education for youth was excellent, but deplored "any expenditure which will tend to develop the military spirit amongst the boys of this country."[4] From the speech of a Brigadier-General delivered before a Vancouver high school audience he quoted: "That nation whose boys can think clearly and shoot straight is the nation that will be able to impose its will upon other nations." Woodsworth commented bitterly that such teaching "is what we have ordinarily termed Prussianism—Prussianism pure and simple, and Prussianism does not look any more attractive to me in a British uniform than it does in a German uniform."

In his attacks on cadet training Woodsworth was supported by Agnes Macphail, E. J. Garland, and other Progressives. They regularly supplied the press with material for sarcastic editorial comment. In 1925, H. E. Spencer was able to read a resolution of the Canadian Council of Agriculture demanding that the annual cadet grant be changed to one for physical education to be administered by the provinces,[5] and Woodsworth caught the Militia Minister, E. M. Macdonald, in a particularly vulnerable point. Macdonald was arguing that cadet training was really educational, and therefore worthy, when Woodsworth reminded him of his party's tenderness towards provincial rights and that the greatest single provincial jurisdiction was the field of education. He clinched the point by reading a letter from a Manitoba M.L.A. proving that the Manitoba government had given no specific authority for cadet training. If Woodsworth was considered to be a crank on this subject, the supporters of cadet training and

[3]*Ibid.*, 1925, pp. 3298 *et seq.*
[4]*Ibid.*, 1922, pp. 1974 *et seq.*
[5]*Ibid.*, 1926, p. 4869.

higher military budgets were open to equally strong criticism of the hollowness of many of their arguments.

Cadet training was, to Woodsworth, one bulwark of an ambitious capitalist society; other outworks of that society also drew his fire. In 1923, for example, the first vote of ten thousand dollars was passed for the national war memorial in Ottawa—the monument which was to be dedicated by George VI in the opening year of the Second World War. Woodsworth criticized the expenditure on many grounds, but primarily because, in a time when essential services were being curtailed, the money could be spent more wisely; and because the monument was essentially of the wrong kind. "May I suggest," he exhorted, "that instead of spending money on the fallen they spend the money for the clothing, feeding and sheltering of the men who had the great misfortune to return to Canada with their lives. It is no fault of theirs if they are not among the so-called glorious dead."[6]

On this occasion King justified his stand to Woodsworth. He did so because Woodsworth had buttressed his charges with evidence of suffering, such as the letter he read from a war widow whose case fell outside the government's rather limited plan of veteran assistance. The Prime Minister declared that he certainly had no thought of "glorifying militarism" but that patriotism and sacrifice must be honoured. "There is a saying," he remarked, "which my honourable friend will recall, to the effect that man does not live by bread alone." And when Woodsworth countered that it was difficult to live without bread, King answered that if it is a choice "I think the majority of men would prefer the spirit of sacrifice to bread."

If Canada were ever to pioneer in a serious effort to cut free from military traditions, to disarm completely and concentrate on international co-operation and internal social welfare, thought Woodsworth, she would have to be certain of her complete political independence. Thus, although he took no part in the debate over the method of negotiating and ratifying the halibut treaty with the United States in 1923, he was in full sympathy with the King-Lapointe assertion of Canada's unfettered treaty-making power. The importance of this final step in the long debate over the right of Canada to conclude her own foreign treaties or to appoint a Canadian minister to Washington in 1926 was not overlooked by Woodsworth; but when the trend was proceeding along lines of which he approved he held his peace. It was upon the shady realm of indefinition that he expended most

[6]*Ibid.*, 1923, pp. 2686 *et seq.*

effort, in an attempt to obtain clear recognition of full political independence or to question the direction of any tentative foreign policy
upon which the government might embark.

While he fully endorsed King's refusal to commit Canada to support
Britain in the Chanak crisis of 1922, he deprecated the government's
negotiation of a trade treaty with Italy while it failed to establish
commercial relations with Russia.[7] Although many were to accuse him
later of blind isolationism, a review of the record indicates that he
recognized the interdependence of the twentieth century earlier and
more clearly than did most Liberals, including the Prime Minister. In
1923 he declared it was impossible to adopt a negative attitude to
European affairs; for example, if Canada saw fit, as she did, to penalize
"forceful revolution" in Russia, she should logically do the same for
Italy. In particular, Woodsworth argued that Canadians should reject
secret diplomacy and hold suspect the foreign policy of any British
government that did not realize the essential iniquity of the Versailles
treaty. Quoting from J. A. Hobson, H. N. Brailsford, F. S. Nitti, J. M.
Keynes, J. H. Thomas, and others, he endeavoured to convince the
House that the British people were "tricked into the war in 1914,"
that Parliament and not the Cabinet should exercise real control over
foreign policy, and that Canada should lead the way in bringing a
revision of the treaty terms of 1919.

Following up this thought, and at a time when the question of
French occupation of the Ruhr was peculiarly aggravated, Woodsworth presented a motion which shocked many members and much
of the press across the country: "That in the opinion of this House it
is in the interest of world peace that Canada should withdraw all
claims on Germany for reparation."[8] The motion touched off one of
the earliest full debates on Canadian foreign policy (as distinct from
earlier debates on exclusively imperial relations). In a tense chamber,
Woodsworth recalled that there had been no real discussion of the
causes of the war while the fighting was in process, and that since
the whole principle of reparations and the harsh treaty rested on the
assumption of Germany's exclusive war guilt, it was imperative to
determine whether that basic assumption was valid. Using the authorities noted above, and adding to them such publications as J. S. Ewart's
Canada and British Wars, and A. J. Knock's *The Myth of a Guilty
Nation*, he expounded the now familiar view that the war sprang from
multiple causes—the French desire to re-possess Alsace-Lorraine, the

[7]*Ibid.*, p. 45.
[8]*Ibid.*, p. 280. For the debate on the motion see pp. 311 *et seq.*

inclusion of Bosnia-Herzagovena in the Austro-Hungarian empire, the truculence of Czarist Russia and the Prussian-controlled German monarchy, the bitter British-German competition in every industrial and colonial field, and the existence of a network of semi-secret treaties and alliances. He suggested to an increasingly restive audience that both Britain and France were fully prepared for war when it came and that between 1909 and 1914 Britain had spent more for war purposes than had Germany.

From J. M. Keynes's books, *The Economic Consequences of the Peace* and *A Review of the Peace Treaty*, and other sources he built up the case for revision, including the removal of economic barriers, impartial adjustment of all colonial claims, guarantees of armament reduction for all nations, the admission of all nations to the League. He felt that not only on economic and political grounds but essentially for moral reasons, the French-led punitive peace should be revised: "We may demand our pound of flesh, but all through the world's history there has run another strain of teaching—that mercy is greater than justice."

With this, the pent-up blast of the traditionalists was released. For once they were even anxious that Mr. Speaker should not rule Woodsworth's motion out of order because, as R. J. Manion said, he must be answered.[9] The Minister of Labour, James Murdock, reminded Woodsworth that the Bible teaches "an eye for an eye" and castigated him for opening afresh the wounds of tens of thousands of Canadian hearts which now would "bleed with the injustice of the proposals that have been discussed before us." H. H. Stevens, the Vancouver Tory, berated Woodsworth for doubting the good faith of the Empire and for referring to the fact that the *Lusitania* had carried war munitions: ". . . He insinuated in that manner of which I say he is a master and which he has used time and again in this country amongst the Canadian people to stir up strife and discord, that there was a question whether the Germans were not more or less justified in that act." Again, said Stevens, Woodsworth lauded his "red revolutionary friends" in Germany who had failed in their courts to convict war criminals, and he had used "soap-box" techniques of blaming the war on captains of finance and industry when these very people had tried

[9]In the middle of Woodsworth's statement the Conservative, W. G. McQuarrie, of New Westminster, raised the point of order that only the Committee of the whole House could deal with a motion to release any sum of money owing to the Crown. The Deputy Speaker's ruling was not ready until the end of Woodsworth's speech, at which point R. J. Manion requested that it be withheld. At the conclusion of the debate the ruling was given that the motion was out of order.

to prevent it. "I challenge him," cried Stevens, "and I challenge everyone who belongs to that peculiar group of economic freaks who owe allegiance to the third international instead of to the British crown to come out frankly and through him debate this question in the proper form—on the floor of the Parliament of this country." That was exactly what Woodsworth was attempting to do, and by comparison with speeches like those of Stevens his was both temperate and thoroughly documented. Stevens added little to his own speech when he questioned Woodsworth's "moral courage."

Although one might question some aspects of Woodsworth's position on reparations, he was the first to admit that it was not dogmatic and that it was open to reason; and, compared to R. J. Manion's argument, its logic was crystal clear. The future Conservative leader said Woodsworth wanted Canadian children to suffer "so that the little boys and girls in Germany might be relieved of the pressure of debt which they would have to pay in the future." The Tory attack was renewed by Hocken of Toronto who, after referring to Woodsworth's peculiar and distorted mentality, and calling him a bolshevist, arrived triumphantly at the conclusion that "there is only one argument that a German can understand, and that is the argument of force. . . ." Mr. Meighen concluded for the Conservatives by stating that only "kinked and super-heated minds" could doubt Germany's war guilt. "Penalties," he proclaimed, "are still the law of this universe. . . . If Germany had been made to pay for her crime in 1870 there would not have been a war in 1914."

Mackenzie King's position was that, since Germany had signed the treaty with its war guilt clause, "that should answer for all time the question of the responsibility of the war." To the suggestion from the scholarly Progressive, W. C. Good, that duress had been applied in the Versailles Hall of Mirrors, King replied, "I think it is unnecessary to answer my honourable friend's question." Then the Prime Minister employed the argument to which he reverted several times prior to the outbreak of the Second World War: that the motion might have an adverse effect on the course of European diplomacy, in this case upon the French stand in the Ruhr occupation.

Such was the calibre of foreign policy debate in 1923. But the lonely voice was not silenced. Indeed, it was strengthened by the presence of some neutrals and a few supporters. Robert Forke, for the "continuing Progressives," paid tribute to Woodsworth's sincerity, while at the same time he thought him mistaken—without elaborating his reasons. Andrew MacMaster, the independent from Brome, while deploring the unprincipled attack on the labour representative, and agreeing with him that Germany was not solely responsible for the war, thought the motion inopportune, as did W. C. Good. Irvine and Garland spoke for the Ginger Group to support the resolution, which was, in Garland's words, "in the essential interest of the economic reconstruction of Europe and of human welfare and peace."

Through all this period it was clear that Woodsworth was functioning consciously as a critic, and that as far as positive policy conclusions were concerned he was advancing on pragmatic lines. In debate, the result from a purely political point of view was not always successful. He was, for example, not perfectly clear about the relationship of collective security to Canadian foreign commitments. He thought that Canada should have "some effective voice" in determining the policy of the League of Nations;[10] otherwise, he suggested, "we may be simply contributing our share to the carrying out of policies that are far from those which would be endorsed by the people of Canada." This was the key problem of any phase of collective security and Woodsworth had no positive suggestion. In the same debate he lauded the League's work in acting as a clearing-house of information, and in developing a court of international justice and the International Labour Organization, but voiced the fear that it was still a league of victors and should somehow be transformed into a "league of peoples" based upon democratic election with the council responsible to the assembly. From the first, that is, Woodsworth could not be accused of being a rock-ribbed isolationist. This was abundantly clear by comparing his comment to the cold logic of C. G. Power who said that if articles 10 and 16 of the League Covenant were binding, Canada had no business being in the League; if those articles were not binding, the League was a mere debating society.

When the cards were actually down on the issue of military commitments, Woodsworth's abhorrence of international force took ultimate control of his position, particularly if the commitment were to an imperial policy. It was this that made him appear an isolationist and that endeared him to many in Quebec. Although on the surface the King-Lapointe-Hertzog view of the Commonwealth, which all through this period was gaining strength, implied the right of each dominion to its own foreign policy, either of peace or war, Woodsworth believed that the legal position was still clouded and that business pressures in both old parties would force automatic Canadian participation in a war declared by Great Britain. He attempted to air

[10]Hansard, 1923, pp. 3993 et seq.

the problem in 1926, with a resolution which at first glance appeared no different from King's position. He moved "that in the opinion of this House Canada should refuse to accept any responsibility for complications arising from the foreign policy of the United Kingdom."[11]

The Prime Minister postponed debate on this motion for a week because, he said, news of such a debate would be a "risk" while at Geneva matters of British foreign policy were being discussed. This gesture, like many similar ones, convinced Woodsworth that King's formal "no commitments" statements were hollow. Supporting his motion, Woodsworth argued that the greatest obstacle in the way of complete Canadian autonomy was that Canada had never asked for it. We must declare, he urged, that the British partnership is one of limited liability. Both these remarks of 1926 seem, in retrospect, of slight importance, for Canada was on the very point of obtaining in the Balfour Declaration most of what Woodsworth claimed. His real point was contained in later sections of the speech where he repeated the Hobsonian analysis of imperialist war. What he was really attempting was a guarantee that future capitalist governments in Britain and Canada would not be able to use even the shadow of an imperial legal bond to get Canada into a war of which she might disapprove.

Henri Bourassa delivered a long supporting speech analysing the history of the imperial relationship and the causes of war and adding a bitter comment on the way in which Canada was committed to article 10 of the League Covenant in 1919. But Bourassa was more fortunate than Woodsworth, for he had not been in Winnipeg in 1919 and it was the Winnipegger who took the brunt of disloyalty charges on this occasion, culminating in the remark of W. W. Kennedy of Winnipeg South Centre that the motion had been put forward simply "to stir up in this country a dissension and discord." The debate was adjourned on the motion of Sir George Perley, who said that Woodsworth's statement was meaningless because Canada had never been asked to accept responsibility—a sidelight either on Perley's knowledge or on his sincerity.

Woodsworth concluded his campaign of initiating debate on foreign policy and national status in this period by a speech in 1927 on the Imperial Conference. This was loudly commended by several admiring French members.[12] Analysing the Balfour report and with copious reference to the work of J. S. Ewart, he underlined those legal facts

11*Ibid.*, 1926, p. 1561. For the debate on the motion see pp. 1765 *et seq.*
12*Ibid.*, 1927, pp. 1757 *et seq.*

which still limited full Canadian autonomy—the Colonial Laws Validity Act, the continuing right of appeal to the Judicial Committee of the Privy Council, the lack of power to amend the B.N.A. Act, and others. Then, developing the programme of British Labour, he criticized the Conference for its refusal to propose a treaty which would bind the signatories to compulsory arbitration of international disputes, and for not planning the early "liberation of the dominated areas" of the Empire. It was all very well, he argued, to talk about equality of status, but the fact remained that there were still many legal qualifications; and with the establishment of an Imperial Defence Committee Canada was in practice bound to the automatic defence of an empire which "in much of its extent is morally indefensible."

While Woodsworth's criticism of the Empire and of Canada's policy in external relations was very much on a socialist basis, it also pointed clearly in the direction in which the Empire was almost inevitably to travel. He was, at least from the historical point of view, riding the wave of the future. It seems odd to reflect that the most common method of denigrating him was to call him impractical—to suggest that he could never be a practical politician. When his more specifically political activities are examined the charge that he was unrealistic is even more difficult to substantiate.

14

A QUESTION OF POLITICS

DURING THESE YEARS AN INTERESTING evolution took place in national politics. The two old parties were recovering their stance after the disruption of the war and the agrarian revolt. On the Left there were skirmishes and the preliminary crystallization of a socialist party. In this, and in the sniping at the defences of political immorality, Woodsworth played a key rôle. Throughout the country he could depend upon organized and vocal support in many areas. The I.L.P. of his own city was perhaps the best example of this, but there were also scores of similar if less efficient groups in other places.

Woodsworth exploited his opportunities to travel across the country and provide a liaison between different elements and sections of the socialist-progressive movement. In 1922, for example, in meetings spread between Vancouver Island and Cape Breton Island, he addressed two hundred different groups varying in nature from the Ottawa Theosophical Society to the Women's International League for Peace and Freedom and the Workers' Party in Toronto. He took part in the Manitoba provincial election campaign, the Winnipeg municipal elections and the Elgin House Conference, and made a detailed personal investigation of the situation in the Nova Scotia mining towns. In between he spread the gospel to farm groups and university clubs.

In Manitoba, the I.L.P. was functioning vigorously although in the long run it ran into serious difficulty in its attitude toward the farmers of the province. In 1923 the party's secretary was able to report that the I.L.P. had won twenty-five seats on the municipal councils and school boards of Greater Winnipeg, The Pas, and Selkirk; that S. J. Farmer had become the first labour mayor of Winnipeg; that West Kildonan and St. Vital had I.L.P. reeves (C. A. Tanner and John

Kelly) and that the party was well pleased with the performance of its member at Ottawa.[1] In the provincial legislature the party was represented by Dixon, Queen, Farmer, Ivens, Tanner, and Bayley. There were several branches of the I.L.P. operative in Greater Winnipeg and at Dauphin and Brandon; the Winnipeg group in particular was developing a remarkable *esprit de corps*. Indeed, there were already signs that the idea of continuity in leadership had developed rather in excess of the optimum.

In the summer of 1923 Fred Dixon was compelled by an incurable illness to resign from the legislature. The loss of his influence at the head of the local party was grievous, since it allowed for a growing tendency toward dogmatism on the subject of farmer-labour relations —the development of a vested interest in the party leadership in local affairs. Some members of the party like S. J. Farmer and Beatrice Brigden supported by Woodsworth and Heaps attempted to keep alive the issue of "broadening out." R. A. Hoey, a Methodist minister and Progressive M.P., attended several party meetings in 1923 and plans for greater co-operation with the farmers were discussed. These plans, however, were not seriously implemented and even the programme of workers' education and of spreading the party organization beyond the province (initiated by William Irvine) was opposed by a group of which John Queen was the leader. At the same time, advances from the Workers' Party were snubbed. The I.L.P., while becoming more narrowly urban, remained securely on the ground of social democracy. This was true, despite the rather doctrinaire resolution moved by Tanner and Queen on the occasion of Lenin's death. The resolution extended sympathy to the Republic of Russia and referred to Lenin as "a man who could never be charged with an attempt to sell his people to the Master class. . . . The workers' movement has lost a valued adviser and a conscientious comrade."[2] In 1925 the party platform came up for review and the minutes of the meeting record that "Comrade Woodsworth went through the platform clause by clause and with the exception of a few minor changes of phraseology the platform was the same as adopted four years ago. . . . It was decided that Comrades Woodsworth and Hyman revise the platform and prepare same for publication."[3]

The problem of national integration of urban labour parties and the

[1]I.L.P. Minute Book, Feb. 9, 1923. (In the possession of the C.C.F. provincial office, Winnipeg.)

[2]*Ibid.*, Feb. 8, 1924.

[3]*Ibid.*, Sept. 16, 1925. Marcus Hyman was a Russian-born, Oxford-educated lawyer of considerable means, who consistently supported the I.L.P.

related one of close co-operation with the farmers (both of which were constantly receiving Woodsworth's attention) continued to come up at the party executive meetings and conventions. In November, 1925, the I.L.P. executive met with "members of the Progressive party for the purpose of discussing the question of closer co-operation between the agriculturalists and the workers in the city." No formal agreement resulted, however, and at a special I.L.P. convention to prepare for the 1926 election it was decided "that the special efforts of the party be concentrated on the two Winnipeg seats [North and North Centre] now held by labour and that with respect to other constituencies your committee be instructed to confer with the party branches concerned in order to determine the action to be taken."[4] (Woodsworth did obtain, in 1927, rescinding of the I.L.P. rule which excluded U.F.M. members from joining the I.L.P., and he hoped that this would lead to greater farm-labour co-operation.)

Questions of party organization and control remained important. For provincial and municipal purposes the party insisted on a strict accountability of its elected representatives not unlike the recall concept of the Progressives. This did not extend in the same degree to the federal I.L.P. members, a situation which was to result in difficult personal relations in the C.C.F.–I.L.P. of the 1930's. According to a resolution of 1923, the "proposed actions of party representatives in legislative bodies" was to come under review of the executive,[5] but by 1926 it was decided this could not apply to the federal field. It was then resolved "that labour be free to take such action at Ottawa as circumstances determined."[6] In the 1925 election campaign Woodsworth stressed the balance of power that might be held through co-operation between the small insurgent group of the Progressives and the labour members.

But if there were divided opinions on the best form of organization the ranks were closed at election time. And increasingly all types of trade union organization recognized Woodsworth as labour's most effective spokesman at Ottawa. In 1925, for example, the O.B.U. plumped for him against "the same old gang of Meighen, M. R. Blake, Bob Rogers, Alf Andrews, Braid and Gideon Robertson." In 1926 the official journal of the Trades and Labour Congress, observing that Woodsworth and Heaps were determined to remain independent of the old parties, commented: ". . . no doubt they can be of the greatest

---

[4]*Ibid.*, Nov. 3, 1925.   [5]*Ibid.*, May 2, 1923.
[6]*Ibid.*, July 13, 1926. No doubt this resolution was influenced by the notable success of the old age pensions negotiations.

service to the workers of this country by so doing."[7] And at all times there was support from the *Canadian Railway Employees' Monthly*, the paper of A. R. Mosher's Canadian Brotherhood of Railway Employees.

In most of his campaigns Woodsworth spent comparatively little time in his own constituency. He had become a national figure, and with enthusiasm accepted the responsibility entailed. In 1925 he was as much interested in being chief speaker at the picnic which endorsed the proposed merger of the Saskatchewan Grain Growers' Association and the United Farmers of Canada (Saskatchewan Section)[8] as he was in getting back to Winnipeg. This attitude was made possible by his own growing prestige and by the smoothly operating electoral machinery developed by the Winnipeg I.L.P.

So well had the I.L.P. rallied general labour approval by 1925 that there were no splinter group labour candidates, and Heaps and Woodsworth carried two of the four Winnipeg seats with majorities of 1,163 and 914 respectively.

In the 1926 election the Liberals put up no candidate in Winnipeg North Centre and in the straight contest with the Tory J. A. Banfield, Woodsworth's majority was increased to over three thousand. Heaps increased his majority also, and Irvine regained his Alberta seat—as a U.F.A. candidate. During the campaign Woodsworth had stressed co-operation with the insurgent farmers, stating that "group government is here to stay." No sooner was the election over than Woodsworth was off for a two-month speaking tour of the Maritimes, spreading the idea of political action in the East. Although in his speeches across the country he clothed his ideas in the garb of class organization for group government, the necessities of the parliamentary system were forcing the Left irresistibly toward a party form of organization. This was not made completely clear until the beginning of the 1930's, and even then the forms adopted by the C.C.F. reflected the background of the Non-Partisan League.

The failure to destroy the party system was, however, implicit in the first major decision taken by the Progressive M.P.'s—not to accept the status of official opposition in the House of Commons.[9] Two

[7]*Canadian Congress Journal*, Jan., 1926.
[8]The Saskatchewan meeting was reported in the *Saskatoon Star*, July 2, 1925.
[9]W. L. Morton's account of this "political failure" of the Progressives, *The Progressive Party in Canada* (Toronto, 1950), chap. v, is very thorough and searching. But it seems to me that he misses the point when he writes of the natural "disposition of third parties to shun responsibility." The Progressives, by their own statements and actions, did not form a political *party* in any sense of

things followed from this. Those Progressives who were concerned
primarily with tariffs and railway rates began to hyphenate their
political name by adding the prefix "Liberal-" and then proceeded to
slide comfortably into the ranks of official Liberalism. By 1927 this
process was virtually complete, and Robert Forke was admitted to
the cabinet as Minister of Agriculture and Immigration. Those Progressives who desired more profound change held out as the "Ginger
Group" and formed a close alliance with the labour M.P.'s.

The process was well under way by the end of 1922. T. A. Crerar,
the first national leader of the Progressives, resigned and was succeeded by Robert Forke. The *Canadian Forum* commented that
Crerar had "lost the art of saying no and could not turn a deaf ear to
flattering tongues. He began with a stock-in-trade of very genuine
ideals but gradually forgot the real mission of the Progressive
party. . . ."[10] Probably the Crerar resignation was the result rather of
his failure to steer the Progressives immediately into the Liberal party,
and thus rescue it from the too-great influence of Sir Lomer Gouin.
This had certainly been the idea of the Dafoe-Sifton-Hudson group in
Manitoba. What else could Dafoe mean when he wrote thus to
Clifford Sifton in 1920: "Assuming that Crerar succeeds in entering
the next Parliament with a following of 75 members, which is not at
all beyond the possibilities, I am satisfied that a fusion of the Liberals
and the farmers for the purpose of carrying on a government will be
quite practicable provided the tariff is made along the lines I have
indicated"?[11] The Manitoba idea of broadening out meant fusion
with the Liberals rather than the creation of a new and independent
farm representation. The U.F.A., and the Morrison faction of the
U.F.O., clung to the idea of group government so tenaciously precisely
because they feared the Liberal designs of the Manitobans. By the
time that Forke took over the Progressive leadership from Crerar
there was already little hope that the Progressives could reform the
Liberal party by prior bargaining with King. By then it was really a
question of how long the cautious ones would resist the Liberal

---

the word. The first minor party of any stature in our history, the C.C.F., certainly
has not displayed this alleged disposition. In Ontario, Saskatchewan, and British
Columbia it has willingly become opposition or government, while in Manitoba
it even made the brief error of joining a coalition government; and who can
doubt the readiness of its present leaders (given the chance) to form at Ottawa
either opposition or government? For that matter, where was E. C. Drury's
disposition to refuse responsibility?

[10]Dec., 1922.
[11]Morton, *Progressive Party*, p. 149n.

magnet, and how soon the genuine radicals would cut clear of the Manitoba "Liberals in disguise."

The *Forum* noted that Forke was a convinced advocate of "fusion" and that he was "not a person of meteoric intellect or a profound parliamentary strategist, but he is no man's fool and has a deep reservoir of Scots caution and commonsense."[12] This was generous. Actually, Forke's nomination by the orthodox Progressives was probably one of the final bits of evidence required by the radicals to propel them leftward.

While the split in the Progressives' ranks was deepening, Woodsworth and Irvine were busy preparing a place of refuge for the recalcitrant "anti-party" men. In the 1923 debate on the Address, Woodsworth obtained a recognized party position when he was allowed to speak fourth—after Forke. Later in the session the Speaker questioned Woodsworth's right to put more than one question on the orders of the day. When Woodsworth explained that he and Irvine could speak through no other leader the Speaker replied: "The honourable gentleman has just called my attention to the fact that there is a fourth party, and on that consideration I will allow the question. I regret that I had ignored the fact."[13]

The explanation sometimes advanced that it was basically a difference of opinion as to the best type of political organization that split the Progressives appears to overlook the more important divisions on questions of legislative policy. It was the decisions made with respect to the Liberal legislative programme that really compelled the splintering of the Progressive movement. Even the vain attempt to obtain acceptance of the pet U.F.A. device of group government shows that it was the achievement of desired legislation rather than the actual political reform that was really sought by the radical farmers. When Irvine presented his 1923 motion that "A defeat of a government measure should not be considered as sufficient reason for the resignation of the government unless followed by a vote of lack of confidence" he supported it with the remark: "It would be better, I think, for all concerned if Cabinets would look for a majority on the issue rather than counting heads before the issue is proposed."[14] The Progressive speakers who followed all indicated that it was the *issues* they were really interested in—that the attack on the party method was an attempt to avoid dictation by caucus and the "big interests" that

[12]*Canadian Forum*, Dec., 1922.
[13]Hansard, 1923, p. 3401.
[14]*Ibid.*, pp. 208 *et seq.*

controlled the old parties. When it was finally shown that the idea of group government was either unworkable or unacceptable, when the Liberals killed even W. C. Good's motions for various experiments in proportional representation, and when the orthodox Progressives began to show their true colours, then the radicals were prepared to reconsider their stand on the subject of party organization. By 1930 they would be ready to accept a broad farmer-labour party with control clearly resting in general party conventions.

The movement of the radical Progressives toward this position was undoubtedly hastened by Woodsworth's almost continual presentation of socialist arguments and motions, and by his consistent support of the radical Progressive fight for such things as banking and tariff reform. It may also have been hastened by the insidious effects of soft Ottawa living upon the more susceptible Progressives, which tended to highlight the corruptibility of those without a cause. The *Forum* noted in the spring of 1923 that "luxurious" Ottawa was already taking its toll: "Was ever four thousand dollars of cold cash so agreeably earned by most of the Progressive members? . . . The feebler characters have succumbed to the lure of what is for them a sybaritic existence."[15] Against this the radicals could place the complete integrity of Woodsworth. They could observe that even while he was purposefully wooing the farmers he would not support any measure for that purpose alone. Thus in the 1924 debate on redistribution he refused to concede the justness of the heated agrarian defence of smaller populations for rural constituencies than for urban ridings, and argued that "there can be no real basis of representation other than population."[16] King was quick to agree with the farmers on this point.

The first big step toward the creation of a genuine farmer-labour party was achieved in 1924. In that year neither Meighen nor Forke moved an amendment to the budget, which proposed only moderate scattered tariff reductions and no tax changes. Both of them no doubt wished to avoid a clear re-statement of Progressive fiscal principles— Forke because he wished to minimize the division in the Progressive ranks and Meighen because he hoped vaguely to win some of them away from the Liberals. It was just this division which Woodsworth desired to emphasize. He seized upon the opportunity to present his own amendment to the budget. He explained his purpose quite frankly, stating that he was making his motion "because I believe that in many respects, although some of us advocate theories that

15April, 1923.   16Hansard, 1924, p. 671.

seem to be very radical in their character, a very considerable number of the members of this House, especially members on the Progressive side, are quite willing to travel a long way in our direction if they are quite sure that we are not advocating anything that is immediately impracticable. So I have tried to draft a resolution in such a form that it will be found to be quite within the range of practical politics."[17]

Actually the resolution which followed, although perfectly consonant with the I.L.P. platform, was virtually the same as that moved by Robert Forke in the previous session. This required the Progressives either to abandon their declared principle or to vote with Woodsworth and against King. The amendment demanded a substantial reduction of the tariff on the necessities of life, graded income tax to bear more heavily on unearned incomes, taxation of unimproved land values and natural resources, and a graduated inheritance tax on large estates. The Liberals were greatly disturbed and the Speaker came close to ruling the amendment out of order. When the Speaker allowed the Woodsworth amendment to stand, Meighen plunged in with a technicality concerning wording, but he too was rebuffed.

According to the *Montreal Star*, when the significance of the amendment was understood "corridors and lobbies were agog, every man suspecting his neighbour of complicity."[18] The still more cynical Toronto *Telegram* reported that "the explosion blew most of [the Progressives] out of the Chamber. They spent the rest of the day in little groups trying to figure out whether they should vote for the principles they pretend to love or for the government that has bought them at a price. Some of them, too, may have thought of the indemnities they draw . . . all of which shows that they are fast learning Liberal ways."[19]

Robert Forke's evasions on this occasion were one classic example in the 1920's of a political leader in trouble. Forke noted that there would be some of his own group who would disagree with him, but that nevertheless the amendment as moved at that time was "not in the best interests of the movement which we represent. . . . I suppose there will be a certain amount of what I may call unholy glee on the part of some who think this places the Progressives in a rather difficult position." He continued by ignoring the Progressive principle of independent voting, and argued that to vote for the amendment and risk a defeat of the government on this "vote of confidence" would not advance the Progressive cause. Then he shifted tack completely and

[17]*Ibid.*, pp. 1460 *et seq.*
[18]April 25, 1924.   [19]April 25, 1924.

argued that since the amendment would not receive a majority it was therefore "only a gesture."

The radical Progressives led by J. T. Shaw, H. E. Spencer, and E. J. Garland contented themselves with parading the obvious fact that the amendment was basically much closer to the official platforms of the Progressives, the I.L.P., and the Liberal party than was the budget. King appealed to the cautious Progressives with his full array of old arguments. The amendment went too far, he explained. It would commit the government to new and untried methods of taxation; any basic tariff change required "expert" advice and would have to await the creation of his proposed tariff board; all the aims of the amendment were being accomplished by the Liberals despite the allegations of "cynics."

Fifteen members followed Woodsworth at 7. A.M. on May 16 to support the principle upon which they had been elected. Although their tiny revolt was overwhelmed by 204 supporters of caution and privilege the "Ginger Group" had found itself and its real leader. The group included at the outset the agrarian support of Robert Gardiner, E. J. Garland, H. E. Spencer, G. G. Coote, D. M. Kennedy, and J. T. Shaw (Alberta); M. N. Campbell (Saskatchewan); W. J. Ward (Manitoba); and Preston Elliott, W. C. Good, and Agnes Macphail (Ontario), together with J. S. Woodsworth, Irvine, and one or two others. The "Ginger Group" expressed the view that political forms and devices, although they might need basic reform, were themselves only a means to reform in the more important social-economic field. They had returned to the Non-Partisan idea.

When the dissident Progressives explained their position to Forke they placed the protest against economic burdens and class government, and the effort to implement a co-operative philosophy, before the fight against party as such.[20] It was becoming evident that in the Canadian climate a protest movement could not long survive if it clung exclusively to the political fetishes of orthodox American progressivism, that is, if it placed its faith exclusively in the political gadgets of direct democracy like the initiative, the referendum, and the recall, or in mild tariff reductions, "trust busting," and railway rate regulation. The Canadian Progressives who did follow this line naturally suffered the same fate as their American brothers of the Populist and Progressive parties. J. D. Hicks has written that it must be the fate of all American "third parties." Thus the absorption of the National Peoples' Party by the Democrats in the United States was a

[20]See the Ginger Group letter printed in Morton, *Progressive Party*, p. 194.

close parallel to the absorption of the conservative Progressives by the King Liberal party in Canada.

The "Ginger Group" was, then, the product of the preceding years of discussion, the influence of the social gospel, the Society of Equity and the Non-Partisan League; the reading of Ernest Gronlund's *Co-operative Commonwealth* and Edward Bellamy's *Looking Backward*; the immigration of men aware of socialist writing and action in the United Kingdom; the experience of war and post-war problems, mortgage companies and banks. It grew out of all these things, and to suggest that suddenly in 1924 or 1930 it began to take on a socialist hue is to ignore a considerable background of socialist thought, including the labour element. It is worth emphasizing this point, since there is an unhistorical tendency among journalists and scholars dealing with this period to under-emphasize the earlier developments. It is equally important to observe that the growing socialist opinion was by no means exclusively "sectional"—it was much more than the "revolt of the West." The acceptance of Woodsworth and Irvine as spokesmen by miners in Nova Scotia, by members of the Canadian Brotherhood of Railway Employees across the country, by the various city labour parties, and tentatively by orthodox trade unionists, proved the contrary, as did the presence in the Ginger Group of Elliott, Good, and Agnes Macphail from Ontario.

During 1924 and 1925 the "co-operating independents," as Woodsworth sometimes termed the Ginger Group, formed almost unconsciously a more cohesive section of the House. They met together in an unofficial and non-coercive caucus, and usually voted together on such things as Woodsworth's 1924 motion to delete the supply item of $600,000 for the completion of the Peace Tower (when there were, as Agnes Macphail remarked, so many cases of desperate need in the country which were the real living memorial of war);[21] W. C. Good's motion to establish the transferable vote in experimental multi-member constituencies as a step toward proportional representation;[22] William Irvine's bill to abolish the death penalty;[23] Agnes Macphail's 1925 motion for prison reform;[24] J. T. Shaw's divorce bill providing equality between the sexes with respect to the grounds for divorce;[25]

[21]Hansard, 1924, pp. 665–6. The vote was 14–124.
[22]*Ibid.*, p. 949.
[23]*Ibid.*, April 11, 1924. A few individuals, such as E. J. McMurray and T. A. Crerar, joined the Ginger Group in the vote, 29–92.
[24]*Ibid.*, 1925, pp. 1265 *et seq.*
[25]*Ibid.*, pp. 3859 *et seq.* This Ginger Group bill mustered sufficient additional votes to pass.

or Irvine's 1925 proposed amendment to the Elections Act which would have allowed labour unions to contribute to political funds.[26]

The Ginger Group, thus, had a sense of identity. But it also held fast to the doctrine of group government. This doctrine received its crucial test when the constitutional crisis of 1926 revealed beyond question the fallibility of the Progressive political panacea. If, however, group government failed the co-operating independents, the constitutional crisis again brought to light the political wisdom of the Ginger Group leader and paved the way for a formal party organization on the Left.

[26]*Ibid.*, pp. 4971 *et seq.* The amendment was lost (53–60) despite the support of most Progressives and some Tories.

15

DEATH OF A DOCTRINE

THE 1926 SESSION OPENED WITH Ernest Lapointe as House leader, since King had lost his seat in the 1925 voting. The Liberals were in a distinct minority. Their lines of support reached down through the orthodox Progressives, through the Ginger Group, and really depended upon Woodsworth and Heaps. At the outset of the session Woodsworth analysed the situation and drew the conclusion that a co-operative government was the logical answer. The two-party system had proven itself inadequate, he declared, as even the seating arrangements of the House illustrated. He himself was now on the "government side," the desk-mate of Henri Bourassa. But, what was much more important, the Liberals with only 41 per cent of the House, had no mandate to govern. The Conservatives, with 46 per cent, also lacked majority authority. The government now, he said, should really be a committee of the House and not of one party. "I am suggesting rather a co-operative arrangement, a council which would be responsible directly to the House and not to any party."[1]

This was again the U.F.A.–U.F.O. favourite idea of group government, and the circumstances, superficially, were favourable to such an experiment. But to anyone who cherished the British political tradition, the likelihood of instability was formidable; and Woodsworth, having stated the theory, turned to pragmatism. At the same time he delivered an indictment of the uninspired old parties which was calculated to counter the sectional and emphasize the national character of the revolt against the *status quo*.[2] He argued that "our forefathers" had the imagination to subdue the forces of nature and to

[1]Hansard, 1926, pp. 25 *et seq.*
[2]*Ibid.*, pp. 629 *et seq.*

set up a political system "which answered the needs of their day and generation." A different problem now confronted Canadians—the problem of how to secure political freedom through the acquisition of economic freedom. But, he continued, the fact that the control of the machinery of production and distribution was in the hands of a small number of people mostly residing in central Canada did not mean that it was "the East" as such that must be reformed. The system was national and must be attacked on a nation-wide front. It was because Woodsworth persuaded the Ginger Group that this was so that he, and not a Progressive, held the initiative of opposition in the 1926 Parliament. To suggest that it was really the Albertans who held the key, places the emphasis a little inaccurately.[3]

Throughout this period the record of Hansard is sprinkled with Woodsworth's motions and bills: for decent salaries for postal workers;[4] for action to "regain for the use of the people the coal mines and water powers which are now being exploited in the interests of private corporations"[5] (enlivened with quotations from American conservationists like Gifford Pinchot and Robert Lafollette); for the amendment of the Civil Service Act by establishing a council of employees on the British Whitley model.[6] But the most significant measure for which he pressed, and which he achieved by an adroit use of political strategy, was federally sponsored old age pensions.

Non-contributory old age pensions as part of an expanding concept of federal minimum standards had been on the agendas of the Trades and Labour Congress[7] and the various labour parties from the turn of the century. The question had been considered by the Royal Commission on Industrial Relations (1919) and in connection with war pensions, but no legislation had resulted. In 1922 the Liberal J. E. Fontaine of Hull obtained passage of a resolution urging the government to consider ways and means of establishing a system of old age pensions, but no action was taken.[8] In 1923 Woodsworth asked if the government would introduce an old age pension measure, to which

[3]W. L. Morton, *The Progressive Party in Canada* (Toronto, 1950), chap. VIII is helpful to an understanding of this difficult parliamentary session.

[4]Hansard, 1924, p. 3280; *ibid.*, 1927, p. 2511.

[5]*Ibid.*, 1926, p. 2561.

[6]*Ibid.*, 1927, p. 594. It is also of interest to note that Woodsworth was the only English-speaking member of the Committee on Industrial and International Relations to give support to the resolution calling for family allowances. The resolution was introduced in 1929 by a French member of the committee and gave voice to the movement sponsored in Quebec by Father Léon Lebel.

[7]See H. A. Logan, *Trade Unions in Canada* (Toronto, 1948), p. 503.

[8]Hansard, 1922, p. 1303.

W. S. Fielding replied, "No decision favourable to the movement has been reached."[9] And when T. L. Church, two months later, asked whether either pension or housing legislation would be brought in, King answered that he could not "give a final answer at this time."[10]

Pressure was building up on all sides, but the King government seemed to owe too much to business to concede this kind of social legislation. By 1924, one barrier had to be let down. A committee was appointed to study the pension question and the House accepted its unanimous report recommending pensions "at the earliest possible moment" for the "deserving" indigent over 70 years of age, the cost to be divided equally between the provinces and the federal government.[11] Before the House committee President Moore of the Trades and Labour Congress pointed to the gross sectional inequalities in Canada and to the nation's backwardness amongst the industrial countries of the world in the matter of social legislation. But there was still no indication that the government intended to act. Indeed, the cabinet old guard, reinforced by anticipation of an almost certain negative in the Senate, remained stoutly opposed. When Woodsworth asked the perennial question about the government's intentions in this matter for the 1925 session, George P. Graham parried with the remark: "I am not in a position to say."[12]

Undoubtedly the government was deeply concerned about the minimizing of its constitutional powers which had resulted from the long series of Privy Council judicial decisions on the B.N.A. Act. It was also acutely aware, in the mid-1920's, of an increase in sectional feeling in Canada. The constitutional straight-jacket was given as a public reason for retarding social legislation. Sectional feeling was a major private reason. But it was precisely this lack of daring in the face of grave social problems that Woodsworth challenged. The mere fact that there were difficulties to be overcome was, to him, the more reason to attack them head on rather than evade them until they might become catastrophic.

In 1925, when the Prime Minister lost his own seat in the general election and saw the first roll-call vote in the House give him a majority of three, he became more responsive to the frequently expressed will of the House on social legislation. Looking on gloomily from the sidelines, King observed that the balance of power, granting Progressive support, was actually held by two men—Woodsworth and

[9]Ibid., 1923, p. 733.
[10]Ibid., p. 2517.
[11]Ibid., 1924, p. 3859.   [12]Ibid., 1925, p. 539.

Heaps.[13] It was not surprising, then, that he should seek means to assure the continued support of these two in crucial votes. He was not unaware of how this might be done, since he had received, prior to the opening of the House, the following letter:

DEAR MR. KING:

As representative of labour in the House of Commons, may we ask whether it is your intention to introduce at this session legislation with regard to (a) provision for the unemployed; (b) old age pensions. We are venturing to send a similar enquiry to the leader of the Opposition.

Yours sincerely,

J. S. WOODSWORTH
A. A. HEAPS

By the time the session opened early in January, 1926, Woodsworth and Heaps were already impatient for a reply. A similar letter to Mr. Meighen had elicited an answer which held out little encouragement, and no doubt King was aware of this.[14] In any event, Mr. Charles Bowman, political editor of the Ottawa *Citizen*, conveyed to the two labour members an invitation from the Prime Minister to have dinner at Laurier House and discuss the situation.[15] Prior to the meeting at Laurier House Mr. Bowman had, on behalf of the Prime Minister, ascertained from H. E. Spencer that the U.F.A. group would support a pensions act, although why King was in any doubt on this point is somewhat mysterious.

During the evening's discussion (at which King, Woodsworth, Heaps, and Bowman were present) Woodsworth sought a pledge that the government would amend the Immigration Act, the Naturalization Act, and the Criminal Code along the lines of his own private bills, and that immediate legislation would be introduced to implement both pensions and unemployment insurance. The last of these items was, the Prime Minister realized, too steep a price for provincial rightists like Lapointe and reactionaries like E. M. Macdonald or Graham. But on the other points, including pensions, he gave a verbal assurance which he later confirmed in a letter for which Woodsworth had pressed him. This letter Woodsworth read into Hansard on January 29.

[13]*Ibid.*, 1926, p. 560.
[14]*Ibid.*, pp. 561 *et seq.* Mr. A. A. Heaps declared (interview with the author, 1952) that their displeasure was made known to Mr. King.
[15]Letter of July 14, 1952, from Mr. Bowman to Mrs. Angus MacInnis. Mr. Heaps' account of these events does not differ from that of Mr. Bowman. Note also Woodsworth's reference to the opportunity King "gave us to present our case in detail" (Hansard, 1926, p. 561); and King's reference to "our interview" (*ibid.*).

Shortly after this private meeting with King, the two labour members had a session with the cabinet which proved how wise they had been to get a written promise. According to Mr. Heaps

there were many of its members who, to say the least, were very lukewarm about the old age pensions. The late Senator Dandurand was amongst these and he stated that he was very uncertain about the Senate approving such a measure. . . . During this session of the Cabinet Senator Dandurand turned to Woodsworth and myself and asked us what the position would be if the Senate rejected the legislation. I replied to this question by reminding him of a similar rejection by the British House of Lords and asked him to consider what happened to the Lords as a result thereof.[16]

King thus found himself thoroughly committed to immediate pension legislation, although he realized that he would have difficulty in carrying such a measure both in his cabinet and in the Senate. Before a final commitment was made at Laurier House, he offered Woodsworth the post of Minister of Labour. When Woodsworth declined the invitation, Mr. Bowman suggested that Mr. Heaps "would be a practical asset to the government as Minister of Labour," but Woodsworth's colleague quickly indicated that he also would decline the invitation. For a new Labour Minister who might slightly redress the heavy rightist weighting of his government, King had to wait until later in the same year when he found Peter Heenan, a Kenora railwayman. The King offer, if Woodsworth had accepted, would have saved the Liberal leader much trouble in the future. In any cabinet that King ever assembled, however, it would have been inconceivable that Woodsworth could have found a place, and there is no evidence that the offer was over repeated.

That a political bargain had been struck none would deny, except the Prime Minister himself. Woodsworth's statement in the House was referred to in the press as the supplement to the Throne Speech, but he did not feel it necessary to defend his action. Like Bourassa, he argued, the labour members were independent and in this case, since their purposes could be advanced by the action, they would vote against the Meighen amendment to the Address (they would vote with the government to accept the Speech from the Throne).[17]

The result was the passage of an Old Age Pensions Bill in May, 1926. It provided that the federal government would pay to any co-operating province one-half of the cost of such pensions. The maximum pension was to be $240, payable to British subjects of seventy years

[16]Letter of Oct. 30, 1951, from Mr. Heaps to Mr. M. J. Coldwell.
[17]Hansard, 1926, pp. 560 et seq.

or over, resident in Canada for twenty years. Even this modest legislation was promptly vetoed by the Conservative Senate majority. When the
bill was re-passed in 1927, after its Senate defeat had helped the Liberals
in the 1926 general election, it was accepted by the Senate. While it
was before the House the second time Woodsworth argued that the
government should pay 75 per cent of the cost to ensure co-operation
by all the provincial governments, that the age should be lowered, and
a larger outside income be permitted to recipients of pensions.[18] None
of these suggestions was incorporated at the time, but during the
depression the federal government extended its contribution to 75 per
cent while still later amendments, and finally a new act, won even
more than Woodsworth sought in 1927.

In his interview with King at the beginning of the session Woodsworth had secured the assurance not only of old age pensions but also
the promise of amendments to the Immigration Act, the Naturalization
Act, and the Criminal Code. This bargain with King was obviously
more significant for legislative policy than was the vague understanding between King and the Progressives; it undoubtedly enhanced
Woodsworth's stature in the eyes of the Ginger Group. And it was
recognized by the Conservatives as being of critical importance in
determining which way the "balance of power" votes would go.

R. B. Bennett, who was himself engaged in a vigorous effort to
succeed Meighen as Conservative leader, assailed the government for
surrendering to blackmail. "Have parliamentary institutions fallen so
low," he enquired, "that our Criminal Code is to be amended that a
government may remain in power?"[19]

This criticism was made during debate on Ernest Lapointe's first
motion (February 2) to adjourn the House until March 15. The motion
was designed to enable the Liberals to reorganize their shattered
forces, allow King to get back into the House through the new constituency selected for him in Prince Albert, and to postpone discussion
of H. H. Stevens' ominous motion for an enquiry into corruption in the
Customs Department. Lapointe's motion marked the beginning of
what historians have named the "constitutional crisis." It might better
be called "the evasion of the customs scandal."

Woodsworth belied the Conservative charges that he had been
"bought," since he voted with the majority to negative the Lapointe
motion and permit preliminary debate on the Stevens' motion.[20] But
this did not appease the Conservatives. Speaker after speaker rose to
excoriate the "bargain," emphasizing the opinion that Woodsworth

18*Ibid.*, 1927, p. 448.   19*Ibid.*, 1926, p. 643.   20*Ibid.*, p. 679.

was primarily responsible for the government's retention of office. The fiery Donald Sutherland of South Oxford proclaimed that the correspondence between Woodsworth and King was "the clearest and most emphatic proof of the fact that there had been bargaining in relation to matters of great public importance in this country with a view to securing support in this House to enable a government which was defeated at the polls to carry on in defiance of public opinion."[21] Later the same individual repeated by implication and by reference to newspaper speculations that King had "purchased" Woodsworth's support. When, upon Woodsworth's request for withdrawal, the Speaker ruled that the remark should be withdrawn, Meighen forced a division in which the ruling was upheld 87–71.

The debate, still technically on the question of a Customs Department enquiry, grew steadily warmer. At one point the Conservative Guthrie referred to Woodsworth as "a front seat" supporter of the government, who had compelled King "to amend three Acts which this government has resolutely refused to touch through the course of four sessions."[22]

Finally, by March 3, Lapointe secured his adjournment of the House; but the tension was not relaxed and Woodsworth continued to be a storm centre. Any and every event that could possibly be given a hostile interpretation was seized upon to discredit him. In this chaotic session occurred what was, perhaps, the classic example of such tactics. During one particularly noisy sitting on the eve of adjournment, enlivened by a series of drinking songs, Bourassa and Woodsworth were deep in discussion. They failed to notice a change in tune to that of the national anthem and continued their talk without rising. The incident was played up in newspapers across the country, particularly by the Tory press. The Toronto *Mail and Empire* reported that Woodsworth and Bourassa had remained "sullenly seated" while the "whole House" sang "The King." Woodsworth raised the report as a matter of privilege, declaring that ". . . at any irrelevant moment when someone calls 'Come on, Ernie,' I do not propose to click heels and come to a salute or do any other form of goose-stepping. . . . No one who knows the animation with which the honourable member for Labelle enters into conversation will say . . . that he was sullenly seated."[23] But such answers were not printed, and the original reports were planted in the public mind with the editorialized accounts of Woodsworth's motion on foreign policy of the same session.

[21]*Ibid.*, p. 739.
[22]*Ibid.*, p. 1460.   [23]*Ibid.*, p. 1666.

In the middle of this boiling political pot was the question of the customs scandal which was to lead directly to a crisis involving the constitutional position of the Governor General. Once the question of supporting King's revised legislative programme had been settled, the problem of his government's shaky administrative record had to be faced, and here both the orthodox Progressives and the Ginger Group fell back again on their individual judgments. Woodsworth was perhaps more consistent than some of his colleagues; and for this, too, he was flailed by the Tories. From the time of his first session he had been distressed by evidence of corruption and indiscriminate patronage on all sides. He vigorously opposed the eager but abortive attempt of the Quebec Liberal M.P.'s to emasculate the Civil Service Commission and restore to uninhibited efficiency the patronage ramp.[24] And as early as the spring of 1923 he endeavoured to draw the government's attention to the very area of laxity in which the customs scandal was growing. He then noted that Canada was being developed as a centre for rum-running to the prohibition-bound United States and asked the government if it were "bringing in any measures with a view to dealing effectively with this matter."[25] In 1923 King's answer was that the government was taking "every precaution." The intervening years were to prove the reverse.

In 1926 the problem of political corruption still occupied a prominent position in Woodsworth's thinking. The Stevens motion of February 2 with its revelations of customs corruption had no doubt further stimulated his thought on the subject. In an article of March, 1926, he laid stress on the vital rôle of money in our political processes. "In the conduct of an election limited to a few weeks," he wrote in the *Canadian Forum*, "money can secure committee rooms, halls, canvassers, transportation, advertising, the press, the pulpit, the radio."[26] In such circumstances it seemed doubly necessary to use the Commons as a check upon the operations of the administrative departments. But complications entered the picture if any particular department or party were to be censured and checked, because, in the alternating governments of the two major parties, records would be found either grey or black indiscriminately as far back as any investigating body had energy to delve. Thus it would also be important to ensure that any investigation of corruption be as impartial and complete as possible. From Woodsworth's point of view the result

---

[24]*Ibid.*, 1922, p. 3075.
[25]*Ibid.*, 1923, p. 2208.
[26]"Grandsons of Confederation," *Canadian Forum*, March, 1926.

would indict "the system" more than any particular government. His part in the customs scandal should be seen against this background.

Following the Stevens motion the Liberals had appointed a special Commons committee to investigate the Customs Department. The interests involved, even at the outset, were somewhat diverse. Obviously any serious degree of corruption in a government department was heaven-sent for an ambitious official opposition already teetering on the brink of office as the result of the 1925 election. And here was an issue on which the rivals R. B. Bennett and C. H. Cahan could give unequivocal support to their precariously perched leader. Business men were incensed by the evasions of the customs regulations by favoured firms and individuals, and, indeed, it was the protests of a business man's protective association that first impelled the Conservatives to action on the subject. It was also one issue on which Meighen could hope for temporary Progressive support—either on the direct ground of corruption or the indirect one of farmer temperance feeling. Finally King's own political life depended upon the outcome of these debates.

By the end of April enough information had been turned up by the Commons committee to indicate a major issue. The "smuggling committee" produced as a starter the story of Captain Zinck, chief Protective Officer at Lunenberg. Zinck's "oversight" of the rum-running operations of enterprising Maritimers was complete. Other evidence proved that for years gangs of smugglers had enjoyed "not merely the tacit connivance of a multitude of Customs officials but in many cases their active co-operation in making a wholesale mockery of the Customs laws of Canada. . . ."[27] Under Hon. Jacques Bureau, deterioration in the morale of the Customs Department had proceeded rapidly, until the point was reached where the competition from wholesale smuggling, both ways across the boundary, and from coast to coast, was felt by significant business groups. The Liberals themselves had been aware of what was afoot, and in September, 1925, Bureau was relieved of his position and given sanctuary in the Senate, in whose holy atmosphere he could be cleansed of such sins as connivance with crooks and the reversal of court sentences passed upon smugglers. George Boivin, appointed to take over the Customs Department, undoubtedly suffered for the sins of his predecessor but also was not free of suspicion. He had, for example, intervened to stay the sentence on Moses Aziz, a convicted smuggler of New Brunswick, in order to have his skilled assistance in the general election. Liquor-

[27]*Canadian Forum*, May, 1926.

laden ships were still reported as leaving Canadian ports with papers designating a South American destination, only to return for fresh cargoes within forty-eight hours.

When the report of the Customs committee came before the House in June, the Liberal tactic was to admit the findings and plead that corrective action had already been instituted. The committee, composed of four Conservatives, four Liberals, and one Progressive with Liberal leanings, had not seen fit to fasten responsibility specifically on the government. Thus the government's motion to accept the report brought forth a tremendous storm of debate, centring on a Tory amendment clearly censuring the government—in short a motion of non-confidence. Woodsworth entered this debate with considerable trepidation. In the midst of almost continuous uproar, with Meighen shouting that he was out of order, Woodsworth patiently explained the reasons for the action he was about to take.

The immediate question, he argued, was essentially a judicial one.[28] But the vote on the report would be decided on party rather than judicial grounds. Therefore the investigation should be reopened by an independent Royal Commission. This was one aspect of Woodsworth's reasoning; a more important one, perhaps, was his abandonment of the group government idea. While he declared in this speech that he *should* be able to vote on such matters without necessarily defeating the government, yet in practice he could not. Thus his vote would have to be cast, in the last analysis, according to whether he preferred a Conservative or a Liberal government. It is true that he was disgusted by the elevation of Bureau to the Senate, and by the attempt to pillory less important individuals, but the whole political analysis of the radical group inevitably concluded that in such things there was little to choose between the two major parties. The only real question of principle involved was whether Conservatives or Liberals would further a desirable legislative programme—and here Woodsworth had already obtained conclusive evidence. Thus, still publicly searching his soul and declaring "I frankly admit that I am open to criticism; I am placing myself in a vulnerable position," he proceeded to move a sub-amendment. This would have removed the element of censure from the Conservative amendment and called for the appointment of a judicial Royal Commission to conduct a total investigation.

Across the country the Tory press scorched Woodsworth as dishonest and disreputable and termed his amendment a whitewash, a

[28]Hansard, 1926, pp. 4921 *et seq.*

"miserable piece of pettifogging and bigotry." In the House Boivin, the unfortunate incumbent Minister of Customs, sat staring straight ahead while the furore around him rose to fever pitch.[29] As soon as Woodsworth had caught the Speaker's eye and moved his amendment, the leaders came in on the run from the lobbies. Meighen immediately challenged the Woodsworth amendment, stating that it was to the main motion and not the Stevens amendment. But the government had staked its all on the Woodsworth amendment and the old Liberal, Lemieux, after a night's sleep on the matter, declared Woodsworth in order.

Again Meighen rose in a white heat. "Do honourable gentlemen recall the loudest assertion of [Woodsworth's] speech," he cried, "that upon which he seemed to have the deepest conviction was a declaration that the most astounding fact of the whole thing was the appointment of Mr. Bureau to the Senate. . . . Will the honourable gentleman tell me where that is in his amendment? His amendment is a lot of eyewash, purposely eyewash, froth and foam, and he knows it. . . ."[30] As Woodsworth had admitted in his speech, his position was open to criticism on these grounds, but he had already given his own reasons for taking that position. He fully expected the Meighen attack and even the harsh words, far more bitter to him, of M. N. Campbell who declared that while he agreed with Woodsworth's analysis of the two-party system he could not accept his readiness "to whitewash one of the worst scandals in the whole history of Canada on the ground of political expediency."[31]

Whether Woodsworth was right or wrong in his definition of where the real question of principle was to be found, the Speaker's ruling that his amendment was in order was a hollow victory for the Liberals. When the vote was taken it was defeated 117–115.

Not technically defeated, since a private member's amendment was being voted upon, still the government had been virtually defeated. When a Progressive sub-amendment was then moved and called out of order by the Speaker, Woodsworth reversed his vote, helping to defeat the Speaker's ruling by a majority of two. The inconsistency of

[29]*Toronto Star*, June 24, 1926. The *Star*'s account of Woodsworth's exchange with Meighen on this occasion suggests that Woodsworth "got the best of it." Other reports of the sitting indicate that Meighen was somewhat warmer than is suggested in the icicle figure portrayed by Mr. Bruce Hutchison in *The Incredible Canadian* (Toronto, 1952), p. 115.

[30]Hansard, 1926, pp. 4983 *et seq.*

[31]*Ibid.*, p. 5019. Bourassa had decided, on similar grounds to those declared by Woodsworth, to vote with the government.

this vote is more apparent than real; since the government was obviously falling, Woodsworth believed the ruling was wrong, and, moreover, a vote on the Speaker's ruling (a procedural rather than a substantive question) is never considered a vote of confidence.

But by this time debate was wearing thin; it was clear that the government was doomed and it remained only to decide in what precise circumstances it would expire. Would those circumstances include a formal vote of censure or would the Prime Minister be able to escape that and go to the country as head of a government, with all the electoral advantage which that implied? King tried first to adjourn the House but the motion for this[32] (moved by the Progressive Beaubien) was defeated by one vote, Woodsworth this time voting for the motion. Finally, at five in the morning, King gave in to the extent of accepting the Progressive sub-amendment. This, it is true, damned the government's policy of interference with the course of justice in the courts, but King professed to see it as being no real censure. In any event, it meant that the House was adjourned without coming to a vote on the main censure amendment of H. H. Stevens. And before it met again King had set rolling the snowball of the "constitutional crisis" with which he could obscure the customs scandal and win an election. Technically the government had not been defeated on any substantive vote although it had failed to carry three successive divisions.

King at once advised Lord Byng, the Governor General, to grant him a dissolution, and the Governor General, with rigid correctness, refused the advice.[33] King resigned precipitously and left to Meighen the opportunity of forming a government. The succeeding events of this spectacular session suggest two points of importance with respect to Woodsworth's position. First, his consistency as compared to the vacillation of most of the Progressives, and secondly his refusal to justify King's advice to the Governor General.

On the first point he appears to have recognized clearly the fact that there was little to choose between a party that could elevate a Rogers or a Roblin and a party that could elevate a Jacques Bureau—in short, that one could go on indefinitely censuring governments of the old parties on such grounds, and having them succeeded by similar governments open to similar pressures. The real issues here

---

[32]*Ibid.*, p. 5088.

[33]The constitutionality of Byng's decision I take to have been fully proven and documented in E. A. Forsey, *The Royal Power of Dissolution of Parliament in the British Commonwealth* (Oxford, 1943).

were twofold: the problem of securing desirable legislation and the specific judicial question of cleaning up corrupt spots as they came to light.

On the second point Woodsworth was not so concerned with the constitutional issue as with the moral. King, he asserted, had not done the courageous thing in seeking a dissolution rather than fight the corruption question through the body in which a vote of censure was pending.[34] On the other hand, Woodsworth saw his own position vindicated in the troubles of Mr. Meighen. On accepting office, Meighen assumed responsibility for the Governor General's refusal to King of a dissolution—a course perfectly permissible to the opposition leader providing he had reasonable assurance of being able to form and carry on a stable government. But this assurance consisted in a very unstable understanding with the Progressives to the effect that they would assist him to complete the unfinished business of the session. On the very record of these Progressives it was obvious that they might bolt at any time if an issue close to their hearts were injected into the debates, and that, as good last-ditchers, they would argue that the government should not consider every substantive vote as involving confidence. Thus Meighen really had no assurance at all of being able to carry on and therefore little real justification for accepting office. Even the necessity of saving the Crown from disrepute or of passing the money supply to carry on ordinary government seems artificial. For, if the Governor General had been unable to find anyone willing to form a government, King could have been recalled and then granted his dissolution (in which case he would almost certainly have lost the 1926 election). It was the consideration that Meighen was "very much deceived if he ever thought that he could carry on without an election" rather than the hollow criticism that his shadow government of acting ministers was illegal, that most impressed Woodsworth about the Tory leader's course in 1926.[35]

In the sequel of Meighen's attempt to carry on a government, the inconsistency of the Progressive position was clearly underlined. First the key Progressive votes supported the government to defeat a sub-amendment by the Liberal Rinfret which would have struck out the censure element of the original Stevens amendment and which called for a Royal Commission to investigate the whole history of the Customs

[34]J. S. Woodsworth, "The Week at Ottawa," July 16, 1926, scrapbook clipping of one of a series of articles printed in various labour and farm journals across the country.
[35]*Ibid.*

Department. Then they helped pass the Stevens censuring amendment. But when, on July 1, the vote on the Robb motion (which formulated the ridiculous Liberal thesis that Meighen's "shadow Cabinet" was illegal) was taken, the key Progressive votes were again switched and the Meighen government was defeated on a straight confidence vote. The Progressives now argued that Byng had been wrong in refusing a dissolution to King and that Meighen's government of acting ministers was unconstitutional.[36] But both these points should have been foreseen. In wavering, the Progressives (basically the critical votes of the Ginger Group) had slaughtered two governments and advanced their legislative programme not one inch.

The lesson of 1926 for the Canadian Left was that the frontier political naïveté of constituency representation and group government would win no national strength; that either to obtain influence in legislation or to implement policy, the party system must be accepted. Political purity would have to be sought not by breaking old parties but by establishing a new one. Even the most steadfast constituency-firsters had for some time been reconsidering their position. As the *Calgary Albertan* editorialized in 1924: although a farmer-labour party was not immediately practicable, the Ginger Group was preparing the way.[37]

The years from 1927 to 1932 witnessed growing concentration on the question of federal political organization. The position of Woodsworth, with a record of political sanity throughout the constitutional crisis, and of integrity since his entrance into public life, was prominent.

[36]See Morton, *Progressive Party*, p. 256.
[37]*Calgary Albertan*, Oct. 9, 1924.

PART III: 1928-1935

16

THE DEPRESSION (I)

CANADIAN PROSPERITY IN THE 1920's moved on to its climax in 1928 and 1929. Yet throughout that whole decade the benefits of prosperity were distributed in total disregard of any principle of equity. Indeed, it was the great inequalities that lent significance to Woodsworth's appeal and formed the basis of his analysis. With economic depression beginning at the end of 1929 and deepening steadily in the early thirties, more and more people gave heed to his declamations—people to whom he had earlier appeared a Cassandra.

The "hungry thirties" were a harvest time of political revolt; yet they were certainly not viewed by Woodsworth as any blessing in disguise. It is true that the spreading disillusionment of the time produced vociferous general criticism of capitalism and that this provided a springboard from which to launch the Co-operative Commonwealth Federation. But the C.C.F. founding meetings at Calgary and Regina were also the maturation of the ideas and experiences of several decades. Thirty-eight cents a bushel for wheat, loss of land, semi-starvation on the prairies, boys on the freight-trains, soup kitchens in the cities—all these injected into old problems a new urgency.

That Woodsworth had mercilessly and consistently castigated a prosperous Canada for its toleration of the grossest inequality of opportunity and welfare, for its failure to honour and safeguard individual liberties of thought and action, and for its unwitting acceptance of American dollar-sign values, indicated that he was concerned primarily with morality. But, as shown in his sparring with King over the interpretation of the "bread alone" passage, he was acutely aware of the necessity of a basic minimum of material well-being; the particular level established for such a minimum was perhaps not as important as that there should be a level. The spectacle of mass destitution, featuring as it did wide regional and class divergencies, sharpened his denunciation of North American capitalism, a denunciation which he transmitted to a widening circle in the country, in the towns, and in the universities.

Despite sporadic evidence of mediocre health, particularly high blood pressure, which kept him in bed over the Christmas season of 1929, he drew increasing satisfaction from the battle. He refused to modify his schedule of meetings from coast to coast—meetings and lectures that averaged close to two hundred a year from 1928 to 1935. From the varying activities of his family, also, he derived great pleasure. His wife continued her support of the women's branch of the labour movement and was a leading member and speaker of the Women's International League for Peace and Freedom. In 1931, Woodsworth observed meetings of the League Assembly in Geneva, as an invited temporary collaborator, and his wife attended sessions of the executive of the W.I.L.P.F. After Geneva their trip was extended to Austria, Russia, Germany, France, and England. In these years, too, his sons and daughters were maturing—completing their university work, travelling in Europe and the East, and going on to further fields in the Sorbonne, the London School of Economics, medical school, journalism, and teaching. Grace and Charles each acted as private secretary to their father at different sessions of Parliament and collaborated in the publication of booklets based on the revelations of Stevens' commission on price spreads and other investigations.[1]

In 1932 Grace was married to Angus MacInnis, who had been closely associated with Woodsworth in the British Columbia Federated Labour Party. This militant Scot from Prince Edward Island had spent his early working years in Vancouver as a street-railwayman, had become an official of his union, a staunch I.L.P. socialist, and in 1930 an M.P.; he was to be one of the fieriest speakers in the young C.C.F. party. Not unlike Woodsworth in some respects, MacInnis was a man completely dedicated, in whose life plan there was little place for recreation. By 1930 he had had considerable political experience. A Vancouver Alderman for five years, F.L.P. candidate at provincial elections in 1924 and 1928, he ousted the federal Liberal, Leon Ladner, in Vancouver South in 1930.

For the greater part of each year the family was widely scattered, but when Woodsworth was in his home in Winnipeg the house at 60 Maryland Street became, like all his "resting" places, a hive of

[1]*Canada through C.C.F. Glasses* (Ottawa, 1934); *Jungle Tales Retold* (Ottawa, n.d.).

activity. People came from all classes in Winnipeg and from across the country to discuss the organizational problems of the C.C.F., the League for Social Reconstruction, the politics of city and province, the comments of the Webbs about Russia, or simply to renew old friendships. And the Winnipeg home, like all aspects of Woodsworth's life, reflected his linking of altruism and personal puritanism. The slight and dignified host, his hair and beard already streaked with white and his health far from robust, made no concession to the stark climate of the prairie capital. More than one of his old colleagues contracted colds in the cool air of the Woodsworth living-room, whose temperature was never permitted to reach the hot-house levels of most Winnipeg houses.

Woodsworth generally managed a holiday of two or three weeks each year, usually on the west coast. But these were likely to be intruded upon by sporadic speech-making, or else to be combined with attendance at summer study groups. In the autumn of 1928 he travelled to Halifax with the tour of the Empire Parliamentary Association, and talked over with other labour leaders of the Commonwealth their mutual problems. In London in 1932 he renewed some of these acquaintances and made others, including George Lansbury, J. C. Smuts, and Mahatma Gandhi. His opinion of Gandhi was that the Indian leader was neither saint nor fanatic, but human, intelligent, and a shrewd bargainer. He returned from his trip to Russia in 1931 with a sober yet optimistic evaluation. Everywhere in the U.S.S.R. he was impressed with the sense of a "people on the march"; the inefficiency which he observed on every hand was balanced by boundless activity, with tangible results in dams and factories. He did not approve the ubiquitous evidence of central authority. But this, he thought, was to some extent countered by the experimentalism in such things as sex equality, education, and "real judgment by peers." While there, he met Maurice Hindus and Anna Louise Strong. Under the guidance of Intourist he was apparently permitted to travel quite freely. In general he was more impressed with the evident economic success of central planning than with the curtailment of civil liberties, although he did not ignore the latter, particularly as it affected education.[2]

Reports of Woodsworth's opinions about Russia, and of his speeches, brought forth adverse comment in most of the press. Although the *Toronto Star*, the Ottawa *Citizen*, *Le Devoir* and sometimes the

[2]See two articles on the Russian tour published in the *Toronto Star Weekly*, Dec. 5, and Dec. 12, 1931.

Winnipeg *Tribune* managed to tolerate him, or even to be mildly laudatory, others were stirred to bitter criticism. The Toronto *Telegram*, for example, reporting a speech he made in 1929 to the Student Christian Movement at the University of Toronto, noted that the meeting was followed by the establishment of a "Fabian Society" by the students. "Petting," thundered the *"Tely,"* "is no longer the chief menace in the university." The Liberal *Globe* on the same occasion saw clear signs of communist influence in the university.[3] Equally informed comments came from the communist *Worker*, such as the headline to an article on Woodsworth: "Pacifist Flunkey of the Ruling Class."[4]

In the House in these years Woodsworth's watching brief was accompanied again by constant recapitulation of the socialist-neutralist position and the demand for immediate action on specific problems. It was probably the debates he instigated that, more than anything else, brought him the support of a large number of "intellectuals"; the university quarterlies, the *Canadian Forum*, and occasionally the editorial pages of papers like *Saturday Night* and the *Free Press* paid tribute to his irritant qualities and, according to their lights, praised or condemned his stand on specific issues. Typical was the comment of C. W. Stanley writing in the *Dalhousie Review* in 1929: "I should like to know whether any readers of the *Review* who are also readers of Hansard think that any other member has instituted debates as excellent as those provoked by Mr. Woodsworth in the past two years."[5]

Early in the session of 1930 Woodsworth began to press the government to define its attitude toward unemployment insurance. At the outset he asked King whether he would assist the provinces in coming together to establish an unemployment insurance scheme. The reply was made with characteristic caution: yes, if the provinces would move first.[6] By April, unemployment was snowballing into a problem of unescapable magnitude. Woodsworth sparked a debate which probably was a major factor in the government's defeat at the polls that year.[7] He granted that the spread of unemployment reflected conditions outside as well as inside Canada, but declared that it was

[3]Toronto *Telegram* and Toronto *Globe*, Jan. 29, 1929.
[4]Toronto *Worker*, June 29, 1929.
[5]*Dalhousie Review*, July, 1929.
[6]Hansard, 1930, p. 107.
[7]*Ibid.*, pp. 1147 *et seq.* In 1933 Woodsworth referred to this debate (*ibid.*, 1932, p. 445), as being the "chief cause" of the Liberal defeat in 1930. Most observers agreed that King's blunder, symbolized by his remark that he would not give a five-cent piece to any province with a Tory government, did much to lose him the election.

no longer possible to argue that its relief could be anything but a national responsibility. In the new context, King's argument that subsidizing the provinces was a "vicious principle" was outdated. The Prime Minister, said Woodsworth, "may represent a constituency in Western Canada but he does not understand the spirit of the West if he thinks he can hide behind the B.N.A. Act when such important questions as this are at stake." The heart of the government's answer, voiced by Heenan, as Minister of Labour, was that "unemployment insurance will be adopted in Canada only after public opinion has been educated to the necessity for such legislation."

Indeed, as the signs of depression increased, the government seemed to grow still more conservative—perhaps the result of representing the West in the cabinet by cautious veterans like Robert Forke and Charles Dunning. The ministry reared like a frightened filly when Woodsworth moved an amendment to the 1930 Coal Bounty Act which would exclude from the act's benefits any company not guaranteeing the eight-hour day, forty-eight hour week, and fair and reasonable wages.[8] The amendment was lost by a vote of 37–62. Both King and Dunning rose to argue that the amendment would discriminate against a single company. Woodsworth and others replied that the entire tariff structure was discriminatory, full of conditions, and that the principle of the amendment might profitably be extended far beyond the coal industry. When, on the motion for third reading of the coal bill Woodsworth moved that it be sent back to committee for amendment, his suggestion was again negatived, but the vetoing majority was decreased and Tory support for his idea had grown. Like the Hoover administration to the south, the King government had overstepped itself in its backward plunge.

When the new Bennett government, in the Special Session of 1930, sought a free hand in the administration of a twenty million dollar relief fund, Woodsworth supported it on the ground that conditions varied greatly across the country. He applauded the change from the previous government's caution which had grown out of King's "obsession with the sense of our constitutional difficulties."[9] But until the pre-election session of 1935 Bennett and his colleagues displayed almost as little constructive statesmanship as had their predecessors. Federal relief continued to be *ad hoc* and inadequate to prevent bankruptcy and near-bankruptcy amongst the municipalities and provinces. Public works were trifling; they were not the product of any such broad principle of human conservation as that which illuminated

[8]*Ibid.*, 1930, pp. 2732 *et seq.*   [9]*Ibid.*, Special Session, p. 166.

the Hopkins-Roosevelt New Deal measures. High tariffs and an Imperial Economic Conference with dubious results on the international flow of trade seemed to exhaust Tory imaginations.

Enraged and frustrated by knowledge of the loss of skills and the degradation of human dignity across the land, Woodsworth proclaimed in the House that "if a government cannot provide the opportunity to work—yes, I will take the responsibility of saying it—that government thereby ceases to have any claim upon the loyalty or obedience of the people."[10] When Bennett stated, in reply to a question from Woodsworth, that the government could not launch an unemployment insurance scheme because it did not yet know all the risks involved, Woodsworth pointed out that there had been little hesitation when railways, coal mines, and steel factories came for assistance—in short, that Canada would never have been built if "all the risks" had been known.[11]

Month after month from 1930 to 1935 Woodsworth voiced the plea for action. It was a prayer supported by ever more graphic word-pictures of the great tragedy which was befalling Canada's working population, her farmers, and her youth. When, finally, in 1935 the Conservative leader reversed himself and brought down, as part of his "new deal" programme, an unemployment insurance bill, Woodsworth acclaimed its good features. But he remarked that it contained no provision for the then unemployed, that it excluded too many classes and ignored British experience of the preceding twenty-five years. His criticism sprang from long study of the problem and it was an integral part of his chosen job as special watch-dog of the working man. A number of major measures of the government carried implications for labour that would not have found clear expression in the House save for the willingness of Woodsworth and his colleagues to remain particularly vigilant. In 1933, for example, the government introduced a bill providing for the elimination of duplicated services between the two great railway systems. Woodsworth's only participation in the debate was to gain assurance of provision for workers displaced in the process. "We are trying," he said, "to provide that the bond-holders shall not suffer, but even in bankruptcy proceedings the last stick cannot be taken out of the house and the family left helpless."[12]

The onset of the depression intensified the problems of class and sectional relationships in Canada. But while these problems of broad economic and social policy had to be faced, other questions involving

[10]*Ibid.*, 1931, p. 623.　　　[11]*Ibid.*, p. 1108.　　　[12]*Ibid.*, 1932–3, p. 4017.

individual liberties and the administration of justice lost none of their importance. In the protection of individual rights Woodsworth was as vigorous in these years as he was in the drive for economic reform.

One area of the administration of justice not only obstructed the business of Parliament but also harboured serious inequities. This was the field of divorce procedure. In the 1920's there were still three provinces (Quebec, Ontario, and Prince Edward Island) in which divorce could only be obtained by means of private bills passed through both Houses of Parliament. The average number of such bills each year between 1926 and 1930 was 183. Each bill had to be considered in some detail by a committee of the Senate, then passed or rejected by that House and, if approved, pushed on to the Commons for the necessary three readings there. In the Commons the bills were usually passed in large blocks seldom receiving detailed consideration by the members. Even so, they cluttered up the order paper, laid upon members a moral responsibility which could not possibly be discharged, and occupied some time; and they took a good deal of time in the Senate. More particularly, the cost of obtaining a divorce under this system was very high and the Senate did not—indeed, could not— consider divorce bills with anything like the competence of a regularly established court of law. In particular, it could not make binding provisions for alimony or the proper maintenance of the children of broken marriages.

Although the number of divorce bills was increasing there were obstacles in the path of reform. The members from predominantly Roman Catholic Quebec formed a solid barrier against the establishment of any divorce court in that province. In addition, the majority of Quebec members took the position that they could not vote to establish a divorce court in Ontario since that would mean extending the legal recognition of divorce. Some of the more artful even argued that such action would be an infringement of provincial rights.

Prior to the 1929 session there had been several attempts to obtain federal establishment of a divorce court for Ontario. In 1928 such a bill, originating in the Senate, never reached the discussion stage in the Commons despite Woodsworth's strenuous efforts to create a virtual blockade against private divorce bills; in 1929 he reopened his private war for an Ontario divorce court by sponsoring the same bill in the House of Commons. The bill, he said, "is a foundling left on my door-step, but since I urged last year that it be given a chance to live, I could not refuse to adopt it this year. Little did I think that the time would come when I would sponsor a bill for the relief of the

Senate. . . ."[13] He proceeded to build an overwhelming case for the bill: the injustice of the existing method, which favoured the wealthy; the 548 Canadian divorces obtained in Detroit courts in 1928; the inability of the Commons or even the Senate to deal properly with what was essentially a legal matter; the need of court directives for alimony and child maintenance; the opinion that, rather than encourage the immorality of divorce, the new method would eliminate much that was morally indefensible as matters then stood; finally, the telling point that it was the method and not the principle of divorce that was in question, since the principle was already recognized by Parliament. He could quote Henri Bourassa on the last point, and from Bourassa he received strong support. The bulk of Roman Catholics in the House, however, voted against the bill, denying the very principle of divorce. Bill number 38 was consequently negatived.

Woodsworth then moved on to fresh ground, where he could display both the power of a determined private member and the inherent weakness of the majority opinion. When the next batch of divorce bills arrived from the Senate he refused to let them slip through unnoticed. Instead, he rose and called for detailed consideration of one of the bills.[14] It was, he argued, beneath the dignity of the House to allow itself to be used as a rubber stamp and it lay heavily on his own conscience to give an automatic assent in such crucially important matters about which he knew nothing. Again he harried the members on the incongruous procedure they were tolerating. They could not, he argued, assume that proper consideration had been given the bills by the Senate divorce committee since in that committee the rules of evidence were not closely adhered to; they did not study the evidence themselves, and if they entered upon the enormous cost of printing and distributing the full evidence of each case to all members they would have such a body of obscene literature on their hands that the galleries would have to be cleared before full debate could ensue. The minds of the members, he declared, would become garbage cans.

He then touched off a series of very bitter comments about himself by stating that he would ask for a roll-call vote on the bills. In that way, he asserted, those opposed to divorce on grounds of religious belief could no longer salve their consciences merely by having the Speaker declare "Carried on division." He himself would vote against the bills, first, because he knew nothing of the details and, secondly, as a protest. Although sorry for the individuals concerned, he declared that the principle must be secured. Before the vote was taken on the

[13]Ibid., 1929, pp. 379 et seq.   [14]Ibid., pp. 1567 et seq.

first test case, Bourassa again braved the wrath of his French colleagues when he said that Woodsworth had "justified the course he has taken when he points out by way of exemplification the consequences of the attitude taken by the House. . . ."

When the vote on the bill was called[15] many members hastened from the House in a vain endeavour to avoid the issue, while the vote itself showed a real split running through party lines. A. A. Heaps, most of the Conservatives and most of the English-speaking Liberals voted for it; the Ginger Group and the French-speaking and Roman Catholic Liberals (except Bourassa) voted against. The Prime Minister was absent. The bill passed by 72–40, but the developing pattern of obstruction threatened the government's whole programme of business.

As the galleries began to fill up, Woodsworth asked the sponsor of another divorce bill on the list to outline the case for the House. He observed that the previous vote had been political and religious rather than judicial; that in a court the jurymen were present when the decision is given, but "half our jurymen ran behind the curtain." But the sponsor of the second bill declined to present the case, with the result that the bill was negatived 65–58. Obviously Woodsworth was gaining ground, and a serious political blockade was possible. The House had, by its second vote, approved the principle that each divorce case should be considered on its merits. But if this were done the ordinary business of the House would have to be set aside for long periods. As long as divorce bills were to go through the House, and as long as unanimous consent was necessary before they could be passed *en bloc* without discussion, the private member held a very high trump card.

When Woodsworth challenged a third divorce bill the top men of both parties felt compelled to defend their position. Charles Dunning, for the government, argued that the Commons could accept in good conscience the findings of the Senate committee. Furthermore, he said heatedly, the House had just turned down a bill to establish an Ontario divorce court and all this opposition was most unjust. Bennett sprang to his aid, pointing out that the work of Parliament was necessarily divided between the two Houses, and in the case of divorce bills the action of the Commons was legitimately a mere formality. As the debate grew warmer the Speaker had frequently to call for order and Woodsworth found his latent support becoming more specific. Bourassa, Agnes Macphail, and now C. G. Power, the Liberal bad boy from Quebec South, were all quick to defend him against the

15*Ibid.*, p. 1585.

charge that his obstructionist tactics were "lowering the dignity of the House." An attempt to obtain debate and clarification of an issue, they and others agreed, could never debase the House. The bill this time was passed 68–47.

The following day another divorce bill was introduced and Irvine called for a vote. This time more members voted and the political implications began to be felt more sharply. Mackenzie King on this occasion voted for the bill, which was passed 99–56.[16] When, a week later, Woodsworth began the procedure of examining bills all over again when they came up for second reading, King rose to appeal for passage of divorce bills for the duration of the session on the understanding that he would consult with those who wished to reform the procedure. Woodsworth agreed to drop his attack temporarily, and a large batch of bills sailed through the three stages in short order.

Woodsworth's key arguments had brought the divorce issue clearly into focus, and by the end of 1929 there was little doubt that reform would follow in the near future. The Senate committee had been shown to fall far short of the standards of procedure and to be lacking the powers of a court of law over civil rights; the existing procedure obviously favoured the wealthy and gave too much publicity to divorce cases. The House of Commons could not correct the deficiencies of the Senate committee because it was not capable of giving the necessary time, or of functioning as a proper court, especially since its votes, when recorded, were transparently based on religious affiliation.

In 1930 Woodsworth reintroduced a bill to establish an Ontario divorce court, observing that similar bills had three times previously been passed by the Senate.[17] On the second reading he reminded the House of the Prime Minister's promise to facilitate reform in this field, noted that the divorce bills of the last session had been allowed through on this understanding, and offered to withdraw his private bill if the government would substitute one of its own.[18] King did not accept this suggestion. Instead he permitted his followers to proceed according to their own views while he himself endeavoured to come down lightly on both sides.

The delaying tactics adopted were interesting. The second reading of the divorce court bill was moved on March 7 without a vote being reached that day. On March 11, while Woodsworth and other supporters were out of the House, the second reading was suddenly reopened and a vote called. The result was a tie which, with the Speaker's casting vote, defeated the motion to "read the bill a second time."[19]

[16]Ibid., pp. 1621 et seq.
[18]Ibid., p. 392.
[17]Ibid., 1930, p. 292.
[19]Ibid., p. 503.

Then, on March 17, the French members who thought they had killed the bill by the snap vote were bitterly disappointed. Since the committee stage (detailed discussion) had not been reached before the vote was taken, William Irvine was able to move again that the bill be given its second reading on May 18.[20] This time, in a reasonably full House, the vote was won, 104–87, with Charles Dunning and many English Liberals voting against the solid French and Roman Catholic bloc.

The prospect of this kind of division must have unnerved the party whips. When King rose, during the committee stage, to state the government's position, he repeated that he was very anxious not to coerce any province. For that reason, he said, he wanted the House to insert a clause which would prevent the establishment of the divorce court until Ontario expressed a desire for it. When the majority indicated its opinion that this was simply a way of preventing or delaying the establishment of the court, King voted for the motion to give the six months' hoist to the bill, which was negatived 108–88.[21]

The next obstruction came from the Speaker who, with strong French support, postponed the third reading of the bill while at the same time endeavouring to get private divorce bills through in the old way. Finally, on May 6, Woodsworth was allowed to move the third reading.[22] An amendment to provide for a permissive petition from the Ontario legislature was defeated, as was a second amendment for a three months' hoist. The latter was supported by the Prime Minister and by French and English Roman Catholics of both parties. The bill was finally passed by a vote of 100–85 and a divorce court was won for Ontario.

It was a long and tricky battle and one which enhanced Woodsworth's national reputation as a skilled parliamentarian. A leading Senate advocate of the bill complimented him by letter, writing, "The success of this matter is entirely due to the courageous manner in which you have fought the question in the Commons. It was no easy task to overcome radical [sic] and religious prejudices that surround a bill of this kind. . . ."[23]

[20]Ibid., pp. 697 et seq.
[21]Ibid., p. 949.
[22]Ibid., pp. 1936 et seq.
[23]Printed in Olive Ziegler, Woodsworth, Social Pioneer (Toronto, 1934), p. 169. The transfer of jurisdiction in Ontario divorce cases from Parliament to the Ontario Supreme Court resulted in an immediate decrease in the number of Ontario divorces. This was the result of the deliberate court procedure of delay between the granting of the decree nisi and the decree absolute. The eventual increase in the divorce rate was undoubtedly due to causes other than the change in jurisdiction.

When still broader issues of civil liberties arose Woodsworth found that, in addition to the support of his farmer and labour colleagues, he could count on strong backing from Henri Bourassa, the doughty French-Canadian independent. Together in 1929 they reaffirmed in long speeches, and on the least favourable ground, their faith in an unqualified right of political and civil free speech, assembly, and publication. Bourassa at times exhibited the curious ambivalence of Roman Catholics in this field and drew the line sharply when the point of blasphemy or denigration of the Church was reached. But he found no difficulty in offering fiery support of Woodsworth's criticism of Judge Coatsworth and the Toronto police commissioners who were waging a violent local war against "the reds." He also agreed with Woodsworth that the exercise of censorship in the case of a Finnish communist newspaper was indefensible and he underlined, for the benefit of a dubious House, the fact that the nature of British liberty involved the acceptance of considerable risks by the state.[24]

As the old hysteria began to spread again, following the growth of unemployment, transiency, and unrest, Woodsworth flooded the pages of Hansard with case histories of police brutality, unwarranted suppression of public meetings, and invasions of private homes. Commenting in 1932 on Bennett's brusque dismissal of a delegation of unemployed men, Woodsworth questioned whether the people of Canada would much longer stand the spectacle of a millionnaire Prime Minister (cries of "Shame") surrounded by a heavy guard lecturing "poor people" because they did not speak to him in the most polite language.[25] When Manion denied that Bennett had had a guard, C. G. Power jumped up to declare that the entire building had been surrounded by tanks and cavalry during the interview.

By 1932, because of the near-collapse of provincial finances, the maritime and prairie governments had abandoned their provincial police forces and the police duty in those regions was assigned to the R.C.M.P. In that year a police reorganization bill was introduced by the government which, amongst other things, provided for the swearing-in of special unpaid constables, most of whom, said the bill's critics, would come from the ranks of private industrial police groups. Memories of 1919 brought Woodsworth to his feet for a lengthy and detailed analysis of the proposed legislation. This centralization of a powerful police force, he declared, "looks in the direction of military repression. . . . It is the transformation of a police force into a military

[24]Hansard, 1929, pp. 2352 et seq.
[25]Ibid., 1932, p. 958.

force."[26] Once again he referred to the evidence of labour spy activity —"a system beneath contempt." Once more the danger was that the country would be led to confuse law and order with the *status quo*, and again Woodsworth, for his efforts, was branded a communist, this time most vociferously by the Conservative Nova Scotian, Isaac MacDougall of Inverness.

But Woodsworth's suspicion of the purposes for which the new model R.C.M.P. would be used was not unfounded. One of the most glaring cases of arbitrary arrest which he aired in the House concerned the apprehension of several foreign-born Winnipeggers, one of whom had lived in Canada for twenty years.[27] All were arrested for immediate deportation under the Immigration Act and were shipped out of town before a writ of *habeas corpus* could be sought. It was alleged, said Woodsworth, that they were communists. But that was not the question. The point at issue was procedural and it was crucial. Justice Minister Guthrie answered that the police had acted for the Immigration Department and that a departmental board would consider the case in Halifax. Here Woodsworth drove home his point. Was it true, he asked the Minister, that men could be arrested without warrant in Winnipeg and be transferred immediately to Halifax? The answer, of course, was "Yes" and gleeful Liberals rose one after the other to denounce the procedure. Apparently the Liberals had forgotten the record of their own government in the Cape Breton coal and iron towns.

Woodsworth turned the screw when he read to the House excerpts from a speech which he had heard delivered by Guthrie to the League Assembly in Geneva. The Minister had told the Assembly that Canada maintained "only such military and air forces as are necessary for the maintenance of law and order within our own borders."[28] Even as the expression of a habit of mind, this was disturbing in view of the massive evidence of expanding repressive machinery. Woodsworth labelled it an insult to Canadian workers. Guthrie's Geneva speech seemed to symbolize, as had Meighen's telegrams of 1919, the doctrine of quick force—the justification of which, should any be thought necessary, being always an afterthought. Thus when Guthrie was explaining his 1933 bill "to more closely regulate the carrying of offensive weapons" he could see little point in Woodsworth's question as to why the carrying of such weapons by the police was not to be similarly restricted, even when Woodsworth referred to the Montreal

[26]*Ibid.*, pp. 2591 *et seq.*
[27]*Ibid.*, pp. 2683 *et seq.*   [28]*Ibid.*, p. 2959.

policeman who had recently shot a man who offered resistance to eviction from his home.[29]

The development of the Bennett-Guthrie coercive state had other ramifications of which the attempt at thought-control, both inside and outside the House, was a spectacular example. The number of books banned in Canada increased sharply and when Woodsworth criticized the "undemocratic" refusal of the Department of National Revenue to publish a list of such books and sought to discover who really was the censor, the government's reply was a total evasion.[30] When Angus MacInnis moved for a debate on the unrest amongst British Columbia relief camp workers (which proved to be the origin of the Regina riot of 1935), in an attempt to settle the question peaceably, his motion was ruled out of order and the Speaker's ruling sustained by the crack of the party whip.[31]

Woodsworth's motion for debate met a similar fate after the relief camp strikers had decided to move to Ottawa with their grievance. Here the government's answer was that the motion was out of order because the agitation, having started two months earlier in Vancouver, was not of "recent occurrence." Instead of allowing debate on the question Guthrie declared the move on Ottawa was controlled by communists. It was, he implied, a distinct menace to the peace and as such required not debate but action. He reported that he had ordered the R.C.M.P. to enforce the Railway Act by preventing the strikers from continuing their riding on freight cars past Regina.[32] This was to produce a repetition on a small scale of the government's technique in the Winnipeg strike, of stimulated crisis and strong-arm suppression. Woodsworth received an opportunity to discuss the results of this policy in the 1936 session.

Throughout the Bennett years Woodsworth maintained a barrage of motions to amend the Criminal Code and the Immigration Act: to strike out section 98 of the Code, to safeguard freedom of assembly, to eliminate the power of deportation after ten years' residence in Canada. The reception given these motions by the government varied, but the result was always a negative. In 1932, when Woodsworth rose to ask leave to introduce the section 98 amendment, Bennett merely shouted across at him "No!" Lapointe hurled back the epithet "Mussolini" at the Prime Minister and finally the Speaker decided that Woodsworth was entitled to "explain" his amendment.[33] The first

[29]Ibid., 1932–3, p. 3513.
[30]Ibid., 1935, p. 1652.
[31]Ibid., p. 2974.
[32]Ibid., pp. 3587 et seq.
[33]Ibid., 1932, pp. 380 et seq.

reading was turned down 72–49. At least in the King Parliaments this amendment had been permitted a decent burial in the Senate.

In 1933 the same amendment reached second reading and a most revealing "debate" ensued.[34] Woodsworth observed that Tim Buck and the other communists who were then in the penitentiary at Kingston had been convicted, under section 98, not of using or of advocating the use of force, but of entertaining certain ideas. The section, he continued, did not define the use of force—it might apply to moral as well as physical force. Those accused under section 98 were assumed to be guilty until proven innocent; property *suspected* of belonging to illegal organizations was seizable; general search warrants were easily obtained; and the definitions of sedition and seditious material would include scores of books in the Parliamentary Library. To all of this and more, the government replied only by reference to the "crisis" and by use of the derogatory innuendo. "If there was reason to pass such a section in 1918 [*sic*]," said Guthrie, "there is certainly reason to keep such a section in force in the year 1933. . . . Section 98 is not in any sense a hindrance to any right-thinking person." John R. MacNicol of Toronto castigated Woodsworth and MacInnis as reds in a long and bitter personal attack. The chief ray of hope was in the strong support given Woodsworth's amendment by Ernest Lapointe. In the vote the second reading was lost 89–45. Even against the intervening Liberal story of reluctance to balance police-militia action with a generous national policy of social welfare, the Tory strangulation of civil liberty in 1919 and during the Bennett régime is a disheartening record.

[34]*Ibid.*, 1932–3, pp. 2006 *et seq.*

17

THE DEPRESSION (II)

For two generations we had an outlet in Western Canada but that outlet is not only closed, the people are drifting back to the East from that country. In the old days we could send people from the cities to the country. If they went out today they would meet another army of unemployed coming back from the country to the city; that outlet is closed. What can these people do? They have been driven from our parks; they have been driven from our streets; they have been driven from our buildings and in this city they actually took refuge on the garbage heaps.[1]

THUS WOODSWORTH IN THE DEBATE on the 1931 budget, questioned whether in Canada there would be evolution or revolution. To support his criticism of the "shamelessly arrogant" budget he drew on both Roman Catholic and Protestant statements. From St. Augustine he reminded the House that "they who possess superfluity possess the goods of others"; from the United Church Conference he repeated the claim that the extended idea of corporate private property must be challenged. The budget proposed to relieve the rich of taxation and to increase the taxation of all others, he argued, since it contained no progressive principle of direct taxation. When he was challenged on his demand for a federal inheritance tax and asked whether he favoured a double inheritance duty (duplicating the provincial levies) he replied, "I would double, treble and quadruple it. . . ."

As the federal division of jurisdiction broke down under the weight of the depression Woodsworth was among the first to call for a redistribution of financial powers between the provinces and the central government. Indeed, revision of the B.N.A. Act had been a primary goal for him since 1922. But he refused to take the Liberal position that nothing should be done in the meantime to undermine provincial

[1]Hansard, 1931, p. 2752.

autonomy. Thus he supported the Conservative government's bill to re-establish federal aid to education in the provinces, a form of subsidy which had been discontinued by King. This policy of federal grants-in-aid, he claimed, was not the "vicious principle" alleged by Lapointe and King, and he castigated them for their "Gladstonian ideas of finance."[2]

As the report of Stevens' Price Spreads Commission was to reveal, and as the later Sirois Commission again underlined, both the war and the depression had hastened the consolidation of control of the Canadian economy in the hands of a relatively small group of individuals and corporations. It was against this background that Woodsworth and his C.C.F. colleagues presented the case for socialism in the 1930's. The Bennett-sponsored Imperial Economic Conference, and higher tariffs, claimed Woodsworth, only obscured the issue of welfare within Canada and benefited exclusively the protected industrialists. Once more, when the Prime Minister brought down the Ottawa trade agreements for quick decision and prohibited general debate upon them, Woodsworth saw the spectre of a puppet Parliament dangling on strings from the hands of the interlocking directorates of Canadian finance and industry. "With us," he declared, "Parliamentary elections are becoming simply a means of deciding who for the next five years will be the big boss." He pointed out that the strengthened party machines, the immense campaign funds, and the ruthless party whips in the House had created the unhealthy situation where in the preceding eleven years only three men had broken with their parties— and these had not been "permitted" to return to the House.[3] Thus it was that Parliament considered no basic changes, while profits and dividends remained high, and one-third of the population of Montreal was on relief. Thus it was that while Canadian textile firms sheltered behind a towering wall of tariff protection, nothing was done to stop their requiring "yellow-dog" agreements from their workers.[4] And for the same reasons, said Woodsworth, when the government finally established the Bank of Canada as a central financial control, it allowed the capital to be privately subscribed. The Bank did, in fact, remain essentially a private institution until the Liberals "nationalized" it in 1938.[5]

The proponents of public ownership and public enterprise found useful arguments in two deals which had been entered into under the King administration. One was in Manitoba (1928) whereby the

[2]*Ibid.*, pp. 1969 *et seq.*   [3]*Ibid.*, 1932–3, p. 432.
[4]*Ibid.*, p. 1445.   [5]*Ibid.*, 1935, p. 459.

federal government sanctioned a lease of water power on the Winnipeg River granted by the Bracken government to the Winnipeg Electric Company. Federal approval was necessary at that time because the prairie governments did not obtain control of their natural resources until 1930. The Winnipeg Electric Company, said Woodsworth in airing the matter in the House, was intent on using the power of the Seven Sisters Falls to the detriment of the Winnipeg city hydro.[6] Failing to get results from the provincial legislature which, indeed, passed a contrary resolution, the Company allegedly made heavy contributions to the Bracken campaign chest and received approval. Then the provincial government applied to King's Minister of the Interior, Stewart, for acceptance of the lease. Stewart promised to consult all the Manitoba M.P.'s before acting on Bracken's request. This he failed to do, although he did seek the opinion of some of the Manitoba members. From Woodsworth's point of view this represented a double aggression against the principle of democracy. At both levels of government the executive had ridden roughshod over the legislature and the power of corporations irresponsible to the public will was greatly advanced, for the Winnipeg Electric Company was simply one unit of the gigantic Power Corporation of Canada which in turn was closely linked to other industrial and financial institutions.

When the Winnipeg Electric Company's lease was confirmed, Woodsworth rose to ask, "what influences have operated here in Ottawa . . . to make the Minister of the Interior disregard his promises made to the Manitoba members of this House. . . . If I had time to read the names of the directors of all these corporations [controlled by the directors of the Power Corporation of Canada] I think we would begin to see how powerful a combination we poor Manitoba members were really up against." With what amounted almost to prescience, he then asked what might happen in the future to the great power sites of the St. Lawrence River and other water courses. Stewart's defence against these charges was that "some Manitoba members" had changed their minds "materially" during the summer; King added that an agreement with Bracken during the summer, which permitted full provincial control over natural resources pending formal transfer of this power, overruled Stewart's prior commitment to the Manitoba members.

Woodsworth also gave strong support to the demand of Robert Gardiner and E. J. Garland for a full investigation of the Beauharnois power contracts—a phase of Canadian government which King was

[6]*Ibid.*, 1929, pp. 440 *et seq.*

to call his valley of humiliation and which the Ginger Group and later the C.C.F. saw as the St. Lawrence "successor to the Seven Sisters steal."[7]

Beauharnois and the Seven Sisters represented merely the grosser aspects of the system which precluded democratic control of the economic life of the nation, subverted political democracy and substituted the maintenance of monopolistic prices for a planned balance between production and consumption. The symptoms of cancerous disease in the system—over-production, mass unemployment, political corruption, extreme contrasts in wealth between classes and regions—now should make it abundantly clear, argued Woodsworth, that nothing but replacement by a different system could solve the problem.

Opportunities to present the socialist case increased during the 1930's. The political atmosphere was filled with challenges to and denunciations of the "capitalist system." In and after the summer of 1932, the American New Deal platform with its acceptance of a considerable measure of planning and federal responsibility for welfare attracted much attention in Canada. The Conservative government itself, with its establishment of a publicly owned radio system and its "new deal" legislation of 1935 opened the door still further to an almost continuous debate about the merits of planning and socialism.

In 1932, for example, Woodsworth and Robert Gardiner suggested to the Prime Minister that if it was right to safeguard the public interest by a national radio commission, then it should be correct for the government to purchase the claims of radium prospectors in the North-West Territories, since the physical welfare of many people might be at stake.[8] In the same year Woodsworth introduced what was to prove the first of an annual series of C.C.F. resolutions: "That in the opinion of this House the government should immediately take measures looking to the setting up of a co-operative commonwealth in which all the natural resources and the socially necessary machinery of production will be used in the interest of the people and not for the benefit of the few."[9]

In a fiery speech supporting the resolution, he quoted from the encyclical of Pius XI on the results of capitalism:

The immense number of property-less wage earners on the one hand and the super-abundant riches of the fortunate few on the other is an unanswerable argument that the earthly goods so abundantly produced are far from rightly distributed and equitably shared among the various classes of

[7]*Ibid.*, 1931, p. 1753.
[8]*Ibid.*, 1932, p. 3283.   [9]*Ibid.*, pp. 726 *et seq.*

men. . . . In the first place, then, it is patent that in our days not alone is wealth accumulated, but immense power and despotic economic domination is concerted in the hands of a few, and that those few are frequently not the owners but only the trustees and directors of invested funds who administer them at their good pleasure. . . .

Here was an excellent description of the nature of the new industrial feudalism, said Woodsworth, and Henri Bourassa added his approval. But Woodsworth did not draw the corporatist-clerical conclusion. Instead, he quoted resolutions of the Alberta Conference of the United Church, and of the farmers' organizations of Alberta, Saskatchewan, and Manitoba, all of which denounced the economic principle of competition and called for the substitution of co-operation and public ownership. "The motive of private gain," he insisted, "is not the one that induces most of us to go along from day to day." As to how the transition could be achieved democratically, he referred members to the Webb's *Constitution for the Socialist Commonwealth of Great Britain.* The resolution was supported by all the members of the Ginger Group, while the few members who remained in the House to hear the debate offered criticism which varied from accusations of impracticability and idealism to J. R. MacNicol's unhesitating announcement that Woodsworth looked to the establishment of a communist dictatorship.

By 1935, Woodsworth was arguing that the resolution had become more practical every year—with C.C.F. mayors in four cities (Winnipeg, St. Boniface, Windsor, and Toronto) a C.C.F. voting strength of 300,000 in the provincial elections in British Columbia, Saskatchewan, and Ontario, C.C.F. official opposition in British Columbia and Saskatchewan, and a carefully considered national programme.[10] The wording of the resolution itself had become more specifically socialist, and now read "A co-operative commonwealth in which the profit motive would be subordinated to that of public service and ruthless competition replaced by collective ownership under democratic control."

Arguing the case in 1935, Woodsworth made full use of Bennett's picturesque language, which had been a characteristic feature of the Prime Minister's radio broadcasts in January. In these talks Conservatives had been notified that they would sponsor a whole network of "new deal" legislation. The Prime Minister, said Woodsworth, had himself provided a comprehensive indictment of capitalism. Did Mr. Bennett realize the meaning of the phrases he had used? " 'In the crash and thunder of toppling capitalism. . . .' Does that mean any-

[10]*Ibid.*, 1935, pp. 691 *et seq.*

thing? Again: 'The old order has gone. It will not return.' Does that mean anything? He goes further in that than I could possibly go. . . ." But when Woodsworth suggested that the Prime Minister had been reading the Price Spreads Report to pick up phrases like "economic parasites," Bennett remained unruffled and told Woodsworth, "I think I got that from the honourable gentleman."

Woodsworth concluded his statement in 1935 with a specific denial of "highly bureaucratic state socialism"; there can be no doubt that he remained fully aware of the totalitarian danger which might lurk either in Tory paternalism or socialist dogmatism. The lines of socialist development in Canada, he asserted, were already vaguely sketched and could be seen in municipal enterprise such as the Toronto Transportation Commission and the Ontario Hydro Commission; provincial hydro-electric; telephones; federal undertakings such as the Bank of Canada, the C.N.R., and the radio commission; and the co-operative field, mainly the wheat pool and consumers' co-operatives. "Along these and kindred lines," he suggested, "we seek to develop the co-operative principle under which the profit motive would be subordinated to the public service." Jean Francois Pouliot remarked that "the only difference between [Woodsworth] and Gandhi is the goat and the spinning-wheel . . . [he and his group] will be the czars of Canada . . . they are czarists. They believe in autocracy. . . ." A few days later Pouliot voted against the Unemployment Insurance and Social Insurance bill.[11]

Woodsworth and his colleagues gave qualified support to Bennett's social legislation of 1034–5. They voted for the measures but criticized their inadequacy and lack of cohesion. In 1934 the government obtained passage of a Natural Products Marketing Act and a Farmers' Creditors Arrangement Act, both designed to alleviate the distress on the prairies. In the 1935 session a much broader programme of legislation was enacted, including national administration of a minimum wage, the forty-eight hour week, a weekly day of rest, and unemployment and social insurance. The anti-trust laws were strengthened (through amendments to the Criminal Code and the Companies Act) and a commission was established to regulate business practices. Finally, the creation of a National Economic Council was authorized to aid the government in any economic planning it might envisage.

Although there were numerous specific points of criticism elaborated by the C.C.F. members, the immediate and essential one was the question of constitutionality. For years the Liberals had seemed to

[11]*Ibid.*, p. 1639.

shelter behind the decisions of the Judicial Committee of the Privy
Council which had whittled down the powers of the federal government almost to the vanishing point; for years Woodsworth had been
assailed for his impractical suggestions of government action which
would automatically run afoul of the narrow "peace-time" constitutional powers of Ottawa; and for years he had advocated, to no avail,
a revision of the B.N.A. Act which would enable the central government to deal with new national problems. Now a Conservative
government admitted the need for national action and proposed a
programme of wide consequence. Woodsworth observed that although
the reforms were good in their immediate purpose, they did not
constitute a basic revision of capitalism but rather they were an
attempt to "stabilize the two classes of producers and parasites"; there
was no proposal to expand government enterprise and no application
of steeply graded income and inheritance taxation. That, he said, was
where he and the Prime Minister must part company. But even
granting the ameliorative aspect of Bennett's new deal, he argued,
"unless some method is evolved of settling the matter of jurisdiction
it is not fair to introduce legislation which may be challenged in the
courts."[12]

This was the crucial point. The C.C.F. and the Liberals were
agreed that the entire block of legislation was *ultra vires* of the federal
powers as those powers were interpreted by the Judicial Committee.
But the Liberals offered no alternative. Woodsworth concluded that
the government's whole programme was an artful dodge to deprive
the Liberals of electoral victory in 1935 and to undercut the growing
political strength of socialism. He was sure that the Conservative
manœuvre, of basing federal authority to enact some of this legislation
upon the treaty-implementing power (section 132) of the B.N.A. Act,
would be unsuccessful, since whenever he himself had suggested this
power to previous administrations he had been told quite distinctly
by the best legal minds that it would not stand up before the imperial
court.

Bennett's legislation professing to implement the labour and other
conventions into which Canada had entered following the 1919 treaty
settlement was indeed declared *ultra vires* by the Judicial Committee
of the Privy Council when it rendered its decision in 1937. The
imperial judges asserted then that the B.N.A. Act did not empower
Ottawa to implement treaty agreements if the legislation impinged
upon property and civil rights or other fields reserved to the provinces.

[12]*Ibid.*, pp. 83 *et seq.*

The judicial argument was that section 132 of the B.N.A. Act, which permitted the central government to perform "the obligations of Canada or of any province thereof as part of the British Empire towards foreign countries arising under treaties between the Empire and such foreign countries" did not apply. This was so because the 1919 treaties and conventions had been signed separately by Canada and therefore were not Empire treaties. The Committee disregarded the fact that the Fathers of Confederation could not write the exact terms to cover such a case. In 1867, Canada did not possess the power to negotiate and sign treaties on her own behalf. The decisions of the imperial judges which since 1883 had consistently favoured the growth of provincial jurisdictions (with the exception of the radio and aviation cases in 1932) may have helped to keep Quebec and Ontario from too drastic an alteration of the federal scheme by unto-ward means; but by the 1930's the continuance of an emasculated central government was intolerable. The movement toward a stronger government at Ottawa was set on foot.

Although the means by which Ottawa increased its power over the provinces in the late thirties, forties, and fifties were various, the result has been a major trend towards increased centralization in Canadian government. In the origin of this movement Woodsworth played a significant rôle. Whether or not it involves serious political dangers in its future development remains a matter for speculation. To the present it has achieved, among other things, a considerable redistribution of wealth between classes and between regions.

In 1935, having assaulted the Bennett legislative programme at its weakest points, Woodsworth placed before the House a motion for a committee to study the best way of amending the B.N.A. Act so as to allow the federal government to deal with "urgent economic problems."[18] He noted that he had several times previously sponsored similar proposals and that in 1931 the government had virtually accepted his suggestion in principle. But no action had been forth-coming. His 1935 motion, however, was formally accepted by Guthrie on behalf of the government and was passed by the House. Although the House committee was established, its discussions bogged down in an interminable debate over which clauses of the "constitution" should be entrenched and thus require unanimous approval of the provinces prior to amendment. This debate became so formidable that the Liberal government was compelled to obtain amendment by the old method of a joint address of both Houses to the British Parliament in

[18]*Ibid.*, pp. 217 *et seq.*

1940 in order finally to create a federal unemployment insurance scheme. But although ponderous, the movement to modernize the federal system and to formalize Canadian independence did not cease to advance. Such important aims as the abolition of appeals to the Privy Council and the right to amend the B.N.A. Act (as it respects the central government alone) without reference to the British Parliament have been more recent markers along the path.

18

THE CO-OPERATIVE

COMMONWEALTH

FEDERATION

THE C.C.F. WAS BORN IN THE WEST, but the West was also acting as midwife at a national event. Much of the writing that has appeared on the origins and nature of the C.C.F. has taken for granted that the movement was, and the party would remain, a prairie farm protest. Already in previous chapters this thesis with its implication has been questioned. The C.C.F.'s ideological background had clear socialist elements; and it sprang from the urban labour movement, from the social gospel of the churches, and from radical intellectuals, as well as from the soil of the wheat belt. To view the C.C.F. as a function only of Saskatchewan grass-roots politics is certainly unhistorical. In particular this view overlooks the critical influence of Woodsworth, who had been working for the creation of a national farmer-labour party since 1918. In the complex events of the opening years of the depression it was the dynamic figure of this urban socialist that provided the essential unifying force for the new political federation. To speak of him as the real founder of the C.C.F. is not exaggeration.

It has already been noted that the early 1930's were favourable to the propagation of socialist ideas and organization. In this atmosphere the socialist labour movement of British Columbia elected Angus MacInnis its first federal M.P. in 1930; the farmers' movements across the country declared for a "Co-operative Commonwealth" and enunciated socialist programmes;[1] independent labour parties in all the

[1]By far the best account of the "socialization" of a farmers' movement is the analysis of Saskatchewan in Martin Lipset, *Agrarian Socialism* (Berkeley, 1950).

industrial towns and cities increased both their membership and influence; Protestant church statements were hostile to the existing economic arrangements and in many cases were socialistic; many branches of the labour union movement, although unionization was still in its infancy in Canada, were prepared to support socialist candidates. A. R. Mosher's influence in the All-Canadian Congress of Labour and the Canadian Brotherhood of Railroad Employees had carried those organizations well into the field of social democracy. With every one of these developments Woodsworth had close contacts, and each recognized in him its chief national spokesman.

Many middle-class and professional people, particularly in the universities, were also taking stock of the situation. "The sin of indifference," defined many years previously by Woodsworth, was coming to be recognized as something more than venial. There seemed now to be a real chance to start effective action for social justice. As F. H. Underhill wrote in the *Canadian Forum* in February, 1931, the real obstacle to Canadian radicalism had been the seemingly tremendous success of American business. "Now," he observed, "the little radical movements which have maintained a precarious existence here since the war will take on new life." Contacts between politically aware professors of Toronto, McGill, and elsewhere became more frequent, and began to take on the aspect of an *entente* between the universities and the radicals. In the spring of 1931, for example, the only members of Parliament to attend the annual meeting of the Canadian Political Science Association were from the Ginger Group.[2] There was some consternation in the press, and this reaction placed in jeopardy the positions of many liberal-socialist professors. Led by the Toronto *Telegram*, a large phalanx of newspapers across the country portrayed Woodsworth as a devil in saint's disguise, corrupting labour, farmers, and youth indiscriminately. Professor Underhill was seen as his archdisciple in the colleges, the dean of a sinister communist conspiracy among the nation's professors. And their mouthpiece was the *Canadian Forum*. Anyone who today reads back through the files of the *Forum*[3] cannot fail to be impressed by the whimsy of the newspaper allegations of communism. At the same time the estimate of its influence (with a circulation of approximately three thousand) was accurate.

Perhaps the chief criticism of this study is that it underemphasizes two factors: (a) the long history of socialist thought in the West, and (b) the fact that the Saskatchewan movement was part of a national one with strong urban and intellectual influences.

[2]*Canadian Forum*, July, 1931.

[3]For a concise history of the *Forum*, see three articles by Carlton McNaught in the *Canadian Forum*, April, May, and June, 1950.

Like other progressive elements in Canada, the *Forum*, after 1929, became more definitely collectivist in its editorial policy; for example, the League for Social Reconstruction (L.S.R.), established in 1932, could count on its close support. In April, 1932, the *Forum* announced the foundation of the L.S.R. "The experience of the last two years," ran the notice, "has produced a growing number of men and women in Canada who have become very sceptical about the ability of our capitalistic system to produce an efficient or happy society. . . . But individual critics are helpless by themselves." To render constructive criticism more effective, a group of professors, professional people, and some business men from Toronto and Montreal had met in February and decided to launch the new group. The article continued: "The founders of the League conceive of it as a kind of Canadian Fabian Society, although they are quite conscious that it does not include in its present membership any Bernard Shaw or Sydney Webb or Graham Wallas or Beatrice Potter."

The purposes of the League were clearly set forth: it was to be a nucleus around which might gather "unattached critical spirits" who could accept neither of the old parties and whose "circumstances do not make it possible for them to join labour or farmer political movements"; it would publish pamphlets, sponsor discussion and study groups, and build up a body of information on such questions as public ownership, planning, and the social services. The basis of membership was similar to that of the Fabian Society: active members must accept the manifesto of the League (social democracy with an emphasis on central planning); associate members, who could attend meetings and receive publications, need only signify general sympathy.

The provisional executive of the L.S.R. in 1932 consisted of Professors F. H. Underhill, F. R. Scott, King Gordon, E. A. Havelock, and J. F. Parkinson. The secretary was Isabel Thomas, daughter of Rev. Ernest Thomas with whom Woodsworth had been closely associated in the early social service work of the Methodist Church. Woodsworth himself accepted the position of honorary president of the L.S.R.—an honour to which he attached particular importance. Although he continued first and foremost to be the representative of the workers, he welcomed with pride the adherence to his cause of a formally organized professional and intellectual group.

There can be little doubt now of the important place occupied in Canadian political life by the L.S.R. Although it was dissolved at the beginning of the Second World War[4] it exercised in its seven years of

[4] An attempt to revive the L.S.R. (under a different name) was made in 1950, with the emphasis on research even more pronounced than in the earlier groups.

life a very widespread influence. Perhaps its primary significance lay in the intellectual prestige it lent to the C.C.F. as a party, and to collectivist planning as a doctrine. Its membership and its close relations with both the C.C.F. and the *Forum* implied the interest, if not the whole-hearted support, of a considerable section of teachers and professional people in Canada.

One is tempted to compare the L.S.R. of the 1930's to the Canada First movement of the 1870's. Both groups sought to define for Canada certain goals, to obtain support for new national policies, and to achieve greater national independence. Both began also with the avowed aim of maintaining political impartiality and both drew inevitably closer to the party which espoused the greater part of their programme. Again, in the 1870's Canada First could boast the best political critic in the country—Professor Goldwin Smith; in the 1930's the L.S.R. could make the same claim for an admirer of Smith's—Professor F. H. Underhill. The peak period of the Canada Firsters, like that of the L.S.R., was the opening of a major economic depression and this helped to create an audience for constructive criticism. Perhaps the sharpest difference between the two groups is that while they both provided ideas which filtered into other parties, the L.S.R. actually helped to found a new national party which, to the time of writing, has continued to live.

The L.S.R. through the work of individual members and of research groups, produced a considerable stream of pamphlets, sponsored lectures, and radio broadcasts and gave informed assistance to the C.C.F. parliamentarians from 1933 on. In the spring of 1933 it was F. H. Underhill acting on behalf of a programme committee (and at the special request of Woodsworth) who drew up the first draft of the C.C.F.'s Regina manifesto.[5] From 1933 to 1939 there were very few meetings of the national council of the C.C.F. which were not attended by one or more members of the L.S.R. The same may be said of the Ontario and Quebec provincial C.C.F. councils.

When in 1935 the League published its *Social Planning for Canada*,[6] it was pilloried by the old parties and welcomed by the Left as the brains trust of the C.C.F. The research committee which collaborated in the production of *Social Planning* included some of the brightest names in the university fields of government, law, history, and economics—Eugene Forsey, King Gordon, Leonard Marsh, J. F. Parkin-

[5]F. R. Scott, Lecture no. 1, in series "Socialism at Mid-Century," Woodsworth House, Toronto, 1951.

[6]Research Committee of the League for Social Reconstruction, *Social Planning for Canada* (Toronto, 1935).

son, F. R. Scott, Graham Spry, and F. H. Underhill. These authors,
freely admitting their heavy debt to Fabianism, also provided a comprehensive historical and critical survey of Canadian conditions and
applied the ideas of planning and social democracy to the Canadian
scene which they described. "Our book," they wrote, "is an attempt to
set out this protest and these proposals in specifically Canadian terms.
It is not a series of doctrinaire generalizations but an attempt to
analyse and prescribe by a group who have tried to visualize a real
and richer 'Canada for Canadians.' "[7] Both *Social Planning* and the
paper-back abbreviated version, *Democracy Needs Socialism* were
influential and provided speakers with useful material. Woodsworth
welcomed the book with a Foreword, noting that "every C.C.F. member ought to be able to give a reason for the faith that is in him."

Social Planning, it is true, appears now to be somewhat dated; its
section on foreign policy, for example, is clearly isolationist and the
volume exhibits, perhaps, a too-exuberant faith in central planning.
But there are few parts of the book that cannot still be read with
profit, not alone for their historical interest. The question of order
versus freedom which so plagues the socialist today is intelligently
discussed and many of the techniques of fiscal and banking control,
marketing, and social security which the volume suggests are now
in process of evolution.

With the L.S.R. established in 1932, and with steady growth of
socialist ideas in the farmers' organizations and trade unions, the time
had again arrived to attempt a national political grouping. The new
endeavour, if a specific point of origin can really be established, was
set on foot at three o'clock on the afternoon of May 26, 1932. The
place was Room 607 of the Parliament Building, William Irvine's
office, which was then being used as the caucus-room of the Ginger
Group. The "co-operating independents" were present and they had
called in a few L.S.R. people and others from Montreal and Toronto.
This meeting passed the resolution which was to result in the Calgary
and Regina Conferences and the founding of the C.C.F. The minutes
of the day read:

Much consideration was given to the matter of dominion organization. A
motion was moved and seconded that a committee be formed to consider
ways and means of carrying out the wishes of the group as expressed during
the discussion—that is, drafting a tentative plan of organization for future
action thereon. Carried. Moved by D. M. Kennedy, seconded by Angus
MacInnis, that J. S. Woodsworth and R. Gardiner be a committee with
power to add to their number.[8]

---

[7]*Ibid.*, p. vii.   [8]J. S. Woodsworth, scrapbook, vol. 1932–7.

Testimony to the amount of informal discussion that had preceded this meeting was the brief note that it was formally adjourned at 3.40 P.M.

By common agreement Woodsworth was chosen temporary president of the new "Commonwealth Party" and others were named to push political organization: Agnes Macphail for Ontario; M. J. Coldwell, head of the recently formed Saskatchewan Farmer-Labour Party, for Saskatchewan; and Robert Gardiner, president of the U.F.A., for Alberta. In Manitoba and British Columbia the I.L.P. and the Socialist Party of Canada respectively took the main organizing responsibility. By August 1 it was possible to hold a joint meeting of the Western Conference of Labour Parties and the U.F.A. at Calgary, and to have representatives from other groups including the United Farmers of Canada (Saskatchewan section) and the Canadian Brotherhood of Railway Employees which was represented by A. R. Mosher. Woodsworth considered it a privilege to move the motion permitting representatives of the L.S.R. to attend the Conference (without voting rights).[9] The 1932 Calgary Conference was held in the Labor Temple under the lowering regard of R. B. Bennett, who was ensconced in the C.P.R.'s Palliser Hotel on the opposite side of the tracks. No doubt the Prime Minister was thinking of that earlier Calgary meeting—the Western Labour Conference of 1919.

At Calgary in 1932, in an atmosphere of informality and earnestness, there was produced a political framework, a provisional executive, and a very general eight-point programme. There appeared to be little friction between farmer and labour representatives. The provisional platform was definitely socialistic, including a modified version of land nationalization,[10] extension of social security legislation, socialization of all health services, "social ownership and control of financial institutions, utilities and natural resources," and the establishment of a planned economy. The purpose of the organization was made even more sweeping in the resolution calling for the establishment of a "co-operative commonwealth in which the basic principle regulating production, distribution and exchange will be the supplying of human needs instead of the making of profits."

In the debate over the name of the new organization Woodsworth proposed "Canadian Co-operative Federation" but the suggestion of

[9]C.C.F. National Council, Executive and Convention Minutes, vol. 1932–6 (C.C.F. National Office, Ottawa).

[10]The original Calgary platform contained fourteen planks, of which the third called for immediate security of tenure for workers and farmers and substitution of a "use-hold" system of land tenure in place of the "present insecurity." Point 3 of the shortened final eight point programme stated simply: "Security of tenure for the farmer."

Walter Mentz (Edmonton) and John Fenstein (Regina) appealed to the majority as being most descriptive both of the nature and purposes of the movement: Co-operative Commonwealth Federation.[11] Much was left indefinite in the way of organizational principles, which were to be hammered out a year later at Regina. But there was no doubt about the enthusiasm and the sense of dedication which permeated this first C.C.F. convention. Nor was there debate as to the man who should appear at the head of the new movement. Although the detailed work of organization was carried on by others—such as M. J. Coldwell, E. J. Garland, Norman Priestley, Angus MacInnis, and Mrs. Louise Lucas—Woodsworth was automatically named president of the first C.C.F. National Council. From the first, the chief organizational principle of the C.C.F. was federalism, and the affiliation both of groups and individuals had to be via the provincial units. Failure to modify this and to provide for national affiliation was one of the chief stumbling-blocks in the way of continuous membership from the beginning of the C.B.R.E.–A.C.C.L. union organizations.[12]

Despite the loose definitions provided by the Calgary meeting, organization was carried on at high speed between the summers of 1932 and 1933. In the West the member organizations conducted an educational campaign; in Ontario and, to a lesser extent, in Quebec and the Maritimes, the C.C.F. provincial councils directly encouraged the establishment of C.C.F. clubs. The organizational *mêlée* produced mild local frictions—in Ontario, for example, the distinction between units of the U.F.O., the Ontario Labour Conference, and the Association of C.C.F. clubs created confusion—but the entire movement vibrated with the enthusiasm of a crusade. Woodsworth and the other leaders stepped up their speaking schedules while volunteer labour across the country wrote, printed, and distributed the pamphlet literature of the movement, of which the keynote was "a call to action." Although, as Woodsworth wrote in September, 1932, "we were starting with not a dollar in the treasury—an immense task ahead,"[13] the feeling of fighting against heavy odds added zeal to the party supporters and organizers. One cannot read through the correspondence files of the C.C.F. without realizing the immense personal sacrifices made by a

[11]The resolution as adopted included the phrase "Farmer-Labour-Socialist," and the full title was used on early literature.

[12]A. R. Mosher, as a member of the provisional executive, attended the Regina Convention and in Aug., 1933, the A.C.C.L. Journal (*Canadian Unionist*) commented: "But the provisional committee found it impossible to make a constitution within which a national labour union could be accommodated and the C.B.R.E. was asked to withdraw. The reason was plausible. The new committee does not contain a single representative of the national unions."

[13]*U.F.A.*, Sept. 1, 1932.

large number of men and women, many of whom are now the party's provincial and federal leaders.

While some sections of the press, like the *Toronto Star* with its columns by C. H. Huestis and Salem Bland (both social gospellers of long standing), gave more than passing support to the C.C.F. in its early years, most of the city dailies expressed fear varying in kind from scepticism to misrepresentation. Some were ludicrous in their first reaction, like *Saturday Night* which wrote in 1932, while thousands of Saskatchewan farmers were on the verge of starvation and loss of land tenure, that the "Western wiseacres" of the C.C.F. were "asking farmers to abandon profits."[14] A tremendous educational effort in Ontario resulted in success for Agnes Macphail when she gained the approval of a U.F.O. convention for affiliation with the C.C.F. provincial council in December, 1932. In the convention she had had the support of visiting speakers like Woodsworth, Irvine, and Bland, and this prompted the *Mail and Empire* to print an editorial entitled "U.F.O. sold out to reds."[15] And although *Saturday Night* later came down to earth on the subject it did ask the C.C.F. leaders in 1933 to consider the question whether the United States would "tolerate" a socialized Canada.[16]

In the twelve months following July, 1932, the movement had grown to one of serious national proportions, although, except in Montreal and Cape Breton Island, it remained weak east of the Ottawa River. When, in August, 1933, the first annual convention was held at Regina, Woodsworth was full of hope. He was, at fifty-nine, already a venerable figure as he faced the convention to proclaim once more his own beliefs and his expectation of independent and positive action from the convention.

In developing a constructive programme [he told the delegates], we face our most difficult task. We are passing through a hitherto untravelled land. We may make mistakes but we must go forward. . . . There are those who would frighten us with the horrible example of failure in England or Germany, or captivate us by idealizing the experiments in Russia. The trouble is that we are inclined to think altogether too much in terms of Europe and in terms of the past. . . . I refuse to follow slavishly the British model or the American model or the Russian model. We in Canada will solve our own problems along our own lines.[17]

These words conveyed more than the vague vision of a national myth. They were addressed to a group which had already smashed

[14]*Saturday Night*, Sept. 24, 1932.   [15]Toronto *Mail and Empire*, Dec. 8, 1932.
[16]*Saturday Night*, Sept. 16, 1933.
[17]*The First Ten Years* (Ottawa, 1942), p. 11.

tradition by acting on the belief that a national political party could be established by democratic means and could be kept free of the control or influence of private or corporate wealth. The idea of frequent and regular conventions composed of democratically chosen delegates as the real authority in the party, and based upon the federal principle, was North American in its origin, reaching back through Canadian and American history to Grits and Jacksonians. The idea of a revolution in the fundamental social field of property ownership to be carried out within an established constitutional framework was basically British, as was much of the terminology of the debates and resulting manifesto. But the men and women who seized upon these ideas were Canadians and they used their knowledge in an attempt to suggest specifically Canadian answers to the economic, political, and constitutional problems of the country. One thing is certain: the Regina convention was conspicuous by the absence of the hired men of big business—the corporation lawyers, the ad-men, and the professional lobbyists.

At Regina a constitution was adopted giving full autonomy to the provincial councils and making them the primary membership centres, with the provisos that the National Council (pending convention decisions) could veto the applications of new organizations for membership and that the final authority in the party in matters of both discipline and programme was to be the annual convention. The qualifications were important, and although there were to be frequent differences of opinion amongst provincial sections, constituent groups, and individuals, the emphatic achievement of a final authority in party matters was all-important. It meant that the procedural *cul de sac* entered by the Progressive movement of the twenties would be avoided by the socialist party of the thirties. The farmers had accepted the idea of a political party without relinquishing the crusading aspect of their earlier activities; they had overcome their previous reluctance to work in organic association with other "classes" in the nation. Put in another way, the essentially conservative social-political ideas of Henry Wise Wood had been replaced by the social democracy of J. S. Woodsworth.

The Regina manifesto (see Appendix) authorized by the 1933 convention left in no doubt the radical nature of the new party. It was remarkably similar to the earlier documents in whose production Woodsworth had been influential: the manifestos of the Federated Labour Party and the Independent Labour Party. The Regina platform opened with a preamble which read in part:

We aim to replace the present capitalist system with its inherent injustice and inhumanity by a social order from which the domination and exploitation of one class by another will be eliminated, in which economic planning will supersede unregulated private enterprise and competition, and in which genuine democratic self-government based upon economic equality will be possible. . . . The new social order at which we aim is not one in which individuality will be crushed out by a system of regimentation. . . . What we seek is a proper collective organization of our economic resources such as will make possible a much greater degree of leisure and a much richer individual life for every citizen. . . .

It closed with the sentence: "No C.C.F. government will rest content until it has eradicated capitalism and put into operation the full programme of socialized planning which will lead to the establishment in Canada of the co-operative commonwealth." The intervening fourteen points set forth proposals for the establishment of a National Planning Commission which would replace the "planning by a small group of capitalist magnates in their own interest" with the planning of "public servants acting in the public interest and responsible to the people as a whole." Social ownership (federal, provincial, or municipal) was to be extended wherever necessary to ensure the success of the national economic plan; co-operative institutions of all kinds were to be encouraged by public authority; financial institutions and all health services were to be socialized either through direct federal action or in agreement with the provincial governments; taxation was to be used for social purposes (both class and regional) and to be steeply graded; security of tenure for the farmer and a labour code for the worker were to be supplemented by a complete system of social insurance. The "contsitution of Canada" was to be modernized by abolition of the Senate and further amendment of the B.N.A. Act "without infringing upon racial or religious minority rights or upon legitimate provincial claims to autonomy so as to give the dominion government adequate powers to deal effectively with urgent economic problems which are essentially national in scope."

The original draft of the manifesto was written (as F. R. Scott puts it) by that "most Shavian of Fabians," F. H. Underhill. This draft was then reviewed by the L.S.R. research committee and later by the C.C.F. National Council, before it was read by Norman Priestley to the delegates at Regina. When it was finally brought to a vote in the convention, the only opposing hand was that of the elderly and respected leader of the Ontario co-operative movement, W. C. Good. Every one of the manifesto's propositions, as well as its statements on external relations and social justice, had been elaborated by Woodsworth in the House of Commons, many of them repeatedly, since 1922.

It was a joy for him to share with the people at Regina in polishing and endorsing the C.C.F. programme, and to receive from them the appointment as president of the party's National Council.[18] He valued this recognition the more because he knew it to be the outcome of a thoroughly democratic process.

In his new position Woodsworth showed a talent for leadership which many contemporary observers failed adequately to assess. His ability as leader was closely related to his emphasis on the inefficiency of a planless capitalism; and perhaps both found their roots in his early Brandon home. Indeed it was always true that Woodsworth seemed to work better and to be happier as a leader than as an undistinguished subaltern. His was a leadership, however, exercised with scrupulous regard for the fundamental source of its authority— the party majority. Combined as it was with an inflexible conviction on certain basic principles such as the immorality of war, this complete acceptance of majority rule would lead to personal tragedy rather than any easy shift of direction in order to retain the lesser good of leadership. When seated at the head of the C.C.F. caucus table Woodsworth always kept a gavel close at hand and used it frequently; and in the 1930's he moved very definitely away from the experimental idea of group government of the 1920's. But when he felt he had lost the support of the majority in 1939 there could be no question for him of an attempt to retain any real share in the party's leadership; this was to be the culminating tragedy of his life.

During 1934 and 1935 the new party, although it still showed exaggerated signs of its federal nature, also demonstrated its vitality. Delegates to the second convention in Winnipeg in 1934[19] could report on provincial growth as follows: British Columbia, 59 branches of the Socialist Party of Canada, 154 C.C.F. clubs, and 7 C.C.F. members in the legislature as the official opposition; Alberta, 1,100 locals (U.F.A., C.L.P., and Economic Reconstruction clubs); Saskatchewan, a steady growth in the Labour party and U.F.C. locals, and 5 C.C.F. members elected to become the official opposition; Manitoba, expansion of the three party affiliates, the I.L.P., the Social Reconstruction Clubs, and the Manitoba Farmers' Section of the C.C.F. Even Quebec and the Maritimes reported the establishment of C.C.F. clubs and the election in Montreal of Alderman Schubert. In Ontario a serious split had been healed and Sam Lawrence elected to the legislature.

[18]C.C.F. National Council, Executive and Convention Minutes, vol. 1932–6. E. J. Garland and Robert Gardiner both withdrew their names from nomination, making Woodsworth's election an acclamation.
[19]Ibid.

The "split" in Ontario grew out of the question of how much support the C.C.F. should give to A. E. Smith, who had been charged with sedition for statements critical of the alleged attempt on Tim Buck's life during the Kingston penitentiary riot. A. E. Smith was at the time one of the leaders of a growing communist drive for a united front—a policy that would quickly have eliminated the C.C.F. as an effective social democratic party. Smith had accused the leader of the C.C.F. of instigating the court action against him. With eight communists languishing in Portsmouth on shaky convictions; with arrests occurring almost daily across the country; with special labour police units multiplying rapidly; with the clear fact that a number of bullets had been fired into Buck's cell (and into no other cells), the mass meetings conducted by Smith's Canadian Labour Defence League contained a dynamic appeal. Yet the plain truth was that the C.L.D.L. was a communist organization designed to attain only communist ends; that to support it without qualification would risk the disintegration of the two-year-old social democratic pary and would lead to a confusion of basic principles—principles which Woodsworth, with most of his colleagues, had long since been agreed upon.

Woodsworth and the other members of the National Council, supported by the Ontario provincial council, decided to refrain from any organic relation with the C.L.D.L. or its meetings. Instead, they protested exclusively through C.C.F. channels against the wildly reactionary Bennett-Hepburn-Taschereau police policies. It was a difficult decision to make in a time of very high tension within the working class.[20] Some individual C.C.F.'ers ignored the official party policy and one section of the Ontario C.C.F. was expelled. The 1934 provincial C.C.F. convention adopted a constitutional amendment providing for disciplinary action in the future.

Throughout this trying episode Woodsworth took a firm stand against any link with communist organizations and because of this was attacked by some elements in his party. The overwhelming majority, however, agreed with him, and gave him steady support as the communists' united front drive went into high gear in the following years. To Woodsworth in these years came a growing volume of letters—letters of enquiry and of encouragement such as one from the United States which asked "Is there any way an American can join your organization?"[21]

[20]A decision, also, which Smith never forgave. See *All My Life* (Toronto, 1947), pp. 163 *et seq.*
[21]J. S. Woodsworth scrapbook, vol. 1932–7.

The evidence concerning this period again belies the rather wide-spread contemporary impression that Woodsworth as a politician was "too idealistic" and therefore ineffectual. In fact, he missed no opportunity to speak out on any issue which needed definition, and he exercised his personal influence in party councils without reserve. The growth of the party in the years of its youth was to no small extent due to the leadership it then possessed. One of the greatest of Woodsworth's contributions to the idea of political parties in Canada was his demonstration of a fact to which generations of politicians before and after him have shut their eyes: adherence to principle strengthens rather than weakens a political party, even in the federal atmosphere of North America. His insistence on this enabled him to keep the C.C.F. a movement as well as a party as long as he was in a position to give it his leadership. Martin Lipset, although he does not draw the same conclusion as that suggested above, does emphasize the same facts about the Woodsworth leadership:

The turning point in the development of the national party can probably be centred in the withdrawal from politics and subsequent early death of J. S. Woodsworth, the Leader of Canadian Socialism from 1921–1940. Woodsworth, who had spent a large part of his life in political isolation trying to build a socialist party, resisted all efforts to achieve rapid party growth through ideological compromise. The newer and younger socialists who joined a going movement wanted power and proceeded to try and get it.[22]

Most political observers and journalists in these years were confused by the nature of the C.C.F. and of its leaders; and many, whether confused or not, wrote under strict injunction to belittle or smear both. Indeed, the political upheaval of the early thirties almost took Canadian journalism back to pre-Confederation days when the *Globe* could refer to its opponents as "oily-mouthed political prostitutes." The journalistic conditions of the time were not conducive to calm appraisal, yet the sheer volume of comment on the C.C.F. and its leadership betrayed serious concern. Toronto's *Saturday Night*, despite a basic liberalism, seemed ever ready to disbelieve the facts of depression and world crisis. That journal, indeed, exhibited a surprising vacillation in its policy. It was able to tell its readers in the autumn of 1931 that in the Far East "Japan represents the forces of order and progress";[23] while in Canada "the sense of security has returned and men of national

[22]M. Lipset, *Agrarian Socialism*, p. 152.
[23]*Saturday Night*, Nov. 28, 1931.

affairs are at last convinced that the depression has broken."[24] A year later it wrote that the newly born C.C.F. was both weak and strong: weak because its members at Ottawa had not voted in unison on Bennett's empire trade agreement; strong because in the debate Bennett ignored King and treated Woodsworth as the real leader of the opposition to the agreement.[25] Commenting on the U.F.O. affiliation with the Ontario C.C.F., *Saturday Night* misread the evidence woefully; either that, or it was endeavouring to drive a wedge into the new party. It credited Agnes Macphail with being the real power in the party's Ontario section because in Ontario the farmers would be the backbone of the party: "She goes in for organization and discipline. The labour man, on the other hand, operates pretty much as a free-lance, as a prophet."[26] A week later Sandwell's journal wrote: ". . . No political organization ever had so much free advertising. People are discussing it everywhere, regarding it with growing respect. . . ."

As the facts gradually revealed themselves to a puzzled *Saturday Night*, the paper began to question more seriously the ability of the C.C.F. leadership. Early in 1933 it wrote, "The extravagant, ill-tempered attacks of the new prophets on the old order repel the sympathy of moderate people, promote fear of the cause they champion, while the stubborn resistance of the stand patters to any new thought only betrays the weakness of their defences. . . ."[27] Then suddenly *Saturday Night* discovered that Agnes Macphail was not the stern disciplinarian it had believed her to be, and it professed to see grave dangers ahead.

The most disturbing feature about the Woodsworth-Macphail organization and its rapid rise to political importance is not the nature of its policies (which, as officially declared, are about as vague and woolly as those of any other left-wing party in any democratic country) but the extreme state of indiscipline in the party and the lack of authority in its leaders which make it impossible to conjecture what the party would do if ever it came to power. . . .[28]

With a return to real liberalism, however, *Saturday Night* offered sympathy to Professor King Gordon, who experienced a fate at Montreal's Union Theological College similar to that visited upon Salem Bland in 1917 in Winnipeg. When it was announced that King Gordon's chair was being discontinued for economic reasons, the paper commented: "By a strange coincidence the instructor in question . . . is

[24]*Ibid.*, Nov. 14, 1931. These comments appeared a few months prior to the change in the editorship from Hector Charlesworth to B. K. Sandwell.
[25]*Ibid.*, Nov. 12, 1932.   [26]*Ibid.*, Dec. 10, 1932.
[27]*Ibid.*, Feb. 11, 1933.   [28]*Ibid.*, Feb. 18, 1933.

in private life a somewhat ardent defender of people who question the perfection of the existing social order, an opponent of Section 98 and a propagandist for the League for Social Reconstruction."[29] But it continued to emphasize the fear of indiscipline and ill-defined objectives in the Woodsworth party, and accused the C.C.F. leadership of endeavouring to establish a state which would be compulsive rather than co-operative in nature.[30]

The *Winnipeg Free Press* gave its readers a similar misinterpretation of Woodsworth and the C.C.F. In the summer of 1934 it declared that the C.C.F. would move to the Left because "there is seemingly no solidarity of views at the top of the party, nor is there the welding force of a strong, competent leader. . . ."[31] This odd interpretation is not so surprising when one considers that the editor of the *Free Press*, as late as 1938, believed David Lewis, the National Secretary of the C.C.F., to be a communist.[32]

If what the *Free Press* and *Saturday Night* alleged concerning weak and divided leadership had been true (or if the even less restrained comments by other sections of the press had had any justification in fact) the C.C.F. could not have withstood the pressure for a united front with the communists. In fact, Woodsworth was the core of opposition to any political compromise tactics and he secured support from the majority of his party for his position. In 1933 and 1934 he had a strong influence in keeping the Ontario C.C.F. away from the united front. He spoke with spirit against political alliance with Social Credit and Conservatives in the Saskatchewan C.C.F. convention of 1936. Although overruled by that convention his advice was proven sound and was later adhered to by the 1939 Saskatchewan convention.[33] Nationally, Woodsworth insisted on a complete rebuff to the direct

---

[29]*Ibid.*, April 8, 1933.

[30]*Ibid.*, July 29, 1933.

[31]*Winnipeg Free Press*, July 12, 1934.

[32]University of Manitoba, Dafoe Papers.

[33]For a discussion of Saskatchewan C.C.F. tactics see M. Lipset, *Agrarian Socialism*, chap. VI. Illustrative of the sharp temporary swing in the thinking of the Saskatchewan C.C.F. Leaders was the difference between two statements made by G. H. Williams. The first was in a letter to M. J. Coldwell (Jan. 30, 1935, C.C.F. files, Regina): ". . . the sooner we reconcile ourselves to out and out socialism and all the abuse that term means, the sooner we will be worthy of the crown of success." The second was in debate in the C.C.F. National Convention of Aug., 1936: "Some say the only way to attain socialism is by being pure socialist and having no truck nor trade with anyone who is not a pure socialist. Now, as a matter of idealism that is fine, but as a matter of practicality it may be political futility. There is only one way to have socialism in Canada and that is to have a socialist government. . . . We learned a good lesson in the last election. . . ."

communist approaches for alliance in the 1935 elections. In the spring of 1935 the C.C.F. National Council received a letter from Tim Buck and Sam Carr, Chairman and National Election Organizer respectively of the Communist party. The letter read in part:

. . . it is the conviction of the Communist federal election committee that the united front is the only guarantee that a great number of working class representatives will be sent into the next House of Commons. . . . We are of the opinion that an agreement can be arrived at between the Communist election committee and the C.C.F., making possible an elimination of any possibility of splits in the working class vote and mutual support on the basis of a minimum programme of immediate needs of the toilers of Canada. . . . Let us set aside the accumulated prejudices and bitterness. . . .

The reply of the C.C.F. National Council over the signature of Woodsworth as chairman was unequivocal:

A few weeks ago at a meeting of the National Council the question of co-operation between the C.C.F. and other political parties was discussed and it was decided that we could not enter into agreements or understandings with other political parties. . . . The C.C.F. is strongly in favour of a united front of all workers. Indeed, to further that end was the reason for the formation of our federation. We consider that we have been fairly success-ful. . . . May I point out that a real united front involves an agreement on fundamentals, and a belief on the part of each co-operating group in the sincerity of the other group. In tactics at least there is no agreement what-ever between the Communist Party and the C.C.F. . . . The overthrow of the C.C.F. rather than that of capitalism would seem to be the main object of the Communist Party of Canada. . . . We have a programme and a policy which we believe fits in with the conditions, traditions and psychology of the people of Canada. . . .[34]

There is little here to suggest the seriously divided councils or dubious direction implied by the Toronto and Winnipeg papers. Indeed, Woodsworth seems to have kept a firm hand on the helm. Photographs of him taken in 1935 show him thinner than ever, with large dark patches under his eyes, and haggard from the immense exertion of his national speaking and organizing tours.

In the summer of 1934 Woodsworth and his wife made a trip to Japan, China, and Korea to visit Woodsworth's brother Harold who was teaching at a missionary college in Japan and to see the East for themselves. The journey confirmed Woodsworth's conviction that the imperialism sponsored by European capitalist nations was ex-ploitive and evil. In these years he spoke increasingly on all questions

[34]J. S. Woodsworth scrapbook, vol. 1932-7.

of Canadian external affairs; in this matter, still more than in domestic policies, his leadership of the C.C.F. was definite.

In the 1930 Commons debate on the estimates of the Department of External Affairs he uttered a revised but wary estimate of the League of Nations, stating that while he had earlier seen it as a league of victors, he now was prepared to support it because it was doing some useful work and because it was the only general international organization.[35] When the 1931–2 crisis developed in Manchuria he declared that Canada should have been pressing Britain and the United States for stronger condemnation of Japan and for the imposition of economic sanctions.[36] But there was no indication either from Bennett or King of an intention to move for reform of the League. When Woodsworth asked, in 1935, whether Canada would regulate the sale of nickel to prevent its going to armament firms, Prime Minister Bennett replied simply that once the nickel was sold to a foreign purchaser it was beyond the power of the government to control.[37]

As the breakdown of the League became evident, with its first important indication in the Manchurian affair, Woodsworth began again to hedge his brief optimism of 1930. In particular, the suspicion of imperialist motives, which he considered to be the explanation of the League's inhibitions, resulted in a renewed concern on his part for increased Canadian independence. In 1931, disapproving the failure of the Statute of Westminster, the Imperial Conferences or the Canadian government to provide a procedure by which Canada could amend her own constitution without reference to the British Parliament, Woodsworth moved the resolution "that in the opinion of this House it is desirable that Canada should have the right to amend her own constitution but that in proceeding to make any amendment scrupulous care should be taken to safeguard the rights of minorities."[38]

Woodsworth pressed for the right to amend, not only because it would imply independence, but also because he believed it necessary to pave the way for long overdue social legislation. He supported his resolution with a lengthy and able discussion of the problems that would have to be settled before an acceptable method of amendment could be defined. With references to the writings of J. S. Ewart, the suggestions of Lapointe and others made at the 1927 Dominion-provincial conference, and the comments of F. R. Scott, E. A. Forsey, Grant Dexter, and R. K. Finlayson, he presented a vigorous refutation of the "compact theory of Confederation." His suggestion was for a

[35]Hansard, 1930, p. 1393.   [36]Ibid., 1932, p. 3437.
[37]Ibid., 1935, p. 2871.   [38]Ibid., 1931, pp. 1466 et seq.

compromise between the demand for unanimous provincial consent, on the one hand, and the legal possibility of unilateral federal action on the other. His speech was centred on the remark: "May I suggest that if our forefathers had brains enough to devise a constitution to meet the needs of their day, we should have brains enough to revise it to meet the needs of our day. . . ." Both Guthrie and Lapointe complimented Woodsworth on his presentation of the case and made their own contributions to the debate. Woodsworth closed the discussion without asking for a vote, because there had been general support for the motion. The motion and the debate were of service to Canada at large, since they constituted a full statement, with adequate publicity, of the problems of constitutional amendment. By 1935 a special Commons committee on the B.N.A. Act had brought in a report advocating the convening of a Dominion-provincial conference to discuss the question of amendments and jurisdictional revision.[39] From the work of this committee, and the decisions of the Privy Council nullifying the Bennett "new deal" legislation, grew the Rowell-Sirois commission on Dominion-provincial relations.

Both inside and outside the House Woodsworth re-defined his own and his party's position on external relations. After the *débâcle* of Manchuria and when the Abyssinian crisis loomed on the horizon, he became increasingly isolationist. During his pre-election speaking tour of British Columbia in 1935 he declared: ". . . If this country seems likely to be embroiled in a war, we should submit the question of Canada's participation in it to a plebiscite. . . . If, after a vote on war, the Canadian people were insane enough to go into another war, I, and I think any C.C.F. government, would resign rather than lead them."[40] In the Commons earlier in the same year he declared: "I believe I would be expressing the opinion of the ordinary man in the street were I to say that if a European war broke out no Canadian troops would be allowed to leave this country to go to Europe."[41] This was all clear and definite; and at first glance it did not differ markedly from the Bourassa position which the veteran Quebecker reiterated in Parliament for the last time in the 1935 session.[42]

There was, however, a rather important point of contrast. When Bourassa viewed British "imperialism" it was with an eye to racial

[39]*Ibid.*, 1935, p. 3817.
[40]Toronto *New Commonwealth*, Sept. 7, 1935.
[41]Hansard, 1935, p. 1564.
[42]Bourassa initiated a full debate on the European situation during this session; Woodsworth made a detailed statement on his and the C.C.F.'s attitude. (Hansard, 1935, pp. 2292 *et seq.*)

defence. He was concerned only with the question of *la survivance*
of the French-Canadian nation within an empire that could either give
it security or send the cream of its youth to slaughter on the fields of
Europe. Woodsworth's position was more complex; he went further
than Bourassa when he depicted the modern world as interdependent,
when he said that a mere declaration of neutrality was not enough,
and that disarmament in itself was an inadequate answer to the question of a foreign policy. He continued to believe that military force
was stupid and could settle nothing, that it was in the hands of
"predatory classes," and that there could be no real peace until
capitalism, the father of imperialism, was destroyed. As an individual
he declared he must refuse to participate or assist in war, yet as a
public representative he must vote on alternative military policies.
Just as in another field he might vote for the electric chair rather than
the gallows, while condemning both, so in external affairs "an international police force under proper control, if that is possible, might be
preferable to world anarchy." The significant thing is that he never
enjoyed the opportunity, in the 1930's, of being able to vote either for
or against such a police force.

"The international world," notes one writer who in 1935 had agreed
with Woodsworth, "was a capitalist chaos in which any conceivable
war was an imperialist adventure. In this context the ringing denunciations of capitalist evils . . . were self-evident truths [and] the avoidance
of foreign entanglements was a positive contribution to peace. . . ."[48]
In the 1935 debate on the European situation (which was forced by
Bourassa) Woodsworth offered what he called a few practical suggestions, a more positive approach than any developed by the governments of the time. He suggested: a separate ministry of external affairs
headed by a specialist in League affairs; a House committee to spend
its full time considering reports from embassies, legations, the League,
and Imperial Conferences; an offer to co-operate with the League in
controlling the export of war materials; official support of the League
of Nations Society and the establishment of international scholarships.
In practice, he argued, there were two great considerations in framing
a valid Canadian foreign policy: Britain ruled a dependent empire for
the defence of which Canada could accept no obligation; the League
as then constituted was an association of European powers and it was
a league of capitalist nations. Canada could choose between three
basic policies: isolation, military alliances, or collective security through
a re-vitalized League. The second, he argued, was discredited. The

[48]Scott, "Socialism at Mid-Century."

third was not yet practical. Thus Woodsworth was left essentially with
isolation—the Bourassa policy—at which he arrived by a somewhat
more tortuous route than that followed by the anti-British French
Canadian.

"I am," he admitted, "close to Bourassa. We have to keep out of the
affairs of Europe; we have to see to it that Canadian boys are not
sacrificed on the battle fields of Europe, or, I may add, of Asia. Yet I
do not think a policy of isolation of that kind will keep us out of war."
Collective security remained the real hope—and that was becoming
dimmer with the passage of each week in 1935. Canada, said Woodsworth, already had to bear her share of responsibility for the weakening
of the League. She had tamely followed Sir John Simon and instead
of pressing for the condemnation of Japan and the imposition of
sanctions, had helped open the door to further Japanese aggression in
North China. Woodsworth bitterly recalled how Bennett had answered
when asked what was Canada's attitude to the Simon report on
Manchuria: the problem should not be discussed, said the Prime
Minister haughtily, because it was *sub judice*.[44] Woodsworth and every
other competent observer of the day knew that the government had
no policy. While Bennett parried Woodsworth's questions in the
House, Cahan was telling the League Assembly that Canada was the
lifelong friend of Japan and that his government earnestly desired a
solution in China which Japan could accept.

Woodsworth desired to exert every effort to keep Canada from
falling into a fresh European conflagration. This would require admission of a Canadian share of responsibility for the iniquities of
Versailles and their result in Nazism, and the weakness of the League.
But at the same time Canada must work for a reform of the League.
He stressed this, but could hold out little positive hope, since he
believed the League to be the instrument of "neanderthal" capitalist
governments, and that real progress toward collective security would
have to await the wider spread of social democracy. Probably his
doubt about producing a good result at any time from the use of force
further weakened his faith in the League—capitalist or reformed.

Thus, neutrality or isolation remained his policy. Officially this was
true also of the C.C.F. until the outbreak of the Second World War.
It was not a policy that cost the party many votes. Canada was being
washed over by the great wave of North American isolationism of the
1930's. Confronted by this wave, neither Bennett nor King tried to
play Canute. Rather, King was to wait patiently until the crest was

44For Woodsworth's question and Bennett's reply see Hansard, 1932-3, p. 1369.

past and had broken behind him on the solid rocks of Anglo-Canadian sentiment and international crisis. When the tide of isolationism receded it left the Liberals still in control. It was to leave Woodsworth face to face with the supreme crisis of his life.

Thus, in these years, Woodsworth was leader in fact as well as in name. This was reflected in the overwhelming demands made upon his time and energy by all sections of the party across the country, and in the authority with which he spoke and wrote. In the election year of 1935 he continued his writing in addition to a very heavy speaking schedule. In April he published a practical analysis of the machinery of Canadian democracy.[45] The most striking aspect of the article was the absence of any reference to group government. Emphasis was placed on the need for some system of proportional representation. The article was critical of cabinet dictatorship, of the function of the Senate, and of the procedures of the House of Commons.

During July, August, and September of 1935 Woodsworth spoke extensively in British Columbia, Alberta (two weeks after Aberhart's provincial victory), and Saskatchewan. At the end of September he made a one-week speaking tour of fourteen Ontario cities and gave several radio addresses. Then on October 5 (nine days before the election) he returned to Winnipeg to take over the campaign in his own constituency. He asserted in September, 1935, that he was confident the C.C.F. would become the official opposition with between fifty and sixty seats.[46] But the conditions for a major C.C.F. electoral advance did not materialize. In Alberta and Saskatchewan the pseudo-radical appeals of the Social Crediters (with their subtle undertones of anti-Semitism and quasi-fascism) made heavy inroads in potential C.C.F. territory. All across the country the Stevens "reconstruction" candidates stole reformist votes for a lost cause which could elect only its leader. The Conservatives were running on a "new deal" platform which appeared entirely out of character and scattered the hereditary Tory vote. Into this political *mêlée* sprang Mr. King with the slogan: "It's King or chaos."

The result of the election confirmed the opinions Woodsworth had expressed in his article about the essentially unrepresentative nature

[45]J. S. Woodsworth, "Political Democracy," *University of Toronto Quarterly*, IV (April, 1935). The article was reprinted in a number of C.C.F. and farm papers in the following month.
[46]Toronto *New Commonwealth*, Sept. 7, 1935.

of Canadian political democracy. The Social Credit party took all the Alberta seats and two others (seventeen in all) with approximately half the vote required by the C.C.F. to elect a total of seven M.P.'s (with over 400,000 votes). The Reconstruction Party, with a vote nearly equal to that of the C.C.F., elected only one member. The King party, with a distinct minority of the national vote, took 171 of the 245 seats in the House. Woodsworth had been right when he foresaw a Tory representation of about forty seats; but even he had under-estimated the effects of the splintering of the opposition and the distorting effect of the electoral system.

Even apart from the effects of the machinery there was a real political chaos confronting the thinking voter. The C.C.F. was very young and was everywhere portrayed as being tinged with communism, while the Social Crediters, the Stevens men, and some Tories all pre-sented themselves as reformers. Probably A. R. M. Lower, in one of his skilful generalizations, gives the best description of the nature of the Liberalism that won in 1935:

Here was the great centre group which had received into its ample bosom frightened Conservatives from one side and those who could not go as far as C.C.F. socialism on the other. The victory was not a tribute to Mr. King, it was not a proclamation in defence of liberty, it was not even a pronounce-ment on the issues of the day. Liberalism, as it emerged in Canada after 1935, was the counterpart of Baldwin conservatism in Great Britain, of *Le Front Populaire* in France, and of Rooseveltian democracy:—it represented the huddling together of frightened people uncertain of their way in a chaotic world.[47]

The election, as far as the C.C.F. was concerned, had been preceded by a number of hopeful signs of increasing maturity in the organiza-tion. The most important of these was the amalgamation of previously separated units of the federation. In British Columbia, for example, the Socialist Party of Canada had merged with the C.C.F.[48] and in Manitoba the farmers' section had merged with the Social Reconstruc-tion Club section, while a move was put on foot to combine the clubs with the I.L.P. in a single provincial organization. But there were also signs of trouble. The attacks on the movement were redoubled and were symbolized in the dismissal of M. J. Coldwell from his position as principal of a Regina school. There were also con-tinuing jealousies within the party, the sharpest of which was seen in

---

47A. R. M. Lower, *Colony to Nation* (Toronto, 1946), p. 519.

48Arnold Webster became the C.C.F. provincial president at the following convention. One of the results of the merger was that in the 1935 federal election the C.C.F. polled the largest vote of any party in British Columbia.

the resistance of the Manitoba I.L.P. to losing its identity within the C.C.F. Woodsworth himself had grown in national prestige, but this only deepened the bitterness of the attacks upon him, and any respectable person who found some justification for his past actions was likely to be confronted with serious difficulties. For example, when Miss Olive Ziegler had completed her biography of the C.C.F. leader in 1934, she took it to a well-known Canadian publishing house where it was accepted for publication. Advertising for the book was issued by the publishers and then someone discovered that the Winnipeg strike had not received the "right" treatment. Miss Ziegler found it necessary to publish the book elsewhere at her own risk.[49]

In his own constituency, although he devoted approximately one week to it, Woodsworth quadrupled his plurality, but even here a miniature illustration of the scattered votes of 1935 could be seen. The vote was: C.C.F., 10,033; Liberal, 6,280; Conservative, 4,710; Reconstruction, 2,480; Social Credit, 1,091. Although M. J. Coldwell and T. C. Douglas both were elected in Saskatchewan, 1935 meant the loss of Gardiner, Spencer, Coote, Garland, and Irvine in Alberta. The defeat of the Albertans was a personal loss for Woodsworth. But the total vote of the C.C.F. was impressive, the problems to be faced were manifold, and the will to fight was not diminished.

[49]Note in Woodsworth's scrapbook, vol. 1932–7.

PART IV: 1935-1942

19

A LEADER'S PROBLEMS

THE FOUR YEARS PRIOR TO THE outbreak of the Second World War
were packed with activity for Woodsworth. It was a time of party
growth and of ever widening recognition of the stature of the C.C.F.
leader. But it was also a period of mounting strain, and this told on
Woodsworth's health. Frictions were developing between sections
within the party, particularly in Manitoba. And the exceedingly complex questions of neutrality and pacifism reached their peak intensity
in September of 1939. In the twenty-four months preceding the outbreak of war a considerable section of the C.C.F. began to slip away
from the oft-repeated party stand on foreign war. This trend was led
to some extent by Woodsworth's daughter and her husband Angus
MacInnis, who in 1936 visited several European countries and thereafter came to the conclusion that the threat of Hitler would have to
be met by force if other means failed. The problem was how to define
more closely the term "imperialist war." Men like M. J. Coldwell,
George Williams, and David Lewis were prepared to concede that
the ambitions of personal dictatorial power might so modify the
purely economic or capitalist causes of war that it would be necessary
for social democrats to take sides in order to secure their own right
to existence for the future. It was a question, perhaps, which can have
no final answer. But it was one on which Woodsworth steadily refused
to modify his position because he considered it to affect his most
deeply held convictions.

These were years in which it was almost literally impossible for
Woodsworth to remain still. The problems of a growing party, the
increasingly voluminous correspondence, opportunities to appeal to
the youth whose lives would be the price of war, and the almost
unbearable responsibility of keeping untarnished his own integrity

permitted him no rest. Throughout the parliamentary sessions he was seldom absent from his seat in the Commons or the desk in his office; he insisted on answering personally the thousands of letters that came to him each year; and on the weekends he was usually to be found addressing meetings anywhere within the transportation radius of Ottawa. Between sessions, when he was not travelling he was speaking at L.S.R., C.C.F., or C.C.Y.M.[1] study groups and camps—the summer schools which were operated in Quebec, Ontario, the prairies, and British Columbia for discussion of socialist theory and the training of leaders.

A story is told of an occasion when he was persuaded to take a brief holiday weekend at Lake Simcoe in Ontario in the middle of a busy summer. His host suggested a drive to Orillia to see the famous Champlain Monument. On the way there they passed the road leading to Couchiching Park, and Woodsworth, without apparent guile, suggested that he would like to see it. Upon arrival it was discovered that the Couchiching conference on international affairs was in full swing; the rest of the day was spent in animated conversation with the delegates and included a speech by Woodsworth.

Yet he never lost touch with the smaller and more personal items of life. He retained his association with old family friends and, as far as he was permitted, refused to allow political differences to intervene; willing always to explain his ideas, he never forced them on his friends. Despite the fact that his income only once reached the figure of five thousand dollars (in the last year of his life), of which a great deal went to the party cause, his acts of generosity and assistance were numerous.

Of all Woodsworth's political satisfactions, the democracy of the C.C.F. was probably the greatest. And there was some irony in this since it was that democracy that led the party on a path he could not follow. In the national conventions, problems were discussed in a most open manner. The line of communication and policy-making was direct—extending from individual members, through local units, through provincial conventions and councils, to national conventions, the National Council and the parliamentary party.[2] At every level of the organization there was the possibility of initiating policy discussion for final debate and decision of a national convention. And there was

[1]The Co-operative Commonwealth Youth Movement, established at the 1934 National Convention with T. C. Douglas as its first president (its first *ad hoc* name was "Youth Rally").

[2]The seven C.C.F. M.P.'s were: J. S. Woodsworth, Angus MacInnis, A. A. Heaps, M. J. Coldwell, T. C. Douglas, C. G. MacNeil, and J. S. Taylor.

a remarkable degree, despite the federal element, of mutual responsibility.

Three items from the November, 1935, meeting of the National Council illustrate the functioning of responsibility and initiation in the party.[3] When William Irvine moved that the C.C.F. members of Parliament should endorse the use of both military and economic sanctions against Italy's Ethiopian adventure the motion was ruled out of order on the ground that it conflicted with the policy declaration of the 1934 convention: "Not a Canadian shall leave the shores of Canada to fight on foreign fields. . . . Canadian neutrality must be maintained rigorously, whoever the belligerents may be. . . ." The second item, a resolution designed to further ensure co-operative policy-making and responsibility, was moved by Angus MacInnis and accepted. It provided that the C.C.F. members of the Commons should report weekly on their activities to the National Council. The third item, indicating the multiple sources of initiative, was the receipt of a report from Professor Underhill. The report was accepted as the basis of action. It called for an amendment to the Federal Elections Act which would require the publication of full reports on all election funds.

The party structure was further strengthened in 1936 when the National Convention approved, on Woodsworth's request, the appointment of E. J. Garland as full-time National Organizing Secretary (with a salary of one hundred dollars a month) and David Lewis, a Montreal Rhodes scholar recently returned from Oxford, as Corresponding Secretary for the National Office.[4] In 1937, on Woodsworth's recommendation, the convention authorized further division of jobs at the party's centre; Woodsworth was thus re-elected President, and M. J. Coldwell was named to the new position of National Chairman.[5] These changes relieved Woodsworth of a considerable amount of worry over party administration, although he never felt absolved from responsibility. The new Chairman, a former high school principal, able organizer of Saskatchewan labour and farm strength, and one of the finest speakers in the House of Commons, was soon recognized as a political figure of real stature and did much to help Woodsworth keep the party united. David Lewis, on a financial shoestring, ran an efficient central office and developed in it a most important second function: it became a centre of research and information.

[3]C.C.F. National Council, Executive and Convention Minutes, vol. 1932–7.
[4]Ibid.
[5]C.C.F. National Convention Minutes, vol. 1936–42.

In Woodsworth's presidential addresses to the two conventions preceding the war, there occur several revealing passages.[6] In 1937 he stated his belief that the continuous educational campaign carried on by all sections of the movement was influencing people in the churches, the universities, the press, the radio, and other fields; these would, in turn, influence their institutions. But he also uttered a vigorous exhortation to all-out action. "Some of us," he said, with a half smile, "who are grey-headed don't want to die in the wilderness. Let us all take the position of Joshua and Caleb, 'Let us go up and possess it; we are able.'" And in 1938 he felt constrained to express the hope that "sectional differences and personal ambitions will be subordinated to the great purpose to which this organization is dedicated." Undoubtedly he was beginning to feel some of the inevitable disappointment of those who set goals for themselves which are simply not attainable within a single lifetime. Those goals were deeply cherished, and although with his mind he knew the most he could hope for was to see steady progress towards them, emotionally it was not easy to approach the end of his life and be left to wonder. It was worse to think that the movement itself might depart from the course which he believed the right one, or that it might be fatally weakened by internal dissension at the critical point in its growth. There was evidence in these years that either or both fates might lie in wait for the C.C.F., and this evidence made hazardous and fearful Woodsworth's path toward his final crisis.

Two incidents may be taken to illustrate the new area of tension in Woodsworth's life. The first concerned the relations of Woodsworth with the President of the Saskatchewan C.C.F., George Williams, and the development of pressures to modify the policy of neutrality.[7] In February of 1937 the C.C.F. sponsored a meeting in Regina to be addressed by Professor King Gordon. The subject of the evening was "neutrality." The chairman of the meeting, Rev. Sam East, made the mistake of announcing that George Williams (who was leader of the C.C.F. opposition in the legislature) did not agree with the views of King Gordon or of the National Council on the subject of neutrality and "pacifism" and therefore was not on the platform. The *Leader-Post* and papers across Canada seized upon this story and obtained a statement from Williams confirming Mr. East's platform remarks. In

[6]*Ibid.*
[7]Information concerning this incident is taken from letters in the possession of Dr. Hugh MacLean; C.C.F. National Council and Executive Minutes, vol. 1937–42; press clippings in Woodsworth's scrapbook; and C.C.F. files, Regina.

the correspondence between Williams and the C.C.F. National Executive, the Saskatchewan leader said that the question of neutrality was still debatable within the C.C.F. and implied that the National Council's position was one of pacifism. The executive replied that the convention's resolution on neutrality was clear and binding, that it did not mention pacifism, and that the place to question it was in the next convention rather than in public.

Woodsworth himself felt very strongly about this incident and when he received an invitation from Williams in the spring to speak at the Saskatchewan C.C.F. summer schools he declined to accept the limitations on foreign policy discussion that were suggested. He was particularly worried because he knew that a majority of the Saskatchewan Provincial Council held "a decided opinion against unrestricted neutrality." In a letter to Dr. MacLean, Vice-President of the Saskatchewan C.C.F., he was definite about the issue:

I am afraid that I cannot alter my position. . . . Both questions [co-operation with other parties, and neutrality] are general rather than provincial. "Neutrality" is distinctly a federal concern. Our federal members and National Executive seemed agreed as to our resolutions. What would Mr. Williams think if a federal representative undertook to interpret Saskatchewan C.C.F. land policy!

But my objection to Mr. Williams' letters is not primarily one of jurisdiction. I have never yet permitted anyone to dictate to me in advance what I may say or not say in regard to matters of vital importance.

If my services are not acceptable in Saskatchewan, I can decline C.C.F. invitations. If I stand in the way of progress or unity in the C.C.F. I can resign from official position. But I will not give up my convictions and freedom!

This cancelling of my Saskatchewan programme disarranges all my summor plans. I am having invitations *direct* from Saskatchewan organizations. I am at a bit of a loss to know how to deal with such. I don't want to cause any friction in the organization; on the other hand, my Saskatchewan connections date back twenty-five years and I did want to get a close view of the drought situation. I am inclined to think I'd better keep out of Saskatchewan until after the national convention.

Here again was stated the core problem of Woodsworth's life: the question of freedom to speak out on all issues of fundamental importance, and the assumption that if institutional requirements inhibit this right, the individual should dissociate himself from the institution. But this time too many of Woodsworth's sympathies were on the side of the institution—indeed, to some extent he *was* the institution. Thus he could more easily see the need of basic unity in the party, and he would attempt every last path of compromise on *forms* before he would take the final step of virtually dissociating himself from it. In this particular instance, through the good offices of Dr. MacLean, Woodsworth and Williams met in Regina with MacLean and M. J. Coldwell present. A temporary basis of agreement was arrived at (although there could obviously be no fundamental unity) and the breach was closed.

The incident was an indication of the temperature of discussion in the party at the end of the thirties. The trend of opinion within the party was, in the face of developments in Europe, beginning to veer slightly away from the unqualified declaration for neutrality of 1936. In the Council meeting preceding the National Convention of July, 1937, a committee was appointed to phrase a foreign policy resolution to present to the convention. The committee consisted of M. J. Coldwell, King Gordon, and George Williams. Its resolution, adopted by the convention, made only one change in the 1936 resolution, which had urged neutrality in the event of "any war." The word "imperialist" was inserted before the word "war." It was the formal announcement of a major policy revision which even Woodsworth would be unable to check.

In the same year another area of internal party trouble boiled over; and it placed an unavoidable further strain directly on Woodsworth. It was not, this time, an issue of general policy but a local question of great intensity. This second incident indicates again the importance Woodsworth placed upon retaining intact the national organization of the C.C.F. and his ability to negotiate with skill in political matters.[8]

In February of 1937 a number of factors induced a special convention of the Manitoba I.L.P. to pass a resolution favouring disaffiliation of the I.L.P. from the C.C.F. provincial organization. The I.L.P., as suggested earlier, had nearly all its roots in Winnipeg, and despite a number of attempts to have it include farmers' locals it had remained essentially an urban labour party. It had refrained from submerging itself in the C.C.F. (as the Manitoba Farmers' Section had already done), clung tenaciously to the use of its name, and objected strenuously to the separate existence in Winnipeg of C.C.F. clubs. A vocal minority in the I.L.P. recognized this as a short-sighted political view and yet was unable to overcome the strong *esprit de corps* particularly of those members who were primarily concerned with

[8]Information concerning this second incident is taken from letters given the author by the late S. J. Farmer; Woodsworth papers; C.C.F. National Council and Executive Minutes, vol. 1937–42; Woodsworth's scrapbook; and interviews with C.C.F. leaders in Manitoba.

municipal politics. An unwise attempt had been made during the C.C.F. Provincial Convention in 1936 to force complete absorption of the I.L.P. by the C.C.F. At the tag end of that convention, after many delegates had left, a resolution was passed declaring that after the next election the I.L.P. should no longer use its own name but only that of the C.C.F.

This unfortunate manœuvre brought to a head the resentment which had been growing among the I.L.P. opponents of a "broadening out" policy. They felt that they were being forced to scrap a well-developed electoral organization centred on municipal and provincial divisions in favour of a loose-knit and untried grouping which made light of class lines. The element in the I.L.P. which led the successful fight for passage of the disaffiliation resolution was headed by John Queen, one of the I.L.P. delegates to the Regina convention of 1933, a successful candidate for the Winnipeg mayoralty, but a man who had been ignored when the first three Manitoba representatives on the C.C.F. National Council were elected. As S. J. Farmer, provincial C.C.F. leader, wrote to Woodsworth at the time, "Personalities to a considerable extent enter into the matter, certain people on each side being disliked or even distrusted by those on the other side. . . . I am frankly at a loss what to do next. It means a bad split in the labour movement in Winnipeg and it seems impossible now to avert it." The positions of Woodsworth and Farmer in particular were unenviable. Both had been amongst the earliest members of the I.L.P.; both had campaigned as I.L.P.–C.C.F. candidates; the one was provincial C.C.F. leader, the other national leader. It was Farmer who first advised Woodsworth of the details of the situation in Winnipeg and in a reply Woodsworth wrote, "Behind these [organizational] difficulties there is the still more fundamental one of a little group who have in the past done good work but refuse to enter upon the larger field. They seem oblivious to the fact that only by taking on a larger work can they even maintain the hold which they have secured. Sooner or later there must be a showdown between the two points of view. . . . I feel that I will have to stand for the larger movement. . . ."

There were, then, three sides to the question for Woodsworth: the prospect of a painful break with old friends (who had been largely instrumental in securing his electoral majorities since 1921); the difficulties of his dual position; and the threat of a crippling division in the Manitoba C.C.F. organization. Here was a danger almost as great as the ominous neutrality question, but it was more readily averted through conciliation. Woodsworth acted with despatch. He introduced the issue at the February meeting of the National Council and obtained the passage of a resolution asking the Manitoba C.C.F. Council to remove the time limit it had imposed for reopening discussion with the I.L.P., and requesting the I.L.P. to suspend action on disaffiliation. He then moved that M. J. Coldwell and A. A. Heaps be deputed to go to Winnipeg and negotiate an agreement on behalf of the National Council between the two sections of the Manitoba party. While Coldwell and Heaps were conducting their negotiations, Woodsworth produced a statement of his own position which carried great weight with both elements of the I.L.P. Reviewing the whole incident, he concluded: "I owed it to the C.C.F., to some of my I.L.P. associates in Winnipeg, and to myself, to make my position clear to the ten thousand people who supported me in the last election. Unless the I.L.P. can alter its decision I must regretfully tender my resignation as a member of the central branch of the I.L.P. I have had to do some hard things in my life; this would be one of the hardest."

The double approach of conciliation and of portraying clearly the inevitable result of a continued rift was successful—so successful that when a motion in the I.L.P. convention was finally made, to drop the old name, the mover was John Queen. But the strain of these events unquestionably told upon Woodsworth, and to the two major incidents just described should be added a number of others only slightly less important: the taut relations in Alberta in 1938 between the U.F.A., the C.L.P., and the C.C.F. clubs, or the sudden appearance in 1939 of the thunder-stealing Herridge party.

To offset the tension and worry of these years, however, there were many encouraging signs. The whole party was successfully warding off the undermining tactics of the communists; the United Mine Workers of Nova Scotia, with their twelve thousand members, affiliated as a body with the C.C.F. in 1938, and the growth of the movement for industrial unions in the rest of the country was bringing a closer political association with organized labour. In the House of Commons, too, Woodsworth found some of the debating load lifted from his shoulders as the party caucus mapped out more precisely the fields of specialization for the little C.C.F. group.

In the House the case for socialism was advanced at every opportunity. Canada, like the United States, failed to emerge from the great depression prior to the outbreak of the Second World War, and this meant that each time the Speech from the Throne described in glowing phrases the return of prosperity, damning evidence to the contrary was not wanting—whether the semi-starvation conditions of the Saskatchewan drought areas or the continuing high unemployment figures of industrial Canada. The rigidity of a semi-monopolized economy led Woodsworth on each presentation of his co-operative commonwealth resolution to draw the conclusion: "The question is not individual enterprise versus bureaucratic monopoly, but rather whether the inevitable monopoly shall be irresponsible and inefficient as at present, or Fascist in type, or democratic. We plead for democratic control in industry."[9]

Nor did the allegations of communism abate. J. R. MacNicol, after 1935 a member of a reduced Conservative representation, frequently led these attacks—often with considerable sarcasm. In 1936 he commented upon the "perennial Woodsworth resolution" thus: "My difficulty arises not because of the resolution itself—it is just as communistic as each of the four preceding ones—but because this session I am sitting close to the honourable member and when I look into his gentle eyes, when I observe his kindly smile, his sympathetic countenance, I know that although in my opinion he preaches communism again in the resolution, he is not a communist."[10] This was followed by a full-scale speech identifying the C.C.F. and the Communist Party and accepting as true every communist claim of a united front.

Although in 1936 the long parliamentary fight of Woodsworth to obtain repeal of section 98 of the Criminal Code was finally successful —the Minister of Justice himself sponsoring the amendment—there were many areas remaining in which a defence of civil liberties was sorely needed.[11] The "Regina riot" of 1935, which had its aftermath in the arrest and conviction of unemployed under section 98, had been, like "Bloody Saturday" in Winnipeg, to a considerable extent aggravated by the unwise use of police force. Woodsworth reviewed the case in the House and asked for an enquiry into the responsibility of the R.C.M.P. Commissioner and Assistant Commissioner. The debate on this served to publicize the issue; to focus attention on a case in which the R.C.M.P. used strong-arm and disastrous methods rather than a calmer strategy; to reduce former Prime Minister Bennett to impotent rage; and to produce only a mild reply from Lapointe, who remarked that nothing should be done to weaken the authority of those charged with responsibility.[12]

[9]Hansard, 1936, pp. 443 et seq.
[10]Ibid., p. 449.
[11]For the last debate on section 98 see ibid., pp. 3903 et seq.
[12]Ibid., pp. 4059 et seq.

With the disappearance of section 98 from the statute book, various defenders of law and order endeavoured to fill the gap by tough policy and in one case by a successful provincial invasion of the federal field of criminal law. In Ontario, Premier Mitchell F. Hepburn, with an eye to the federal Liberal leadership, was building up his private army (special police force) preparatory to riding in full force against the new industrial unionism. In Quebec, Premier Maurice Duplessis, on the basis of a tortured interpretation of the British North America Act, secured passage of the Padlock Law enabling him to close up any building (including private houses) in the province, which he might consider to have been used for communist ends. The legislation did not define communism (or what might be meant by the phrase "tending to propagate communism"); there was no need of definition because the Premier had told the legislators that communism could be felt. These two premiers, protecting central Canada against the dangers of trade-union growth, seemed almost to be classed by the federal Minister of Justice with the R.C.M.P. as agents whose authority should not be undermined.

In 1937 Woodsworth launched an attack against the wholesale curtailment of civil liberties, using four specific cases to illustrate the need for constructive and protective federal action.[18] In Sarnia, he noted, where the "sit-down" strike method had been tried in the Holmes Foundry, the management had armed gangs with axes and rods to attack the factory and some workers' homes. The result was a "riot" and the imprisonment without bail of a number of union leaders. Lapointe had commented, upon receipt of this news, that the full powers of the state would be used to crush any sit-down strike. Here again was the legalistic method of suppressing effects without impartially investigating causes. Once more the doctrine of provincial rights was being used to justify the federal Big Brother stepping in on the "right side" only.

The other three cases selected by Woodsworth were all from Quebec. All showed the application, even more specifically, of the same principles applied to the Sarnia riot. The Duplessis police had entered the offices of the Unemployment Relief Commission's headquarters in Montreal. Without a warrant they had ejected the director, Brigadier-General Panet, and seized the records. There was no protest from Ottawa. In Montreal also, seven officials of a trade union (the Joint Board of Amalgamated Clothing Workers) had been seized in their homes in the dead of night by special provincial officers and

[18]*Ibid.*, 1937, pp. 2298 *et seq.*

given no bail until their appearance in court. They were faced with the nebulous charge of conspiring to injure business and prevent others from working. "Did our Minister of Justice," asked Woodsworth, "upon these arrests in Montreal hasten to interpret the law as he did in the case of the sit-down strikers?"

The fourth item was a blanket indictment of the Padlock Law. Woodsworth reviewed the various aspects of the law. There was not the slightest doubt that the act denied the most basic British liberties. It deprived individuals of property without due process of law; it prescribed arbitrary arrest procedure; it placed the burden of proving innocence upon the accused persons; and in subtler ways it slashed to ribbons the whole concept of civil liberty. Worried editorials from journals as cautious as the *Financial Post* and the *Winnipeg Free Press* had already said as much, and questioned whether the act was *intra vires* of the province's jurisdiction. The government, declared Woodsworth, did not hesitate to interpret the law quickly with respect to corporate property rights in Sarnia or to send the constitutionally dubious Bennett "new deal" legislation to the courts for testing. Here was a much more serious question of immediate importance. Lapointe, he argued, should either send the act to the courts or declare it *ultra vires* himself and use the federal power of disallowance as an assertion that there existed the means of protecting Canadian citizens in Quebec against lawlessness and violence and that the resources of the Dominion would be used to ensure the rights and liberties of all Canadian citizens.

Rising to reply to this formidable barrage, Lapointe employed the defensive weapons of provincial rights and official dignity. Of the first three items, he said, he was not in possession of official knowledge. Of the Quebec law he had no official copy. When Woodsworth rose and offered him a copy he stated: "I have not the bill, but when the bill comes to me it will come in an official regular way, not through the agency of the honourable member for Winnipeg Centre." The Minister then launched on a white-hot tirade. Woodsworth, he implied, had gone off at half cock; his observations had been premature; and in proposing the use of the disallowing power (which, said the Minister, had not been used for many years, since 1924, in fact) Woodsworth was advocating an arbitrary policy.

The Padlock Law remained on the books. And when Premier Hepburn opened his war against the C.I.O. strike at General Motors in Oshawa, the federal government stood with all its authority behind Toronto. As in Winnipeg in 1919, the Oshawa employers had refused to deal with the industrial union committee, asserting that they would negotiate only with "their own men." Tempers grew warm and Hepburn overruled the mayor of Oshawa who had declared that he was in no fear that the situation was beyond local control. On the ground that the C.I.O. was subversive and led by foreign agitators Hepburn asked for R.C.M.P. reinforcement in defending the American-controlled automobile firm. Lapointe, as Woodsworth noted in the debate which he obtained on the subject, was quick to send the Mounted Police to be held in reserve at Toronto.[14]

By 1938 the argument that federal disallowance of the Padlock Law would be either anachronistic or arbitrary was wearing thin. For when the Alberta government acted against the interests of the chartered banks its legislation was promptly disallowed by the federal government, on the ground that Alberta had invaded a federal field of jurisdiction. A fresh light was thus shed upon the nature of federal-provincial relations and Woodsworth reintroduced the question of the validity of the Padlock Law and of Ottawa's attitude towards it.[15] No sooner had he introduced the question than Lapointe leapt angrily to his feet. The Commons could not ask a minister to use the power of disallowance, he thundered, until after the minister had presented his report on the questionable legislation to the Governor in Council; thus Woodsworth was out of order. When the dust had subsided Woodsworth remarked that he was not asking for the immediate use of disallowance, but rather that the Padlock Law be referred to the Supreme Court for an opinion on its validity.

Deprived of his point of order, the Minister of Justice became still more angry. When Woodsworth remonstrated that the Commons must never cease to be a forum to which grievances can be brought, Lapointe replied, "There is no grievance here." His meaning was, of course, that there could be no grievance as far as Woodsworth was concerned since Woodsworth did not live in Quebec. Woodsworth countered this by appealing to the rights of Canadians to civil liberty no matter what province they might move to or travel through, and to the fact that Duplessis had called the C.C.F. into question, thus obviously threatening it with action under the obnoxious law. He then listed some of the more glaring of many police actions taken under the law—actions which had caused the formation of the Canadian Civil Liberties Union headed by eminently respectable citizens, and petitions against the act by such reputable bodies as the Canadian Bar Association and the Social Service Council.

[14]*Ibid.*, pp. 2811 *et seq.*   [15]*Ibid.*, 1938, pp. 3368 *et seq.*

In the face of the legal and constitutional analysis of the Civil Liberties Union and the Bar Association it is perhaps little wonder that Lapointe would not ask the Supreme Court for an opinion which would almost certainly have nullified the Quebec law. Thus again Quebeckers rose to tell Woodsworth that this was none of his business, that it concerned exclusively the province of Quebec. It mattered little that Woodsworth could read off a list of raids, searches and confiscations, and summarize the situation thus: "Twice every three days for six months the provincial police have carried out execution without judgment, dispossession without due process of law; twenty times a month they have trampled on liberties as old as Magna Carta."

The Padlock Law was to stay and the federal government, while perhaps disapproving its lack of restraint, accepted its philosophy. Commenting on the unemployment situation in Vancouver, which was to be settled by tear gas and the outbreak of war rather than by a government employment policy, Lapointe said: "In spite of the fact that the words are so unpleasant to the honourable member for Winnipeg North Centre, I do desire to say that the reign of law must continue in this country, that peace and order must prevail."[16]

In another direction Woodsworth made definite progress in the regular 1939 session.[17] This was the culmination of a campaign for a positive legal guarantee of labour's right to join unions—a right which had been recognized only in the most negative way hitherto. Woodsworth had twice introduced a bill (in 1936 and in 1938) designed to amend the Criminal Code to prevent employers "from refusing to employ or from dismissing employees or conspiring with others therefor for the reasons that they are members of a trade union." The bill provided severe penalties for violation of its provisions. In 1936 the bill failed because it was shunted to the end of the session; in 1938 the government endorsed the principle but refused to act because the legislation would affect the ubiquitous "property and civil rights" reserved to the provinces. The entire support of organized labour was behind what the Trades and Labor Congress called "the Woodsworth bill";[18] and in 1939 when Woodsworth reintroduced it for the third time he produced enough arguments to make untenable the government's 1938 reasons for inaction. The Criminal Code already defined scores of crimes which affected property and civil rights; and the proposed bill in any event dealt primarily with intimidation and

[16]Ibid., p. 4023.
[17]Ibid., 1939, pp. 1077 et seq.; pp. 3296 et seq.
[18]H. A. Logan, Trade Unions in Canada (Toronto, 1948), p. 417.

conspiracy (as R. B. Bennett had pointed out in the 1938 debate). Woodsworth suggested that if the House accepted the bill it might well add a clause safeguarding the right to organize, as well as to join unions.

Although the Woodsworth bill itself did not reach third reading, the pressure for it had become so great that the Minister of Justice reversed his previous stand and himself introduced a similar bill which not only passed but received the royal assent from George VI during the monarch's Canadian visit. Such legislation as this, or the final nationalization of the Bank of Canada, resulted from years of patient argument.

The halting reform of these years has been described by Liberal historians as a line of cautious advance. And doubtless the Prime Minister was dogged by almost innumerable defenders of the *status quo*. In any matter of federal social legislation the chief spokesman of Quebec, Ernest Lapointe, was ready to insist on the political dangers of invading provincial jurisdiction. In the continuous debate about the proper fields of public and private enterprise there were always substantial defenders of the latter in the cabinet. Several questions about this period will no doubt be answered by the biographers of Mackenzie King. How far, and in what ways did King really push for the advancement of the welfare state; to what extent were his tentative moves primarily concessions to public opinion and leftist pressure?

To socialists, the snail's pace of reform was explained fairly simply: in terms of property and bigotry. In the House and in their newspapers they offered many illustrations to substantiate their interpretation. The privileges and purposes of property, for example, seemed to be evidenced by Charles Dunning's speaking in 1939 for the Canadian *rentier* class. He was opposing, for the government, the motion of A. A. Heaps to lower the pensionable age from seventy. The Minister of Finance asked, "Do we not concentrate too much on the seven or eight hundred thousand people who are on relief tonight and think rather too little of that great body of our middle class represented by those four million who have some savings . . . who are attempting to make provision for their own security by way of life insurance? They are the great burden-bearers of this nation, the great middle-class of this country. . . ."[19]

Again, the door to another needed piece of legislation seemed to be held closed by the hand of bigotry. In 1938 Woodsworth sponsored a Senate divorce bill to widen the grounds of divorce to include deser-

[19]Hansard, 1939, p. 1613.

tion, cruelty, and insanity.[20] The government would have let the bill drop quietly from the order paper without debate; and apparently no one except Woodsworth was prepared to take the political risk of fathering it in the Commons. All the arguments against divorce in general and against widening the grounds upon which divorce was obtainable were summarized by Lapointe. But his main argument was that the incidence of divorce had increased in Ontario as a result of the establishment of a divorce court there. This was arguable; also it veiled the material consideration. Woodsworth replied, ". . . Let me point out to my right honourable friend that before that legislation was enacted it took a considerable amount of money to see a divorce case through Parliament. Therefore only people who had money to spend to come to Ottawa and to employ lawyers could secure a divorce. My idea of justice is that it ought to be just as possible for poor people as for wealthy people to secure relief." He pointed out that the bill was designed not to encourage the breaking of homes but to salvage something from the wreckage of homes already broken; and in the process, to discourage immorality. His argument that "the state must not allow itself to become a policeman to enforce certain religious beliefs or practices" was effectively crushed by a vote of 102–53. Although it was officially a non-party vote, the Liberals had kept most of their non-Catholics in line.

The power of the Prime Minister and his cabinet in controlling so effectively the votes of the majority party in the House continued to bother Woodsworth as it did other liberals in Canada. Besides the day-to-day criticism in debates, Woodsworth focused particular attention on this question at the time of the abdication crisis in 1937. His purpose in making an issue of King's handling of this tricky constitutional procedure was twofold: to reveal the full extent of the extraordinary power wielded by the Prime Minister and to obtain a clarification of the constitutional relationship of Canada to the United Kingdom.

When Edward VIII decided to abdicate in December, 1936, the governments of the Dominions were all advised (December 9). The Instrument of Abdication was signed by the King on December 10 and the British Parliament met to pass the legislation necessary to give effect to the abdication and to debar from the succession any issue of Edward. The parliamentary action was necessary because the Act of Settlement which governed the royal succession contained no provision for abdication. The abdication did not become final until after

[20]*Ibid.*, 1938, pp. 3845 *et seq.*

Edward VIII had assented to this legislation (on December 11) and the Parliament had thus consented to the procedures adopted. In Canada, Parliament was not specially summoned to deal with this constitutional situation. Instead, the cabinet requested and assented to the British Act of Succession on behalf of the Dominion of Canada, because there was not, in the Prime Minister's opinion, enough time to summon Parliament. This procedure was technically permissible since the Statute of Westminster employed the word "Dominions" rather than the term "Dominion Parliaments" in section 4 dealing with United Kingdom legislation which would affect the Dominions.[21]

When the Canadian Parliament did assemble in January, 1937, the government immediately sought the passage of an address of loyalty to George VI and it was at this stage that Woodsworth rose to voice objections.[22] He declared that the Prime Minister had usurped the powers of Parliament, that the cabinet should not have taken the action it did, that the address should not be passed until after the Succession Bill was debated and passed, and that the oath of allegiance to George VI should not have been administered to the members. When Parliament had been prorogued, he asserted, all members were pledged to Edward. "Why should the Liberal party be in a position to decide who is to be King of the Canadian people?" he asked. If the Prime Minister can decide matters such as this he can also declare war. The time element was not critical, he argued: "Surely if the King of the United Kingdom can be distinguished for legal purposes from the King of Canada, then the recognition of the King of the United Kingdom as King of Canada can wait until there is time to call Parliament. If the selection of the King of Canada is of such minor importance, the question arises: why a King at all?"

[21]See Statute of Westminster (22 Geo. V, c. 4). As with several other aspects of this statute, the procedure outlined is ambiguous. The preamble, for example, says, "any alteration in the law touching the Succession to the Throne or Royal Style and Titles shall hereafter require the assent as well of the Parliaments of all the Dominions as of the Parliament of the United Kingdom. . . ." Section 4 reads: "No Act of the Parliament of the United Kingdom passed after the commencement of this Act shall extend or be deemed to extend to a Dominion as part of the law of that Dominion unless it is expressly declared in that Act that the Dominion has requested, and consented to, the enactment thereof." There certainly is room to argue that King was evading, at the very least, the spirit of the statute. The problem was not an imperial one, for the procedure followed by King was perfectly acceptable to the United Kingdom government, see Declaration of Abdication Act, reprinted in Dawson, *The Development of Dominion Status, 1900–1936* (Oxford, 1937), p. 452. It was a question whether Canadians would allow their Prime Minister to decide such matters on his own authority and only later obtain the sanction of the parliamentary rubber stamp.

[22]Hansard, 1939, pp. 4, 13 *et seq.*

Such argument caused considerable fluttering in loyal breasts and after the address was passed the Prime Minister gave a fuller statement of his actions during the crisis. He reiterated his plea about time being of the essence. Then, rather ironically, in view of his general external policies, gave this reason: "If there ever was a time in British history when it was of importance that the unity of the British Empire should be demonstrated to all the world, it was when a question affecting the Crown itself was under consideration." Here, in one sentence, was illustrated the contradictory nature of King's foreign policy. Parliament, he had asserted, must always be supreme, and Canada must guard jealously her right to independent action in external affairs. Those twin principles were logically destroyed in this debate. Yet down to the outbreak of war in 1939 the Prime Minister insisted that he had no prior commitments and that it would be left to Parliament to declare Canadian policy. On these grounds he refused all formal declarations concerning Canada's right to remain neutral, and gave to most Canadians the impression that his own policy was one of neutrality. Was this because he knew that Canadians dislike, above all else, the clarification of fundamentals; or was it because he himself remained in doubt about where he was going? Possibly it was both, yet the evidence leads strongly to the conclusion that actually Canada was committed to the support of any British action in a major European war of aggression.

In any case, the Canadian press did little to enlighten its readers on the subtleties of the constitutional question and its implications. Most papers reported that the Conservative C. H. Cahan and Woodsworth were together in their opposition to King's procedure in the abdication crisis. Actually the two men agreed only on the unconstitutionality of the government's action with respect to Canada; they did not agree on the theory of the divisibility of the Crown. Cahan pointed out that although the British act was quite sufficient, in his opinion, to secure the succession, the Canadian government's order-in-council consenting to it had no statutory authority, and that no order-in-council can be valid without such authority. Herein was the beginning of a continued Conservative–C.C.F. critique of government by order-in-council.

At the time of this constitutional debate none knew how imminent was the outbreak of war; but all sensed the urgency of the external relations aspect of the discussion. How important were the warnings against abuse of orders-in-council and the power of the chief minister was to be revealed in war and post-war policy.

20

WAR

IN THE PRECEDING CHAPTERS considerable attention has been paid to Woodsworth's attitude to war. This was never an easy thing for his closest friends to define during his lifetime. The passage of time has not simplified the task.

In many ways Woodsworth was a fighter himself and he had no particular distaste for violence *per se*. He believed that there were occasions when one must use force to discipline children, and in his youth we have seen that he could admire the soldiery of Germany. His pacifism, then, was not an inherent repugnance to the use of physical force. It was primarily a reasoned thing and it was intimately related to his social thought. No one who ever observed the vigorous little man bristle with fiery indignation in his denunciation of sweatshops and armament profits could miss the close connection. In the final analysis it was his estimate of capitalism that produced his pacifism.

Capitalism, Woodsworth believed, was both exploitive and inefficient. In its exploitive aspect it sacrificed the human individual on the altar of profit. In its inefficient aspect it found only war as an answer to its periodic economic unbalance or depression. War itself could settle no basic problems because the causes of war grew out of capitalist profit-seeking and would remain active until the profit motive was replaced by democratic planning and production for use. Granting these premises, the conclusion followed that the only sane policy of any social democrat was to fight against his country's involvement in foreign war and to press for the social revolution at home.

To this general analysis Woodsworth added the moral fervour of his temperament. He found it morally disgusting that anyone could recommend the principle of competition within a society and then reason that since this was a "natural" principle, warfare between nations was also "natural."

We might well ask now: at what point and in what manner did his pacifism become more than the result of political-economic reasoning? Because, while it was not religious in any formal sense, it came to have a high emotional content not dissimilar to that of the religious pacifist. The answer will be best understood by those who have read John Stuart Mill's essay on utilitarianism.[1] This is not to suggest that Woodsworth became a utilitarian in the exact philosophic sense, but that the process by which sentiment, emotion, or fervour can become attached to principles originally perceived by the mind alone is perhaps best described in Mill's revised utilitarian terms. When Mill describes how the reasoned morality of his utilitarianism can dictate actions of public service and co-operation (as opposed to the earlier and simpler hedonistic calculus), and how all the emotions evoked by religion may become active in support of such morality, he gives the answer to our problem.

"In the golden rule of Jesus of Nazareth we read the complete spirit of the ethics of utility."[2] Like Mill, Woodsworth saw the Christian revelation as "intended to inform the hearts and minds of mankind with a spirit which should enable them to find for themselves what is right, and incline them to do it when found, rather than to tell them, except in a very general way, what it is."[3] It may be recalled that Woodsworth at Oxford had defined his own problem in almost exactly these terms;[4] that he had early reached a position where he thought that the church should not lay down any absolutes of belief. He had concluded then that any valid ethical system must be the result of historical and personal experience, that it might be informed by Christian as well as other revelation, and that it must remain open to modification. He thus could use the precepts of the Sermon on the Mount without attaching to them an absolute meaning stemming from a supernatural interpretation. His own central principle he had defined as brotherhood; and the evolutionary nature of social ethics he had frequently emphasized in such aphorisms as: "The nineteenth century made the world a community; the twentieth century must make it a brotherhood."

Now to such reasoned social ethics, implying the goals of social democracy, Woodsworth had attached a very strong emotional bias which nevertheless left him free to adopt or reject various practical alternatives. That is, his position on domestic questions remained relatively undogmatic. To the position of pacifism in international

[1]J. S. Mill, *Utilitarianism*. See especially chap. IV.
[2]*Ibid.*, chap. I.
[3]*Ibid.*   [4]See p. 15, *supra*.

affairs, also arrived at originally by reasoning, he had attached an even stronger emotional bias. But in this second area he came very close indeed to dogmatism and this was the real centre of his personal tragedy in September, 1939.

It was not only that he found himself having to oppose what appeared to be a generally accepted national purpose; nor that he was in opposition to many who had been close to him in establishing the C.C.F. These things he had faced before, and although they were deeply distressing, they could be borne again. But by 1939 there could be no certainty that the causes of the second German war were overwhelmingly the result of capitalism; there was doubt whether the basic purposes of brotherhood, of socialism, would be advanced by allowing Hitler to expand his empire, opposed only by moral force.

Against this doubt Woodsworth posed the questions: did the First World War assist social progress or did it merely create the causes of its successor; would not a second large war only create the causes of a third; and would not the steady advance of militarist preoccupation undermine completely the principles of brotherhood and co-operation which socialists should hold pre-eminent? In 1939 the case for opposing force with force seemed much stronger than it had been in 1914. It will probably remain an open question whether Woodsworth's stand in 1939 was influenced more by his rational conviction or by his emotional attachment to the pacifism which had been such an important aspect of his reputation for integrity.

Whatever may be the answer to this (possibly artificial) question, it was Woodsworth who spoke most clearly for Canada's conscience at the outbreak of war. In the several years preceding that catastrophe it was Woodsworth above all others who compelled the increasing debate on external affairs in the House of Commons—debate which, if it did not influence the government to the adoption of a positive policy, at least provided a record of the ostrich-like Canadian refusal to see things as they were and to attempt to alter them.

On each occasion that a specific question of foreign policy was raised by the Left in these years there was an automatic attempt in the House to reply by referring either to the dangerous subversive elements within Canada, or to the crucial nature of the European "balance" which it would be suicidal for Canada to endanger. As F. H. Underhill wrote in 1937, advocating a neutrality declaration, "We are getting closer to the condition of mass hysteria that will make all sane discussion of our national policy impossible."[5]

In 1936 after Germany had violated the Versailles treaty by formally

[5]*Canadian Forum*, March, 1937.

repossessing the Rhineland, Bennett and King both made statements in the House agreeing that Canada should keep out of the ensuing negotiations because she was not a signatory of the Locarno treaty.[6] Woodsworth pointed out that Canada was a signatory of the 1919 treaty and asked what was the attitude of the government as a member of the League and in view of the violation of the earlier agreement. King's answer illustrated the way in which he based a "do-nothing" policy upon fear of the consequences of open discussion and action: "May I say . . . the attitude of the government is to do nothing itself and if possible to prevent anything occurring which will precipitate one additional factor into the all-important discussions which are now taking place in Europe. . . ." To this the Prime Minister added the additional bogey of Quebec; did Woodsworth, he asked, wish to keep Canada united or not?

Both King and Woodsworth could agree that war was an evil; they differed widely in their estimates of how evil it was. Woodsworth was prepared to refuse any part in war and to run risks to guard against its outbreak. King, while he argued that Canada must not commit herself in advance, knew that in the last analysis she was thoroughly committed at every stage; and he refused to run the preliminary risks (both internal and external) involved in an attempt at collective security. Thus he and Lapointe stamped out the one brief Canadian move to make the League effective by imposing genuine economic sanctions against Mussolini. The "Riddell" incident[7] proved beyond doubt that the Canadian government would take no overt decision as to what was right or wrong in peacetime foreign policy, and that it was not prepared to take risks to establish the idea of collective security. Until Britain and France declared themselves on any issue, King refused to take a stand. He would not even consider Woodsworth's suggestion that Canada advocate the use of article 19 of the League Covenant to revise the treaty settlement and thus eliminate some of the areas of European friction.[8] Anomalously, while King was staying "neutral" and refusing a formal declaration of Canada's right to remain neutral in a war declared by Britain, Woodsworth was pressing for an effective League, the diminution of national sovereignties, and a formal declaration of Canadian neutrality.

Woodsworth placed the question of neutrality in a motion in 1937

[6]Hansard, 1936, pp. 1332 et seq.
[7]For a brief account of this incident see R. A. MacKay and E. B. Rogers, *Canada Looks Abroad* (Toronto, 1938), p. 105; or G. P. de T. Glazebrook, *Canadian External Relations* (Toronto, 1950), pp. 409 et seq. An "inside" account is in W. A. Riddell, *World Security by Conference* (Toronto, 1937).
[8]Hansard, 1936, pp. 3873 et seq.

which declared that Canada would remain neutral in any war no matter who were the belligerents.[9] He was able to assert that this was official C.C.F. policy (as of the 1936 convention). Because neither the Canadian government nor the British government had done anything to implement the principle of collective security, he argued, the next war would be one of the old alliances, of the defence of an unjustifiable empire. Since this was so, Canada had every right to take advantage of the Monroe Doctrine and not sacrifice herself to the ambitions of imperialists and munitions makers. But because the government knew it was committed, even in the days when there was a chance of influencing British policy, because the government wished to appear isolationist in Quebec, it not only smothered the C.C.F. motions but gave very dubious answers to questions asked in the House. When Woodsworth questioned the 1937 increase in Air Force estimates and asked against whom the government planned to use the non-defensive bombing planes,[10] Lapointe replied: "Can there be anything more ludicrous than that question? . . . Can [Woodsworth] cite any country in the world, any Parliament in a civilized country, where, when they organize their defence, they broadcast to the world that they are arming against this or that country. . . . We have no enemies, I hope; in fact, I know we have no enemies. . . ." The Minister of Justice concluded his remarks by stating that Woodsworth was saying the same things as the communists; and by denying that Canada was "preparing for participation in wars outside Canada." He did not explain what the bombers were to do inside Canada.

Against this policy of not letting the left hand know what the right hand was doing, Woodsworth appealed in vain for sanctions, or the clear prohibition of the export of munitions or war materials to Japan, Germany, and Italy (such as the government was prepared to enforce against both sides in the Spanish civil war). Each time this suggestion was made a government spokesman countered it with the "wait and see" answer. In 1938 it was Lapointe who asked Woodsworth whether he thought Canada should take the lead and apply sanctions alone against Japan.[11] Woodsworth replied, "I do not think I can accept a code of morals that affirms that we shall not do anything until somebody else does it. I submit that we are guilty— I use the word advisedly— of assisting an aggressor nation to kill men, women and children in China. . . ." This stung King, who sprang to his feet to say,

The government is just as concerned as [Woodsworth] is about the well-being and welfare of the women and children of the Orient, in Spain or in

---

[9]Ibid., 1937, pp. 237 et seq.
[10]Ibid., pp. 1157 et seq.   [11]Ibid., 1938, pp. 380 et seq.

any other part of the world. But what this government is particularly concerned about is the wellbeing and welfare of the Canadian people. If my honourable friend wishes to know in a word what the policy of this country is with respect to matters affecting war, let me tell him that it is to seek in every possible way to avoid taking any step which may be responsible for this country either directly or indirectly being drawn into war. . . .

The difference between the two men was that King was willing to commit Canada to war in defence of a policy for which he refused all responsibility, and which he made no effort to alter; Woodsworth would refuse to commit Canada to any war, given those conditions.

As the crisis approached, as Austria fell and Czechoslovakia slipped, as Munich was reached, the degree of the government's prior commitments became clearer each time it denied them. Through the nightmare months Woodsworth could scarcely conceal the rage which trembled in his voice as he sought vainly to force the government to declare its true policy and allow the people to see things as they were. By the spring of 1938 even Toronto's *Saturday Night*,[12] usually quick to note anything of the fanatic in Woodsworth, could observe that "for once the C.C.F. leader has a full legion of sympathizers" in his attempt to discover the government's foreign policy. When Ian Mackenzie, the Minister of National Defence, stated in Toronto that Canada must stand by Britain, Woodsworth declared: "He was speaking not for himself but for the government. It is a catchy slogan. . . . Has Canada no opinion of her own? We ought to know that. Otherwise it is a case, as in the last war, of 'ready, aye, ready'. . . . Has the Liberal government taken that stand? If it has not, I would like the Liberal government to say so."[13]

Again the reply came from a nervous Lapointe: "Does my honourable friend want to split the country right away?" The memories of the 1917–18 conscription crisis hovered over the Liberals but did not carry enough weight to alter real policy. The shipments of British gold to Canada, the mushrooming of munitions orders from the United Kingdom, the preliminary discussions for the air training scheme—on all these and many more facts of preparation and commitment the government would give no official information to the House. Ian Mackenzie could, indeed, tell Woodsworth at the end of the 1938 session, with respect to two hundred million dollars' worth of munitions orders placed by the United Kingdom government in Canada: "I wish to assure him at once that the Department of National Defence has played no part either directly or indirectly in these negotiations. With reference to any orders to be placed in Canada, we have no more

[12]*Saturday Night*, March 5, 1938.   [13]Hansard, 1938, pp. 3214 *et seq.*

information than is in the possession of the honourable member. . . ."[14]

In 1939, upon news of the Nazi coup in Czechoslovakia, Woodsworth called again for an effort to use the League machinery for the long overdue prohibition of the export of war materials to the Fascist countries, the supertaxing of goods from those nations, and a specific declaration of the right of neutrality. While Canadian metals were flowing freely into Germany and Japan, King again made a lengthy statement.[15] He now clearly implied Canada's immediate readiness to support the "peace and freedom-loving nations" but on the demand for a declaration of the right of neutrality (a right which was at least dubious in 1939) he remarked, "Why divide Canada to provide against a contingency that may not arise, or if it does, may not come until the situation has materially changed? The same consideration of the overwhelming importance of national unity which has led this government to decline to make premature and inappropriate statements of possible belligerency prevent it from recommending actions to declare possible neutrality. . . ." And so, right up to the brink of war, the bogey of disunity was used to manœuvre the nation into a declaration of war, without open debate and without attempt to influence the course of events.

It is now evident that from the time of the Commonwealth Conference of 1937 to the outbreak of war, Prime Minister Chamberlain was fully aware of King's decision that Canada would be at Britain's side in the event of a major aggressive war in Europe. Although King did not wish to face the political difficulties of obtaining a clear-cut statement of this policy in the House, both he and Ernest Lapointe knew well that to stay out of such a war would be a greater danger to Canadian unity than to enter it. On many occasions in the 1930's Lapointe stated that legally Canada was still committed by any British declaration of war. With Lapointe as the political key to Quebec it is difficult to see how a statement of the government's actual policy could have caused a racial disruption of Canada. At the same time, the C.C.F., after 1937, was not prepared to split Canada on such a policy either.[16] If politics is the art of the possible, it should be recognized that statesmanship is the art of making things possible —and that the latter art was without an exponent in the Canadian government.

And so the grisly summer of 1939 was somehow endured. The

[14]*Ibid.*, p. 3706.

[15]*Ibid.*, 1939, pp. 2047 *et seq.*

[16]For the argument that the King-Lapointe use of the "threat to Canadian unity" was a bogey, see Kenneth McNaught, "Canadian Foreign Policy and the Whig Interpretation: 1936–1939," Canadian Historical Association, *Report, 1957*.

British, the French, and the Russians failed to sign a mutual security agreement, the Russians and the Germans concluded a non-aggression pact, and Hitler sent his Panzer divisions into a Poland whose security had finally been guaranteed by the United Kingdom. Haggard with the strain, Woodsworth went on September 6 to the emergency C.C.F. National Council meeting, called after the British declaration of war and the summoning of the Special Session of the Canadian Parliament. In addition to the regular members of the Council, the C.C.F. members of Parliament and provincial presidents had been invited in order to get as representative a group as possible.[17] The full attendance of this session of the Council (which was held on September 6, 7, and 8) was twenty-eight, with fourteen visitors including Mrs. Woodsworth and Agnes MacPhail, the only non-C.C.F.-er present. The delegates from British Columbia and Manitoba came with the knowledge that their provincial parties were strong for non-participation; feeling in the other provincial sections was less definite, except that Saskatchewan leaned towards an endorsement of participation in the war. The entire morning and the afternoon of the first day were given to a discussion of the nature of the war, of Canada's interest, and finally of the proper official attitude of the C.C.F. As the debate proceeded, one or two opinions were changed, but all knew that a deep and wounding split could not be avoided.

Finally it was moved that a committee be appointed to draft a statement, which would reflect the majority opinion. This was to be the compromise statement recommended by the group of which M. J. Coldwell was chief spokesman. But before that motion was put, Woodsworth, seconded by S. J. Farmer, moved "That this Council refuses to discuss any measure that will put Canada into the war." Woodsworth and those who agreed with him argued that all the known preliminary facts of the war placed it clearly within the national convention's definition of "imperialist war," and that to consider a reversal of the convention's resolutions on foreign policy would be to shatter the spirit of the movement. He was overruled, however, when it was agreed (not unanimously, according to the minutes of the meeting) not to put his motion to a vote; the main motion to appoint a committee to frame a statement was then passed unanimously. The arguments for neutrality were doomed when the majority of the C.C.F. Council reversed its previous official policy. While the committee worked over a compromise between neutrality and the

[17]The account of this Council meeting is based upon C.C.F. National Council and Executive Minutes, vol. 1937–42; items in Woodsworth's scrapbook, vol. 1938–42; and interviews with C.C.F. leaders.

all-out war effort advocated by Williams and Heaps, the Council decided on a declaration against entering a "national government," and named a committee to draft a report on peace aims.

On the morning of September 7 the Council opened debate on the draft statement on war policy. This time the lines had hardened and no opinions were changed. When the vote was taken (after six members of the twenty-eight with voting rights had had to leave) it stood at 13–9 for accepting the committee's statement. At least one of the nine, George Williams, opposed the compromise because it called only for qualified support of the war effort, and particularly because it declared against an expeditionary force. By a not-too-comfortable majority neutrality had been rejected, the official policy of the National Convention at least seriously modified, and the stand of the party's leader repudiated.

Although the policy change was violently opposed by those who followed Woodsworth, and although it came as a distinct surprise to many members of the party, it was one which had long been anticipated by the men who carried it through the Council. These were the same leaders who had piloted the foreign policy plank in the 1937 convention, and they had become increasingly concerned about the party's tradition of absolute neutrality since that time. Furthermore, they felt sure that they could, in a crisis, outgeneral the neutralists. Although there was no personal antipathy in the cleavage of opinion, still the importance of the policy issue meant some very sharp clashes of will. Certainly as early as Munich the non-neutralists were convinced that they could produce a change in policy at the party's centre. One of them wrote from Ottawa to George Williams in September, 1938, that it was "already decided" that if Britain declared war, Canada must accept the situation but that for various reasons Canada's best contribution would be economic. The writer added that no statement should be issued "until we know whether it will be war."[18]

In the 1939 Council meeting the debate on the compromise statement continued through the whole day and long into the night. When the crucial vote was taken at least one of the women present wept to see the movement so deeply divided. As National Chairman, M. J. Coldwell presided and Woodsworth sat with apparent calm, his wife beside him at the table. When at last the vote was taken, he rose in his place and said to the weary group: "You all know, as I know, what this must mean. . . ." Then he placed before the meeting his resignation both from office and from the party. It was an irrevocable move. But none of his colleagues was prepared to accept the fact of his

[18]Letter to G. H. Williams, Sept. 28, 1938 (C.C.F. files, Regina).

complete dissociation from them and he was persuaded to let the question wait over until the following morning.

The events of the Council's meeting on Friday, September 8, were both important and anti-climatic. It was agreed that Woodsworth should be permitted to give in the House that evening an unqualified statement against the case for Canadian participation in the war; that this should not necessitate his resignation from the party; but that it should be recognized that the official party position would be stated by M. J. Coldwell. In effect, Woodsworth's position in the party became at that moment an honorary one. Yet at least part of the reason for the decision to permit a separate statement by Woodsworth was to give expression to the very considerable body of party opinion that was not represented by the compromise statement.

The other business of the Council that day included the decision to distribute copies of the official statement to Council members and provincial offices; the acceptance of a cable from Arthur Greenwood (acting leader of the British Labour party) which noted that a struggle was being entered "to put a final end to methods of violence and the use of force to achieve national purposes . . ."; a motion to reaffirm the principles of the position taken at Regina; and finally a motion declaring that a special national convention of the party was unnecessary at that time. As the National Secretary wrote to George Williams, "another national meeting [even of the Council] would only serve to aggravate divisions in our ranks and would solve nothing."[19]

Here it might be noted that, when it was announced in January, 1940, that there would be an early federal election, the C.C.F. National Executive again decided that, because of the short notice, there would not be time to call either a meeting of the National Council or a national convention.[20] The party thus was to fight the 1940 election officially on the basis of the Council's statement of September, 1939. This statement called for material assistance to Britain but pronounced against an expeditionary force. The function of the C.C.F. was seen as holding a watching brief over civil liberties and war contracts, the advocacy of nationalization of all war industry, a steep tax schedule, and the enunciation of a peace programme.[21] But since this policy

[19]See letters: Williams to David Lewis, Dec. 2, 1939; Lewis to Williams, Dec. 15, 1939 (C.C.F. files, Regina).

[20]C.C.F. National Council and Executive Minutes, vol. 1937–42.

[21]A "Special Bulletin" was issued by the National Secretary on Sept. 12, 1939, explaining the issuance of the National Council's statement of war policy. Sent to National Council members, provincial officers, and the C.C.F. press, it stated that Woodsworth remained president with the unquestioned support of every section of the movement: "The National Council statement nowhere expresses

was not endorsed by a convention (and indeed seemed to many to run counter to the last convention policy), members of the C.C.F., and candidates, felt free to interpret it as they saw fit. Some C.C.F. candidates ran on an anti-war platform, some on an all-out support of the war, and others on the official platform of limited liability.[22] In Winnipeg, for example, Woodsworth was elected in North Centre on the basis of his anti-war speech in the House, while in the adjoining constituency of Winnipeg North, A. A. Heaps was defeated on a full participation platform.

Parliament met on September 7, 1939, while the C.C.F. Council was still hammering out its compromise position. The Governor General's speech said that the government would seek authority "for co-operation in the determined effort which is being made to resist further aggression and to prevent the appeal to force instead of to pacific means. . . ."[23] It seemed ambiguous, and the speech of the seconder of the Address did little to clarify the government's position: "It cannot be reasonably contended, after due reflection," said J. A. Blanchette, "that it would not be wise to co-operate to a reasonable extent with France and England in the present conflict, taking into account, however, our resources and our capacity, and without sacrificing our vital interests. . . ." But this ambiguity was also a bridge over which could pass all those, including King and Lapointe, who had allowed the country to assume that they had been seriously considering neutrality. King had not been influenced by O. D. Skelton's argument "that the surrenders and the hypocrisy of appeasement from Ethiopia onward had undermined all the moral purposes for which the war ostensibly was to be fought. . . ."[24] And few in the House doubted the now firm intention of the government, particularly when R. J. Manion, for the Conservatives, rose to congratulate Blanchette on his "moderate and reasonable address."

King himself knew that on the next day, when he would definitely enter his new wartime rôle, he would face no substantial opposition. He was able to tell the House on September 8 that a few days earlier M. J. Coldwell "was kind enough to come to my office where he informed me that unfortunately his leader was far away but that he

---

support of Canada's entry into the war. It was based on the assumption that Canada had been committed to a war policy by the government and then proceeded to outline the limits and conditions which should govern Canada's assistance to the allies."

[22]M. Lipset, *Agrarian Socialism* (Berkeley, 1950), p. 116; C.C.F. press clippings, 1940.   [23]Hansard, 1939, Special Session, pp. 1 *et seq.*
[24]Bruce Hutchison, *The Incredible Canadian* (Toronto, 1952), p. 250.

himself wished at once to express his appreciation of the situation. He asked me to realize that when co-operation was necessary in so great a cause, I would find the members of his party ready to do their part." The Prime Minister knew then that Woodsworth was already in fact "deposed."

Before making his speech on September 8, he and Woodsworth spent nearly two hours together in the Prime Minister's study. No doubt King at that time gave to Woodsworth the most significant reasons that would justify the impending war declaration; and received from Woodsworth confirmation that the statement against the war would have to be made.

Toward the end of his long speech,[25] knowing he was to be followed by Woodsworth, the Prime Minister remarked that "there are few men in this Parliament for whom, in some particulars, I have greater respect than the leader of the Co-operative Commonwealth Federation. I admire him in my heart because time and again he has had the courage to say what lay on his conscience regardless of what the world might think of him. A man of that calibre is an ornament to any Parliament. . . ."

The compliment did not make what Woodsworth was about to do any easier. But there were parts of King's speech which could not be let pass and which brought the fire back into Woodsworth's eyes. The Prime Minister had said, for example, that he had never doubted that "If the time ever came when the world should again be threatened as it was in 1914 by a war, the end of which no one at the time could see, my honourable friend [Manion] and myself would be found instantly side by side. . . ." How could this in all honesty be made to gibe with King's steady reiteration in the late thirties that Canada was through with crusades in foreign fields? In his speech the Prime Minister with pride pointed to all the steps of preparation started as far back as 1938—the munitions contracts, the air training scheme, the readying of the democratic arsenal—which he now said had been necessary because "it was our duty as citizens of Canada to stand to a man in the defence of this country and at the side of Britain. . . ." However, King had said, the momentous question of peace or war "is not decided yet"—that would be done by the adoption or rejection of the Speech from the Throne: the government in asking adoption of the address now proposed "to hold to all the treaties we have entered into. . . ." Finally, in specific anticipation of Woodsworth's remarks, he declared that when the forces of good oppose the forces of evil no

[25]Hansard, 1939, Special Session, pp. 19 *et seq.*

one can stand idly by: "You can persuade men; you can convert them, but there are times—and history is there to record them—when if force had not been opposed by force there would have been no Christianity left to defend. . . ."

Here were the arguments that Woodsworth must refute in justifying the stand he was about to take. He rose to speak in a silent chamber—a silence established by the years of integrity behind him and by the virtual warning issued by the Prime Minister that he would be accorded a full hearing. With the galleries packed, with his wife and two of his sons among the watchers, and with his own party about him yet not all with him, he began his speech:[26] "I could almost wish that [the Prime Minister] had not said what he did because I am afraid that tonight I must rather disappoint him and disappoint some of my other friends in this House. . . ." He made it clear that he did not speak for his party's official policy but that he was proud to belong to a group which permitted the voicing of a basic dissent.

Then Woodsworth presented his answer to King. Was this war, he asked, really a conflict between the forces of good and the forces of evil? Hitler might be "a very devil incarnate" but "you cannot indict a great nation and a great people such as the German people. The fact is we got rid of the Kaiser only to create conditions favourable to the rise of a Hitler." We did not take the League seriously, he argued, and time after time we condoned the violation of international covenants. Now we proposed to defend Poland, a creation of the Versailles treaty, and Danzig, a former German territory. All the right, he cried, is not on one side. "More than that, we have been willing to allow Canadians to profit out of the situation. The Prime Minister may talk about preventing profiteering now, but Canada has shipped enormous quantities of nickel and scrap iron, copper and chromium to both Japan and Germany. . . . I submit that if any shooting is to be done the first people who should face the firing squad are those who have made money out of a potential enemy. . . ."

There were other questions of fact that should be more plainly stated, he declared. The lawyers differed, for example, as to whether or not the country was already at war. It was dishonest to the rest of the world to appear neutral and receive a stream of war supplies across the border if we were legally at war. But if we were at war, what then was Parliament to decide? "If . . . we are still able to decide to keep out of war, then I would hold up both my hands to keep out of war. . . ."

[26]*Ibid.*, pp. 41 *et seq.*

This indeed was a question which at that very moment was being decided. Canada probably was, by constitutional precedent, at war; yet the separate Canadian declaration that followed in itself altered the precedent and secured for the future the right of neutrality. But this point of fact the government did not define while the debate was on, and this lent weight to Woodsworth's remark that "truth is one of the first victims of war." Woodsworth sought to make the moral problem more clear when he said, "I have every respect for the man who, with a sincere conviction, goes out to give his life if necessary in a cause which he believes to be right; but I have just as much respect for the man who refuses to enlist to kill his fellow men and, as under modern conditions, to kill women and children as well, as must be done on every front. These facts ought to be faced."

Then, in burning sentences, this venerable man summed up his case. The Prime Minister, he said, had appealed to religion.

Well, I left the ministry of the church during the last war because of my ideas on war. Today I do not belong to any church organization. I am afraid that my creed is pretty vague. But even in this assembly I venture to say that I still believe in some of the principles underlying the teachings of Jesus, and the other great world teachers throughout the centuries. . . . War is an absolute negation of anything Christian. The Prime Minister, as a great many do, trotted out the "mad dog" idea; said that in the last analysis there must be a resort to force. It requires a great deal of courage to trust to moral force. But there was a time when people thought that there were other and higher types of force than brute force. Yes, if I may use the very quotation the Prime Minister used today, in spite of tyrants, tyrants as bad as even Hitler is today, in spite of war-makers—and every nation has them—as Lowell reminds us:[27]

"Truth forever on the scaffold, Wrong forever on the throne,
"Yet that scaffold sways the future, and, behind the dim unknown,
"Standeth God within the shadow, keeping watch above his own. . . ."

It requires a great deal of courage to carry out our convictions; to have peace requires both courage and sacrifice. . . . Yes, I have boys of my own and I hope they are not cowards, but if any one of those boys, not from cowardice but really through belief, is willing to take his stand on this matter and, if necessary, to face a concentration camp or a firing squad, I shall be more proud of that boy than if he enlisted for the war.

The single interruption came at this point when the Conservative Mr. Tustin cried "Shame." The interjection prompted Woodsworth to be very emphatic in his conclusion:

I said I wanted to state my conviction. Now you can hammer me as much

---

[27]Woodsworth had referred earlier to King's quoting of the entire seventy lines of J. R. Lowell's "The Present Crisis." It had been, he said, rather prostituting it to use it to justify war.

as you like. I must thank the House for the great courtesy it has shown me. I rejoice that it is possible to say these things in a Canadian Parliament under British institutions. It would not be possible in Germany, I recognize that . . . and I want to maintain the very essence of our British institutions of real liberty. I believe that the only way to do it is by an appeal to the moral forces which are still resident among our people, and not by another resort to brute force.

Woodsworth sank back into his seat, his dissent voiced. The machine of the majority rolled on. J. T. Thorson (Selkirk), the chief English-speaking non-C.C.F. advocate of neutrality in the 1930's, now declared that an issue had arisen where Canada could not stand aside. M. J. Coldwell assured the government of co-operation. That was the policy, he declared, "not only of the majority of our Parliamentary group but of our National Council, which met for two days this week, and which represents the concensus of the leaders of our movement from coast to coast." A French-Canadian motion condemning participation in war outside Canada was negatived and the main motion passed without recorded vote. When the Speaker declared the address carried, Woodsworth rose to say "There were some of us opposed to the main motion." And the final answer came back: "Only one member rose."

It would be easy to say Woodsworth had been "nobly wrong"; that his fallacy was proven by the strong voice of the majority. But one question must remain to plague us. Did that majority have then, and does it have now, a better answer than Woodsworth's to the tragic facts of the twentieth century: the increasing resort to mass war with its accompaniment of chronically debased human values, the growing militarization of democracy, and the mounting pressures on the individual to conform to majority ideologies?

Hitler and all he stood for were consumed, perhaps, in the Berlin funeral pyre of 1945. But there was another funeral pyre in that year. It started with two blinding flashes and was presided over by two pillars of flaming cloud. The forces of right had given their answer to the forces of evil. But what actually was consumed in the fire-clouds over Hiroshima and Nagasaki?

In 1939 that future was unknown. To Woodsworth, it nevertheless was certain. A Vancouver paper, reporting his speech, phrased what many felt: "True to the principles he has so consistently advocated, this kindly, courageous man nailed his colours to the mast and sailed off on the lonely route where conscience is the only compass."[28]

28Vancouver *Daily Province*, Sept. 10, 1939.

21

EPILOGUE

IN EFFECT, SEPTEMBER, 1939, ENDED Woodsworth's political career. Within eight months he suffered the stroke from which he never really recovered. In the final two years of his life he did not relinquish his association with the C.C.F. but of necessity it became increasingly tenuous, and was maintained through individuals more than through organizational channels.

He could never really accept a party policy which declared that the very existence of democratic institutions throughout the world was at stake—and then said that Canada should send guns but no men. He could and did co-operate to the limit of his strength, and beyond, in the C.C.F. effort to secure Canada against a repetition of the worst inequalities occasioned by the First World War. He could not forget that in the special war session of the House he had voiced not only his own views but those of a very considerable number of C.C.F. members. In a voluminous mail, the letters commending his stand seemed to obliterate the protest of the Conservative women voters of Winnipeg North Centre who had immediately demanded his resignation. Even the official party newspaper in his own province could write: "Mr. Woodsworth's contention that wars settle nothing, that the last war settled nothing, has certainly been proven correct. Who can say that he may not be right again? Certain it is that there are thousands of people all across the country who agree with Mr. Woodsworth."[1]

The election of March, 1940, Woodsworth fought with much of his old fire. Warning against conscription and the rapid growth of order-in-council government, calling for the nationalization of all war industries and an end to the "cost plus" psychology, he still made it

[1]*Manitoba Commonwealth*, Sept. 15, 1939.

clear to his constituents: "If you people elect me, you must take me as I am."[2] They did re-elect him, although his majority was reduced.

There was a meeting of the C.C.F. National Executive in May, 1940. Its business was to review the election and it was decided that since a Canadian expeditionary force was already overseas by cabinet action it was not possible to refuse to vote the necessary supply for its maintenance. The further decision was taken that only conscription for overseas service would be opposed, and that more effective economic aid should be advocated. It was during the discussion that Woodsworth suffered a stroke which left him partially paralysed for months, and from which he was not to recover.

To the National Convention of October, 1940, Woodsworth wrote,

It is improbable that I shall be able to take responsibility for an executive position. . . . Further, on the important question of war policy my personal position differs from that of the majority of the executive and, I take it, from that of the majority of our members. It is not fair either to the organization or to myself that I should occupy an executive position under these circumstances. . . . Needless to say, I retain the heartiest interest in the work of our movement and treasure the fellowship which has persisted in spite of our differences in conviction. . . .[3]

Rather than accept such complete severance of its leader from the party, the Convention created the office of Honorary President, abolished that of President, and re-elected M. J. Coldwell National Chairman with Angus MacInnis Vice-Chairman.

This demonstration of loyalty, indeed, of love, together with the blood of the parliamentarian which ran so strongly in his veins, dictated a courageous attempt to resume his place in the House of Commons. In his convalescent retirement in British Columbia he summoned his remaining strength, and in October, 1941, journeyed with his wife once more to Ottawa. The trip cost him much. To the thunder of applause which greeted him the exhausted crusader could not rise in acknowledgment, yet it was perhaps the greatest tribute of his life and a tribute to the British traditions which he had so vigorously sought to maintain. A few hours later, after the personal and non-partisan greetings in the House lobby, a second stroke was so serious that even he was forced to concede that his active life was over.

When the end came in March, 1942, it was typical that the family rites had been arranged by Woodsworth himself. There was the sing-

2*Winnipeg Free Press*, March 18, 1940.
3C.C.F. National Council and Executive Minutes, vol. 1937–42.

ing of a few hymns which to him had conveyed the message of peace and brotherhood; a testimony to his work and a declaration of faith in the vision of the kind of world he had striven to realize. There was no adherence to formula, but an unquestionably spiritual theme ran through the message spoken by Miss Mildred Fahrni whom Woodsworth had selected for this privilege. Eloquent of his undiminished conviction was the fact that Miss Fahrni was, in unpretentious fashion, a disciple of Gandhi. It may be of interest also to note here that during his final illness, when discussing religion, Woodsworth had said privately that his own feelings were best expressed in Lowell's poem "The Present Crisis."

After the family service and the cremation, Woodsworth's family took the urn containing his ashes aboard Charles Woodsworth's boat. Of this part of the day, Woodsworth's son wrote:

Dark clouds rode the sky and a stiff breeze whipped up a choppy rolling sea as we put forth into the waters off English Bay. . . . It was a stormy day but the wind blew with a clean freshness, the clear cold waves breaking in foaming white crests, good to behold. It was a day which in many ways symbolized the turbulent yet transparently honest and cleansing character of the man whose memory we were honouring.[4]

As the ashes were scattered on the water about midway between Jericho Beach and Spanish Banks, they were followed by a tiny piece of shamrock—for the strong and gallant woman upon whose belief and support Woodsworth had been able to rely for so long.

Across Canada there were more formal ceremonies of commemoration as well as many quiet and private ones, such as that conducted by the General Council of the United Church in its board room. The suggestion of M. J. Coldwell that the C.C.F. could best honour its founder through the creation of a research foundation was warmly received by all sections of the party and in due course "Woodsworth House" in Toronto was established to fulfil this purpose.

It would be possible to quote many glowing tributes delivered at the time of Woodsworth's death; perhaps it is wisest to select two from non-socialist sources. J. F. Pouliot, the French-Canadian independent, said: "I shall remember him as a born gentleman. Those who had conversation with him will never forget the kindly glance in his eye. He will be remembered for his integrity, his sincerity and his indomitable courage." The *Ottawa Journal*, conservative in its politics, wrote: "J. S. Woodsworth was of that brave British company; of the

---

[4]Unpublished personal sketch of his father by Charles Woodsworth.

men who were never terrified by principalities and powers; one who all his life blueprinted a dream of what he hoped would be a better Canada, and who was on the side of the underdog. As he goes out without a stain on his armour, well may the common crowd salute him."[5]

Above all, Woodsworth was a protestant. His inherited family background was certainly this; but more, protestantism seemed rooted in his very nature. It was this, joined to the ever mounting evidence that he was incorruptible, that endeared him to the working class.

He was, too, a profound admirer of the British reform tradition. Thus his reform zeal was a mixture of utilitarian rationalism and Christian Socialism. Although he came to Christian Socialism through its American version of the "social gospel," his political application of the doctrine was fundamentally British.

But not only was he a natural protestant, he was a leader by instinct; and for a protestant to wish to lead is always dangerous. In Woodsworth the combination produced both tragedy and fulfilment. It might well be argued, indeed, that his whole life was a creative tragedy. If it is true that Woodsworth could see few of the virtues of conformity, and often found it impossible to work with those who admired those virtues, it is also clear that when he joined the ranks of the working class it was his passion for social justice that had led him there. That passion gained much for the ordinary men and women of Canada.

As with many protestants there was a good deal of the puritan in Woodsworth. But although some of the effects of that puritanism were apparent to his family, his final aim was not puritanism but achievement of the good life for all members of the social brotherhood. If there was anything of the martyr in him he did not consciously feel it. Martyrs, if they recognize themselves as such, become bitter. There was too much of the joy of battle in Woodsworth ever to permit bitterness in defeat.

Although as a politician Woodsworth was frequently charged with being doctrinaire, he had an abiding suspicion of dogma. And, as he grew older, his refusal to accept intellectual absolutes was strengthened by fear that such devices are customarily employed in the defence of social privilege. His scepticism was reflected in his refusal to proclaim that his or any political platform could provide a final solution to the problems of society. This same scepticism prevented him from accepting the pretensions of Russian communism.

Woodsworth's place in the history of Canada is sure. While he never

[5]*Ottawa Journal*, March 24, 1942.

held public political office his influence upon legislation was greater than that of many men who have experienced long years of political power. But, more important, he gave dramatic expression to one of the principles of the Canadian nation—the protest against the North American compulsion to uniformity. Although he frequently talked of Canada as being an American nation, and certainly held suspect the class-power traditions of the old British Empire, in fact he was far more British in thought than he was American. Undoubtedly his zeal in public affairs was increased by the common heritage of North Americans: the feeling that much could be done in a country still in its youth. But, like other great Canadians, he saw the libertarian traditions of the British parliamentary system as the surest guarantees of a creative Canadian society.

Because Woodsworth carried his protestantism to the most extreme pacifist position, and because this was put to the test in the greatest crisis of the twentieth century, the popular assessment of him is likely to remain blurred. But the farther we move from him in time, the more clearly he will be seen as one of the most important influences on the growth of our social conscience and our survival as an independent nation.

Like all prophets Woodsworth was greatest as critic. And as such he lived essentially in isolation—an isolation the more complete because of his moral courage.

APPENDIX

Appendix

CO-OPERATIVE COMMONWEALTH FEDERATION PROGRAMME

ADOPTED AT FIRST NATIONAL CONVENTION
HELD AT REGINA, SASK., JULY, 1933

THE C.C.F. is a federation of organizations whose purpose is the establishment in Canada of a Co-operative Commonwealth in which the principle regulating production, distribution and exchange will be the supplying of human needs and not the making of profits.

We aim to replace the present capitalist system, with its inherent injustice and inhumanity, by a social order from which the domination and exploitation of one class by another will be eliminated, in which economic planning will supersede unregulated private enterprise and competition, and in which genuine democratic self-government, based upon economic equality will be possible. The present order is marked by glaring inequalities of wealth and opportunity, by chaotic waste and instability; and in an age of plenty it condemns the great mass of the people to poverty and insecurity. Power has become more and more concentrated into the hands of a small irresponsible minority of financiers and industrialists and to their predatory interests the majority are habitually sacrificed. When private profit is the main stimulus to economic effort, our society oscillates between periods of feverish prosperity in which the main benefits go to speculators and profiteers, and of catastrophic depression, in which the common man's normal state of insecurity and hardship is accentuated. We believe that these evils can be removed only in a planned and socialized economy in which our natural resources and the principal means of production and distribution are owned, controlled and operated by the people.

The new social order at which we aim is not one in which individuality will be crushed out by a system of regimentation. Nor shall we interfere with cultural rights of racial or religious minorities. What we seek is a proper collective organization of our economic resources such as will make possible a much greater degree of leisure and a much richer individual life for every citizen.

This social and economic transformation can be brought about by political action, through the election of a government inspired by the ideal of a Co-operative Commonwealth and supported by a majority of the people. We do not believe in change by violence. We consider that both the old parties in Canada are the instruments of capitalist interests and cannot serve as agents of social reconstruction, and that whatever the superficial differences between them, they are bound to carry on government in accordance with the dictates of the big business interests who finance them. The C.C.F. aims at political power in order to put an end to this capitalist domination of our political life. It is a democratic movement, a federation of farmer, labor and socialist organizations, financed by its own members and seeking to achieve its ends solely by constitutional methods. It appeals for support to all who believe that the time has come for a far-reaching reconstruction of our economic and political institutions and who are willing to work together for the carrying out of the following policies:

1. PLANNING

The establishment of a planned, socialized economic order, in order to make possible the most efficient development of the national resources and the most equitable distribution of the national income.

The first step in this direction will be setting up of a National Planning Commission consisting of a small body of economists, engineers and statisticians assisted by an appropriate technical staff.

The task of the Commission will be to plan for the production, distribution and exchange of all goods and services necessary to the efficient functioning of the economy; to co-ordinate the activities of the socialized industries; to provide for a satisfactory balance between the producing and consuming power; and to carry on continuous research into all branches of the national economy in order to acquire the detailed information necessary to efficient planning.

The Commission will be responsible to the Cabinet and will work in co-operation with the Managing Boards of the Socialized Industries.

It is now certain that in every industrial country some form of planning will replace the disintegrating capitalist system. The C.C.F. will provide that in Canada the planning shall be done, not by a small group of capitalist magnates in their own interests, but by public servants acting in the public interest and responsible to the people as a whole.

2. SOCIALIZATION OF FINANCE

Socialization of all financial machinery—banking, currency, credit, and insurance, to make possible the effective control of currency, credit and prices, and the supplying of new productive equipment for socially desirable purposes.

Planning by itself will be of little use if the public authority has not the power to carry its plans into effect. Such power will require the control of finance and of all those vital industries and services, which, if they remain in private hands, can be used to thwart or corrupt the will of the public authority. Control of finance is the first step in the control of the whole economy. The chartered banks must be socialized and removed from the control of private profit-seeking interests; and the national banking system thus established must have at its head a Central Bank to control the flow of credit and the general price level, and to regulate foreign exchange operations. A National Investment Board must also be set up, working in co-operation with the socialized banking system to mobilize and direct the unused surpluses of production for socially desired purposes as determined by the Planning Commission.

Insurance Companies, which provide one of the main channels for the investment of individual savings and which, under their present competitive organization, charge needlessly high premiums for the social services that they render, must also be socialized.

3. SOCIAL OWNERSHIP

Socialization (Dominion, Provincial or Municipal) of transportation, communications, electric power and all other industries and services essential to social planning, and their operation under the general direction of the Planning Commission by competent managements freed from day to day political interference.

Public utilities must be operated for the public benefit and not for the private profit of a small group of owners or financial manipulators. Our natural resources must be developed by the same methods. Such a programme means the continuance and extension of the public ownership enterprises in which most governments in Canada have already gone some distance. Only by such public ownership, operated on a planned economy, can our main industries be saved from the wasteful competition of the ruinous over-development and over-capitalization which are the inevitable outcome of capitalism. Only in a regime of public ownership and operation will the full benefits accruing from the centralized control and mass production be passed on to the consuming public.

Transportation, communications and electric power must come first in a list of industries to be socialized. Others, such as mining, pulp and paper and the distribution of milk, bread, coal and gasoline, in which exploitation, waste, or financial malpractices are particularly prominent must next be brought under social ownership and operation.

In restoring to the community its natural resources and in taking over industrial enterprises from private into public control we do not propose any policy of outright confiscation. What we desire is the most stable and equitable transition to the Co-operative Commonwealth. It is impossible to decide the policies to be followed in particular cases in an uncertain future, but we insist upon certain broad principles. The welfare of the community must take supremacy over the claims of private wealth. In times of war, human life has been conscripted. Should economic circumstances call for it, conscription of wealth would be more justifiable. We recognize the need for compensation in the case of individuals and institutions which must receive adequate maintenance during the transitional period before the planned economy becomes fully operative. But a C.C.F. government will not play the role of rescuing bankrupt private concerns for the benefit of promoters and of stock and bond holders. It will not pile up a deadweight burden of unremunerative debt which represents claims upon the public treasury of a functionless owner class.

The management of publicly owned enterprises will be vested in boards who will be appointed for their competence in the industry and will conduct each particular enterprise on efficient economic lines. The machinery of management may well vary from industry to industry, but the rigidity of

Civil Service rules should be avoided and likewise the evils of the patronage system as exemplified in so many departments of the Government today. Workers in these public industries must be free to organize in trade unions and must be given the right to participate in the management of the industry.

4. AGRICULTURE

Security of tenure for the farmer upon his farm on conditions to be laid down by individual provinces; insurance against unavoidable crop failure; removal of the tariff burden from the operations of agriculture; encouragement of producers' and consumers' co-operatives; the restoration and maintenance of an equitable relationship between prices of agricultural products and those of other commodities and services; and improving the efficiency of export trade in farm products.

The security of tenure for the farmer upon his farm which is imperilled by the present disastrous situation of the whole industry, together with adequate social insurance, ought to be guaranteed under equitable conditions.

The prosperity of agriculture, the greatest Canadian industry, depends upon a rising volume of purchasing power of the masses in Canada for all farm goods consumed at home, and upon the maintenance of large scale exports of the stable commodities at satisfactory prices or equitable commodity exchange.

The intense depression in agriculture today is a consequence of the general world crisis caused by the normal workings of the capitalistic system resulting in: (1) Economic nationalism expressing itself in tariff barriers and other restrictions of world trade; (2) The decreased purchasing power of unemployed and under-employed workers and of the Canadian people in general; (3) The exploitation of both primary producers and consumers by monopolistic corporations who absorb a great proportion of the selling price of farm products. (This last is true, for example, of the distribution of milk and dairy products, the packing industry, and milling.)

The immediate cause of agricultural depression is the catastrophic fall in the world prices of foodstuffs as compared with other prices, this fall being due in large measure to the deflation of currency and credit. To counteract the worst effect of this, the internal price level should be raised so that the farmers' purchasing power may be restored.

We propose therefore:

(1) The improvement of the position of the farmer by the increase of purchasing power made possible by the social control of the financial system. This control must be directed towards the increase of employment as laid down elsewhere and towards raising the prices of farm commodities by appropriate credit and foreign policies.

(2) Whilst the family farm is the accepted basis for agricultural production in Canada the position of the farmer may be much improved by:
   (a) The extension of consumers' co-operatives for the purchase of farm supplies and domestic requirements; and
   (b) The extension of co-operative institutions for the processing and marketing of farm products.

Both of the foregoing to have suitable state encouragement and assistance.

(3) The adoption of a planned system of agricultural development based upon scientific soil surveys directed towards better land utilization, and a scientific policy of agricultural development for the whole of Canada.

(4) The substitution for the present system of foreign trade, of a system of import and export boards to improve the efficiency of overseas marketing, to control prices, and to integrate the foreign trade policy with the requirements of the national economic plan.

5. EXTERNAL TRADE

The regulation in accordance with the National plan of external trade through import and export boards.

Canada is dependent on external sources of supply for many of her essential requirements of raw materials and manufactured products. These she can obtain only by large exports of the goods she is best fitted to produce. The strangling of our export trade by insane protectionist policies must be brought to an end. But the old controversies between free traders and protectionists are now largely obsolete. In a world of nationally organized economies Canada must organize the buying and selling of her main imports and exports under public boards, and take steps to regulate the flow of less important commodities by a system of licenses. By so doing she will be enabled to make the best trade agreements possible with foreign countries, put a stop to the exploitation of both primary producer and ultimate consumer, make possible the co-ordination of internal processing, transportation and marketing of farm products, and facilitate the establishment of stable prices for such export commodities.

6. CO-OPERATIVE INSTITUTIONS

The encouragement by the public authority of both producers' and consumers' co-operative institutions.

In agriculture, as already mentioned, the primary producer can receive a larger net revenue through co-operative organization of purchases and marketing. Similarly in retail distribution of staple commodities such as milk, there is room for development both of public municipal operation and of consumers' co operatives, and such co-operative organization can be extended into wholesale distribution and into manufacturing. Co-operative enterprises should be assisted by the state through appropriate legislation and through the provision of adequate credit facilities.

7. LABOR CODE

A National Labor Code to secure for the worker maximum income and leisure, insurance covering illness, accident, old age, and unemployment, freedom of association and effective participation in the management of his industry or profession.

The spectre of poverty and insecurity which still haunts every worker, though technological developments have made possible a high standard of living for everyone, is a disgrace which must be removed from our civilization. The community must organize its resources to effect progressive reduction of the hours of work in accordance with technological development and to provide a constantly rising standard of life to everyone who is willing to work. A labor code must be developed which will include state regulation of all wages, equal reward and equal opportunity of advancement for equal services, irrespective of sex; measures to guarantee the right to work or the right to maintenance through stabilization of employment and through unemployment insurance; social insurance to protect workers and their families against the hazards of sickness, death, industrial accident and old age; limitation of hours of work and protection of health and safety in industry. Both wages and insurance benefits should be varied in accordance with family needs.

In addition workers must be guaranteed the undisputed right to freedom of association, and should be encouraged and assisted by the state to organize themselves in trade unions. By means of collective agreements and participation in works councils, the workers can achieve fair working rules and share in the control of industry and profession; and their organizations will be indispensable elements in a system of genuine industrial democracy.

The labor code should be uniform throughout the country. But the achievement of this end is difficult so long as jurisdiction over labor legislation under the B.N.A. Act is mainly in the hands of the provinces. It is urgently necessary, therefore, that the B.N.A. Act be amended to make such a national labor code possible.

8. SOCIALIZED HEALTH SERVICES

Publicly organized health, hospital and medical services.

With the advance of medical science the maintenance of a healthy population has become a function for which every civilized community should undertake responsibility. Health services should be made at least as freely available as are educational services today. But under a system which is still mainly one of private enterprise the costs of proper medical care, such as the wealthier members of society can easily afford, are at present prohibitive for great masses of the people. A properly organized system of public health services including medical and dental care, which would stress the prevention rather than the cure of illness should be extended to all our people in both rural and urban areas. This is an enterprise in which Dominion, Provincial and Municipal authorities, as well as the medical and dental professions, can co-operate.

9. B.N.A. ACT

The amendment of the Canadian Constitution, without infringing upon racial or religious minority rights or upon legitimate provincial claims to autonomy, so as to give the Dominion Government adequate powers to deal effectively with urgent economic problems which are essentially national in scope; the abolition of the Canadian Senate.

We propose that the necessary amendments to the B.N.A. Act shall be obtained as speedily as required, safeguards being inserted to ensure that the existing rights of racial and religious minorities shall not be changed without their own consent. What is chiefly needed today is the placing in the hands of the national government of more power to control national economic development. In a rapidly changing economic environment our political constitution must be reasonably flexible. The present division of powers between Dominion and Provinces reflects the conditions of a pioneer, mainly agricultural, community in 1867. Our constitution must be brought into line with the increasing industrialization of the country and the consequent centralization of economic and financial power—which has taken place in the last two generations. The principle laid down in the Quebec Resolution of the Fathers of Confederation should be applied to the conditions of 1933, that "there be a general government charged with matters of common interest to the whole country and local governments for each of the provinces charged with the control of local matters in their respective sections."

The Canadian Senate, which was originally created to protect provincial rights, but has failed even in this function, has developed into a bulwark of capitalist interests, as is illustrated by the large number of company director-ships held by its aged members. In its peculiar composition of a fixed number of members appointed for life it is one of the most reactionary assemblies in the civilized world. It is a standing obstacle to all progressive legislation, and the only permanently satisfactory method of dealing with the constitutional difficulties it creates is to abolish it.

10. EXTERNAL RELATIONS

A Foreign Policy designed to obtain international economic co-operation and to promote disarmament and world peace.

Canada has a vital interest in world peace. We propose, therefore, to do everything in our power to advance the idea of international co-operation as represented by the League of Nations and the International Labor Organization. We would extend our diplomatic machinery for keeping in touch with the main centres of world interest. But we believe that genuine international co-operation is incompatible with the capitalist regime which is in force in most countries, and that strenuous efforts are needed to rescue the League from its present condition of being mainly a League of capitalist Great Powers. We stand resolutely against all participation in imperialist wars. Within the British Commonwealth, Canada must maintain her autonomy as a completely self-governing nation. We must resist all attempts to build up a new economic British Empire in place of the old political one, since such attempts readily lend themselves to the purposes of capitalist exploitation and may easily lead to further world wars. Canada must refuse to be entangled in any more wars fought to make the world safe for capitalism.

11. TAXATION AND PUBLIC FINANCE

A new taxation policy designed not only to raise public revenues but also to lessen the glaring inequalities of income and to provide funds for social services and the socialization of industry; the cessation of the debt creating system of Public Finance.

In the type of economy that we envisage, the need for taxation, as we now understand it, will have largely disappeared. It will nevertheless be essential during the transition period, to use the taxing powers, along with the other methods proposed elsewhere, as a means of providing for the socialization of industry, and for extending the benefits of increased Social Services.

At the present time capitalist governments in Canada raise a large proportion of their revenues from such levies as customs duties and sales taxes, the main burden of which falls upon the masses. In place of such taxes upon articles of general consumption, we propose a drastic extension of income, corporation and inheritance taxes, steeply graduated according to ability to pay. Full publicity must be given to income tax payments and our tax collection system must be brought up to the English standard of efficiency.

We also believe in the necessity for an immediate revision of the basis of Dominion and Provincial sources of revenues, so as to produce a co-ordinated and equibable system of taxation throughout Canada.

An inevitable effect of the capitalist system is the debt creating character of public financing. All public debts have enormously increased, and the fixed interest charges paid thereon now amount to the largest single item of so-called uncontrollable public expenditures. The C.C.F. proposes that in future no public financing shall be permitted which facilitates the perpetuation of the parasitic interest-receiving class; that capital shall be provided through the medium of the National Investment Board and free from perpetual interest charges.

We propose that all Public Works, as directed by the Planning Commission, shall be financed by the issuance of credit, as suggested, based upon the National Wealth of Canada.

12. FREEDOM

Freedom of speech and assembly for all; repeal of Section 98 of the Criminal Code; amendment of the Immigration Act to prevent the present inhuman policy of deportation; equal treatment before the law of all residents of Canada irrespective of race, nationality or religious or political beliefs.

In recent years, Canada has seen an alarming growth of Fascist tendencies among all governmental authorities. The most elementary rights of freedom of speech and assembly have been arbitrarily denied to workers and to all whose political and social views do not meet with the approval of those in power. The lawless and brutal conduct of the police in certain centres in preventing public meetings and in dealing with political prisoners must cease. Section 98 of the Criminal Code which has been used as a weapon of political oppression by a panic-stricken capitalist government, must be wiped off the statute book and those who have been imprisoned under it must be released. An end must be put to the inhuman practice of deporting immigrants who were brought to this country by immigration propaganda and now, through no fault of their own, find themselves victims of an executive department against whom there is no appeal to the courts of the land. We stand for full economic, political and religious liberty for all.

13. SOCIAL JUSTICE

The establishment of a commission composed of psychiatrists, psycho-
logists, socially minded jurists and social workers, to deal with all
matters pertaining to crime and punishment and the general administra-
tion of law, in order to humanize the law and to bring it into harmony
with the needs of the people.

While the removal of economic inequality will do much to overcome the
most glaring injustices in the treatment of those who come into conflict with
the law, our present archaic system must be changed and brought into
accordance with a modern concept of human relationships. This new system
must not be based as is the present one, upon vengeance and fear, but upon
an understanding of human behaviour. For this reason its planning and
control cannot be left in the hands of those steeped in the outworn legal
tradition; and therefore it is proposed that there shall be established a
national commission composed of psychiatrists, psychologists, socially
minded jurists and social workers whose duty it shall be to devise a system
of prevention and correction consistent with other features of the new
social order.

14. AN EMERGENCY PROGRAMME

The assumption by the Dominion Government of direct responsibility
for dealing with the present critical unemployment situation and for
tendering suitable work or adequate maintenance; the adoption of
measures to relieve the extermity of the crisis such as a programme of
public spending on housing, and other enterprises that will increase the
real wealth of Canada, to be financed by the issue of credit based on
the national wealth.

The extent of unemployment and the widespread suffering which it has
caused, creates a situation with which provincial and municipal governments have long been unable to cope and forces upon the Dominion government direct responsibility for dealing with the crisis as the only authority
with financial resources adequate to meet the situation. Unemployed
workers must be secured in the tenure of their homes, and the scale and
methods of relief, at present altogether inadequate, must be such as to
preserve decent human standards of living.

It is recognized that even after a Co-operative Commonwealth Federation Government has come into power, a certain period of time must elapse
before the planned economy can be fully worked out. During this brief
transitional period, we propose to provide work and purchasing power for
those now unemployed by a far-reaching programme of public expenditure
on housing, slum clearance, hospitals, libraries, schools, community halls,
parks, recreational projects, reforestation, rural electrification, the elimination of grade crossings, and other similar projects in both town and country.
This programme, which would be financed by the issuance of credit based
on the national wealth, would serve the double purpose of creating employment and meeting recognized social needs. Any steps which the Government

takes, under this emergency programme, which may assist private business, must include guarantees of adequate wages and reasonable hours of work, and must be designed to further the advance towards the complete Co-operative Commonwealth.

Emergency measures, however, are of only temporary value, for the present depression is a sign of the mortal sickness of the whole capitalist system, and this sickness cannot be cured by the application of salves. These leave untouched the cancer which is eating at the heart of our society, namely, the economic system in which our natural resources and our principal means of production and distribution are owned, controlled and operated for the private profit of a small proportion of our population.

No C.C.F. Government will rest content until it has eradicated capitalism and put into operation the full programme of socialized planning which will lead to the establishment in Canada of the Co-operative Commonwealth.

Index

331

tours West (1919), 97–8; influence of Winnipeg strike, 99; on strike, 115, 116; edits strike newspaper, 120–1; strike articles, 124–7; seditious libel charge, 124–8; arrested, 128; and Labour Defence Committee, 132–3; on Canadian capitalism, 133–4; and strike trials, 135–6; and Labour Church, 136–9; and Manitoba elections (1920), 136, 140; combines rationalism and revivalism, 139; and Federated Labour party (1920), 141–4; moves to Vancouver, 141; financial problems, 141, 160; on "professional politicians," 143; secretary, Labour Church, 143–7; on unemployment, 145–6, 150, 166–7, 179, 183, 186, 218, 234–6, 293; and group government, 145, 157–8, 167–8, 209–28 *passim*; non-labour support of, 146–7; and labour politics in Winnipeg (1921), 147–53; joins Independent Labour party, 148; elected to Parliament, 152–3; position (1922), 157–61; on religion, 158–9; and education of his children, 159–61; on cadet training, 160; rôle at Ottawa, 161–4; relations with press, 162–3; as parliamentarian, 163; first Commons speech, 165–7; on Mounted Police, 168–70; and repeal of 1919 amendments, 170–1, 243–4, 289; on King's policy in Cape Breton crisis, 173–80; on private banks, 187–92; in Quebec, 193; on military expenditures, 193–6; and foreign policy debates, 194, 300–4; and political independence of Canada, 197–202, 271–2; on League of Nations, 201–3, 232, 271–4, 301, 304; and I.L.P. organization, 204–7; and Ginger Group, 209–14; and old age pensions, 215–20; customs scandal and constitutional crisis (1926), 220–8; influence during depression, 230–1; health in 1930's, 232–4; visits Russia, 233–4; and reform of divorce procedure, 237–41; on government depression policy, 246–54; on hydro-electric projects, 247–9; on stronger central government, 252–4; as "father" of C.C.F., 255–65; and C.C.F. split in Ontario, 266; visits Far East, 270; on communist united front, 270; compared with Bourassa, 272–4; and 1935 election, 275–7; and C.C.F. division on war, 281, 284–6; as party leader, 281–8; on right to organize and join unions, 283–4; and defence of civil liberty, 289–94; and divorce laws, 294–5; on abdication of Edward VIII, 295–7; neutrality resolution (1937), 301–3; and C.C.F. emergency council meeting (1939), 305–7; in Special War Session (1939), 308–12; and election of 1940, 313–14; stroke and last days, 314–17; place in Canadian history, 316–17

Woodsworth, Mrs. James, 5, 30–1, 86n
Woodsworth, Mrs. J. S. (Lucy L. Staples), 23, 31, 130, 161, 305
Woodsworth, Richard, 3–5
Worker, Toronto, 234
Workers' Alliance, 136, 149
Workers' Educational Association, 44
Working class, J.S.W. member of, 92–8

"YELLOW DOG" CONTRACTS, 113, 117
Young People's Forward Movement, 46–52

ZANETH, CORPORAL, 169
Ziegler, Olive, 277